The United States and Human Rights addresses the place of human rights in U.S. policy, both domestic and foreign. The contributors are leading analysts of international human rights, some having considerable experience working with human rights organizations and others providing expertise from such fields as law, developmental anthropology, political science, and public diplomacy.

The first part of the book deals with human rights issues in American society. The contributors focus on how international human rights standards could improve American society in several areas, including health care, the labor force, and refugee and immigration affairs. Other essays analyze why the United States has been hesitant to ratify human rights treaties. The second part of the book deals with human rights issues in American foreign policy, considering both stated ideals and the practical application of those ideals. Of particular interest are the impact of public opinion on humanitarian assistance and support for democracy abroad, and how the persistent issue of universal human rights affects U.S. relations with the United Nations, human rights organizations, indigenous peoples, and particular countries.

David P. Forsythe is Charles J. Mach Distinguished Professor of Political Science at the University of Nebraska. He is the author or editor of many books, including *Human Rights and Peace: International and National Dimensions* (Nebraska 1993).

UNIVERSITY OF NEBRASKA PRESS
Lincoln NE 68588-0484
www.nebraskapress.unl.edu

EDITED BY DAVID P. FORSYTHE

The United States and Human Rights

•

LOOKING INWARD AND OUTWARD

University of Nebraska Press

Lincoln and London

Publication of this volume was assisted by grants
from the University of Nebraska Research Council and
the G. E. Hendricks Fund of the University of
Nebraska Foundation.

Library of Congress Cataloging-in-Publication Data
The United States and human rights: looking inward
and outward / edited by David P. Forsythe. p. cm.–
(Human rights in international perspective : v. 5)
Includes bibliographical references and index.
ISBN 0-8032-2008-1 (cloth: alkaline paper)
1. Civil rights – United States. 2. Human rights.
I. Forsythe, David P., 1941– . II. Series.
KF4749.U55 2000 342.73'085–dc21
99-41949 CIP

Contents

DAVID P. FORSYTHE

Foreword

The Fifteenth Hendricks Symposium sponsored by the Political Science Department at the University of Nebraska–Lincoln was made possible by the generosity of an alumnus of the university. Mr. G. E. Hendricks had a lively interest in American politics and became especially concerned about the limitation of public discussion in this country at the start of the Cold War. Therefore, from 1949 to 1957 he gave the University of Nebraska Foundation a substantial sum of money to be used to deal with "current controversial political questions in a non-partisan, unbiased manner."

The Political Science Department chose to focus the fifteenth in this series of discussions on the United States and internationally recognized human rights. This is certainly a current and controversial topic. Americans are now once again debating with considerable vigor such topics as whether health care should be guaranteed by the state as a fundamental human right and whether the death penalty should be an appropriate penalty for common crime, especially when committed by the young or the mentally impaired. Americans, through their elected officials in Washington, must also confront controversial human rights issues in foreign policy, such as whether the United States is obligated to act to stop genocide in foreign countries.

The department assembled a group of especially talented people in September of 1996 to address human rights issues as they appeared in both U.S. domestic and foreign policy. Our participants included political scientists and lawyers. Two ambassadors also took part in our discussions. A number of people wore both an "academic" and a "practical" hat, as some participants represented an intergovernmental or nongovernmental organization as well as an academic discipline. The result was a stimulating meeting that led to this volume.

We are especially grateful to Ryan Hendrickson, then a doctoral candidate in our graduate program, who ably served as the conference coordinator. He was backed up by our excellent support staff of Jan Edwards, Monica Merry Mason, and Helen Sexton. Barbara Ann J. Rieffer, while a work-study student for the department, helped in numerous ways, including editing several of the revised chapters. A number of departmental members also participated in the meeting, including William Avery, Michael Combs, Philip Dyer,

John Hibbing, Jeff-Spinner-Halev, and Andrew Wedeman. We also were happy to have the participation of Brian Lepard from the Law College and Joseph Stimpfl from the Office of International Affairs.

AMBASSADOR HARRY G. BARNES JR.

Preface

The Fifteenth Hendricks Symposium at the University of Nebraska in September of 1996 addressed a number of issues that I had confronted as a U.S. Foreign Service officer and more recently as director of the Human Rights and Conflict Resolution Programs at the Carter Center in Atlanta. In each of these professional positions I have been faced with the sorts of dilemmas raised in the various sections of this book that resulted from that symposium. Often a fundamental dilemma results from the contrast between U.S. pronouncements and subsequent action, which is to say from the contrast between our righteousness and lack of right action. This dilemma frequently stems from the larger tension between justice based on human rights and peace based on what is possible in a given context.

Let me start with righteousness. Having lived in a number of different countries, I became used to foreigners' contradictory attitudes toward the United States. Even in societies dominated by totalitarian regimes there was considerable admiration for, and envy of, U.S. material and political accomplishments. And even from democratic countries people were often critical of the United States as well. Authoritarians and democrats alike frequently found Americans expressing a moral superiority, which many foreigners viewed as quite hypocritical, because Americans did not seem to understand the weaknesses in their own society.

If ever there were a time for Americans to develop a critical perspective on their own country, that time is now when we are the world's only superpower. During the Cold War we could easily compare ourselves with the Soviet Union, knowing such a comparison was to our advantage. Now we must learn to measure ourselves against our proclaimed ideals of human rights, including democratic freedoms. These ideals are part of the International Bill of Human Rights. We should not fear such measurement. As Jimmy Carter might put it, to those to whom much is given, much is expected.

A fundamental part of this measurement is stressed in several of the chapters of this book, namely ratification of human rights treaties. The United States is conspicuous by its failure to ratify a number of these multilateral conventions and by its insistence that a number of reservations accompany ratification. The United States also usually requires specific national legislation to supplement ratification. Still, a small milestone was passed in 1995 when the United States submitted its first report to the UN Committee on Human Rights, at least recognizing the right of that international body of experts to review the U.S. record in light of the UN Convention on Civil and Political Rights. Many Americans would be surprised to learn that the committee, made up of nongovernmental experts from a balanced range of countries, was critical of some U.S. policies in this domain. As part of this review process, a number of public meetings were held in the United States, including one at the Carter Center, with support from the U.S. Departments of Justice and State. These meetings provided a useful opportunity to discuss how the UN Civil and Political Covenant should impact the United States.

Two chapters in this volume review the debate as to whether it is better for the United States to ratify human rights treaties with reservations or not to ratify until the highly restrictive reservations can be avoided. I believe that future U.S. reservations should be subject to a sunset clause, causing them to terminate automatically unless the Senate explicitly agrees to continue them. With this procedure we could gauge our experience under the conventions and then decide whether to continue the reservations.

It is unfortunate that as of early 1997 a number of human rights treaties still await the advice and consent of the Senate, including the Convention on the Elimination of Discrimination against Women, the Convention on the Rights of the Child, and the Convention on Economic, Social, and Cultural Rights. The last was signed by President Carter some twenty years ago. While speaking at the International Human Rights Council at the Carter Center in late 1996, Carter recalled how he himself had initially not fully understood the importance of the Socio-Economic Covenant. He became a strong supporter when he realized that people without access to adequate health care or housing, or people forbidden to use their own language, could not really exercise their rights of freedom of speech or assembly. If one were seriously ill and without care, or homeless, or could not communicate in public in his or her own language, the civil and political rights so dear to Americans would become meaningless. Programs dealing with health and food are thus integrated into Carter Center activities from a human rights perspective.

Against the background of this brief discussion of perceived American moral superiority and yet need to measure our society against international standards, let me now turn to that old problem of peace versus justice. My work at the Carter Center seems to produce a type of schizophrenia. My conflict resolution role points toward promoting peace by reducing violence and suffering. My human rights position suggests we should be wary about sacrificing moral principles for possibly temporary gains. My own experience tells me that tactical compromise is sometimes right, sometimes not. This is not the vacuous statement it appears to be.

Former President Carter went to Bosnia in December of 1994 to try to negotiate a cease-fire and resumption of peace talks. He negotiated with two persons subsequently indicted for gross violations of internationally recognized human rights — Radovan Karadzic, the chauvinistic political leader of Bosnian Serbs, and General Ratko Mladic, the brutal Bosnian Serb commander. The fact was that they had sufficient power to stop the fighting and atrocities and negotiate a peace agreement. President Carter's team made sure that human rights issues were part of the discussions. These included access for the International Committee of the Red Cross to detention centers where abuses were being reported by the media, and free passage for humanitarian assistance to civilians in dire straits. Similar provisions were later incorporated into the 1995 Dayton Agreement, which did wind down the fighting and greatly reduced the atrocities. We were criticized at the time for dealing with international criminals, but we achieved — at least indirectly — some improvement "on the ground." Our role at that point was not to pursue legal justice for human rights violations through judicial proceedings but to seek practical human rights improvements through diplomacy and compromise.

On the other hand, in the 1980s the second Reagan administration began publicly to urge much greater respect for human rights, including a prompt return to democracy, in authoritarian Chile. To back up those words, for the first time in the UN Human Rights Commission, we co-sponsored a resolution critical of Chile. Partly because of U.S. influence in the Western Hemisphere and partly because of an ingrained Chilean tradition of legalism, U.S. active support for the resolution induced more Chilean attention to human rights problems. In this case it proved correct not to compromise quietly with General Pinochet's authoritarian government but to publicly and officially demand principled changes.

Likewise, in the 1970s the U.S. Congress demanded that communist countries, or those with "command economies," improve their record on emigration or forego Most Favored Nation status in trade with the United States. In light of this firm congressional action, I was able to negotiate the first MFN agreement with Romania in return for its relaxation of barriers to emigration. Under this agreement a number of those who had been persecuted by the Romanian communist authorities were allowed to leave.

It is not always easy to tell what leverage for human rights will work best. It is sometimes only with hindsight that one can evaluate whether a firm stand for justice or tactical compromise is the best course of action. Contemporary China provides an excellent example of this difficulty. Partway through its first term, the Clinton administration delinked trade and human rights. Despite periodic objection from some of the human rights groups noted in this book, and from some members of Congress, the administration maintained quiet diplomacy on human rights issues. On trade matters, however, it did use its leverage to win economic concessions. Early in 1997 it appeared unlikely that the second Clinton administration would return to its early policy of a firm and public opposition to certain Chinese policies that violated international rights standards. The administration apparently believed that private markets and trade would loosen Chinese repression, as seemingly had happened in places such as South Korea and Taiwan. The administration may have also concluded that overt pressure only worked on small and weak countries. Even then, U.S. efforts to pressure the military government of Burma/Myanmar into recognizing the outcome of free and fair elections had not proven successful at the time of writing.

On the basis of my own experience I tend to side with the more pessimistic authors of the chapters of this book, because it is so much harder to advance human rights effectively in other countries than it is to preach about them from a distance. Yet I am still convinced that public and firm support for human rights abroad does have its place in U.S. diplomacy. Public stands in favor of "justice" remind those people whose government may ignore human rights that such standards are acknowledged elsewhere. Thus people can hope and work for eventual change in their own countries. As I learned in Pinochet's Chile, the sense of U.S. solidarity with like-minded people in other countries can be a very powerful force.

But, to come full circle, the authors in this book do us a great service in reminding us that international human rights is not just for others. We in the democratic countries have a moral obligation to practice at home what we preach abroad. For those of us in the United States concerned with human rights activism, this moral obligation implies a long-term lobbying effort with Congress, with the current administration, and with the public. There must also be a greater educational effort over time, so that the next generation understands that there need be no difference between international and

American human rights standards. In this latter regard I note with some satisfaction that the Human Rights Program of the Carter Center organized in 1996 a course for the staff of the teacher's training college in Ethiopia. The program was devoted to bringing international human rights standards into the school curriculum and from there into the lives of students in Ethiopia. We would all do well to support comparable courses in the United States.

DAVID P. FORSYTHE

Introduction

There are surprisingly few books that deal with the United States and international human rights — and virtually none that deal with the subject in a Janus-like fashion encompassing both domestic politics and foreign policy. Surveys of the human rights literature indicate that no definitive book provides an overview either of international human rights and American society or of U.S. foreign policy and human rights. Our book thus breaks new ground, treating internationally recognized human rights as a two level political "game" that encompasses both domestic and foreign factors. We provide perspectives from law, qualitative political science, quantitative political science, public diplomacy, and nongovernmental action. Human rights is very much a transnational or "intermestic" subject as well as an interdisciplinary one.[1]

No one has ever purported to present a book on universal human rights and American society. A book by the Canadian sociologist Rhoda Howard discusses international human rights and national societies in general, with primary attention to Canada but only passing reference to the United States.[2] Howard shows, among other things, that Canada has a stronger sense of community than does the United States. Howard believes, not unlike Mark Hong in his postscript to this volume, that New York — if not the entire United States — seems "callous, cruel, an exaggeration of the right of the individual to disregard all others in pursuit of his own fortune." Howard argues for an implementation of international human rights leading to social democracy. Although she holds Canada deficient in the attention it gives to social and economic rights, she finds the United States to be woefully lacking in this regard. It is socioeconomic rights, she argues, that make civil and political rights most meaningful and help counteract the class bias in rugged capitalism that allows the leisured classes alone to use their civil and political rights to maximize their interests. It is particularly socioeconomic rights, she says, that contribute to a greater sense of community.

Beyond the Howard analysis, pathbreaking in its efforts to discuss international human rights in relation to North American societies, there are precious few shorter analyses looking at American society through the prism of international rights.[3] As Jack Donnelly has written, Americans think international human rights are something for others, not for themselves.[4]

In our book, in the first section looking inward on American society, three chapters focus on human rights and policy choices. The opening chapter, by Audrey Chapman, discusses health care from a human rights perspective. In her tightly argued analysis, she lays out ten specific guidelines for dealing with health care as a human right. She then discusses various health care proposals in the United States through the mid-1990s, evaluating them in light of the ten guidelines.

Ultimately, she concludes that although the American public superficially is in favor of guaranteed health care, the public has not generated effective demand on Congress to make changes. This lack of concerted pressure, in her interpretation, stems from undesired tradeoffs that would be involved — for example, more governmental regulation and/or some sacrifice on the part of those currently favored to provide better coverage and services for those currently less fortunate. She also finds a lack of national leadership on behalf of a new social arrangement featuring a universal right to adequate care. Her basic conclusion is fairly pessimistic: American society lost a major opportunity for significant correction of fundamental ills during the mid-1990s, and neither the several states nor the federal government is likely to make significant improvements in universal health care coverage in the foreseeable future. She continues to advocate that a human rights perspective is an important feature of future debates about American health care.[5]

Kelly-Kate Pease argues, in chapter two, that recent trends in economic theory and practice have been detrimental to certain segments of American society. She finds attention to at least some socioeconomic policies in American society, just as Chapman found some debate on health care as a human right from 1945 to 1995. Pease notes, as did Chapman, that the U.S. commitment to socioeconomic rights is uncertain at best and argues that increased attention to these rights is precisely what is needed to offset the negative effects of certain recent economic trends.

Specifically, Pease argues that economic globalization combined with the dominance of neo-classical economic theory has been detrimental to socioeconomic rights in the United States. She cites data on the real minimum wage over time as well as on patterns in unionization and its effects to buttress her argument. Pease believes the state should indeed intrude into economic policy matters, although she notes the problem of "prisoner's dilemma" in these international business matters. If the United States increases the real minimum wage and encourages unionization while others do not, there will be economic costs to pay. Successful international competition will become more difficult. Her interpretation is a welcome addition to the debate on global markets, for much of that literature has been uncritically bullish. She joins George Soros, the brilliant financier and advocate of democracy, in questioning certain types of capitalism and the extreme individualism that sometimes accompany what in other times was called robber baron capitalism.[6]

Finally, in this first section, Mark Gibney emphasizes how the United States accepts into American society those persons who are recognized as refugees in foreign countries, arguing that they should be allowed into the country more on humanitarian than on expediential grounds. In short, he argues that whereas after the Cold War the United States has treated asylum seekers who come here directly as a first country of sanctuary increasingly in terms of whether or not they are persecuted, our government continues to treat refugees held in foreign centers as primarily a potential economic resource. The United States treats them, he says, as we treat migrants who are allowed entrance if they can provide economic skills to American society. Gibney wants more humanitarianism and less expediency in our refugee admissions policy and urges that we give more attention to serious persecution rather than to purely economic factors. At least, as Gibney notes, contemporary Western (including American) restrictions on all forms of immigration are relatively mild compared to earlier eras when immigration laws, at least in the United States, were openly harsh and racist.[7]

In a second section to part one on human rights and American society, we discuss the related question of U.S. ratification of human rights treaties. It is sometimes easily forgotten, inside the Washington beltway as well as outside, that they have — or are designed to have legal — impact within the United States. A small amount of literature already exists on that subject.[8] The three new chapters presented in this volume are all provocative and make the following points.

Barbara Stark chronicles some of the socioeconomic ills in American society to argue that ratification of the UN Covenant on Social, Economic, and Cultural Rights, plus good faith application, would help correct those problems. The United States shows the second greatest gap among OECD (Organization for Economic Co-Operation and Development) countries between the wealth of the upper and lower 20 percent of the population. Her analysis fits well with the Chapman and Pease chapters and the Donnelly chapter later on. The common point can expanded. According to the 1995 Human Development Report published by the UN Development Program, the United States fares well overall.[9] This would be expected from a report focusing on per capita income, longevity, and literacy, because all three factors reflect wealth. This country, however, shows a number of specific deficiencies. In general, the United States is in second place behind Canada in a ranking of all countries on the basis of life expectancy, adjusted literacy, and per capita income. But women's nonagricultural wages are only 75 percent of male wages, suggesting systematic gender discrimination. Australia, by contrast, pays women at 90.8 percent of males. Moreover, in the United States the lowest 40 percent of households receive just 15.7 percent of national income, the second largest gap among OECD countries. This suggests a systematic disregard for the welfare of the less fortunate and a type of rugged capitalism that authors such as Howard criticize.

On the basis of her analysis, Stark urges foreign parties to pressure the United States to ratify the Socio-Economic Covenant, believing that this foreign pressure could be effective in the U.S. political process. Stark also believes that the mood in the United States is not definitively set against an increase in socioeconomic entitlements, despite welfare reform that has shrunk the U.S. welfare safety net. In this regard she is more optimistic than Chapman, who is fairly pessimistic about immediate advance on health care as one type of socioeconomic right.

In a forthcoming work Stark projects in more detail what may transpire in American society.[10] If foreign pressure on behalf of the Socio-Economic Covenant is combined with changed domestic pressure, momentum may build for U.S. adherence to this human rights treaty. If middle-class Americans, who tend to be more politically active and have more political clout than lower-class Americans, genuinely fear for their jobs, their health care, and their social security, they may join with foreign parties in providing a successful push for socioeconomic rights in the United States.

In a second chapter on human rights treaties, Christina Cerna believes that because the United States has ratified the UN Covenant on Civil and Political Rights, there should be few obstacles to U.S. ratification of the American Convention on Human Rights. Cerna argues that the United States should ratify this latter convention, even if with reservations, to participate in the legal regime created by the treaty and to further undermine American ideological opposition to human rights treaties. She suggests that undesirable reservations could be rescinded in the future. She believes that hemispheric human rights agencies would be more effective if the United States exercised leadership on the basis of its ratification of the American Convention.

Cerna's analysis should be read against the background of deep American suspicion of human rights treaties prior to the second Reagan administration.[11] That administration, ironically the most unilateralist in American history since 1945, successfully urged ratification of the 1948 Genocide Convention. The Bush administration then followed with the controversial U.S. ratification of the UN Covenant on Civil and Political Rights. It was controversial abroad, but not at home, because our government argued it was not obligated to make any changes in its domestic law. It was also noncontroversial within this country, because U.S. citizens were not afforded the right to bring petitions to the UN Committee on Human Rights, claiming that their rights under the treaty had been violated and that efforts via national remedies had been exhausted.

Contesting Cerna's argument in favor of U.S. ratification of the American convention even with controversial reservations by whatever name, William Schabas notes that U.S. reservations, understandings, and declarations concerning the UN Covenant on Civil and Political Rights have provoked bilateral and multilateral opposition. He especially notes the position of the UN Human Rights Committee that monitors the Civil-Political Covenant. He believes that this UN agency is on good ground in contesting some of the U.S. attachments to its ratification, because in his view the committee is acting in conformity with other developments in international law.

Thus, unlike Cerna, Schabas does not believe the United States should attach reservations and similar measures to human rights treaties that, at a minimum, raise the question of whether they are incompatible with the basic meaning and purpose of a treaty. Cerna, however, finds fault with the international community for objecting to reservations. These can be peeled away later, she says, similar to Ambassador Barnes's comments in the Preface. Moreover, the international community has not been systematically rigorous in contesting the reservations of certain other states. The Islamic states have deposited a number of dubious reservations to their adherence to the UN Convention on the Rights of the Child. Yet challenges to those reservations are lacking. So why not, she argues, accept questionable U.S. reservations as the price of formal adherence? She is thus more accepting in the short run of controversial reservations that might be politically necessary to secure ratification. Meanwhile, the Canadian Schabas believes the United

States has to play the game of international relations by the international legal rules, even if this creates domestic difficulties. After all, he argues, the point of ratification is to produce beneficial changes, not to endorse a questionable status quo. Similar to Stark, Schabas believes in the efficacy of international pressure against questionable U.S. decisions. All three chapters capture well the interplay of foreign and domestic factors inherent in the subject of U.S. consent to human rights treaties.

These first six chapters fit well together, showing, among other things: the imperfections of American society; the relevance of international human rights norms to these imperfections; the international and domestic obstacles to developing an international human rights paradigm in and for American society; the blending of political, economic, legal, and ethical factors; and the transnational or intermestic nature of the subject matter reviewed. All reflect both domestic and international considerations.

When focusing on American society against the background of international human rights, one might do well to recall West European experience. Between the early 1950s and fall of European communism, the European Convention on Human Rights was formally adhered to by a variety of democratic governments (excluding Greece from 1967–74, which continued legal adherence during military rule). Despite the fact that, Greece excepted, all parties to the convention during the Cold War were liberal democracies, the European Commission and Court on Human Rights did not lack for business. The central point is that even genuine liberal democracies violate civil and political rights on occasion or in certain situations.[12] Thus there is need for an international protective system to counteract these violations.

With regard to the second main focus of this work on U.S. foreign policy, there are several books on selected aspects of this subject. Among more recent works, Steinmetz looks at rights and U.S. policy toward governments under siege, such as in Iran, Nicaragua, and the Philippines.[13] Nolan looks at the interplay of rights and security on certain aspects of U.S. diplomatic history, including policy toward the Soviet Union and also toward the United Nations.[14] Among slightly older works, Muravchik wrote a polemic attacking the Carter record.[15] Mower did a more balanced comparison between the Carter and Reagan administrations.[16] Newsom edited a work surveying the making of U.S. human rights policy, focusing attention on a few foreign countries.[17] And there are still older works dating back to Van Dyke in 1970.[18] Many shorter treatments of issues are relevant to U.S. foreign policy and human rights, including a 1995 summary analysis or overview.[19] None of the studies accomplishes what is set out below.

In part 2, which focuses on foreign policy, the first section deals with public opinion and also both American and transnational interest groups. Ole Holsti presents a quantitative analysis, suggesting among other things that whatever one might say about American exceptionalism and a moral streak in American political culture, there is little public support for a moral crusade abroad on behalf of human rights. Indeed, human rights turns out to be a fairly controversial and partisan issue. Holsti's conception of international human rights reflects mostly a largely liberal Democratic concern, to which a number of other political circles object. Thus, even after considerable attention to international human rights by both Democratic and Republican administrations especially since 1976, a domestic consensus in support of those rights still fails to manifest itself relative to foreign policy. This situation was predicted by Sandy Vogelgesang, among others, toward the end of the Carter administration.[20] Moreover, the failure of the United States to lead international institutions into decisive efforts to end atrocities in places such as Bosnia and Rwanda during the 1990s gives considerable pause for thought about American moral rhetoric. Likewise, by 1996 it was clear that the Clinton administration was not prepared to sacrifice economic interests in places such as China for the cause of human rights.

In a related piece, Ellen Dorsey first indicates why human rights NGOs found fault with the Clinton record on human rights. Then she indicates the prospects for change in that record. She analyzes the forces at work that have limited the effect of human rights NGOs as they try to change U.S. foreign policy on rights. Her restrained forecast fits exactly with Holsti's point that one cannot expect from the American public a concerted effort to pressure Congress into changing Clinton's disposition toward caution on the question of U.S. action for rights abroad.

Given that, as Henry Kissinger has noted, all U.S. presidents since Woodrow Wilson have identified their administrations with the promotion of democracy abroad, and because the Clinton administration's rhetoric fits perfectly with this historical pattern, a second section in part two looks at the place of democracy in U.S. policy abroad.[21] Jack Donnelly reminds us that the issue is not democracy per se but liberal democracy in which free and fair elections are combined with a number of protections of human rights. Thus the U.S. goal should not be simple pursuit of democracy but of rights-protective and hence liberal democracies. It is worth recalling, however, what was noted above, that liberal democracies may also violate human rights but not exactly in the same ways and to the same extent as various authoritarian or illiberal democratic states. After reviewing both procedural and substantive democratic standards, Donnelly rightfully pays special attention to the fate of vulnerable groups in society when adversely affected by democratic state capitalism. Donnelly concludes with an important point: just as civil rights have liberalized democracy, socioeconomic rights have liberalized capitalism.

Stephen Zunes follows up Donnelly's general analysis with special attention to U.S. foreign policy, democracy, and rights in the Middle East. Zunes argues that an American bias against Arab and Islamic peoples, a bias in favor of Israel and other allied governments, and various strategic considerations have undermined U.S. attention to international human rights, including democratic rights, in this region. He also notes, as does Christopher Joyner in the subsequent chapter, that democracy and rights-protective regimes have not prospered in the Islamic world, suggesting that there may be aspects of particular versions of Islam that are not conducive to liberalism and democracy. Zunes also observes that some human rights NGOs, knowing that Congress is not going to allow significant pressure on Israel, have chosen to focus on other rights issues as a tactical, rather than ideological, matter. Zunes provides a fresh and perceptive analysis of U.S. foreign policy in the perpetually unsettled Middle East. He basically argues that there are limits to what the international community attempts in the Middle East on behalf of democracy and rights *because* of U.S. foreign policy. Joyner tends to argue that democratic developments have not been impressive in that region *despite* U.S. policy. This is a distinction that indeed does make a difference.

Joyner shares much of Zunes's analysis, although Joyner seems more optimistic that the United States can nudge states such as Morocco and Jordan — over time — to at least a more liberal if not a more democratic stance. Joyner emphasizes that Islam is not a culture or civilization set in stone. Interpretations change, along with dominant secular and religious groups. Islamic states, too, are subject to the same processes of economic and cultural globalization affecting other parts of the world. However, one has not seen the same extent of democratization in the Middle East that has occurred in Eastern Europe and Latin America and even in much of Africa since the end of the Cold War. In addition, a number of Middle Eastern governments felt threatened by various parties and causes. Fundamental civil rights almost always suffer during times of armed conflict and perceived threats to governmental security.[22] It follows that liberal democracy is also difficult to sustain during times of war and public emergency.

A final section in Part 2 looks at several multilateral aspects of U.S. foreign policy in relation to universal rights. Linda Keith and Steven C. Poe suggest that the International Monetary Fund (IMF), with the United States controlling the largest bloc of votes, has contributed to increased repression in many developing countries through its structural adjustment programs. The authors discuss the dilemma of whether some short-term pain may be necessary to produce long-term gain, for example, whether some repression may be necessary to move a country along the path to eventual sustainable development. They also raise the troubling point of whether some repression, hopefully short term, may be necessary to implement unpopular structural adjustment programs, which in a Hobbesian choice may be preferable to a descent into ethnic conflict or civil war if economic changes are not carried out. Thus IMF structural adjustment programs may correlate with some curtailment of rights; but it is not clear that persons in places such as Zaire are better off for their government's having balked at IMF austerity measures. Keith and Poe explain through their clear quantitative analysis why international financial institutions such as the Fund and also the World Bank have come under such criticism for their impact on various human rights. But they significantly broaden the debate by looking at long-term choices and the consequences of not implementing austerity measures.

George Kent addresses a subject related to failed states and other situations of extreme distress, namely humanitarian assistance. After clarification of terms and trends, Kent develops a model of desirable humanitarian assistance. He argues that those in dire straits should have a recognized right to humanitarian assistance, and more affluent states a duty to respond. Thus, rather than emphasize the right of states to intervene, he stresses the obligation of states to respond effectively to the positive right of individuals in distress to receive international assistance. Kent addresses the practical problem of how to get such a right recognized and applied in places such as the U.S. Congress, which controls the budget, and the State Department. Congressional support would be crucial for such a vision to become reality.

Kent has developed a liberal model focusing on the rights of individuals. A central question concerns how to implement such a model in a world in which states frequently pursue nonliberal policies focusing not on individual need but elite preference. State leaders, especially in parts of the global south, are not known historically for their love of discourse about state obligation. They much prefer to articulate claims based on the rights of state sovereignty. When states fail, as in places such as Liberia and Somalia, it is precisely because over time elites do not rule on the basis of a sense of obligation to the nation but to enrich themselves and the political groups that supported them. These elites are naturally not much moved by arguments based on moral obligations on behalf of the "nation." Even where elites may demonstrate genuine concern for the welfare of a large part of the nation, the history of colonialism and imperialism mitigates against easy acceptance of foreign intrusion into what was traditionally considered domestic affairs. Kent's model is likely to prove workable only if over time diplomacy is able to produce state agreement to his morally appealing vision.

Robert Hitchcock also focuses on assistance, in this case U.S. development assistance through the Agency for International Development. He believes that the U.S. record in combining a concern for economic growth with respect for various human rights, including the rights of indigenous peoples, is inconsistent. He finds some grounds for optimism, at least regarding growing sensitivity and related rhetoric about protecting indigenous peoples. However, Hitchcock also believes that the reality of U.S. Official Development Assistance is often injurious to these vulnerable peoples. Thus he finds the U.S. record on these questions to be similar to that of the World Bank (which is not surprising given the U.S. influence within that international financial institution). The Bank at least talks more about paying attention to the rights of vulnerable groups, especially when they are dislocated by economic projects. But the overall Bank record on various types of human rights issues, including those pertaining to indigenous peoples, leaves much to be desired.[23]

Hitchcock's rich analysis shows additionally that one should be careful about sweeping generalizations pertaining to the United States in general and to AID in particular. The United States has taken some steps to protect indigenous peoples, as in Indonesia, but its record is much less salutatory in other places. Nevertheless, Hitchcock shows very clearly that the thrust of U.S. development assistance has been historically mostly toward economic growth even when that pursuit is accompanied by hardship for vulnerable groups. But this is precisely the model of U.S. development at home, historically speaking. Once again we see that a state's conception of its foreign policy, in this case development assistance and indigenous peoples, is directly related to its domestic evolution. For this reason states that have the most generous programs of official development assistance in foreign policy have the largest welfare states at home.[24] The United States has not shown much interest in socioeconomic rights at home, relatively speaking, as demonstrated by earlier chapters. Thus it has not shown consistent and systematic interest in socioeconomic damage to indigenous peoples caught up in "development" projects. Some grounds for optimism remain, however, as Hitchcock shows how congressional and NGO pressures have effectuated some change over time at AID.

Finally, Patrick Flood examines the U.S. record at the United Nations with regard to two mechanisms employed by the UN Human Rights Commission: country-specific measures and the thematic measures. The UN Human Rights Commission, traditionally the hub of UN diplomacy for human rights, and now only partly upstaged by the new (1993) UN High Commissioner for Human Rights, has for several decades focused the diplomatic spotlight on both selected governments and on general problems. Thus the commission has voted to create special rapporteurs for countries such as Chile and for general problems including enforced disappearances. Through his case studies, Flood concludes that neither UN mechanism may be superior to the other, that each works best when multilateral pressures are combined with bilateral efforts, and that the United States at times has played an active role in advancing diplomatic protections of human rights through the United Nations. Flood quotes from several U.S. reports and position papers, as he himself represented the United States in Geneva through the U.S. diplomatic mission to international organizations there.

In a unique postscript, Ambassador Mark Hong of the Republic of Singapore, a state that has been in the middle of the global debate about human rights, suggests that there may be reasons for convergence between U.S. views and Asian views on human rights. He argues that both the East and West agree on such things as family values, the need for order, and a shrinking of the welfare state. Ambassador Hong suggests that what has been described as a Western-Asian debate may be a false image. He argues that just as some Asian states have adopted a number of policies on democracy and related human rights, so some in the West seem to be rethinking what he calls an extreme version of individualism. He believes that many Asians are more concerned with preservation and creation of jobs, personal security, and some basic needs such as clean air and water. Ambassador Hong also believes that many Westerners will come to appreciate the effects of severe overpopulation on conceptions of individual rights.

Some experts, such as Rhoda Howard, might agree with parts of his argument — for example, about excessive individualism in the West — but for different reasons. Others would say that a generational, rather than a regional or cultural, debate was at issue between the United States and Singapore. In this view, the first generation of hard working and superachieving people was more interested in material success, discipline, and order; and a later generation, accustomed to affluence, became more interested in issues of personal freedom and expression. There is some evidence that South Korea and Taiwan in Asia have traveled precisely this road and that eventually Singapore perhaps will too, especially after passing from the political scene of Lee Kwuan Yew and those who engineered the dramatic improvement in Singapore's economy from 1965 to 1995. Elections in Singapore in 1997 did little to resolve debates about whether the ruling elite had fashioned an attractive model of political development, which included interpretations of human rights, because the elite, as usual, so manipulated those elections that a serious opposition never had a chance to articulate an alternative model.

In sum, this book will probably leave its readers with two general thoughts. First, the United States that sees itself as a shining city on a hill and a beacon to others regarding human rights and democracy[25] has many problems at home that certainly could benefit from review within the framework of international human rights. American exceptionalism, as a mythology and self-image of exceptionally good commitment to personal freedom, should not be confused with empirical evidence showing fundamental problems in American society.

Second, U.S. rhetoric about advancing rights and democracy abroad should not be confused with the reality of the impact of U.S. policy. This is not to say that U.S. policy is always opposed to international human rights. That is not the case at the United Nations, or regarding indigenous peoples, and so forth. It is remarkable how many times certain U.S. ambassadors interceded on behalf of human rights and human dignity in places such as the former Yugoslavia.[26] The record of Ambassador Harry G. Barnes Jr. in Chile during some of the Pinochet years is also noteworthy. The United States, similar to other industrialized democracies and most intergovernmental organizations, for example, currently manifests a multimillion dollar official program of democracy assistance. But it remains true to say that at times the United States is not as protective of internationally recognized human rights through its foreign policy as it could be. This book has demonstrated some of the reasons for that shortfall, as well as the prospects for progressive change.

Suffice it to say that human rights in foreign policy presents innumerable dilemmas. No one subject captures the total complexity, but the issue of U.S. support for international criminal courts comes close. Ambassador Barnes refers to some of these dilemmas in his Preface. The Clinton administration, against the background of a congressional backlash against the Somali adventure in particular and UN use of force in general, was not eager to have IFOR arrest indicted war criminals in the former Yugoslavia. A vigorous attempt to arrest the likes of Slobodan Milosevic might have undermined the Dayton peace accords, leading to a resumption of fighting and atrocities, plus IFOR casualties and a damaged re-election bid for President Clinton (contributing to the victory for a more nationalistic and unilateralist Bob Dole). Numerous others, however, believed it was vital to lasting peace in the Balkans to end legal impunity for those who had committed war crimes, genocide, and crimes against humanity. Once the U.S. election had passed, and with Milosevic under domestic pressure in modern Yugoslavia because of his authoritarian ways, the Clinton White House by early 1997 was being pressured by various groups to be more assertive in bringing gross violators of human rights to legal justice. The debate continued, with conflicting reports of what might transpire.

This book reviews a number of these dilemmas in U.S. foreign policy on human rights, as well as delving into the domestic politics that undergird, for better or worse, a concern for rights abroad. The result is a sophisticated discourse on the United States and human rights.

Notes

1. Jack Donnelly, "Post–Cold War Reflections on the Study of International Human Rights," *Ethics & International Affairs* 8 (1994): 97–118; and Claude E. Welch Jr. "International Human Rights: A Guide to Collection Development," *Choice* 28 (January 1991): 741–747.

2. Rhoda Howard, *Human Rights and the Search for Community* (Boulder CO: Westview, 1995).

3. See especially, Beth Stephens, "Hypocrisy on Rights," *New York Times*, June 24, 1993, A13, who notes that while the United States was preaching universal human rights at a UN conference in Vienna, it was engaging in its own form of particularism regarding socioeconomic rights, the death penalty, and interdiction of asylum seekers.

4. Jack Donnelly, *International Human Rights* (Boulder CO: Westview, 1993).

5. Audrey Chapman, ed., *Health Care Reform: A Human Rights Approach* (Washington: Georgetown University Press, 1994).

6. Georg Soros, "The Capitalistic Threat," *Atlantic Monthly* 279 (February): 1997.

7. See, for example, Wayne A. Cornellius, Philip L. Martin, and James F. Hollifield, eds., *Controlling Immigration: A Global Perspective* (Stanford: Stanford University Press, 1994); Gil Loescher, *Beyond Charity: International Cooperation and the Global Refugee Crisis* (New York: Oxford University Press, 1993); and Myron Weiner, *The Global Migration Crisis: Challenge to States and to Human Rights* (New York: Harper Collins, 1995).

8. See, for example, Richard Lillich, *U.S. Ratification of the Human Rights Treaties* (Charlottesville: University Press of Virginia, 1981); and Hurst Hannum, *Materials on International Human Rights and United States Constitutional Law* (Washington DC: Procedural Aspects of International Law Institute, 1985).

9. UNDP, *Human Development Report 1995* (New York: Oxford University Press, for the UNDP, 1995).

10. Barbara Stark, *Critical Theory and Economic Rights in the United States: The Other Half of the International Bill of Rights*, forthcoming.

11. See further, Lawrence J. LeBlanc, *The United States and the Genocide Convention* (Durham: Duke University Press, 1991); and Natalie Hevener Kaufman, *Human Rights Treaties and the Senate: A History of Opposition* (Chapel Hill: University of North Carolina Press, 1990).

12. Donald W. Jackson, *The United Kingdom Confronts the European Convention on Human Rights* (Gainesville: University Press of Florida, 1997).

13. Sara Steinmetz, *Democratic Transition and Human Rights: Perspectives on U.S. Foreign Policy* (New York: SUNY-Albany, 1994).

14. Cathal J. Nolan, *Principled Diplomacy: Security and Rights in U.S. Foreign Policy* (Westport CT: Greenwood Press, 1993).

15. Joshua Muravchik, *The Uncertain Crusade: Jimmy Carter and the Dilemmas of Human Rights Policy* (Lanham: Hamilton Press, 1986).

16. A. Glenn Mower Jr., *Human Rights and American Foreign Policy: The Carter and Reagan Experiences* (Westport CT: Greenwood, 1987).

17. David D. Newsom, ed., *The Diplomacy of Human Rights* (Lanham: University Press of America, 1986).

18. Vernon Van Dyke, *The United States, Human Rights, and World Community* (New York: Oxford University Press, 1970).

19. David P. Forsythe, "Human Rights and U.S. Foreign Policy: Two Levels, Two Worlds," *Political Studies* 43 (1995): 111–130; also published as a chapter in David Beetham, ed., *Politics and Human Rights* (Oxford: Blackwell's, 1995).

20. Sandy Vogelgesang, *American Dream, Global Nightmare: The Dilemma of U.S. Human Rights Policy* (New York: Norton, 1980).

21. Henry Kissinger, *Diplomacy* (New York: Simon & Schuster, 1994).

22. Steven C. Poe and C. Neal Tate, "Repression of Human Rights to Personal Integrity in the 1980s: A Global Analysis," *American Political Science Review* 88 (December 1994): 853–873.

23. Catherine Caufield, *Masters of Illusion: The World Bank and the Poverty of Nations* (New York: Holt, 1996).

24. Alain Noel and Jean-Phillipe Therien, "From Domestic to International Justice: The Welfare State and Foreign Aid," *International Organization* 49 (summer 1995): 523–555.

25. T. Davis and S. Lynn Jones, "City on a Hill," *Foreign Policy* 66 (1986): 20–38.

26. Warren Zimmermann, *Origins of a Catastrophe: Yugoslavia and Its Destroyers* (New York: Times Books, 1996).

The United States and Human Rights

PART 1

Looking Inward on American Society

SECTION 1
Human Rights and Policy Choice

1

The Defeat of Comprehensive Health Care Reform

•

A Human Rights Perspective

•

AUDREY CHAPMAN

The United States presents a series of paradoxes with regard to the right to health care. Although Americans have a disposition to frame claims in the language of rights, this country is the only major industrialized democracy that fails to recognize a universal entitlement to health care. Survey after survey finds the overwhelming majority of the population believes that there should be a right to health care, but this support does not get translated into legislative action. Although the United States has gradually legislated a substantial role for the government in financing health care, particularly during the mid-1960s, there seems to be little consensus about public responsibility in the health care sector. Despite the highest levels of health spending in the world, both in absolute terms and on a per capita basis, over 43 million Americans, most of whom are employed or are dependents of someone who is employed, lack basic health insurance coverage. This chapter will explore prospects for reforming the health care system in the direction of realizing a right to health care in light of this legacy and the failure of the 1993–94 comprehensive reform initiatives.

Background Trends

Four trends accounted for the momentum in the early 1990s toward comprehensive health care reform. The first is escalating health costs. With spending on health care increasing in the period prior to 1993 at an annual rate of 12 to 15 percent and exceeding the annual inflation rate, the cost of health care was straining the economy and state and federal budgets. An aging population, leading to a growing demand for health care and a need for more care for the chronically ill, and the increasing use of sophisticated and expensive equipment created pressures on financial resources in virtually all industrialized countries. In the United States these factors were further compounded by commercialization of the health care industry, the absence of controls over the deployment of expensive technology, and the comparatively high earnings of many people in the health care sector.[1]

The second trend was increasing gaps in health insurance coverage and persistent inequities in access to health care. Despite the highest levels of health care spending in the world, more than 40 million persons, nearly 20 percent of the nonelderly population, were without health insurance, and another 60 million had inadequate coverage. Between 1988 and 1993 the rate of coverage through private, employer-sponsored plans fell from 67 to 61 percent.[2] Welfare legislation, which permits states to withdraw Medicaid benefits from legal immigrants and confers greater freedom in allocating federal welfare grants, is likely to increase these numbers substantially.

Ethnic minorities, particularly African Americans, Latinos, and Native Americans, are far more likely than other groups to have inadequate health insurance.[3] A 1993 profile of the uninsured population indicated that 60 percent of the uninsured had incomes below 200 percent of the poverty level.[4] Most uninsured persons, 84 percent, were workers or dependents of workers who did not receive health insurance through their employment. Slightly more than half of these workers without health benefits were full-time employees. As might be expected, persons without insurance had more difficulty gaining access to health care, so that when the uninsured finally saw a doctor their health problems were more likely to be serious and difficult to treat.[5] Death rates among low-income populations were twice the rates of the highest income groups.[6]

The third trend accounting for the momentum toward change was a lack of security about obtaining and retaining health insurance coverage. As health care became more and more expensive, insurance premiums escalated, resulting in increasing numbers of Americans who could not afford to buy insurance. Group health insurance premiums for families cost an average of $5,232 in 1993; employees covered through their place of employment typically were required to contribute at least 30 percent of the total.[7] Individual insurance rates were even higher. Even if individuals were able to afford insurance, there was no assurance that they would be able to secure coverage. To cope with financial pressures and, in the case of for-profit companies, to maintain profits, health insurers decreased the availability of community-rated insurance, under which anyone who applies for coverage is accepted, and instituted experience ratings that enabled them to exclude those deemed high risk from coverage. Increasing health costs have also led many large firms to self-insure, enabling these employers to limit liability for chronic and expensive conditions.

These policies made many people hostage to their current jobs to retain their health insurance and made others "medically uninsurable," as insurers denied coverage both for numerous pre-existing conditions and for those considered likely to develop such conditions, no matter how minimal the risk. The bipartisan Health Insurance Portability and Accountability Act of 1996 has made it more feasible for workers to carry their health insurance from job to job and limits, but does not eliminate, the ability of insurance companies to deny coverage to persons with pre-existing conditions.[8] Perhaps for the first time, anxieties about the scope, security, and cost of health insurance coverage have become a major preoccupation of the middle class.

Fourth, there was evidence of serious inadequacies in the American model of health care, with its reliance on treatment rather than on prevention and its investment in high technology rather than in basic health care. Although the United States had the most advanced medical technology, the largest ratio of doctors to population in the world, and the highest hospital bills, the country fared worse than other developed countries on many health indicators. For example, the United States ranked (from best to worst) nineteenth in infant mortality, twenty-eighth in the rate of infants born at low birth weights, fifteenth in the rate of maternal mortality, and ninth in life expectancy, worse in some cases than Hong Kong, Singapore, Jordan, or Costa Rica.[9] The American Public Health Association described this situation as a "public health crisis."[10]

The Right to Health Care

What does a human rights approach to health care reform entail? How should it be defined and conceptualized? Several major international human rights instruments recognize the right to health care in the context of a more inclusive right to health. The Universal Declaration of Human Rights (1948), the principal standard by which human rights are identified today, states that "everyone has the right to a standard of living adequate for the health and well-being of himself and of his family, including food, clothing, housing and medical care and necessary social services."[11] Article 12 of the International Covenant on Economic, Social and Cultural Rights (1976), a treaty intended to make more specific and binding the obligations of governments to protect the social, economic, and cultural rights enumerated in the Universal Declaration, "recognizes the right of everyone to the enjoyment of the highest attainable standard of physical and mental health," and to that end, mandates that state parties to the Covenant (governments that have ratified the instrument) undertake the following steps to achieve full realization of this right:

a. The provision for the reduction of the stillbirth rate and of infant mortality and for the healthy development of the child.

b. The improvement of all aspects of environmental and industrial hygiene.

c. The prevention, treatment and control of epidemic, endemic, occupational and other diseases.

d. The creation of conditions which would assure to all medical service and medical attention in the event of sickness.[12]

The World Health Organization (who) has also recognized a right to health. Language in the preamble to its constitution states, "The enjoyment of the highest attainable standard of health is one of the fundamental rights of every human being without distinction of race, religion, political belief, economic, or social condition." The who formula links the right to health to a definition of health as a "state of complete physical, mental and social well-being and not merely the absence of disease or infirmity."[13] In 1977 the World Health Assembly reaffirmed that health is a basic human right and a worldwide social goal essential to the satisfaction of basic human needs and the quality of life. It set the goal of "Health for All by the Year 2000," the attainment of a level of health that would permit all citizens to lead a socially and economically productive life. Two years later the Declaration of Alma-Ata further linked the "Health for All" goal to rectifying inequalities in the health status of people both within and between countries.[14]

The constitutions of a number of countries include a right to health or health protection, but this right, however, is rarely an individual, immediately enforceable right. It is more likely to be a programmatic or policy right that articulates goals.[15] Although not as broad as a right to health, the right to health protection encompasses attention to the public health context of curative medicine. Thus a right to health protection goes beyond medical intervention to include preventive measures, such as the provision of potable water and improvement of environmental conditions. The distinction is sometimes articulated as the right to health care when one is sick and the right to health protection to prevent the population from becoming sick.

For any right to health care, health, or health protection to be effectively implemented, this entitlement must be translated into specific obligations and commitments consistent with the resource levels of a society. This is a difficult and complex task. Many appeals to a right to health or health care are little more than rhetorical exercises. Enumeration of a basic human right to health in key international human rights instruments has not been paralleled by conceptual development specifying the content of this right. In contrast to civil and political rights, international standards for economic, social, and cultural rights do not rest on foundations of extensive domestic jurisprudence. Moreover, there have not been effective international mechanisms to promote the intellectual development of these rights. The major UN body responsible for oversight of the International Covenant on Economic, Social and Cultural Rights, the Committee on Economic, Social and Cultural Rights, has not had either the resources commensurate with this task or the effective cooperation of states parties to this treaty. Some critics of rights-based approaches therefore argue that the concepts of individual rights in general and a right to health care in particular are overloaded to the point of meaninglessness.[16]

In April 1992, well before the inception of comprehensive health reform efforts, the Science and Human Rights Program of the American Association for the Advancement of Science (AAAS), with the assistance of the Robert Wood Johnson Foundation, initiated a project to explore the implications of recognizing a right to a basic and adequate standard of health care in the United States and to assess the benefits and problems in doing so. One of the project's priorities was to conceptualize the scope and limitations of a right to health care in an advanced industrialized country. Between September 1992 and May 1993 the project sponsored two planning and evaluation meetings and four substantive consultations that brought human rights specialists together with health care providers, health policy analysts, bioethicists, and health care economists. On the basis of these deliberations, the project proposed recognition of a right to a basic and adequate standard of health care consistent with society's level of resources. The project also concluded that the right to a basic standard of health care could not be achieved, even in a more affluent society, apart from wider issues of health protection. Hence securing a right to health care was understood as a component of a broader effort that acknowledges the dynamic relationship between health conditions and health status on the one hand and investments in public health as a meaningful and effective strategy to reduce the cost of health services as well.[17]

The two project publications, *Exploring a Human Rights Approach to Health Care Reform* and *Health Care Reform: A Human Rights Approach*, developed the concrete requirements and implications of recognizing a right to health care. In summary form, they are as follows:

1. a universal legal entitlement to basic health services that is guaranteed equally to all citizens and residents and cannot be withdrawn;

2. structural reforms to rectify inadequacies and inequities in the current health care system so as to assure that all have equal access to quality health care;

3. treatment of health care as a social good to be distributed according to principles of justice rather than as a commodity to be distributed by market forces for the financial benefit of health care providers;

4. affirmative action measures to bring the health status of the most disadvantaged and vulnerable communities up to mainstream standards;

5. a health care paradigm which stresses preventive and primary care rather than curative health services;

6. meaningful public participation in setting priorities for the health care system, shaping health care policy, and making major decisions about benefits and delivery systems;

7. affordable health care which is publicly financed;

8. effective monitoring of the system so as to identify inadequacies and to rectify them;

9. meaningful potential recourse for those who do not receive adequate health care;

10. priority accorded to public policies conducive to health protection, such as effective regulation to preserve or restore clean air and water, reduce exposure to toxic substances, and assure work place safety.[18]

If these criteria are fulfilled, then the substantive core of a human rights approach is being met.

Legislative and Policy Framework in the United States

As early as 1798, Congress passed a law establishing the Relief of Sick and Disabled Seamen, which provided medical care for merchant marines. One of the first public programs enacted was the Emergency Maternal and Infant Care Act in 1943 to ensure that the spouses and children of low-ranking servicemen would be able to receive health care. In 1948 the Hospital Survey and Construction Act furnished federal funds to build hospitals in underserved communities, with the requirement that these funds offer a certain amount of charity care. In 1956 Congress extended federal health care benefits to dependents of military servicemen and women through the Civilian Health and Medical Program of the Uniformed Services.[19] The Indian Health Services, a distinct federally funded health care service, was created in 1955 on the basis of federal treaty obligations.[20]

These programs paved the way for the enactment of Medicare and Medicaid, the two most comprehensive medical services entitlements established to date. In 1965 the Social Security Act was amended to create Medicare as a federal health insurance program with a uniform eligibility and benefit package for those over 65. In 1972 coverage was extended to people with chronic renal disease, as well as to the disabled under 65 who had received disability benefits for two or more years. Although Medicare is often considered an entitlement to comprehensive health care for all persons over 65, the Part A entitlement covers only hospital costs. Physicians' and other outpatient services are supplied only if a premium is paid for Part B. These provisions, as well as the inclusion of lifesaving dialysis and kidney transplants within the program, confer an acute care orientation.

The 1965 amendment to the Social Security Act that created Medicare also established Medicaid, but the latter was more a consolidation and expansion of federally financed state programs for certain broad categories of needy recipients than a uniform or comprehensive entitlement. Medicaid, although limited in its coverage, provides a more comprehensive array of benefits than Medicare, including early periodic screening and treatment services for children and long-term care services for persons who are functionally impaired. However, eligibility criteria and benefits vary among the states and even within a particular state over time,[21] and low reimbursement rates limit access to health care by discouraging the participation of health care providers. Medicaid has also been more vulnerable than Medicare to budget cuts and an erosion in coverage. To contain Medicare costs, states have made eligibility requirements increasingly stringent: in 1989, thirty-two states set the maximum income level for public assistance eligibility at less than 50 percent of the federal poverty level standard.[22]

Court decisions have recognized a limited right to lifesaving treatment.

Hospitals are legally obligated to provide care to the underserved if the condition is life-threatening. Antidumping laws have also been enacted in response to egregious cases of hospitals denying care in emergency situations. The rulings and legislation, however, stem primarily from a sense that there is an obligation to act when an individual's life is at stake, rather than from recognition of a right to health care. Moreover, there have been few efforts to prosecute hospitals that turn away emergency patients.[23]

Although this country has gradually legislated a substantial role for the government in financing health care, it has done so with little clarity about the underlying rationale. Debates over extending entitlements have usually focused on the needs of specific groups and have avoided broader ethical issues about government responsibility in the health care sector. Policies and programs that provide a legal right to limited health care services through public programs were enacted from a recognition that society in general and hospitals in particular have a responsibility to provide health care for certain categories of vulnerable persons and to all individuals in emergency circumstances.[24] Nevertheless, advocates have generally been reluctant to employ rights language or to try to generalize these obligations.

Proposals for Comprehensive Health Care Reform in the United States

The defeat of the Clinton administration's health care reform initiatives in the 103rd Congress represents the fourth time in the past fifty years that the president or other key political leaders have unsuccessfully sought to enact comprehensive health care reforms. As in many other industrial democracies, the issue of national health insurance reemerged in the United Sates in the years following World War II. In 1948 President Truman introduced proposals for national insurance. A President's Commission on the Health Needs of the Nation reporting in 1953 concluded that "access to the means for the attainment and preservation of health is a basic human right."[25] These proposals for national health insurance and recognition of a right to health care were unsuccessful. In the early 1970s the increasing cost of medical care renewed discussions of national health insurance for all. Sen. Edward Kennedy of Massachusetts, a strong proponent of reform, introduced two bills, and the Nixon administration put forward a plan as an alternative to the Kennedy proposals.

In 1980 a President's Commission for the Study of Ethical Problems in Medicine and Biomedical Research was given a mandate by the Carter administration to study the "ethical and legal implications of differences in the availability of health services as determined by the income or residence of the person receiving the service."[26] Perhaps the most influential public study and report on access that focused on ethical issues, "Securing Access to Health Care for All," concluded that society has an ethical obligation to ensure equitable access to health care for all and that equitable access to health care requires that citizens be able to secure an adequate level of care without excessive burdens.[27] Nevertheless, the report explicitly chose not to frame its conclusions in terms of the moral or human right of individuals to health care but instead used the language of ethical obligation. Political factors played an important role in determining the commission's position on the right to health care. By the time the commission was making final decisions on the form and content of the report, the Reagan administration had taken office and a majority of the commissioners were Reagan appointees. The conservative political climate characterizing the early years of the Reagan administration was inimical to putting forward a proposal for a major and costly new social program, particularly one that would be understood to underwrite an unlimited new entitlement.[28]

For nearly a decade there was little momentum for health care reform. Then President Bush mentioned a right to health care in his 1991 State of the Union Address, Harris Wofford won election to the U.S. Senate from Pennsylvania, campaigning on a health care reform platform, and the 1992 Democratic platform incorporated a provision advocating a right to health care. In January 1993 Rep. Ed Pastor of Arizona introduced a nonbinding concurrent resolution resolving that it was the sense of Congress that "access to health care services is a fundamental human right" and that all legislative proposals by the president and Congress concerning national health care reform should be based on recognition of this fundamental right.[29] According to public opinion polls, support for national health insurance reached a forty year high of 66 percent in 1992. Voters in the 1992 election ranked health care as the third most important issue to consider in their choice of a president. By 1993 when President Clinton had taken office, health care had moved up to second place among the issues that Americans most wanted the government to address.[30]

Like the 1983 President's Commission, the Health Security Plan developed by President Clinton's expert Task Force on Health Reform refrained from using a rights formulation. And like the 1983 commission, the Clinton administration's failure to propose recognition of an explicit right to health care appears to have resulted from the reluctance to advocate for a new legal entitlement as well as from political decisions to avoid controversy and reach out to the broadest potential political constituency. Nevertheless, the American Health Security Act, first described in a September 1993 presidential address to the nation and then published as a 1342 page bill, proposed to guarantee comprehensive health coverage for all Americans regardless of health, employment status, or geographic location. The claim was that the plan was based on the bedrock assumption that all Americans must be guaranteed health coverage that, in President Clinton's words, "can never be taken away." Proponents argued that a true commitment to universality served as a fundamental dividing line between the president's proposal and others that did not commit to or define the means of achieving universal coverage.[31] Consistent with a human rights approach, the plan had provisions precluding any health plan from denying enrollment to an applicant because of health, employment, or financial status or charging some patients more than others because of age, medical condition, or other factors related to risk.[32]

Nevertheless, despite this rhetoric, the bill fell far short of providing a right to health care. Of the ten criteria listed above as defining a human rights approach, the Health Security Act conformed only with respect to its proposed grievance procedures. Its most serious deficiencies were its provisions to exclude undocumented aliens from coverage and to postpone extending coverage to the nearly 40 million Americans who lacked health insurance. Another problematic feature was its disregard for the welfare of the poorest and most vulnerable groups. Several of the proposed financial provisions would have taken resources away from low-income groups and illegal aliens so as to extend benefits for the middle class without imposing new taxes. This author conducted an analysis of the Health Security Act during the debate and assigned it an overall grade of C+ from a human rights perspective.[33]

Assessing the Failure of Comprehensive Reform Initiatives

Analyses of the defeat of comprehensive health care reform in 1993 and 1994 identify a variety of problems. Certainly, inadequacies in the manner in which the Clinton administration managed the process contributed to the debacle: the administration's failure to engage the public and/or the medical profession in the development of the plan, the absence of meaningful public debate, and the inability of the Clinton administration to articulate its vision to a confused, sometimes frightened public.[34] A second line of explanation focuses on the role of special interest groups and the millions of dollars they spent on their mass media campaigns to discredit the plan and subvert health care reform. Institutional and political obstacles, such as ideological conflict and the institutional fragmentation of Congress, were another factor. Some analysts have also noted that a Democratic president with an activist agenda is seriously handicapped in gaining support from the public in a context in which Democratic local party organizations have all but disappeared and organized labor is weak.[35] Others believe the problem was in the nature of the plan — its complexity, its poorly understood provisions, and its seeming creation of a large, new government bureaucracy. Still other analysts point to more long-term obstacles, such as the decline in concern about social issues and social welfare, a rise in concern about economic issues, and, most importantly, distrust of and frustration with the government.[36] The next section of this chapter will review these and other analyses and explore their implications for realizing a right to health care in the future.

COMMITMENT TO UNIVERSALITY

A right to health care is based on the principle of universality, the recognition that all members of society have equal moral claims and have to be treated with uniform standing and status. The principle of universality acknowledges that all persons, without regard to their purchasing power, social status, or personal merit, are entitled to basic and adequate health care. A human rights approach, based on justice rather than on efficiency, does not recognize any valid grounds for withholding health care from the poor, the unemployed, or individuals with pre-existing conditions or hereditary proclivities to disabilities or illness. Universality requires that a basic and adequate standard of health care be guaranteed to all citizens and residents. Though legal recognition by itself cannot guarantee secure and meaningful access to basic health care, legislative provision of a guaranteed standard of health care is a prerequisite. Although many countries distinguish between citizens and noncitizens or among citizens, legal residents, and others in according rights, excluding some groups, such as illegal aliens, is inconsistent with human rights criteria and is counterproductive, because it increases the likelihood that others will be exposed to communicable diseases.[37]

In surveys of attitudes toward health care, the American public has consistently expressed a belief that health care is a right and that the government is obligated to ensure health care for those who are too poor to pay for it. The public has held this conviction for more than sixty years. A 1938 Gallup poll reported that 81 percent of adults nationwide stated that "government should be responsible for medical care for people who can't afford it." [38] More recent polls elicited a similar figure. A 1987 Harris poll found almost universal agreement (91 percent) with a statement that "everybody should have the right to get the best possible care — as good as the treatment a millionaire gets." [39]

Why then is it so difficult to translate these convictions into reforms that will move toward the goal of universality? One interpretation of the failure of the health care reform points to the superficiality of the commitment to universality and the unwillingness of those with health care to make sacrifices on behalf of those who are without. Opinion polling expert Daniel Yankelovich suggests that what most people really mean when they say they support universal coverage is the following: "We don't believe anybody should be deprived of care because of money. We support the president's goal of insurance for all that can never be taken away, but only if the nation can afford it and it doesn't limit choice of doctors or raise taxes or cause employers to cut jobs." [40] James Mongan offers a similar explanation: "Even though poll after poll consistently shows that a strong majority of the American people favor the concept of universal coverage, the majority evaporates quickly when people are asked about their willingness to pay, via increased taxes or related employer and individual mandates, which are viewed as the equivalent of taxes." [41] He claims that economic malaise, based on a perception that real income is stagnating and that families are having to work harder to stay even, results in greater self-centeredness and a lack of willingness to sacrifice on behalf of others. [42] However, neither author offers real data to support his contentions.

Another potential line of interpretation is based on data showing that the moral commitment to the uninsured is combined with other core values that may be difficult to reconcile with universality. An analysis of these other core values was conducted by a team headed by Robert Blendon, chair of the Department of Health Policy and Management at the Harvard School of Public Health, who identified the following: a desire to achieve personal peace of mind, a lack of self-blame, a limited willingness to sacrifice, a reasoned self-interest in the changes that are enacted, a distrust of government, and a healthy cynicism about the behavior of major institutions. Underlying and interacting with this mix is a sense of anxiety and vulnerability about losing one's own benefits. All this adds up at the least to a fundamental ambivalence and contradictory attitudes about going forward with the kind of comprehensive reform required to achieve meaningful universality. Further complicating matters, surveys also show a lack of knowledge of the details of any reform proposals or even of the contents of one's own health insurance coverage.[43]

Even more significantly, no recent political leader has sought to harness the commitment to universality into a coherent national movement in favor of a right to health care. It is revealing that the health care debate focused on the details of specific proposals rather than on broader consideration of the goals and objectives of health care reform. As will be noted further on, a decision about establishing a fundamental right requires a national debate and the reshaping of the social covenant among members of a society and between them and their government. This national debate never took place. Nor did the Clinton administration or other political leaders deal realistically with the costs of universality and ask people to make sacrifices on behalf of those who lacked access to health care. Survey data suggest that such an appeal would have struck a responsive chord.

It is sometimes said that human rights are won by the people, not granted from above. Viewed from this perspective, the problem is not so much that the commitment to universality is superficial but that it has lacked leadership and an organizational base. Or to put it another way, no campaign on behalf of achieving universality ever began. Survey data suggest that the public was more inclined than the politicians to embrace a right to health care, but no one came forward to organize a grassroots movement and become its voice. Moreover, the need for political organization is particularly great in a political system in which those favoring the status quo have the advantage of significant resources and power, as in the United States. Airing a few commercials by public interest groups arguing for a right to health care, as occurred in 1993–94, does not substitute for a grassroots movement. If my analysis is correct, meaningful health care reform will require an explicit commitment to a right to health care as well as a well-organized mass movement promoting its achievement.

ROLE OF THE GOVERNMENT

A rights approach vests primary responsibility in governmental authorities. In all the countries that currently provide an entitlement to health care, the central government plays a major role in managing and leading the health care system. Obligations of government are both negative — not to violate — and positive — to uphold or implement. Relevant responsibilities encompass formulating a framework or plan through which to promote progressive realization as well as undertaking specific policies and actions intended to achieve that goal. In addition, legal recognition means that the content of the right should be used as a standard of evaluation for all public policy formulation: A criterion for evaluating prospective public policies in other fields is whether they are consistent with legal rights. Where there is a legacy of discrimination or inequities related to a right, as in this country, governments have a particular responsibility to rectify and redress this pattern. In the U.S. context, this translates into the need for a vigorous affirmative action policy with regard to health care, one component of which would be to give priority to minority health issues and the problems of the poor. The duty to protect requires according public health protection a high priority in the health care system and in public policy formation.

However, there is a fundamental contradiction in this country. Surveys indicate that Americans are dissatisfied with their health care system, more so than citizens in several other countries, but at the same time they do not trust the federal government to reform the health care system. Cross-national surveys indicate that Americans experience more problems in paying hospital and medical bills, obtaining care when needed, and being treated fairly when ill than Canadians or Germans. In addition, Americans spend more each year for their health care. A serious lack of public confidence in federal health care authorities marks the greatest cultural difference between Americans and citizens of other countries in comparative health opinion surveys. Analysts do not know, however, whether these attitudes reflect something specific to the federal role in health care or reflect a general antipathy toward the federal government.[44]

Many analyses of the failure of the Clinton health plan point to overwhelmingly negative attitudes toward the government as a key factor. Although a majority of Americans favored federally sponsored health care reform, their distrust of government undermined one of the key preconditions for achieving such reform. The data cited in these analyses are as follows: In 1965 when the Medicare program was enacted under President Johnson, 69 percent of Americans said that they trusted the federal government to do what is right most of the time, but in March 1993 when the Clintons convened their task force on health care reform, the level of trust had dropped to 23 percent. At the same time that the Clinton planners were proposing to institute an elaborate new bureaucracy and promulgate new health care regulations, 65 percent of Americans told pollsters that the federal government controlled too much of their daily lives; 69 percent agreed with the statement that when something is run by the government, it is usually inefficient or wasteful; and 60 percent favored a smaller government with fewer services.[45]

Nevertheless, other data temper these findings. For example, evidence suggests that Americans' attitudes toward governmental activism and regulation of the health care system have shifted from strong laissez-faire statism, often attributed to the public, to a more moderate pragmatism. Moreover, distrust of the government was outweighed by an even greater distrust of the health care industry. In various 1993 polls the public's acceptance of government activism increased when the purpose of the intervention became more specific and concrete. Polls indicate that in 1993 Americans were particularly receptive to government-imposed price controls to limit the amounts charged by private health insurers, drug companies, doctors, and hospitals. According to the surveys, the public also supported government controls to restrict increases in health care spending — even if that meant some health care services would become harder to obtain.[46] These data suggest that the public was ready for the development of a new public philosophy based on a greater role for the government, but no political leaders or movement assumed the role of articulating and giving voice to it.

If Americans began the health care reform debate with misgivings about the appropriateness and effectiveness of using government to reform the health care system, the defeat of efforts to do so inevitably bequeathed a legacy of greater ambivalence, distrust, and cynicism. Seen in this light, the defeat of government-initiated health care reform became something of a self-fulfilling prophecy. It left both politicians and citizens wary of renewed initiatives.

HEALTH CARE AS A SOCIAL GOOD

Employing rights language designates health care as a fundamentally important social good to be considered differently from other goods and services. In applying rights discourse, a society assigns priority to a particular human or social attribute and accepts responsibility for its promotion and protection. A logical corollary of health care being understood as a fundamentally important social good is that the health care system itself should be evaluated by a social or community standard in terms of its ability to promote and protect the general health and well-being of the population as a whole. Designating health care as a right therefore changes the status of health care from a commodity regulated primarily by market forces for the financial benefit of health care providers to a social good to be distributed according to principles of justice.[47]

The dilemma is that many of the components of a human rights approach are currently the subject of contention. Ethicist George Khushf describes the competing visions of society as follows: "On one side, there is an emphasis on social solidarity and equity, an understanding of society as community, a confidence in government, and a skepticism about the capacity of the market to promote efficiency or justice. On the other side, there is an emphasis on pluralism and moral diversity, a distinction between communities and society, a skepticism about the capacity of government to solve social problems, and a confidence in a free market, especially in its protection of individual liberty and responsibility."[48]

Applied to the health care debate, at one end of the ideological spectrum are those, including human rights advocates, who would like to see health care treated as a social good to be made available to all members of society, regardless of a person's ability to pay for it, with at least basic health care uniformly available to everyone. At the other end are those persons who have been dubbed the "food people." This label reflects the disposition of members of this group to consider health care just another basic private consumption good, such as food or housing, or as House Republican Leader Dick Armey put it, "Health care is just a commodity, just like bread, and just like housing and everything else."[49] The "food people" regard the procurement and financing of health care to be primarily the responsibility of the individual and assume that it is quite appropriate for the quantity, timeliness, and quality of health care to vary with household income.[50]

The lack of a moral consensus about basic societal values affected efforts to bring about significant reform of the health care system. Even the deliberations of the ethics group of the President's Health Care Task Force apparently reflected this conflict.[51] Although the ethics group did manage to draft an inventory of ethical principles and values that might ideally inform health care reform, it could not offer a coherent moral vision. As one member of the ethics group commented, "While it would be uplifting to think that a shared moral vision was at the root of health care reform, and the Ethics group had effectively surfaced and neatly defined this shared vision, there is little evidence to confirm such a claim. . . . It would be more accurate to say that shared dissatisfaction with the present health care system, rather than a shared moral vision, has shoved health care reform to center stage."[52]

The so-called food people won the health care reform battle of 1993–94, but the manner in which they did so does not support the contention that their position is shared by the majority of the American people. For one thing, they did not fight openly, making the claims their ideological position represents. Instead, as Uwe Reinhardt points out, their initiatives were camouflaged behind soothing code words, such as "empowerment," "personal responsibility," and the "freedom to choose whether or not to be insured," all of which are relevant only to those already insured and/or affluent Americans.[53] However, while the "food people" may be a numerical minority, they are overwhelmingly supported by those with the most to lose if significant health care reform were to take place — pharmaceutical corporations, for-profit health-related companies and institutions, health care providers, and health care professionals. As the outcome of the 1993–94 reform efforts attests, these groups have the incentive and resources to block health care reform. Their economic and political power constitutes the most significant obstacle to achieving the right to health care.

Establishment of a New Paradigm

One of the AAAS project's conclusions regarding a human rights approach to health care reform was the need for a new framework or paradigm based on a preventive rather than curative approach to health.[54] The current U.S. health care model was deemed to be fundamentally inadequate for the following reasons:

1. It concentrates resources in curative care rather than dealing with the underlying determinants of health and public health measures.

2. It is based on a dual-tier system in which the poor are given a different standard of medical care than the middle and upper classes.

3. It favors training of and treatment by specialists rather than a focus on primary health care by family physicians or general practitioners.

4. Health care is treated as a for-profit commodity rather than as a social or public good.

5. There are great disparities in the availability of health services across ge-

ographic locations, leaving many urban centers and rural areas seriously underserved, without the institutional means to correct this problem.

6. There are no mechanisms to control the cost of medical care by regulating the deployment of high technology innovations, reducing the cost of pharmaceuticals, focusing investments in preventive/primary care, or limiting tertiary care services.

Many of the participants also believed that the principles of a market-driven health care system were inconsistent with basic features of a human rights approach. In a market-oriented system, health care is treated as a commodity, not as a priority social good or a right. A health care system controlled by market forces lacks mechanisms to assure public control, accountability, and recourse for violations of human rights. Stressing self-interest and economic incentives as the driving forces seriously weakens or perhaps even undermines the community welfare standard intrinsic to a human rights approach. By making access to and the quality of health care services dependent on financial resources, a market-driven system inhibits or precludes universality of access. There are few incentives and many disincentives for a market-oriented health care system to be responsive to the special needs of neglected and disadvantaged groups. Providers intent on maximizing profits will prefer acute care practices, because preventive and primary care are less lucrative.[55]

The failure of fundamental health care reform partly reflected the inability or unwillingness of politicians or the public to confront the fundamental inadequacies in the U.S. model. None of the proponents of health care reform was willing to address issues related to the inappropriateness or cost of our current model of health care, and beneficiaries of the current system had few incentives to remind the public of problems. No one discussed the need to undertake structural changes in the system or emphasized that universality would require public choices and sacrifices. The proposed Clinton package added some public health initiatives and preventive care services and provided incentives for training primary care physicians, but it did not deal with other issues, such as the proliferation of high cost technologies, the aging of the population, and the apparent insatiability of the public demand for health care. Therefore it is not surprising that the public assumes that it can have it all: universality, access to unlimited services, and unlimited high technology innovations, all without new taxes or fees.

In the period since the defeat of the health care reform initiative, the system has become even more retrogressive. Given the conclusion that commercialization of health care contradicts fundamental aspects of a human rights approach, it is disturbing that for-profit managed care providers are one of the principal beneficiaries. Moreover, in practical terms Congress has given de facto sanction to an income-based three tier system: (1) uninsured Americans who are poor or near-poor and families of persons who work full time at low wages and salaries will have to rely on a patchwork of public hospitals and clinics, which, in the aftermath of draconian welfare legislation and increasing pressure from managed care providers, will be even more underfunded than in the past; (2) the employed broad middle class will be increasingly enrolled in health maintenance plans that will limit patients' choice of doctor and hospital and withhold some care that patients and their physicians judge desirable; and (3) affluent Americans will continue to benefit from open-ended, fee-for-service health care without rationing in any form.[56]

PUBLIC PARTICIPATION

A human rights approach underscores the importance of public participation in shaping health care policy and the accountability of major health care institutions to the broader public. The recognition of new rights and entitlements requires a broad political consensus that can only result from meaningful public consultations. This process represents political action in the most profound sense through which a community redefines the nature of its ties and obligations to its members. The legitimacy of both the process and the specific definition of the right to health care depends on the broadest possible involvement of citizens. Meaningful participation entails the careful design of a process through which issues are identified and forums provided that encourage citizen input into the debate. Setting the agenda for health care reform cannot and should not be the prerogative of medical professionals, health care providers, or public policy elites. In addition, health care users should be represented on all decision-making boards so that oversight and control do not become the prerogative only of health care professionals. Further, a human rights approach entails the accountability and transparency of major institutions in the health sector.[57]

Several analysts have castigated the Clinton administration for failing to create and sustain a meaningful public debate over health care reform. According to Daniel Yankelovich, "As far as the public is concerned, the great health care debate never took place."[58] He attributes the defeat of the Clinton health reform plan, as well as the repeal of catastrophic coverage for the elderly in 1989, to this massive failure of public deliberation. Yankelovich describes the electorate and the nation's leadership class (in which he includes leaders of medicine, industry, education, the legal profession, science, religion, and journalism, as well as national and community political leaders) as "carrying out a bizarre dialogue of the deaf" with each other across a void of misunderstanding and misinterpretation.[59] According to Yankelovich, it reflected a "disconnect" between the American public and its leaders. As he describes the process, "Technical experts designed it, special interests argued it, political leaders sold it, journalists more interested in its political ramifications than its contents kibitzed it, advertising attacked it. There was no way for average Americans to understand what it meant for them. The political reality is that Americans were not prepared to and did not, in fact, deliberate on the scope, magnitude, and nature of the reforms the Clinton plan proposed."[60]

Yankelovich believes that the plan lost public support because its opponents found it easy to raise the public's fears about a proposal that they did not understand. This analysis led Yankelovich to conclude that successful reforms in the future depend on the nation's ability to rectify this "disconnect" and carry out genuine public deliberation on this significant topic. To that end, Yankelovich proposes a strategy for stimulating a five year process of public deliberation on health care.[61]

Others have been less sanguine that it is possible to hold a meaningful public debate on health care reform. Some analysts suggest that the problems that Yankelovich cited appear to be indicative of deeper issues than just a need for better information and communication. The survey data indicate that not only did the American public have little knowledge of the specifics of the various 1993–94 health care proposals, but it also had no decisive view of the details of the proposed legislation eventually passed in August 1996 to make health insurance coverage portable from job to job.[62] Several analysts question whether it is realistic to expect a substantial portion of the public to enter into, and sustain interest in, a complex process of deliberation that might extend over several years.[63] Others point to a decline in concern about social issues and social welfare and a rise in distrust and frustration with government.[64] If these critics are right, then Yankelovich is too optimistic about the prospects for constructing a meaningful health care debate.

AFFORDABLE AND PUBLICLY FINANCED HEALTH CARE

One of the innovations in the human rights approach developed through the AAAS project is the emphasis on a meaningful right's being affordable as well as publicly financed. There was a consensus that recognition of a right to health care requires that society remove financial barriers to basic and adequate health care. This means that the quality and scope of basic health services need to be the same for all persons regardless of their financial status, and the means by which the health care system is financed needs to be equitable and fair. To balance these commitments, the scope of the entitlement should be linked to the resource levels available in a particular society so that the total cost of health care is affordable on a societal level. The objective is to seek a national consensus on a cost-conscious standard of care.[65]

These financial considerations were dealt with inadequately or not at all by the abortive health care reform process. As noted above, there was a lack of willingness by elites to acknowledge the fundamental deficiencies in the high-cost curative care paradigm prevalent in the United States or to address the fundamental causes of runaway costs, such as the proliferation of high-cost technologies, the comparatively high level of provider fees, and commercialization of the health care sector. To avoid alienating health care professionals and providers, the Clinton administration did not deal realistically with containing health care costs or imposing limits on health care spending. Seemingly, there was an unspoken agreement not to mention the "r" word, "rationing." The Clinton administration's decision not to propose a tax increase, other than a cigarette tax, to finance its plan further suggested that more people could be covered, more benefits added, and more bureaucracies established without additional cost. This decision may have backfired: In an October 1993 survey, eight in ten Americans thought that the Clinton plan would cost more than the president estimated.[66] This sense of hidden costs undoubtedly helped to undermine the administration's credibility.

Despite conventional wisdom that Americans are unequivocally antitax as well as antigovernment, the data are open to a different conclusion. As one group of analysts points out, survey results purporting to show that Americans oppose tax increases to finance health care may be an artifact of the manner in which the questions were asked. Americans' attitudes appear to depend on whether they perceive concrete, specific gains. Other factors shaping Americans' views are whether the proposed new taxes are linked to potential future savings and whether respondents can identify alternative sources of financing, such as employer contributions. It is noteworthy that in a January 1993 survey about two thirds of those questioned supported tax-financed national health insurance. Support slipped during consideration of health care reform to about 50 percent.[67] Nevertheless, these figures suggest that the public was more open than Congress to single-payer, government-financed health care reform.

With the failure to enact fundamental health care reform in 1993–94, the American political system lost a significant opportunity to renegotiate its fundamental social covenant. Despite the failure to shape the choices in human rights language, the public appeared to have been at least potentially willing to embrace many elements of a human rights approach to health care reform, most notably a commitment to universality. Other dimensions of a human rights approach, such as a central role for the government, were more problematic. Still others, including the levying of taxes to finance health care, the adoption of a new paradigm, and the imposition of cost savings measures, may or may not have been issues. It is difficult to know because they were not addressed.

In the aftermath of the defeat of health care reform proposals, prospects for fundamental and meaningful systemic reform appear to be much reduced. As noted previously, many of the trends and problems that shaped a national consensus in favor of significant reform persist or are even getting worse. Nevertheless, the historic opportunity to address them may have been lost, at least for the foreseeable future. The experience seems to have confirmed the public's apprehension about the ability of the federal government to institute meaningful changes and increased its alienation from the political system. It has also made potentially progressive political leaders even less willing to take political risks and deal realistically with the inadequacies of the health care system. Ironically, their obfuscation and lack of political will contributed significantly to their failure in the first place.

Incremental national or state level health care reform may be the only current option. Neither is likely to address the worst problems. For one thing, it is virtually impossible to institute systemic changes on an incremental basis. Moreover, it is unlikely that most states will be inclined or able to enact comprehensive insurance expansions or engage in serious cost containment efforts, even if current federal barriers that inhibit innovative reforms are removed. State-based reforms are a poor substitute for a national health insurance program for a variety of reasons. First, it will be very difficult for any state to find the necessary money to provide universal coverage. Second, state innovation is limited by the fear of a business exodus in the face of comprehensive reforms and/or the state becoming a magnet attracting uninsured persons.[68] Even if states surmounted these obstacles, a variable level of coverage and benefits at the state level would be inconsistent with the requirements of a national human rights approach. Thus it appears that significant violations of the right to health care will persist in this country for the foreseeable future.

Notes

1. Robert Pear, "Health Care Costs Up Sharply Again, Posing New Threat," *New York Times*, January 5, 1993, 1.

2. John Holahan, Colin Winterbottom, and Shruti Rajan, "A Shifting Picture of Health Insurance," *Health Affairs* 14 (winter 1995): 254.

3. Michael Millman, ed., *Access to Health Care in America* (Washington DC: National Academy Press, 1993).

4. Diane Rowland, Barbara Lyons, Alina Salganicoff, and Peter Long, "Special Report: A Profile of the Uninsured in America," *Health Affairs* 14 (spring 1994): 284.

5. Rowland et al., "Profile," 284–286.

6. Millman, *Access*, 3.

7. Rowland et al., "Profile," 285.

8. Judith Havemann, "President Signs Insurance Portability Bill into Law," *Washington Post*, August 22, 1996, A9.

9. American Public Health Association (APHA), *America's Public Health Association Report Card: A State-by-State Report on the Health of the Public* (Washington DC: APHA, 1992), 2.

10. APHA, *America's Public Health Association, Report Card*, 1.

11. "A Universal Declaration of Human Rights," *The International Bill of Rights* (New York: United Nations, 1985), 8.

12. *International Covenant on Economic, Social and Cultural Rights.* Adopted and opened for signature, ratification, and accession by U.N. General Assembly Resolution 2200 A (XXI) on December 16, 1966. Entered into force on January 3, 1976.

13. World Health Organization, "Preamble to the Constitution," in *The First Ten Years of the World Health Organization* (Geneva: WHO, 1958).

14. Genevieve Pinet, "Human Rights and the WHO Health for All Indicators," paper prepared for the American Association for the Advancement of Science Consultation on Standards and Indicators to Monitor the Achievement of the Right to Health Care, February 26, 1993, Washington DC.

15. See, for example, Hernan Fuenzalida-Puelma and Susan Scholle Connor, eds., *The Right to Health in the Americas: A Comparative Constitutional Study* (Washington DC: Pan American Health Organization, 1989), 608.

16. See, for example, Daniel Callahan, *What Kind of Life: A Challenging Exploration of the Goals of Medicine* (New York: Touchstone Books, 1990), 56.

17. Audrey R. Chapman, *Exploring a Human Rights Approach to Health Care Reform* (Washington DC: American Association for the Advancement of Science, 1993), 19–20.

18. This list is drawn from the rephrased version of the major components of a right to health care in Audrey R. Chapman, "A Human Rights Approach to Health Care Reform," in *Health Care Reform: A Human Rights Approach*, ed. Audrey R. Chapman (Washington DC: Georgetown University Press, 1994), 149–164.

19. Janet O'Keefe, "The Right to Health Care and Health Care Reform," in Chapman, *Health Care Reform*, 36–39.

20. Timothy Taylor, "The Needs of Native Americans," presentation at the AAAS Right to Health Care Consultation: Defining a Minimum Adequate Standard of Health Care, November 13, 1992.

21. President's Commission for the Study of Ethical Problems in Medicine and Biomedical and Behavioral Research, *Securing Access to Health Care: The Ethical Implications of Differences in the Availability of Health Services*, vol. 1 (Washington DC: U.S. Government Printing Office, 1983), 146–154.

22. "Including the Poor, Health Policy Agenda for the American People: The Final Report of the Ad Hoc Committee on Medicaid," 1989. Cited in *Health Care Crisis in America Fact Sheet* (Minneapolis: Bioethics Consultation Group, 1989).

23. O'Keefe, "Right to Health Care," 39–41.

24. Theodore R. Marmor, "History and Politics of Health Care Reform," in Thomas J. Bole III and William B. Bondeson, eds., *Rights to Health Care* (Dordrecht, Netherlands: Kluwer Academic Publishers, 1991), 26–27.

25. *President's Commission on the Health Needs of the Nation* (Washington DC: U.S. Government Printing Office, 1953), 3.

26. "President's Commission for the Study of Ethical Problems," *President's Commission*, 6.

27. *President's Commission*, 3–5.

28. Dan W. Brock, "The President's Commission on the Right to Health Care," in Chapman, *Health Care Reform*.

29. House Concurrent Resolution No. 56, 103rd Congress, 1st session.

30. Robert J. Blendon, Mollyann Brodie, and John Benson, "What Happened to Americans' Support for the Clinton Health Plan?," *Health Affairs* 14 (summer 1995): 12.

31. Walter A. Zelman, "The Rationale Behind the Clinton Health Care Reform Plan," *Health Affairs* 14 (spring 1995): 10.

32. *Health Security: Preliminary Plan Summary* (Washington DC: U.S. Government Printing Office, 1993), 1.

33. Audrey R. Chapman, "Assessing the Clinton Administration's Health Security Act," in Chapman, *Health Care Reform*.

34. Daniel Yankelovich, "The Debate That Wasn't: The Public and the Clinton Plan," *Health Affairs* 14 (spring 1995): 7–36.

35. Margaret Weir, "Institutional and Political Obstacles to Reform," *Health Affairs* 14 (spring 1995): 102–103.

36. Drew E. Altman, "The Realities Behind the Polls," *Health Affairs* 14 (spring 1995): 24–26.

37. Audrey R. Chapman, "A Human Rights Approach to Health Care Reform," in Chapman, *Health Care Reform*, 149–150.

38. Quoted in Yankelovich, "Debate," 12.

39. Yankelovich, "Debate," 12.

40. Yankelovich, "Debate," 15.

41. James J. Mongan, "Anatomy and Physiology of Health Reform's Failure," *Health Affairs* 14 (spring 1995): 101.

42. Mongan, "Anatomy," 101.

43. Robert J. Blendon, John Marttila, John M. Benson, Matthew C. Shelter, Francis J. Connolly, and Tom Kiley, "The Beliefs and Values Shaping Today's Health Reform Debate," *Health Affairs* 13 (spring 1994): 274–298.

44. Robert J. Blendon, John Benson, Karen Donelan, Robert Leitman, Humphrey Taylor, Christian Koeck, and Daniel Gitterman, "Who Has the Best Health Care System? A Second Look," *Health Affairs* 14 (winter 1995): 220–230.

45. Blendon, Brodie, and Benson, "What Happened to Americans' Support?," 12–13.

46. Blendon et al., "Beliefs and Values," 294–295.

47. Chapman, "A Human Rights Approach to Health Care Reform," in Chapman, *Health Care Reform*, 151–152.

48. George Khushf, "Ethics, Politics, and Health Care Reform," *Journal of Medicine and Philosophy* 19 (October 1994): 397.

49. Quoted in Uwe E. Reinhardt, "Turning Our Gaze from Bread and Circus Games," *Health Affairs* 14 (spring 1995): 33.

50. Reinhardt, "Turning Our Gaze," 33.

51. See, for example, the differences in perspective in the articles in a special journal issue edited by George Khushf on "The Ethical Foundations of Health Care Reform: Clinton and Beyond," *Journal of Medicine and Philosophy* 19 (October 1994): 78.

52. Laurence J. O'Connell, "Ethicists and Health Care Reform: An Indecent Proposal?" *Journal of Medicine and Philosophy* 19 (October 1994): 421.

53. Reinhardt, "Turning Our Gaze," 34.

54. Chapman, "A Human Rights Approach to Health Care Reform," in Chapman, *Health Care Reform*, 52–60.

55. Chapman, "A Human Rights Approach to Health Care Reform," in Chapman, *Health Care Reform*, 52.

56. Reinhardt, "Turning Our Gaze," 34.

57. Chapman, "A Human Rights Approach to Health Care Reform," Chapman, *Health Care Reform*, 156–157.

58. Yankelovich, "Debate," 10.

59. Yankelovich, "Debate," 8.

60. Yankelovich, "Debate," 8–9.

61. Yankelovich, "Debate," 20–23.

62. Blendon et al., "Beliefs and Values," 280–283; Adam Clymer, "Public Lacks Strong Opinions on Health Bill, Survey Shows," *New York Times*, July 31, 1996, A13.

63. Reinhardt, "Turning Our Gaze," 36; and Mark A. Goldberg, "Public Judgment and the Prospects for Reform," *Health Affairs* 14 (spring 1995): 31–32.

64. Drew E. Altman, "The Realities Behind the Polls," *Health Affairs* 14 (spring 1995): 24–26.

65. Chapman, "A Human Rights Approach to Health Care Reform," in Chapman, *Health Care Reform*, 155–156.

66. Blendon, Brodie, and Benson, "What Happened to Americans' Support?," 16–17.

67. Blendon et al., "Beliefs and Values," 290–292.

68. Michael S. Sparer, "Great Expectations: The Limits of State Health Care Reform," *Health Affairs* 14 (winter 1995): 191–202.

2

Economic Globalization and American Society

•

KELLY-KATE PEASE

The post–Cold War international environment has been conducive for democratic reforms in the former Eastern bloc and Soviet successor states, as well as the former authoritarian states aligned with the West. The international community has cheered the improved human rights records of many of these states while remaining gravely concerned by human rights violations in places such as Chechnya, Bosnia, Somalia, Iraq, Rwanda, and Burundi. The focus of the human rights community has been on gross violations of human rights occurring as a result of the breakdown of civil order or violent conflict. Less attention is paid to the status of internationally recognized human rights in the United States and the other advanced industrialized states. The dominant human rights discourses generally center on U.S. human rights policy abroad or the subordination of human rights to sovereignty or foreign policy considerations. What is often overlooked, however, is that globalization and the growing dominance of neoclassical economic ideology pose serious structural challenges to the actualization of human rights in the United States and abroad, particularly with respect to economic and social rights. If current trends continue, civil and political rights may also be undermined.

I seek to partially fill the void in the human rights literature regarding the status of, and challenges to, human rights in the United States by making three interrelated arguments. First, I argue that while the United States has conceived of human rights only as civil and political rights, economic and social rights were, at the very least, interactive with civil and political rights in both political and economic theory. Although this interaction has not been expressed using international human rights language, it is implicit in the economic ideology that dominated international economic relations from 1945 to 1981. The human rights debate during the Cold War was not about whether economic and social rights were human rights per se as much as it was about ideological differences regarding strategies for actualizing these rights.

The tendency on the part of U.S. scholars to consider only civil and political rights as human rights results from the divorce of human rights discussions from their formative economic factors. My second related argument is that current understandings of human rights can be enhanced by examining the relationships between conceptions of human rights and economic ideology. Human rights are usually conceptualized and justified in terms of legal or political theory while ignoring the companion economic theory. Liberalism is just as much an economic philosophy as it is the political philosophy that justifies civil and political rights. I explore the theoretical debate regarding which category or generation of rights should be given priority using an economic interpretation of the evolution of internationally recognized human rights. This analysis shows that different understandings of human rights are grounded in economic, as well as political, traditions.

Third, I argue that the globalization (internationalization) of the U.S. economy has led to diminished socioeconomic human rights in the United States. The declining status of social and economic rights can be attributed to: (1) neoclassical/liberal ideology that relegates the state to the role of a laissez-faire umpire (enforcing contracts and property rights), and (2) the inherent logic of a relatively uncontrolled global market. These forces, coupled with the historical practice and enforcement of human rights, have contributed to the evolving consensus that human rights are increasingly being defined only as political and civil rights. The central theme of this research is that economic considerations, whether ideological or practical, substantially affect the discourses on human rights and certainly influence their definition and implementation.

The Interaction of Human Rights in International Law

A growing body of international law is devoted to several kinds of human rights: civil and political rights; economic, social, and cultural rights; and collective rights. The first post–World War II international law to recognize human rights is the UN Charter (1946), in which Articles 55 and 56 levy a duty on states to respect human rights and establish the protection of human rights as priority for the United Nations. Not a warrant for intervention, these provisions articulate general goals without defining strategies for actualizing them. Article 55 states:

With a view to the creation of conditions of stability and well-being which are necessary for the peaceful and friendly relations among nations based on respect for the principle of equal rights and self-determination, the United Nations shall promote:

a. Higher standards of living, full employment, and conditions of economic and social progress and development;

b. Solutions of international and economic, social, health, and related problems; and international cultural and educational cooperation; and

c. universal respect for, and observance of human rights and fundamental freedoms for all without distinction as to race, sex, language or religion.

Article 56 requires states to take joint and separate action to achieve these purposes.

Articles 55 and 56 reflect more than just a passing reference to human rights. Human rights were included in the charter at the insistence of the United States, and the United Nations itself is the centerpiece of the U.S. hegemonic order.[1] Human rights legitimized U.S. hegemony, and, more important, Article 55 reveals what Ruggie has termed the "compromise of imbedded liberalism."[2] This compromise, which is also reflected in the charters of the World Bank and the International Monetary Fund (IMF), recognizes that states must have a positive role in affecting national economic goals such as full employment and economic development. The state is permitted a variety of actions such as tax and spending programs to pursue these goals while at the same time maintaining a basic commitment to free trade and free market principles.[3] The Great Depression experience is remembered by the compromise of embedded liberalism, as is the importance of social and economic rights to international peace and stability.

The Universal Declaration of Human Rights, a resolution passed by the UN General Assembly in 1948, spells out political and civil rights (for example, the right to life, liberty, and political participation), economic and social rights (the right to work, form unions, and to social security), and collective rights (the right to self-determination). Although not immediately binding international law, the Universal Declaration of Human Rights served as the foundation of the international human rights regime as an expression of the will of the international community.[4] The drafters of the resolution intended to follow up with a binding treaty or covenant that would have placed duties and obligations on states.[5]

The binding international law that was supposed to follow the Universal

Declaration of Human Rights was a long time in coming. The International Covenant of Civil and Political Rights and the International Covenant on Economic, Social, and Cultural Rights did not open for signature until 1966 and were delayed in large part because of Cold War tensions and the related divisiveness regarding the status of social and economic rights relative to political and civil rights.[6] The United States emphasized Soviet violations of civil and political rights to justify and legitimize its Cold War policies. The Soviet Union accentuated segregation in the U.S. South, the systematic denial of political and civil rights of African Americans, and the lack of attention paid to economic rights. Developing states sought to actualize cultural and collective rights as well as certain economic rights. The lag between the Universal Declaration and the International Covenants was caused by fundamental political divisions within the international community. These political divisions were not just about the primacy of state sovereignty over authoritative international norms or differences of political opinion. They were reflective of deep-rooted ideological differences that are essentially economic: capitalism versus socialism, the "haves" versus the "have-nots."

The distinction between the different categories of human rights has given rise to the debate as to whether one category of rights should be given preference over another. After all, the right to life (a political right) would seem to take priority over the right to a paid holiday (an economic right). The following section provides a brief overview of the variations of this debate and also integrates an economic interpretation. This synthesis demonstrates the interaction of economic and social rights with civil and political rights in the United States. It also sets the foundation for consideration of evidence that suggests that economic and social rights in the United States are threatened by the globalization of the U.S. economy.

Political/Civil Rights versus Economic/Social Rights

The debate regarding if and when certain human rights should be given preference over other human rights consists of overlapping arguments, grounded in different philosophical traditions. One side of the debate argues that civil and political rights must first be guaranteed before economic and social rights can be actualized. Variations of this argument use the concepts of first and second generation rights and positive and negative rights. First generation rights are often thought of as civil and political rights, and their intellectual precursors are liberals such as Adam Smith, John Locke, and

John Stuart Mill. The idea that "man" has an inalienable right to life, liberty, and the pursuit of happiness (property) entails both negative and positive human rights.[7] Negative human rights, such as the right to life, free expression, and association, require the forbearance of the state for the most part. Human beings have the right to be free from government interference to pursue their self-interests. Theoretically, the individual knows better than the government regarding what is best for the individual and, therefore, should be free to maximize his or her self-interest. According to one observer, negative human rights shield the individual from abuse and misuse of political authority.[8]

Positive rights differ from negative rights in that they require action on the part of the state. Political and civil rights, such as the right to political participation, nondiscrimination, and equal protection under the law, enable individuals to influence and control government. Armed with these rights, individuals will ensure the forbearance of the government and also be able to affect their personal goals. Individuals maximizing their self-interest in a maximally free market provide the greatest good for the number. This explanation, albeit an oversimplification, suggests that civil and political rights, which can require extensive state action to implement and enforce, are required first so that individuals can then pursue a family, a home, an education, and so forth. In other words, empower individuals with civil and political rights (both positive and negative) and they will actualize for themselves economic and social rights. The inherent assumption of this reasoning is that the market will provide the means for individuals to pursue economic and social rights.

The opposite side of the debate holds that economic and social rights, which are often referred to as second generation rights, must first be guaranteed before civil and political rights can have any meaning. What good is the right to vote if the individual is starving? So-called second generation rights grew out of the shortcomings of market capitalism. The abuses and failings of capitalism have been addressed by such ideologically divergent thinkers as Marx, Hobson, Lenin, and Keynes.[9] Marx and Marxist scholars have provided the most comprehensive critique of liberalism and capitalism, and, therefore, a brief summary of the critique is presented below.

According to Marx, capitalism faces three economic laws: the law of disproportionality, the law of capital concentration, and the law of the falling rate of profit.[10] The law of disproportionality rejects the equilibrium assumed by liberals between supply and demand. Supply does not necessarily create demand, because capitalism's capacity to produce goods and the wage-earner's capacity to consume are often in disequilibrium. This is due to cyclical depressions, recessions, and other market fluctuations. During these periods of economic crises, the wage earner is impoverished, because his or her earnings do not permit the consumption of the available goods and services. The disproportionality between supply and demand is exacerbated by falling wages, as competition in the market and the drive to maximize profits force wages down, limiting the worker's purchasing power.

The law of concentration holds that competition and the demands of the market require greater efficiency, productivity, and capital investment. As the market weeds out the less efficient, capitalism evolves to the point where wealth is concentrated into the hands of the fittest. "With the petite bourgeoisie being pushed down into the swelling ranks of the impoverished proletariat, the reserve army of the unemployed increases, labor's wages decline and the capitalist society becomes ripe for social revolution."[11] The concentration of wealth leads to monopoly and oligopoly in which businesses have incentives to set prices artificially high and wages artificially low.

The law of the falling rate of profit is that as capital increases in supply, the marginal rate of return declines and the incentive to invest in job-creating ventures also declines. Coupled with labor-saving technologies, unemployment rises and further impoverishes the working class. For Marxists, these laws indicate that capitalism could collapse under the weight of its own contradictions.

In light of this critique of liberalism, it is not surprising that Marxist analyses of human rights have tended to focus on positive economic and social rights, such as the right to employment and for just reward, to unionize, and to food and shelter. Political and civil rights are meaningless until economic and social rights are realized.[12] Simply possessing civil and political rights does not translate into the actualization of social and economic rights, because the market-based system of private property threatens, not enhances, the economic and social rights thought to be necessary for human dignity. The status of most people in the late nineteenth and early twentieth century, along with the Great Depression, suggests that Marxist arguments have considerable merit.

Marxists were not the only ones to recognize the short-comings of capitalism and the consequences for economic and social rights. Keynesian-inspired liberals have argued that the laws identified by the Marxists can be nullified through state intervention. The law of disproportionality can be nullified by the state through demand management. Demand can be increased or curbed through tax and spending programs and an adjustable monetary policy. The effects of the law of concentration can be avoided through antitrust legislation, income redistribution — including a progressive income tax — and direct and indirect government subsidies. Governments could also support unions and promote regional and small businesses. The law of the falling rate of profit could be invalidated by extensive government support of education, health care, and research that increased the efficiency of all factors of production.[13] Keynesian economics lent considerable support to the idea that the government has a responsibility to provide positive second generation rights.

To say that the United States falls neatly on the classical liberal side of the debate is misleading. After the Depression and World War II, the U.S. position on human rights at home and abroad was based on a number of considerations. At home, political and civil rights were still given preference but buoyed by Keynesian and New Deal economics; the interactive nature of first and second generation rights was at the very least implicit. The state appropriately had a role in securing an adequate standard of living and making sure everyone had access to employment. The state should manage the economy to avoid the cyclical booms and busts by leveling the peaks and valleys associated with the often volatile market. The contradictions of capitalism could be corrected by the state through demand management and a variety of government initiatives and programs. Unemployment was addressed through the 1946 Employment Act, which gave the U.S. government the responsibility to promote maximum employment, and the Humphrey-Hawkins Act of 1978 required the government to reduce unemployment to a minimum of 4 percent by 1983 and to maintain that level.[14] Poverty and homelessness were addressed through direct subsidies such as Social Security, Aid to Families with Dependent Children (AFDC), Unemployment Insurance, Medicare, Medicaid, Food Stamps, and educational assistance.

Legislation such as the Civil Rights Acts, Affirmative Action, and the Voting Rights Act were designed to correct violations of civil and political rights within the United States. These extensive government programs, coupled with federal monitoring, show the interaction of political/civil and social/ economic rights at home. The United States clearly recognized that economic and social rights were important human rights, even though it was not a formal party to the international covenants.[15]

The state intervention became even more institutionalized in Europe.

Welfare states emerged in part because of the strong state role required for rebuilding war-torn economies. The United States even encouraged the welfare state in Europe as part of its hegemonic role. The welfare state was seen as a more attractive alternative to Soviet-styled socialism after World War II. Furthermore, by permitting state intervention in the national economies of Europe, the United States was able to gain the states' deference to its leadership in the international economy, particularly as it related to the Bretton Woods system. This represents the compromise of embedded liberalism and is, in essence, what economists call the neoclassical-Keynesian synthesis.[16]

U.S. human rights policy has rarely been consistent with its rhetoric or its policy at home. On the one hand, the United States condemned the Soviet Union and its communist allies for systematically denying civil and political rights. On the other hand, the United States tolerated the systematic denial of civil and political rights by its allies in the developing world on the grounds that a strong arm was a necessary bulwark to communism. What is often forgotten is that a strong arm was also necessary to implement development plans and create markets in the Third World. Mass participation, which involves civil and political rights, coupled with urbanization, population growth, and mass literacy were seen as threats to development.[17] Democratic reforms such as the right to vote, freedom of association, freedom of the press, and the right to participate in government placed too many demands on a developing state's economy. The state was pressured to provide for social welfare and social security, goods it could ill-afford.

So, in somewhat of a contradiction of past human rights rhetoric and classical liberal ideology, a circular argument for human rights in the developing world was formed. Civil and political rights were subordinated until market reforms could be enacted and institutionalized. Then political and civil rights could be granted so that individuals could pressure the state and pursue their economic and social rights.[18] In other words, limiting civil and political rights is justified under certain circumstances. Anticommunism and the demands of the market required the subordination of civil and political rights.

The relatively poor state of internationally recognized human rights in the developing world has been well documented.[19] The dependent position of many developing states in the international economy makes it difficult for governments to actualize economic and social rights. Even states that have achieved remarkable growth, development, and comparative wealth have poor records not only on promoting economic and social rights but also civil and political rights. Until recently, Hong Kong, South Korea, Chile, Brazil, Singapore, Malaysia, and Mexico were not exactly shining examples of states that promoted and protected civil and political rights. Yet, their market reforms and export-led development strategies are to be emulated.

Civil and political rights do appear to be taking hold in some former authoritarian and totalitarian states in the post–Cold War era. However, abuses of civil and political rights continue to be accepted in the name of market reforms and structural adjustment. Moreover, economic, social, and cultural rights once provided by former communist governments are sacrificed to the economic "shock treatment" said to be necessary to transform the former command economies into market economies. The same type of circular argument discussed above is used to justify the denial of human rights.

The collapse of the Cold War order has not translated into a friendly environment to actualize human rights. On the contrary, human rights, particularly second generation rights, are at risk. Observers have recognized that this is a problem in the developing world and former Eastern bloc and the Soviet successor states.[20] However, economic and social rights in the advanced industrialized states are also at considerable risk. These rights were not major issues in the past, because these wealthy states provided for a relatively comfortable life for the vast majority of their citizens. In the following section, the dominance of neoclassical ideology minus Keynes and the globalization of the U.S. economy are cited as two factors that threaten economic and social rights in the United States.

Globalization and Neoclassical Economics

Neoclassical economic theory has gained prominence since the early 1980s largely because it was embraced by Ronald Reagan and Margaret Thatcher as a policy alternative to Keynesian economics. Intellectually indebted to Milton Friedman, neoclassical economic theory prescribes a dramatically curtailed role for the state in redistributing wealth and regulating the market. The welfare state is seen as the major impediment to free trade in that it seeks to protect national industries and jobs. It is inefficient and interferes with the logic of the market.

Neoclassical economic theory is different from classical theory because instead of focusing on what makes nations wealthy, it centers on what promotes efficiency.[21] It differs from Keynesian-inspired liberal theory in that it argues that government is not the solution to the nation's economic woes but the problem. The supply-side variation of neoclassicism argued that the stagflation of 1970s (high unemployment and high inflation) was caused by too many burdens placed on businesses (the suppliers). Taxes, government support for unions, price controls, and governmental regulation caused stagflation. The supply side of the equation must be addressed, and the solution is to provide tax cuts to businesses and then get the state out of the market.

This ideology is especially compatible with the globalization of the U.S. economy that began in the 1950s and was accelerated during the 1980s. The initial phase of globalization was led by U.S. multinational corporations that invested principally in raw materials and extractive industries, particularly oil.[22] The production process entailed exporting of raw materials from the periphery to the core where those resources were used to make manufactured goods. These goods were then exported abroad for sale. This initial phase generated an enormous amount of wealth for the United States and its multinational corporations, because the good-paying manufacturing jobs were located in this country and U.S. corporations were competitive internationally as a result of their access to the world's cheap raw materials. The win-win situation for U.S. private and corporate citizens is reflected in the words of one General Motors chairman, "What is good for GM is good for the country, and what is good for the country is good for GM."

The next phase of the globalization process was ushered in by the growing protectionist mood within the developing world. In the 1970s developing states sought to renegotiate existing international economic agreements in an attempt to address their deteriorating terms of trade.[23] A debt and stagnation problem had resulted from importing expensive manufactured goods and oil and exporting cheap raw materials. U.S. multinationals responded by shifting their production strategy from ownership or managerial control over extractive industries to horizontal direct foreign investments whereby plants and subsidiaries produced the same goods everywhere. In other words, U.S. multinationals sought to forestall protectionist measure by locating manufacturing in the developing world. This contributed to a net loss of manufacturing jobs in the United States.

The unemployment situation in the United States was mitigated by social welfare programs and job programs provided by the U.S. government at considerable expense. However, the election of Ronald Reagan ushered in the new era of economic policy guided by neoclassical ideology heavily influenced by supply-side arguments. The welfare state, though not eliminated, was scaled back considerably. Furthermore, the Reagan administration was committed to further trade liberalization internationally and continued global integration. The unemployed had little choice but to take jobs in the low-paying service sector of the U.S. economy, one of the only sectors of economy not exposed to international competition.

The U.S. economy has continued to globalize; however, the investment emphasis has shifted from horizontal to vertical where the outputs of plants and subsidiaries serve as the inputs to other plants and subsidiaries.[24] Intercorporate alliances have formed whereby largely U.S.-owned multinational corporations cooperate with foreign multinationals in achieving global economies of scale. These corporations are the most efficient in the marketplace, because they have access to global pools of capital, labor, and resources. The analogy of the world as a global factory, at least for many U.S. corporations, is apropos.[25]

Globalization of markets and production poses significant challenges to the state, because the state's ability to affect national goals is greatly reduced. The state is sensitive if not vulnerable to exogenous forces, such as inflation or volatility in (global) markets, over which it has little control. Globalization also challenges a state's economic sovereignty, because it demands that the state yield its right to determine economic outcomes and distribute resources within its territorial jurisdiction. For the pure neoclassical economists, this sovereignty should be yielded to the global market, because it is the most efficient way to distribute resources, goods, and services. Efficiency becomes synonymous for what is just and fair, and, in what appears to be a case of collective amnesia, the neoclassical economists assume that the global market will provide the means for individuals to pursue economic and social needs.

For most other liberals, however, economic sovereignty is ceded to the international organizations governing the market. Participation in the global market presents states with a "dilemma of common aversion. Dilemmas of aversion refer to situations in which actors must coordinate their polices by agreeing on some set of rules or conventions, to avoid mutually undesirable outcomes."[26] States benefit from participating in a maximally free trading system; however, states acting unilaterally and resorting to "beggar thy neighbor" policies during economic instability can disrupt or even destroy the very system that brings them wealth. Hence, states create and participate in international organizations. Interdependence does not breed harmony, but it does provide incentives to cooperate.[27] The long-term costs of resorting to self-help measures usually outweigh the short-term benefits. States, therefore, seek to exercise some managerial control over the economy by working through international organizations and regimes. The formation of the European Union, the World Trade Organization, and North American Free Trade Agreement is evidence of states' willingness to cede some economic sovereignty for continued economic growth. These institutions are arguably the pillars of authoritative economic governance in the nascent new world order.

Developing states' complaints regarding the "layered governance" of the World Bank and IMF are well documented.[28] The basic criticism of these institutions is that they are a mechanism through which the developing states are exploited by the advanced industrialized states. The World Bank and the IMF are largely great power directorates serving the interests of the core states. Many fail to recognize, however, that the loss of economic sovereignty has also occurred in the advanced industrialized state, and globalization has not benefited many segments of U.S. society.

Since the 1970s the status of social and economic rights in the United States has been in decline, and the statistics are compelling. The right to work is one of the most basic economic rights — that is, everyone has a right to seek work, and for every person that wants a job, one is available. Unemployment statistics empirically indicate the percentage of the workforce actively looking for work but unable to find it. The unemployment rate, therefore, reflects the status of the right to work in the United States. Although everyone has the right to work in legal theory, unemployment figures show the extent to which that right is actualized. In 1973 the unemployment rate was 4.9 percent.[29] In 1979 the rate was 5.8 percent. In 1989 the unemployment rate dropped to 5.3 percent. In 1993 it increased to 6.8 percent. On this very superficial basis, unemployment increased during the rapid globalization of the late 1980s and the early 1990s.

Unemployment calculations do not include the underemployed. The underemployed are those who are either involuntary part-time or overqualified for their current position. For the same years cited above the underemployment rates were 8.2 percent, 9.7 percent, 9.8 percent, and 12.6 percent, respectively.[30] Again, the increases in underemployment correspond with globalization and provide an empirical dimension to the extent Americans are working for just reward.

A better indicator of the extent to which Americans are working for just reward is the minimum wage, which was raised to $5.25 in 1997. Although there is no internationally recognized standard relating to just reward, the United States as a society has defined it in terms of a minimum wage. The minimum wage was first introduced in the 1930s, because the market-determined wage could not provide a standard of living necessary for human dignity. According to Mishel and Bernstein, the minimum wage was $2.90 in 1979. When this wage is adjusted to 1993 dollars, it is worth $5.66. The actual minimum wage in 1993 was only $4.25, however. Seen in this light, the minimum standard for just reward was worth less in 1993 than in 1979.[31]

Market-based capitalist economies have structural unemployment of around 4 percent, hence zero unemployment is not a realistic goal. This is why U.S. legislation required an unemployment rate of 4 percent, not 0 percent. In essence, liberals write off a 4 percent of would-be workers to the structure and the nature of the market economy. A state mandated-minimum wage creates additional unemployment, and the higher that wage, the higher the unemployment. Hence, the trade-off is between lower real wages or higher unemployment. This trade-off is illustrated between the unemployment rates in France and the United States — 12 percent and 6.8 percent, respectively in early 1997. French policy does not permit a lowering of the real wages; hence, France has a higher unemployment rate and a higher number of people on public assistance.

The liberal focus on the trade-off between wages and unemployment obfuscates the issue germane to actualizing economic and social rights. In market economies many individuals are presented with the choice of unemployment or working for declining, or worse, less than subsistence wages. In other words, the market is unable to provide a decent standard of living for a large percentage of the individuals governed by it. In the past, states were able to soften the effects of their largely national markets by redistributing the wealth through progressive income taxes and mandating a minimum wage that would lift individuals out of poverty. With a global market but no real authoritative governance, states are faced with a classic prisoner's dilemma. If all states were to cooperate and set uniform standards, then all potentially could benefit from a maximally free market. However, state competition for jobs and investment provide incentives to defect (to lower living, working, and environment standards to attract investment and jobs) at the expense of others. As long as some states are willing to defect, all will be forced to defect, and the result is a suboptimal outcome for all.

The debate within the United States about raising the minimum wage illustrates how globalization affects the state's ability to set economic and social policy. Raising the minimum wage, it is argued, will make U.S. businesses uncompetitive in the market. At home, businesses would have to compete with imports produced by cheap foreign labor. Abroad, exports would be unattractive because of the increase in U.S. labor costs. However, Americans working for the minimum wage are not making a living wage. With a large supply of labor, the price of that labor in the market falls. Today, the supply of available labor has dramatically increased by globalization and integration. Most Americans now compete in a global workforce. However, that global workforce is not governed by any uniform labor law. The result is a leveling downward of wages worldwide, not just in the United States.[32] This includes the real wages of most Americans, not just minimum wage workers, in spite of longer hours and increased productivity.[33] The downward trend occurs in spite of record profits for U.S. corporations. The well-being of American corporations is no longer necessarily related to the well-being of Americans.[34]

Another basic economic human right is the right to organize and join unions. Several authors of this book point out that the right to organize and join unions is in fact a fundamental political or civil right of association. However, many human rights violations that have occurred in the so-called free world during the twentieth century have not been against individuals who want to freely associate so they can determine where to put a school or a stop sign. Many human rights violations have occurred against people who sought to organize labor and challenge the dominant market-based ideology. U.S. constitutional law is filled with landmark cases in which the Supreme Court upheld the denial of basic civil and political rights of labor organizers and communist party members.[35] The gross and systematic violations of human rights in the Western Hemisphere have been largely perpetrated against labor organizers or suspected communist sympathizers. The victims of human rights abuses in Haiti, Brazil, Chile, Argentina, El Salvador, Guatemala, Nicaragua, and Honduras were not targeted because they wanted to associate per se; they were targeted because they wanted to associate for specific economic purposes. Clearly, certain types of association have been less protected than others, which is why there is a human rights interaction between the right of freedom of association and the right to form and join unions.

The right to form and join unions was recognized when the U.S. government passed the National Labor Relations Act (1935). This act emphasized collective bargaining requiring employers to bargain in good faith with unions. It also established the National Labor Relations Board to prosecute violations of workers rights.[36] In spite of the past success of unions, the percentage of the American workforce represented by unions has significantly declined. In 1979 union coverage hovered around 25 percent of the workforce but declined steadily to around 18 percent in 1985.[37] After an increase in 1986 to 22 percent, union coverage declined to around 16 percent in 1992.[38]

Little doubt exists that union members on the whole fare better than nonunion members in terms of wages, insurance, and pension coverage. In 1989 union members made 25.7 percent more per hour than nonunion workers, and they received 111.1 percent more in insurance and 117.1 percent more in contributions to pension plans than did their nonunion counterparts.[39] If unions continue to be successful, then why is America de-unionizing? There are three interrelated reasons. The first is that American workers no longer perceive union membership as an advantage.[40] The demonization of unions by the Reagan and successive administrations has caused many to view unions as the source of many of the nation's economic ills.

Secondly, and relatedly, the neoclassical ideology places emphasis on the market determining wages, not on the state or unions.[41] Thirdly, capital mobility effectively prevents the formation of unions and undermines their bargaining position. Globalization creates a huge labor market without uniform labor laws or practices. According to one observer studying the effects of NAFTA, it is the nature of free trade and capital mobility that threatens the organization rights of workers. "The threat of such relocation will inhibit U.S. workers' effort to organize and engage in meaningful collective bargaining with their employers. Where workers are already unionized, the collective bargaining process will likely be reduced to union acceptance of less than favorable management offers which guarantee that workers will not lose their job."[42]

Globalization and neoclassical ideology erode the right to organize from above and below. The state should not support unions because it interferes with the market and free trade. This in turn encourages antiunion practices on the part of business. Even if the state wanted to actively promote and support unions, the logic of the global market makes it impossible for unions to be effective because of the very real threat of relocation and the loss of jobs altogether. The right to organize in the United States is increasingly a hollow right.

This analysis has thus far only shown that the erosion of the rights to work, for just reward, and the right to organize have occurred at the same time that the U.S. economy has globalized and that neoclassical ideology ascended to prominence in policy-making circles. It has not proved any causal relationship between the variables, although it does assume such a relationship. In fact, this causal relationship is assumed by many policy makers in the United States and Europe who are trying to cope with the loss of jobs via policy tools that have been rendered either obsolete by ideology or useless by market externalities. Hence, in an ironic twist of policy fates, the United States and its European allies have once again discovered the importance of the interaction of economic and social rights with political and civil rights. This is evidenced by the words of Secretary of State Warren Christopher in his speech "America's Fundamental Dedication to Human Rights":

> With the expansion of global trade, worker rights take on renewed urgency. The new World Trade Organization will have to face the effects of workers rights on trade.

The universal right most pertinent to the workplace is freedom of association, which is the foundation on which workers can form and organize trade unions, bargain collectively, press grievances, and protect themselves from unsafe working conditions. In many countries, workers have far to go in realizing their rights.[43]

There is an interdependency between economic rights abroad and those at home, and the ill-effects of this interdependency cannot be managed by the state alone. International organizations such as the World Trade Organization, EU, and NAFTA provide the best hope for promoting and protecting economic rights if development and sovereignty issues can be overcome. The Clinton administration has argued that "unfair" labor practices translate into unfair trading practices because they give businesses that benefit from the lack of regulation and enforcement an unfair competitive advantage in the market.[44] French, German, and U.S. officials are pushing to empower the World Trade Organization to review labor practices and set minimum labor standards.[45]

Skepticism abounds regarding the potential effectiveness of the World Trade Organization, or NAFTA for that matter, setting minimum standards. On the one hand, the neoclassical free traders argue that Western efforts to make labor rights an issue are a form of protectionism designed to keep jobs at home. The implementation of a so-called social clause "appeals equally to rich-country self-interest and self-righteousness."[46] The World Trade Organization was created to help eliminate nontariff barriers to trade, and therefore it should not erect them.

The U.S. and European states also face serious sovereignty issues. Can these international organizations set adequate standards? Even if these states seek to maintain a higher standard than the international minimum, the logic of the market cannot be escaped. Business will locate where their operating and labor costs are lowest. This inevitably translates into reduced taxes (which affects the state's ability to provide social welfare). States that want to attract investment are forced to reduce regulations on businesses. Governments cannot require businesses to provide insurance, full-time employment, and retirement benefits. The result is a leveling downward of economic rights and social rights.

In the past, the state has been one of the greatest threats to internationally recognized human rights. It has also been one of the greatest protectors of human rights, having been challenged from above and below to respect and promote human rights at home.[47] Globalization and neoclassical ideology present serious structural problems for the state, because globalization negatively affects the state's capability to promote and implement human rights. Neoclassical ideology justifies that impotence. Hence, it is not surprising that the human rights discourses that are invariably influenced by ideological or practical economic considerations have returned to the idea of basic or fundamental human rights. Basic human rights are rights that are fundamental to a life of minimum dignity, such as the right to a minimum level of physical and economic security.[48] In other words, human beings are only entitled to "basic needs," meaning that they must not be physically harmed by the state or any other party under the state's jurisdiction. Persons are entitled only to subsistence. All the other rights articulated under the Universal Declaration of Human Rights and related covenants are either not really human rights or are of secondary importance. With the idea of basic human rights, the obligations of states become minimal: refrain from harming humans beings, and provide minimum food and shelter for those that cannot help themselves.

Many observers have argued that certain civil rights must be included as basic human rights so that individuals can make a claim when their rights are violated and may improve their standard of living.[49] But what is participation in a government that can do nothing for you either because of the demands of the global marketplace or an ideology that removes the state from the market? Recall that enforcement of political rights, such as the right not to be discriminated against, requires extensive state intervention in the market. Yet government efforts to end discrimination in the market are under attack. Furthermore, the institutions governing the global market are not democratic.[50] WTO meetings are closed, and there is little input by traditionally underrepresented groups such as labor unions and environmental groups. Classical liberal theory prescribes civil and political rights to influence the institutions governing the lives of individuals. Yet those rights do not exist at the international level. Increasingly, many traditional civil and political rights are becoming as hollow as social and economic rights.

This research has argued that the divergent understandings of human rights are influenced by changing economic realities and ideologies, and the United States does not fit neatly into the neoclassical category. The post–Cold War order contains some new and serious challenges to U.S. efforts to implement and protect human rights at home. Economic and social rights are clearly threatened in the United States and elsewhere. The current trend, influenced by globalization and neoclassicism, appears to be leading to a lowest common denominator approach to defining, promoting, and protecting human rights. If this trend continues, it will be a major setback for the human rights revolution.

Notes

1. George Modelski argues that during the world power phase in the cycle of world (hegemonic) leadership, the world leader consolidates its power and establishes international organizations to legitimize its dominant position. See George Modelski, *Long Cycles in World Politics* (Seattle: University of Washington Press, 1987).

2. See John Gerald Ruggie, "International Responses to Technology: Concepts and Trends," *International Organization* 36 (summer 1982): 557–584.

3. Gilpin argues that the compromise of embedded liberalism was the foundation of U.S. hegemony in the international economic system. See Robert Gilpin, *The Political Economy of International Relations* (Princeton: Princeton University Press, 1987), 132–133.

4. Krasner defines a regime as "principles, norms, rules, and decision-making procedures around which actor expectations converge in a given issue area." See Stephan Krasner, "Structural Causes and Regime Consequences: Regimes as Intervening Variables," *International Organization* 36 (summer 1982): 185.

5. See Jack Donnelly, *International Human Rights* (Boulder CO: Westview Press, 1993), 10.

6. See Donnelly, *International Human Rights*, 7–10. Also see Adamantia Pollis and Peter Schwab, eds., "Human Rights with Limited Applicability," in *Human Rights: Cultural and Ideological Perspectives* (New York: Praeger, 1979), 1–18. David P. Forsythe, *The Internationalization of Human Rights* (Lexington MA: Lexington Books for D.C. Heath, 1991), 121–127.

7. The general tendency to conceive of economic and social rights as positive rights is misleading. The task of providing many of these rights may have fallen to governments; however, rights such as the right to marry and participate in the cultural life of the community are relatively negative. Donnelly points out that all human rights "require both positive action and restraint by the state if they are to be effectively implemented." See Donnelly, *International Human Rights*, 26.

8. See Burns H. Weston, "Human Rights," in Richard Pierre Claude and Burns H. Weston, eds., *Human Rights in the World Community: Issues and Action* (Philadelphia: University of Pennsylvania Press, 1990), 17.

9. See David McLellan, ed., *Karl Marx: Selected Writings* (1859; Oxford: Oxford University Press, 1977); John Hobson, *Imperialism: A Study* (1902; Ann Arbor: University of Michigan Press, 1965); John Maynard Keynes, "National Self-Sufficiency," *Yale Review* 22 (1933): 755–769; and V. I. Lenin, *Imperialism: The Highest State of Capitalism* (1917; New York: International Publishers, 1939).

10. The analysis of these laws is drawn from Gilpin, *Political Economy*, 36–64.

11. Gilpin, *Political Economy*, 36.

12. See Bilahari Kausikan, "Asia's Different Standard," *Foreign Policy* 92 (1993): 35; and Anatoly Muvchan, *Human Rights and International Relations* (Moscow: Progress Publishers, 1982), 110.

13. Note table 1 in Gilpin, *Political Economy*, 59.

14. For an overview of these acts, see J. Bradford De Long, "Keynesianism, Pennsylvania Avenue Style: Some Economic Consequences of the Employment Act of 1946," *Journal of Economic Perspectives* 10 (summer 1996): 41–53.

15. Sovereignty issues were clearly important at least domestically for the United States. The United States did not become party to the Covenant on Civil and Political Rights until 1992 and is not party to the Covenant on Economic, Social and Cultural Rights. The reasoning for not becoming party to these treaties is that the U.S. Constitution and federal law provided for most of these rights, and the treaties would represent a higher law.

16. Neoclassical economic theory represents twentieth-century liberal economic thought.

17. See Samuel P. Huntington, "Political Development and Political Decay," *World Politics* 17 (1965): 386–430. Also see Samuel P. Huntington, *Political Order in Changing Societies* (New Haven: Yale University Press, 1968).   ·

18. See, for example, Jeanne J. Kirkpatrick, "Double Standards in Human Rights," *Current Policy*, no. 353, U.S. Department of State, November 24, 1981.

19. For an excellent overview of the literature regarding the status of human rights, see Jemi Osinbajo and Olukonysola Ajayi, "Human Rights and Economic Development in Developing Countries," *International Lawyer* 28 (fall 1994): 727–742.

20. See Donnelly, *International Human Rights*.

21. See Adam Smith, *Wealth of an Inquiry into the Nature and Causes of the Nations* (1976; New York: Modern Library, 1937).

22. This review of the role of multinational corporations in the globalization of production is drawn from Gilpin, *Political Economy*, 231–262, and George Modelski, ed., *Transnational Corporations and World Order* (San Francisco: W. H. Freeman, 1979).

23. For an overview of the developing states' position, see Stephan D. Krasner, *Structural Conflict: The Third World Against Global Liberalism* (Berkeley: University of California Press, 1985).

24. See Gilpin, *Political Economy*, 231–262.

25. Some have challenged the notion of globalization, arguing that the European and Japanese multinationals still manufacture most of their products at home. See Laura D'Andrea Tyson, "They Are Not U.S.: Why American Ownership Still Matters," *American Prospect* (winter 1991).

26. Stephan Krasner, "Global Communications and National Power: Life on the Parieto Frontier," *World Politics* 43 (April 1991): 338.

27. Robert Keohane, *After Hegemony: Cooperation and Discord in the World Political Economy* (Princeton: Princeton University Press, 1984).

28. See Barry J. Riddel, "Things Fall Apart Again: Structural Adjustment Programmes in Sub Saharan Africa," *Journal of Modern African Studies* 30 (March 1992): 53–69; Paul Mosely, "Policy-Making Without Facts: A Note on the Assessment of Structural Adjustment Policies in Nigeria, 1985–1990," *African Affairs* 91 (April 1992): 227–241; Alicia Korten, "Cultivating Disaster: Structural Adjustment and Costa Rican Agriculture," *Multinational Monitor* 14 (July–August 1993): 20–23; and Anthony G. Hopkins, "The World Bank in Africa: Historical Reflections on the African Present," *World Development* 14 (December 1986): 1473–1474.

29. Lawrence Mishel and Jared Bernstein, *The State of Working America 1994–1995* (New York: M. E. Sharpe, 1994), 205. The years 1973, 1979, and 1989 represent peak years in which the business cycle is high. The economy is strongest during peak years, and unemployment is the lowest. The year 1993 is the latest year for which data were available.

30. Mishel and Bernstein, *State of Working*, 205.

31. Mishel and Bernstein, *State of Working*, 172.

32. See Jeremy Brecher and Tim Costello, *Global Village or Global Pillage: Eco-*

nomic Reconstruction from the Bottom Up (Boston: South End Press, 1994), 19–28; Robert B. Reich, *Work of Nations* (New York: Vintage Press, 1992).

33. Mishel and Bernstein, *State of Working*, 112–114.

34. Reich, *Work of Nations*, 8.

35. See *Schenck v. U.S.*, 249 U.S. 47 (1919); *Debs v. U.S.*, 24 U.S. 211 (1919); *Abrams v. U.S.*, 250 U.S. (1919); *Whitney v. California*, 274 U.S. 357 (1927); *Dennis v. U.S.* 341 U.S. 494 (1951).

36. Timothy A. Canova, *Monologue or Dialogue in Management Decisions: The Duty to Negotiate and the Efficiency of Dialog* (Stockholm: Juristforlaget, 1990), 14.

37. Mishell and Bernstein, *State of Working*, 165.

38. Mishell and Bernstein, *State of Working*, 165.

39. Mishell and Bernstein, *State of Working*, 166.

40. Canova, *Monologue*, 11.

41. See the attack on neoclassical view of labor rights in Edward Balls, "Toddlers with Brick Menace the World: Labor Standards in Future GATT Talks," *New Statesman and Society* 7 (June 24, 1994): 25.

42. Charles W. Nugent, "A Comparison of the Right to Organize and Bargain Collectively in the United States and Mexico: NAFTA's Side Accords and Prospects for Reform," *Transnational Lawyer* 7 (spring 1994): 222.

43. Warren Christopher, "America's Fundamental Dedication to Human Rights," *U.S. Department of State Dispatch* 6 (February 6, 1995): 75.

44. See Bruce E. Stokes, "The New Linkage," *National Journal* 26 (June 25, 1994): 1509; Susumu Awanohara, "Hard Labour: Dispute Over Workers' Rights Sours U.S.-Indonesia Ties," *Far Eastern Economic Review* 156 (May 13, 1993): 13; Shada Islam, "Here Comes Trouble: Western Countries Link Asian Workers' Rights to Trade," *Far Eastern Economic Review* 159 (April 18, 1996): 82.

45. Islam, "Here Comes Trouble," 82. Also see John Chowcat, "Flexible Unionism," *New Statesman and Society* 8 (October 17, 1995): 31.

46. Edward Balls, "Toddlers," citing *The Economist*.

47. Forsythe, *Internationalization*.

48. See Henry Shue, *Basic Rights: Subsistance, Affluence, and U.S. Foreign Policy* (Princeton, Princeton University Press, 1980); Jack Donnelly, *Universal Human Rights in Theory and Practice* (Ithaca: Cornell University Press, 1989); and Robert O. Matthews and Cranford Pratt, eds., *Human Rights in Canadian Foreign Policy* (Kingston: McGill-Queens University Press, 1988).

49. Shue, *Basic Rights*; Donnelly, *Universal Human Rights*.

50. See Robert Weissman, "Secrets of the WTO," *Multinational Monitor* 15 (October 1994): 9; Ralph Nader, "Drop the GATT," *The Nation* (October 10, 1994): 368; Brecher and Costello, *Global Village*.

3

In Search of a U.S. Refugee Policy

•

MARK GIBNEY

Immigration, broadly defined, has become a very hot social and political issue. The dominant, perhaps overwhelming, sentiment in the country in the
mid-1990s — as evidenced by the strong support for Proposition 187 in California, as well as the restrictive legislation passed by Congress in September 1996 — was that there are simply too many foreigners flooding into the
United States. The fear is that foreigners threaten to take our jobs, threaten
to take our security, threaten to take our hard earned tax dollars, and quite
possibly something of even greater importance, threaten to take away our
very way of life.[1]

In many ways such nativist sentiments are easy to understand, if not to defend. For one thing, there is nothing really new about them. From the Alien
and Sedition Act in 1798, to the rise of "America First" parties in the middle
part of the nineteenth century; from the exclusion of the Chinese later that
century, to the exclusion of the Japanese during this one; and from the racist
National Origins Quota systems of the 1920s, to the perpetuation of such
ugly values through the McCarran-Walter Act that was law from 1952 until
the period of Civil Rights reform in 1965, throughout American history there
has been virulent (and at times violent) opposition to foreigners (or certain
kinds of foreigners) that has coincided quite uneasily with the notion of the
United States as a "nation of immigrants."

When set against the backdrop of U.S. immigration history, the present-
day backlash against aliens might even be considered mild. Still, the sentiments thereby expressed are real enough; and they need to be examined and
addressed. Why is it that nativist sentiments are once again coming to the
fore? I will suggest that there are several reasons, all of which build on one
another. The first is that there has been a substantial and continuing increase
in the number of aliens coming to the United States in the past two decades.
Along with that is the manner in which some arrive here, thereby confirm-
ing for many that we have "lost control over our borders." And finally, in an
increasingly cold and hostile world (or what is seen as such), what is deduced

from all this is that there is no end in sight in terms of those who will make every effort to migrate here.

There are, of course, other phenomena that one could point at to explain the rise in native sentiment, such as the changing ethnic composition of immigrants or domestic factors such as the state of the U.S. economy. My aim, however, is not necessarily to provide an exhaustive list. Instead, I am far more concerned about the larger consequences of nativist thinking, whereby all aliens, and all alien claims, become indistinguishable from one another. At that point it simply becomes "us" versus "them" — all of them — and this is the point that we are rapidly approaching.

This chapter opposes the current thinking that treats all alien claims as being one and the same and instead suggests that some groups of aliens have much stronger claims for admission than others. The problem, as we explore in part 3, is that U.S. immigration policy itself has done much to blur some important distinctions that exist between alien groups. I will focus on two distinctions that I believe are vital to maintain. The first is that between asylum seekers and illegal aliens.[2] As I will show empirically in part 3, contrary to popular sentiment, there is very little evidence that aliens are abusing our asylum system by filing frivolous claims. Rather, the overwhelming majority of those who have applied for asylum in the United States are those one would expect to do so: individuals from countries experiencing extraordinarily high levels of political violence. This was certainly the case in the 1980s, but the data indicate that it continues to be true in the 1990s as well.

The second distinction is between immigrants and refugees. Immigrants are invited to the United States for permanent residence and eventual citizenship, if the alien so chooses. Our country's immigration policy is based on two principles: family reunification and the needs of the U.S. economy. Thus, in almost all cases the invitation to become one of us is offered to those who either have family members in this country or have particular economic skills. Contrast this with the refugee population. Refugees, in their truest form, are individuals in desperate circumstances. By definition, these are individuals who have a "well-founded fear of persecution" and have fled their home country. In granting refugee status to a person we are offering protection to a vulnerable individual. In essence, I argue that there is virtually no connection between immigration and refugee admissions, aside from the act of allowing aliens to come to our country. Yet what I will show, again through empirical analysis, is that the United States essentially has had no refugee policy as such — only an immigration policy disguised as a refugee policy.

Why focus on U.S. refugee/asylum policy? Although no nation-state is obligated to admit any aliens if it so chooses, under international law all nation-states are bound by the principle of *nonrefoulement* to avoid sending refugees back to their home country when harm might be done to them.[3] *Nonrefoulement*, unfortunately, does not go nearly far enough. Political violence continues to increase in the world, victimizing millions of people and placing many times that in danger.[4] Yet the vast majority of these individuals have essentially no connection with the United States or with any of the other industrialized Western countries. Instead, if they are able to find refuge at all it will be within other areas of their own country (precipitating the explosion in the number of internally displaced persons) or else in a nearby country where safety can be found (although the prospects of this continue to dim). We can either continue to ignore the consequences of political violence in the world (much as we ignored being one of the causes of violence and resulting refugee flows during the Cold War), or we can attempt to be part of some humane or humanitarian solution. Or to phrase this another way, we can continue to pretend that we have a serious and broad refugee policy, or we can actually *have* such a refugee policy. This is the focus of part 4.

The Muddled Nature of Alien Claims

There is little question that current nativist sentiments have been fueled, in large part, by the increased number of aliens migrating to the United States. Between 1981 and 1990 the United States admitted 7,338,062 immigrants for permanent residence in this country, nearly double the number of immigrants from the previous decade and representing the highest level of net migration to the United States in its history.[5] The numbers for the current decade are even higher. Factoring in aliens who legalized their status under the 1986 Immigration Reform and Control Act (IRCA), the United States "admitted" 1.8 million aliens in 1991; 973,977 in 1992; and 904,292 in 1993.

Note that these numbers do not include refugee admissions, which now are approximately 75,000 per year. This number also does not include nonimmigrants, those who visit the United States for work or pleasure. In 1993 millions of nonimmigrants arrived in the United States, most for a short visit to this country but some for a much longer period of time. Although in theory it is easy to differentiate between immigrants and nonimmigrants — the difference between permanent residence and possibly citizenship in this country, on the one hand, versus transitory residence — in practice the distinction has not always been an easy one to make. For one thing, certain non-immigrant visas allow "visitors" to stay in the United States for years. Beyond this, many of those who ultimately gain entry into the United States as permanent resident aliens had previously lived here in some capacity as a non-immigrant. In this way (and perhaps *only* in this way) marriage partners and sponsoring employers can be found (and permanent residence achieved). Finally, it is certainly not unknown for nonimmigrants who are out of status to make every attempt to somehow remain in this country nonetheless — and they are quite often successful.

Finally, the numbers given above do not include the population of illegal aliens residing in this country, itself estimated in the millions. When Congress passed IRCA, the bill was heralded as the solution to the country's illegal alien problem. In exchange for the legalization of long-term residents and agricultural workers who labored here for a relatively short period of time, a system of employer sanctions was instituted, for the first time in American history making it a federal offense to hire an illegal alien. The new law, however, has produced very little change.[6] Countless numbers of aliens continue to reside — and work — in the United States illegally.

It is not simply the number of aliens migrating to this country or the manner of admission (where even much of "legal" migration has a shading of "illegality" to it). It is also the sense that conditions will only continue to grow worse. The world around us is now commonly thought of as destitute and hostile.[7] Who, then, would not want to leave wherever and migrate to the United States — by whatever means possible? The ultimate result of this kind of thinking, however, is that all aliens, and all alien claims, soon become indistinguishable from one another. More than this, all become suspect.

The problem with this mindset is that it ignores important differences between and among aliens. For example, without examining the data it would be very easy to blend together those applying for asylum in the United States and the illegal alien population. Both groups tend to be, in overwhelming numbers, poor, non-white, and from countries south of the United States. Moreover, only a small percentage of asylum seekers (this is particularly true of Central American applicants) are granted refugee status. Yet, as we will see in the next section, what distinguishes the asylum seeker population is the fact that nearly all have been fleeing countries experiencing gross levels of human rights abuses. In a similar way, political violence should also be a distinguishing feature between refugees and immigrants. However, as we will also see in the next section, such a distinction does not exist in U.S. policy.

Human Rights and the Granting of Refugee Status

For most of our country's history, no distinction has been made between refugees and other immigrants, although many of those who migrated to this country certainly did so because of what we would now think of as human rights abuses in their home country. One of the most visible examples of the nonrecognition of the special needs and claims of "refugees" occurred in 1938 when the United States turned away a boatload of Jewish schoolchildren on the U.S.S. St. Louis on the basis that the German quota for that year had already been filled. The ship eventually returned to Germany with its passengers.

Following World War II, certain provisions were made for refugees and displaced persons; however, these efforts were essentially ad hoc responses to the exigencies created by the war. It was not until passage of the 1965 Immigration Act that a special category for refugee admissions was created, allocating 17,400 slots each year for those purposes, although the law was restricted to refugees from communist countries or the Middle East. Despite the new provision in the law, refugees were more commonly admitted through the use of the attorney general's "parole" power. Through this extralegal mechanism, hundreds of thousands of Cubans and Vietnamese were admitted to the United States, in occasional mass waves, between 1965 and 1980.

The Refugee Act of 1980 was an attempt by Congress to rein in this pell-mell and standardless refugee admission system. The new law set a baseline for the admission of 50,000 refugees per year, removed the ideological and geographic restrictions that had existed under the 1965 Immigration Act, and essentially made the definition of "refugee" under U.S. law consonant with the UN definition.[8] Despite these changes, however, refugee admissions continued to reflect foreign policy considerations, as nearly all of the refugees admitted to the United States during the 1980s were from communist countries.[9]

Refugee Admissions and Asylum Adjudications in the 1980s

Rather than engaging in what seemed to be an endless and ultimately fruitless debate regarding the continuing existence of an ideological bias in U.S. refugee policy (a point that seemed more than evident), I have examined instead the relationship between levels of human rights violations in the world and the refugee and asylum response of the U.S. government. Data for this study come from a project that I have directed the past decade, the results of which are called the Political Terror Scale (PTS). Each year more than 140 countries were coded on a scale of 1–5, with 5 representing the very highest levels of political terror and 1 representing the lowest.[10] The data for this coding came from two different yearly sources: The State Department Report on Human Rights Practices and the Amnesty International Report. In the construction of this index for each year, all reports were scaled as if the information contained in them were accurate and complete. Thus any biases to be found in the annual reports of the two organizations should be evident in the indices. (Scores for selected countries can be found at *www. unca.edu/~mg.bney.*)

A human rights analysis informs refugee decision making in two ways. First, the greater the level of human rights abuses in a country, the more likely is the *probability* that individuals living there would suffer persecution, all else being equal. Second, levels of human rights abuses can also inform us of the *severity* of persecution. That means there is a difference between, say, political imprisonment for one's ideas, as opposed to more pernicious behavior such as torture, rape, and disappearances. All are human rights violations, and all would meet the "persecution" standard for refugee purposes. However, the point is that there is a qualitative difference between imprisonment and these other abuses that a human rights analysis can reflect.

In terms of refugee analysis, we expected to find a direct relationship between levels of political terror and the creation of refugee flows. This turned out to be true: The vast majority of refugees in the world are from countries experiencing "gross levels of human rights abuse"—what we have defined as countries with a political terror score of Level 4 or Level 5. What we also expected to find, this time from the receiving side, is that a country would generally tend to admit refugees from Level 4 or Level 5 countries. Not only are there many more refugees in the world from these countries, but, as explained previously, both the probability and the severity of persecution would be higher in those countries. What we found for the United States, however, was quite mixed.

In terms of refugees admitted through the overseas processing procedure, during the 1980s there was virtually no relationship between levels of political terror in other countries and the American response. Instead, notwithstanding admission criteria that gave preference to those in serious plight, the vast majority of refugees admitted to the United States during the

Table 3.1: Human Rights and Asylum Applications, 1980–89

I Level	II Asylum applications	III As % of total applications	IV No. granted	V As % of those granted asylum	VI Acceptance rate by level
Amnesty International					
5	54,293	33.9	17,926	41.6	33.0
4	40,894	25.5	10,355	24.0	25.3
3	55,951	35.0	12,382	28.7	22.1
2	6,456	4.0	2,181	5.1	33.7
1	464	0.2	57	0.1	12.2
NC	1,771	1.1	158	0.3	8.9
Total	159,829		43,059		
State Department					
5	37,627	23.5	20,783	48.2	55.2
4	91,529	57.2	14,306	33.2	15.6
3	22,243	13.9	6,192	14.3	27.8
2	6,128	3.8	1,544	3.5	25.1
1	547	0.3	65	0.1	11.8
NC	1,755	1.0	169	0.4	9.6
Total	159,829		43,059		

1980s were from countries experiencing only "fair" levels of human rights abuses. Individuals from countries suffering from gross levels of human rights abuses were, almost without exception, ignored by U.S. refugee admission policy. Consider data from 1989, when the United States admitted 98,076 through its overseas refugee program. Fully 56.2 percent (using Amnesty International as a data source) of these "refugees" were from Level 2 countries; and *only 45 individuals* (representing 0.0 percent of those admitted) were from a Level 5 country (again using Amnesty as a data source). The results were only slightly different using the State Department as a data source: 6.7 percent of the refugees were from Level 5 countries and 7.8 percent from Level 4, but fully 39.6 percent were from Level 3 countries and 43.5 percent from Level 2.

Asylum adjudications for this period provide us with slightly different results, which are shown in table 3.1.[11] Contrary to the repeated charge made throughout the Reagan and Bush administrations that asylum applicants were abusing the system by filing unfounded claims, a very substantial portion of those who applied for asylum from 1980 to 1989 were from countries experiencing "gross" levels of human rights abuses. For example, of the 159,829 asylum applicants filed during the decade, fully 95,187 (using Amnesty) or 129,156 (using the State Department) were from either a Level 4 or Level 5 country (columns 2 and 3). Not only were most applicants from countries experiencing gross levels of human rights abuses, but so were those who were successful (columns four and five). According to State Department Reports data, an incredible 81.4 percent of the successful asylum applicants in the 1980s were from either a Level 4 or Level 5 country (the comparable number using Amnesty was 65.6 percent). What tempers these results somewhat, however, is the fact that this preponderance of successful Level 4 and Level 5 applicants simply appears to be a function of the larger number of applicants from those levels (as evidenced by the inconsistent acceptance rates within levels, column 6), although the 55.2 percent acceptance rate for Level 5 applicants (using the State Department) is most encouraging and seemingly reflective of human rights considerations.

In sum, what we found for the time period of 1980–89 was that of the two means of obtaining refugee status in the United States — applying for asylum in this country or being selected through a refugee selection process overseas — there was a much stronger connection to levels of human rights abuses in other countries in the former than in the latter. These results are quite surprising, because overseas refugee processing allows the U.S. government (and the governments of other countries as well) to "pick and choose" the refugees it wishes to select for admission. Asylum applications, on the other hand, are by and large beyond the control of the government. What we found for 1980–89, however, is that the system was by no means abused in this manner. Instead, the overwhelming majority of those who applied for asylum were from countries experiencing gross levels of human rights abuses.

Human Rights and the Granting of Refugee Status Post Cold War

The year 1989 was a watershed year, because it marked the end of the Cold War and the death of politics as it had been carried out since the end of World War II. Communism fell in one Eastern Bloc country after another, and some semblance of democratic rule was established in its place. The brutal

civil wars in Central America were also beginning to wind down, partly out
of sheer exhaustion, but also because of their insignificance to the United
States and the Soviet Union. The same phenomena occurred in a number of
African countries as well. There was a lot of talk at this time of a "new world
order." The question we attempt to answer is whether these sea changes in
the world's geopolitical system brought about any change in U.S. refugee/
asylum policy.

REFUGEE ADMISSIONS

Most aspects of U.S. refugee policy have remained the same following the
end of the Cold War, while other parts of it have changed, or give some indication of change. The emphasis on admitting refugees from communist (or
former communist) countries has certainly continued, although there has
been some modification of policy. As had been the case the decade before,
"refugees" from the Soviet Union (more accurately now, the former Soviet Union) continued to dominate, representing nearly half the admissions
each year: 49,385 (1990), 39,116 (1991), 61,714 (1992), 49,559 (1993), and 44,095
(1994). Yet, this has not been a widespread Eastern Bloc phenomenon. Instead, in each of the other former Warsaw Pact countries there has been a
sharp decline in the number of "refugees" admitted to the United States.
Quite typical is Romania. In 1991, 4,803 refugees were admitted to the United
States, but by 1994 that number had dwindled to 267.

Countries still under communist rule (and this is now a very small subset
of the nation-states in the world) have continued to send substantial numbers of refugees to the United States. Refugee numbers from Vietnam and
Laos have remained high, reflecting foreign policy concerns and commitments from a previous era but certainly showing no indication of changed
geopolitical events.[12]

Setting aside ideological issues, once again, and focusing on the relationship between levels of political terror in the world and the refugee response
of the United States, there have been some interesting and noteworthy developments. Table 3.2 provides this data for the period 1990–95.

Refugee admissions in 1990 and 1991 essentially showed no change from
the decade before. Once again, exceptionally few refugees from Level 5 countries were granted admission to the United States. Of the 110,117 refugees admitted to this country in 1990, only 136 were from a Level 5 country (using
either Amnesty or the State Department Report as a data source). In 1991 this

Table 3.2: Human Rights and Refugee Admissions, 1990–95 (%)

Level	Amnesty International	State Department	Amnesty International	State Department
	1990		1991	
5	136 (0.1)	136 (0.1)	1,134 (1.1)	2,911 (2.9)
4	9,040 (8.2)	11,387 (10.3)	8,933 (8.9)	47,146 (47.0)
3	84,246 (76.5)	89,517 (81.2)	72,922 (72.7)	31,543 (31.4)
2	14,495 (13.1)	6,877 (6.2)	15,209 (15.1)	15,977 (15.9)
1	246 (0.2)	471 (0.4)	—	821 (1.8)
NC	1,954 (1.7)	1,729 (1.5)	2,031 (2.0)	1,831 (1.8)
Total	110,117		100,229	
	1992		1993	
5	9,700 (7.6)	12,340 (9.7)	5,838 (5.1)	10,235 (9.0)
4	9,479 (7.4)	5,648 (4.4)	8,235 (7.2)	1,804 (1.5)
3	6,241 (4.8)	40,440 (31.7)	4,939 (4.3)	63,372 (56.0)
2	98,108 (77.0)	1,787 (1.4)	88,267 (77.0)	31,834 (28.1)
1	249 (0.2)	1,718 (1.3)	115 (0.1)	149 (0.1)
NC	3,633 (2.8)	65,387 (51.3)	5,758 (5.1)	5,758 (5.1)
Total	127,410		113,512	
	1994		1995	
5	16,527 (14.4)	16,522 (14.4)	15,625 (16.3)	47,416 (49.6)
4	45,587 (39.8)	45,784 (39.9)	40,762 (42.6)	4,678 (4.8)
3	4,219 (3.6)	36,644 (32.0)	2,617 (2.7)	10,027 (10.5)
2	33,204 (29.0)	6,586 (5.7)	32,182 (33.6)	32,482 (34.0)
1	110 (0.0)	116 (0.0)	3,413 (3.5)	161 (0.1)
NC	14,824 (13.0)	8,819 (7.7)	977 (1.0)	973 (1.0)
Total	114,471		95,576	

number increased to 1,134 (Amnesty) and 2,911 (State Department); however, these numbers represented only a very small percentage of those admitted to the United States that year. This upward trend continued in 1992 and beyond, so that by 1994 14.4 percent of the refugees were from Level 5 countries (and a substantial number from Level 4 countries, reflecting the increased violence in the Russian republic).

What brought about these changes? One partial explanation involves U.S. military involvement. Consider the admission patterns from Iraq and Somalia, two countries that have experienced gross human rights abuses for many years but which had not sent refugees to the United States until American troops were sent there. The United States granted admission to 73 refugees from Iraq in 1990 and 812 in 1991, but in 1992 that number surged to 3,889 and it has stayed at these levels since then. Refugee admissions from Somalia have shown a similar pattern. While only 52 Somali refugees were admitted to the United States in 1990, these numbers increased to 305 in 1991, 1,690 in 1992, 2,802 in 1993, and 4,900 in 1994, before dropping to 2,435 in 1995.

Although the involvement of the American military apparently plays a significant role in increasing refugee flows from the countries where these actions take place, something else seems to be going on as well. For example, after years of making little attempt to share the substantial burden of refugees from the former Yugoslavia, in 1994 the United States suddenly granted admission to 8,790 refugees from Bosnia and 8,412 in 1995. The same kind of phenomenon has occurred in Sudan as well. Prior to 1994 the United States had granted admission to only a handful of refugees from Sudan; however, that year 1,229 refugees were admitted and 1,654 the following year. In 1992 the United States admitted 899 refugees from Liberia and 1,034 the following year; this was in marked contrast to the 72 refugees granted admission between 1988 and 1991. However, since that time the number of refugees has decreased significantly (150 refugees were admitted in 1995), although the levels of political terror have remained the same.

In sum, there is at least some indication that U.S. refugee policy is beginning to reflect human rights concerns. What should aid this shift is the expansion of the first priority category, announced in September 1994. This category is for "groups of special concern to the United States to be established as needed by nationality." For Fiscal Year 1995 these specified groups were: Bosnia, Burma, Cuba, Haiti (later suspended), Iran, Laos, Vietnam, and the former Soviet Union. In addition, however, this priority category also now includes: cases referred by a U.S. embassy or by the UN High Commissioner for Refugees (UNHCR), including persons in immediate danger of loss of life; former political prisoners; UNHCR-referred vulnerable cases (for example, women at risk or torture survivors); and those from UNHCR's list of persons for whom other durable solutions are not available and whose first asylum situation is not feasible in the long run.[13]

Part 4 suggests what U.S. refugee admissions could look like. Suffice to say at this point that the increased refugee flows from such countries as Sudan and Bosnia — countries experiencing extraordinarily high levels of human rights abuses — are encouraging and hopefully an indication of future policy. Yet, there are still many more situations where U.S. refugee involvement is nonexistent.[14] Part of this could be resettlement options that are available in other countries (although these opportunities, at least in terms of finding a "safe" country, are disappearing).[15] Still, consider the extraordinarily precarious situation facing so many Rwandan refugees, and compare this to the grand total of thirty refugees admitted to the United States in 1994 from that devastated country.

ASYLUM ADJUDICATIONS

U.S. asylum adjudications have also experienced some change from the previous decade, although here, too, there has been far more continuity (see table 3.3).

The most noteworthy aspect is what we have already seen before: a majority of those applying for asylum in the United States are from countries experiencing the very highest levels of political terror. Using the State Department as a data source, 59 percent of those who applied for asylum between 1990 and 1995 were from either a Level 4 or Level 5 country (column 3). This, again, is contrary to the public perception that asylum seekers are abusing the system. Instead, as was true of the previous decade, most asylum seekers are from countries we would expect asylum seekers to come from. The converse of this is also true in that very few asylum seekers are from "safe" countries. According to the State Department, only 8 percent of the asylum seekers were from a Level 1 or Level 2 country (column 3).

In terms of acceptance rates, once again a majority of those granted asylum from 1990–95 were from countries experiencing the highest levels of political terror. According to State Department data, 58.6 percent of those granted asylum were from a Level 4 or Level 5 country (column 5). Perhaps

Table 3.3: Human Rights and Asylum Applications, 1990–95

I Level	II Asylum applications	III As % of total applications	IV No. granted	V As % of those granted asylum	VI Acceptance rate by level
Amnesty International					
5	16,472	13.5	6045	18.6	36.7
4	50,297	41.2	11,633	35.7	23.1
3	22,886	18.7	6464	19.8	28.2
2	21,740	17.8	4803	14.7	22.0
1	1,621	1.3	135	0.4	8.3
NC	8,880	7.2	3453	10.6	38.8
Total	121,896		32,533		
State Department					
5	20,524	16.8	7837	24.0	38.2
4	51,511	42.2	11,257	34.6	21.8
3	31,048	25.4	7863	24.1	25.3
2	8,044	6.5	1772	5.4	22.0
1	1,922	1.5	193	0.5	10.0
NC	8,847	7.2	3611	11.0	40.8
Total	121,896		32,533		

the most notable change from the previous decade is that the acceptance rate for individuals from Level 5 countries — for *both* Amnesty and the State Department — was considerably higher than it was for the other levels of political terror (column 6). Using Amnesty as a data source, 36.7 percent of the Level 5 applicants were successful, and this number was even higher (38.2 percent) using the State Department Reports as a data source.

One of the strengths of a human rights analysis is that it seeks to move public discourse away from simple ideological and geopolitical concerns. Instead, it allows us to group countries according to their level of political terror, which then allows a more insightful analysis of the refugee/asylum response of the United States. The risk at the other end, however, is that there is too much abstraction. To rectify this, table 3.4 is presented showing asylum acceptance rates for 1994, with countries grouped by averaging their Amnesty and the State Department political terror scores (see table 3.4).

Table 3.4: 1994 Asylum Acceptance Rates

Level	Country	No. Accepted	No. Applied	%	Level	Country	No. Accepted	No. Applied	%
5.0	Afghanistan	86	154	55.8	3.0	Bangladesh	64	304	21.0
	Bosnia	127	136	93.3		Cuba	384	571	67.2
	Burma	71	108	65.7		Ecuador	4	66	6.0
	Columbia	30	227	13.2		El Salvador	148	2520	5.8
	India	523	1646	31.7		Ghana	36	253	14.2
	Iraq	110	148	74.3		Mali	3	33	9.0
	Liberia	206	408	42.9	2.5	Albania	28	87	32.1
	Sierra Leone	36	334	10.7		Bulgaria	26	330	7.8
	Somalia	125	165	75.7		The Gambia	1	40	2.5
	Sudan	168	209	80.3		Honduras	78	907	8.5
	Turkey	2	39	5.1		Ivory Coast	12	85	14.1
	Yugoslavia	416	842	49.4		Jordan	19	198	9.5
4.5	Haiti	96	2213	4.3		Romania	122	891	13.6
4.0	Brazil	2	95	2.1		Senegal	4	57	7.0
	Cameroon	65	141	46.0		Ukraine	150	364	41.2
	Egypt	34	195	23.4	2.0	Armenia	56	439	12.7
	Ethiopia	534	1115	47.8		Guyana	1	37	2.7
	Guatemala	315	4427	7.1		Jamaica	0	40	0.0
	Iran	416	646	64.3		Laos	64	289	22.1
	Lebanon	50	260	19.2	1.5	Trinidad	0	42	0.0
	Mexico	5	4475	0.1		Tobago			
	Pakistan	157	993	15.8	1.0	Czech	2	27	7.4
	Peru	265	920	28.8		Poland	3	494	0.6
	Russia	408	1028	39.6					
	Syria	396	516	76.7					
	Yemen	9	80	11.2					
3.5	China	307	1011	30.3					
	Nicaragua	313	1834	17.0					
	Philippines	51	1792	2.8					
	Sri Lanka	45	104	43.2					

Note: Not coded: Croatia, Israel, Fiji, and the former Soviet Union.

Even a casual glance reveals two things. First, there are many more countries (and asylum applicants) experiencing very high levels of political terror than countries with fair or low levels. Second, asylum acceptance rates, for the most part, seem to reflect human rights concerns. Consider a few Level 5 countries. The asylum acceptance rate for Sudan was 80 percent; percent for Bosnia, 93 percent; and percent for Afghanistan, 55 percent. These are all impressive numbers. On the other hand, only 5 percent of the Turkish asylum applicants were successful (reflecting political considerations), and 13 percent of the Colombian applicants were accepted (indicating geographical as well as political concerns). Very low success rates were also experienced for Mexico and Brazil — two Level 4 countries that year). On the other end of the spectrum, there are not nearly as many countries (or asylum applicants) from countries with an average political terror score of 2.5 or below, and the acceptance rates are commensurate with the differences in human rights abuses in those countries. Notwithstanding these findings, there is still a very strong public perception that our asylum system is rampant with abuse.

What an American Refugee Policy Could Look Like

In theory, there are very few ways in which it would be possible for the United States to make a more positive contribution to the world than through the admission of refugees. Without attempting to sound melodramatic, the U.S. government's refugee policy could, quite literally, mean the difference between life and death for substantial numbers of individuals each year. And at the risk of sounding hopelessly naive, I would argue that perhaps there is no purer way for the United States to protect the human rights of others than through a refugee admission policy that focused on meeting the needs of the most desperate among us.

In fact, the United States has, on one level at least, been very generous in terms of the number of refugees it has admitted. During the 1980s the United States admitted nearly 1 million refugees and close to 600,000 for the first half of the 1990s. Particularly for a Western country, these numbers are extraordinarily high. The problem, as indicated by the data in part 3, is that the United States has not necessarily been admitting refugees through its overseas refugee admission program, as evidenced by the relatively mild forms of persecution in nearly all the countries where refugees are migrating from. Thus, I would argue, the United States has been admitting "immigrants" but labeling these individuals "refugees." Although there is nothing wrong with admitting immigrants as such, the appropriate manner for doing so is by some other means (such as through normal flow immigration channels). Admitting immigrants as refugees not only cheapens the concept of refugeehood, but much more importantly, it thereby deprives others — real refugees — of an opportunity for safety in this country.

The End of the Cold War

For decades, U.S. refugee policy has served the ends and the goals of American foreign policy. This was certainly true before 1980 when refugee admissions were limited by law to individuals from communist countries or from the Middle East (although nearly all were from the former). Refugees fleeing communist regimes were taken as proof positive of the evils of those regimes and the superiority of our way of life. The 1980 Refugee Act offered the promise of some change, but this opportunity was missed.

The promotion of ideological solidarity is a commendable goal for U.S. foreign policy and perhaps for refugee admissions as well.[16] The problem — at least in terms of refugee admissions — is that by the 1980s the worst abuses of communist rule had long been over. To be sure, all these countries were governed by repressive regimes, and nearly all the population suffered the daily indignities and duplicities of life in a communist country.[17] But with virtually no exception these were not countries marked by large-scale political violence. Still, the United States readily responded to this repression but in doing so essentially ignored the claims of millions of individuals who were brutalized by far more violent regimes. Whatever justification there may have been at one time for focusing U.S. refugee policy on the claims of individuals from communist countries has certainly passed by now. The Cold War is over; the Lautenberg Amendment expired in 1996.[18] It is time to create a new U.S. refugee policy.

Creating a New Refugee Policy

The term "burden sharing" receives a lot of attention in the refugee literature, but it is a term essentially devoid of meaning because it is a concept in search of implementation. Consider, however, an American refugee policy that was premised on the concept of burden sharing and which made a concerted effort to protect those in grave danger. Under such a policy we could admit, say, 40,000 refugees a year. This would be a sharp reduction in the numbers we currently take in and even 10,000 below the baseline established under present law. The difference is that we would be admitting real refugees as opposed to disguised immigrants. One means of achieving this would be to actively recruit (for lack of a better term) those in the most desperate of circumstances. This, after all, is why we grant individuals refugee status in the first place. However, rather than granting permanent residence to those taken in, as we do presently (which is another indication of the lack of distinction between immigrants and refugees under present policy), we should instead only offer a temporary safe haven until danger has passed.[19]

What are the advantages of this kind of refugee system? To point out the obvious, the proposal's greatest strength is that it would reduce human misery in a way that present policy seldom does. Quite obviously, the United States cannot admit anywhere near the number of people who are in need of such assistance, but this is also a manner in which we could (safely) become involved in some of the worst human crises on the planet. Imagine, for example, if the United States had offered a safe haven to several thousand Rwandan refugees, either during the 1994 genocide, or at any time since then. What would this accomplish? The most important would be that thousands of people would be given safety — a safety that did not (and presently does not) exist. Beyond this, however, such an involvement also would have provided the United States (along with the other Western countries) the opportunity, as well as the impetus, to begin to address the political quagmire that gave rise to this utter brutality in the first place. Would this ensure a lessening of ethnic tension, or would it mean that hostilities would not persist? Of course not. But, I would argue, it would have represented a much better policy — politically as well as morally — than the one that we have pursued — which has been little more than to sit back and watch the horror unfold.

A number of objections would be made to the proposal outlined above. One is that in admitting a substantially different "class" of refugees, there would be far more difficult problems of assimilation than we presently face. This much is conceded. However, with temporary admission the norm (and permanent residence the exception), the assimilation of refugees is not a goal to be pursued, at least not initially. Related to that, another objection might be that, based on the apparent lack of political willpower to deport unsuccessful asylum applicants, any "temporary" admission of refugees would easily turn into something like we have at present: permanent residence. This, however, is due in large part to poor administration, an unfortunate hallmark of the Immigration Service.[20] This should not be a reason for not attempting to create a refugee system.

The strongest objection to such a proposal may be that it threatens to create a further "mess" in this country's alien admissions — and don't we have enough going on in this area already?[21] Though I would most definitely agree with the premise, I do not accept the conclusion. U.S. alien admission policy has certainly been ill conceived, but this is also a reflection of how it has attempted to be all things to all people: to employers who enjoy cheap labor, to families who wish to be reunited in this country (but who could, in most instances, be reunited back in the home country), to a public that wants the benefits of aliens without the presence of aliens, to well-entrenched interest groups who promote admission of their own "refugee" group only, and so on.

Because of this, I suspect that little will change. We will, most certainly, make stronger efforts to prevent illegal aliens from entering and working here; but, we will make no real effort to deal with the reasons why they are flocking here in the first place.[22] We will continue to placate those who have family members who wish to migrate to the United States, as well as the needs of the business community, although the numbers might well decline in the short run. What will not be questioned, however, is the 10:1 ratio of immigrants to refugees, a policy that somehow seems to be etched in stone.[23] We can point to the cruelty of the 1938 St. Louis incident without realizing that we are doing essentially the same thing now. Humanitarianism is nice in theory but apparently has severe limits in practice. In sum, U.S. alien admission policy, for all intents and purposes, will pretty much stay its present course. All I would ask for, then, is for a U.S. refugee policy that makes a much deeper contribution to the cause of human rights in the world than the one that we have at present.

Notes

I would like to thank Carolyn Johnson, a statistician with the Immigration and Naturalization Service, who has been very helpful in gathering data for this paper. I would also like to thank David Forsythe for his most useful comments on an earlier draft.

1. This, in essence, is the theme of Peter Brimelow's book, *Alien Nation: Common Sense about America's Immigration Disaster* (New York: Random House, 1995).

2. An asylum seeker is an individual who applies for refugee status while in the

United States. I use the term "illegal alien" to describe those who have entered the United States without inspection, although it is noteworthy that a substantial portion of the "illegal" aliens in this country are nonimmigrants who are out of status.

3. Article 33 of the 1951 Convention Relating to the Status of Refugees protects against the return of an alien "where [the refugee's] life or freedom would be threatened on account of his race, religion, nationality, membership of a particular social group or political opinion."

4. Mark Gibney, Clair Apodaca, and James McCann, "Refugee Flows, the Internally Displaced and Political Violence (1980–1993): An Exploratory Analysis," in *Wither Refugee?* ed. A. P. Schmid, (Leiden, Netherlands: PIOSM, 1996).

5. Although there was more immigration, 8.8 million, to the United States during the decade of 1900–1910, there was also considerable emigration as well. Jeffrey S. Passel and Barry Edmonston, *Immigration and Race in the United States: The 20th and 21st Centuries* (Washington DC: Urban Institute, 1992).

6. See, generally, Kitty Calavita, "Employer Sanctions Violations: Toward a Dialectical Model of White-Collar Crime," *Law & Society Review* 24 (1990): 1041–1069.

7. Reflecting (or perhaps creating) this mood are such articles as Robert Kaplan's "The Coming Anarchy" in the February 1994 issue of *Atlantic Monthly*, or that by Matthew Connelly and Paul Kennedy, also in *Atlantic Monthly* (December 1994), "Must It Be the Rest against the West?," which uses the analogy of alien hordes arriving at our shores en masse.

8. Section 101(a)(42)(A) of the Immigration and Nationality Act defines a "refugee" as: "any person who is outside any country of such person's nationality or, in the case of a person having no nationality, is outside any country in which such person last habitually resided, and who is unable or unwilling to return to, and is unable or unwilling to avail himself or herself of the protection of, that country because of persecution or a well-founded fear of persecution on account of race, religion, nationality, membership in a particular social group, or political opinion."

9. Arthur Helton, "Political Asylum Under the 1980 Refugee Act: An Unfulfilled Promise," *Michigan Journal of Law Reform* 17 (1984): 243–264.

10. Level 1: Countries are under a secure rule of law, people are not imprisoned for their view, and torture is rare or exceptional. Political murders are extremely rare. Level 2: There is a limited amount of imprisonment for nonviolent political activity. However, few persons are affected and torture and beatings are exceptional. Political murder is rare. Level 3: There is extensive political imprisonment or a recent history of such imprisonment. Execution or other political murders and brutality may be common. Unlimited detention, with or without a trial, for political views is accepted. Level 4: The practices of Level 3 are expanded to larger numbers. Murders, disappearances, and torture are a common part of life. In spite of its generality, on this level terror affects those who interest themselves in politics or ideas. Level 5: The terrors of Level 4 have been extended to the whole population. The leaders of these so-

cieties place no limits on the means or thoroughness with which they pursue personal or ideological goals. For further information on these human rights measures, see Mark Gibney and Matthew Dalton, "The Political Terror Scale," in *Human Rights and Developing Countries*, ed. David Cingranelli (Greenwich CT: JAI Press, 1996).

11. Owing to the enormous backlog of asylum cases, it often takes years for a case to be adjudicated. Because I am speaking in terms of raw numbers, an "application" is made the year that the INS makes a determination on a case, not when the application was actually made.

12. The admissions from Vietnam since 1988 have been: 17,626 (1988), 21,865 (1989), 26,023 (1990), 27,441 (1991), 26,921 (1992), 30,920 (1993), 33,204 (1994), and 28,653 (1995). For Laos: 14,561 (1988), 12,799 (1989), 8,667 (1990), 9,212 (1991), 7,964 (1992) 6,853 (1993), 5,999 (1994), and 3,323 (1995).

13. Thomas Alexander Aleinikoff, David Martin, and Hiroshi Motomura, *Immigration: Process and Policy*, 3rd ed. (St. Paul: West Publishing Co., 1985), 739.

14. In addition to Rwanda, there are many other countries with a high score on the PTS but with no or very few persons admitted into the United States. Afghanistan, Angola, and Bosnia, *inter alia*, fit into this category. See U.S. Committee for Refugees, *1995 World Refugee Survey* (Washington DC: U.S. Committee for Refugees, 1995).

15. Gibney et al., "Refugee Flows," 14.

16. Michael Walzer, *Spheres of Justice: A Defense of Pluralism and Equality* (New York: Basic Books, 1983), 49.

17. One of the best accounts of the constant misery of life under communist rule is Ivan Klima's novel, *Judge on Trial* (New York: Alfred A. Knopf, 1993).

18. Section 599D, Immigration and Nationality Act, 8 U.S.C. Sec. 1157, note. The act provides preferential treatment for individuals from the former Soviet Union, Estonia, Latvia, Lithuania, Vietnam, Cambodia, and Laos.

19. See, generally, Bill Frelick and Barbara Kohnen, "Filling the Gap: Temporary Protected Status," *Journal of Refugee Studies* 8 (1995): 339–363.

20. It is not merely the administration of U.S. asylum policy that has been lacking. As Frelick and Kohnen point out, the Immigration and Naturalization Service does not even keep track of whether aliens whose TPS status has expired ever leave the United States.

21. A policy that might be given more thought is for the United States to house "its" refugees in other countries — much as we did with Haitian and Cuban refugee flows.

22. David Forsythe has suggested that my assessment might be too harsh in that the United States does provide official democracy assistance to between thirty-five and fifty countries, costing some $700 million each year, trying to create liberal democracies in the world. Although there certainly have been a good number of success stories — Haiti, El Salvador, and Nicaragua immediately come to mind — there

are still far too many countries where the U.S. government exhibits scant concern with respect to human rights conditions, to refugees, or even to whether a democratic form of government exists or not. See the chapter by Zunes in this volume.

23. See generally, Mark Gibney, *Strangers or Friends: Principles for a New Alien Admission Policy* (Westport CT: Greenwood Press, 1986).

The United States and Human Rights Treaties

4

U.S. Ratification of the Other Half of the International Bill of Rights

•

BARBARA STARK

The end of the Cold War marked a breakthrough for human rights in the United States as well as in the rest of the world.[1] Since the collapse of the Soviet Union, the United States has ratified the International Covenant on Civil and Political Rights (the "Civil Covenant") and the International Convention on the Elimination of All Forms of Racial Discrimination (the "Race Convention" or "ICERD"), and President Clinton has sent the Convention on the Elimination of All Forms of Discrimination Against Women (the "Women's Convention" or "CEDAW") to the Senate for approval.[2] The Clinton administration pledged to press for ratification of the International Covenant on Economic, Social and Cultural Rights (the "Economic Covenant" or "ICESCR"), recognizing that the United States could not credibly claim to be the "world leader in human rights," while ignoring rights recognized everywhere else.[3] The United States is now the only major industrialized democracy that has not yet ratified the Economic Covenant.[4]

This chapter briefly reviews the development of human rights law since World War II, focusing on the erasure of economic rights in the United States during the Cold War. I will then explain how the end of the Cold War not only eliminated a major obstacle to U.S. ratification of the Economic Covenant but created major incentives for ratification as well. At the same time, because of the domestic "war on welfare" and declining U.S. economic hegemony, the need for ratification of the Economic Covenant has never been greater.[5] I conclude that these factors, together with the support of the executive, make ratification a practical objective, and it explains why the domestic human rights community should make ratification a priority.

International Human Rights

The human rights atrocities of World War II proved to a shocked world that even "advanced," "civilized" states, such as Germany, could not be depended on to assure the basic "human dignity" of their own people.[6] Lead by the United States, the world powers declared that the people of the world had fundamental human rights beyond those established under their own national laws, rights that the states themselves could not abrogate.[7] Virtually every state in the world endorsed this limit by accepting the UN Charter and the Universal Declaration of Human Rights.[8]

The states did not consider the human rights provisions of the UN Charter and the Universal Declaration binding at first.[9] In fact, they agreed from the beginning on the need for a more specific legal instrument.[10] In 1952 the General Assembly decided that two Covenants would be necessary.[11] The Civil Covenant assures familiar "negative" rights, similar to those in the U.S. Constitution, and the United States ratified it in 1992.[12] The Economic Covenant assures less familiar "positive" rights, which are not protected under the U.S. Constitution.[13] These include rights to food, shelter, health care, and education.[14] The two Covenants, together with the Universal Declaration, comprise the International Bill of Rights.[15] They are globally recognized as equal, indivisible, and interdependent.[16] Neither Covenant may be neglected at the expense of the other.

The Covenants are intended to serve as law.[17] By ratifying them, a state takes a major step toward enabling its own people to assert rights against the state itself.[18] The Covenants provide the basic legal frameworks for those human rights neglected — or worse — under a state's own law. The international community, however, has lacked the political will to develop mechanisms, or devote sufficient resources, to effectively support these frameworks. Thus, paradoxically, human rights remain dependent on the very domestic legal systems they are intended to supplement, or even supplant.[19]

During the Cold War: Economic Rights as a Soviet Threat

Although the United States was eager to "declare" international human rights after World War II, it was more hesitant about domestic implementation.[20] Some believed that we had an already well-developed constitutional jurisprudence of civil and political rights. Others were concerned that the world would be scandalized by still-legal segregation and other forms of state-condoned racial discrimination.[21] International civil and political rights were seen as both redundant and as an invitation to unfriendly foreign states to criticize the United States.[22]

The rights set out in the Economic Covenant were viewed with even more suspicion. As Roosevelt's promise of "freedom from want" receded from public memory, economic rights were linked to our new arch-enemy, the Soviet monolith.[23] Because the United States linked economic rights with the Soviets during the Cold War, it was impossible for the domestic human rights community to draw on international human rights for the economic rights that were — and still are — missing from domestic law.[24]

It was difficult enough for domestic human rights advocates to convince their fellow Americans that international human rights were not some foreign conception, that they were not only compatible with our own jurisprudence but deeply grounded in American constitutionalism.[25] In this country, human rights advocates explained, human rights were not opposed to "state values"; rather, they embodied them. The domestic human rights community expanded the American notion of "rights" as grounded in American legal instruments, particularly the Constitution, to include the broader "human rights" of those denied their civil and political rights in other countries.[26] The American human rights community established itself as a political player by focusing on violations of civil and political rights by foreign states. The domestic community thus legitimated the civil and political half of the "human rights idea," despite often vigorous opposition and its marginal status as law.[27] Its influence contributed to a culture of respect for those international human rights most similar to our own, and its tireless efforts contributed to the 1992 ratification of the Civil Covenant and the 1994 ratification of the Race Covenant.[28]

While international critics have faulted the domestic human rights community for neglecting economic rights, the politics of the Cold War made it impossible for the already-struggling domestic community to do otherwise.[29] Senator John W. Bricker proposed an amendment to the Constitution requiring an act of Congress before any human rights treaty could become law in the United States. This was supported by opponents of civil rights and only defeated because the Eisenhower Administration promised that it would not adhere to human rights treaties.[30] Senator Joe McCarthy and his cohorts were openly hostile toward economic rights and vilified those who espoused them. Few domestic groups concerned with economic rights survived the 1950s. Those that did prudently steered clear of the Economic Covenant with its troublesome associations with foreign policy.[31]

Domestic human rights rhetoric remains universalized and abstracted, reflecting the universal and abstract level of law to which, until 1992, the United States had acceded.[32] It also remains partial, a ragged half of a cleft body of human rights law. While its rhetoric speaks deeply to shared aspirations, even those idealistic law students most receptive to human rights law question its relevance to their future practice.[33] Although human rights everywhere depend primarily on domestic law, the domestic human rights community lacks ties to the domestic constituencies that could support such law in the United States and make it concrete.[34] The paucity of domestic applications and the abstracted tone of the discourse inhibit the growth of a human rights constituency in the United States.

The human rights community is all too aware of the dearth of domestic human rights law. Though there may be normative consensus with respect to civil and political rights, at least insofar as they are compatible with our own constitutional jurisprudence, that jurisprudence often makes them redundant for Americans protected by the Constitution.[35] Although economic rights have not been overshadowed by domestic jurisprudence in the same way, the domestic human rights community has contributed little to the public debate on economic rights that is finally surfacing in this country.[36]

By focusing almost exclusively on the experience of those denied political and civil rights abroad, the domestic human rights community has emphasized the differences between their circumstances and our own, their repressive regimes, and our Constitutional protections. Though the human rights community insists that human rights law is "real" law, rather than the political posturing of states, human rights law rarely functions like "real law" here. The use of human rights rhetoric in connection with military "humanitarian intervention" by the Reagan and Bush administrations in Grenada and Panama, moreover, appeared to be political posturing even to many otherwise staunch supporters of human rights.[37] In doing so the domestic community has not only alienated many in the international human rights community, it has snubbed its "natural [domestic] constituenc[ies]" — women, men of color, and the poor — by ignoring the economic rights issues that most concern them.[38]

After the Cold War: Ratification as a Practical Objective

International human rights have been marginalized in this country because of domestic law and rhetoric as well as foreign policy concerns. The civil and political rights set out in the Civil Covenant were resisted by opponents of domestic civil rights and eclipsed by an otherwise robust domestic jurisprudence.[39] The economic rights set out in the Economic Covenants were not only fatally linked with the Soviets but preempted by the rhetoric of "opportunity."[40] But the Soviets are gone, the Cold War is over, and opportunity means little to growing numbers of Americans. These changes have produced domestic as well as international incentives for ratification. As these changes become more pressing, and the links between them better recognized, ratification becomes an increasingly practical objective.

DOMESTIC INCENTIVES

The American Dream has lost its luster. The difference between the best paid 10 percent and the worst paid 10 percent of Americans "is wider than in any other large industrialized State," and inequality has grown in this country between 1980 and 1991.[41] The social costs of increasing polarization are borne by all of us.[42] Even the middle class feels the need for a dependable "safety net," although it remains unwilling to pay for it.[43] While President Clinton renewed his promise to "rebuild the economy and with it the American Dream," he stressed in his 1995 State of the Union Address that opportunity is only part of that dream: "Opportunity and responsibility, they go hand in hand; we can't have one without the other, and our national community can't hold together without both."[44]

Not since 1965 have so many Americans lived in poverty.[45] For many of these poor Americans, infant mortality rates, life spans, and health problems are closer to those of the Third World than to those of other Western industrialized democracies.[46] Their inadequate housing and schools, lack of healthcare, and job opportunities have been recognized as international human rights issues for at least fifty years.[47] Ironically, even the federal Agency for International Development (AID) has realized that it need not go abroad to promote human rights. AID, "which spent the Cold War fighting communism with foreign aid and helping poor countries like Bangladesh immunize children . . . has found a new customer for its services: America's inner cities."[48]

Americans generally think of human rights law as protection for oppressed people in distant places, people denied their civil and political rights.[49] The Economic Covenant offers protection for the oppressed in this country, including those denied basic welfare rights taken for granted in every other Western industrialized democracy.[50] Welfare rights are what the United States lacks as a nation, what Americans hardly have words for, just as those in other nations hardly have words for the civil and political rights that many take for granted here.[51]

The Supreme Court has consistently held that the U.S. Constitution does not assure welfare rights.[52] Nor can the American political process be depended on to do so.[53] As the November 1994 election again confirmed, the political process cannot be relied on to protect the most vulnerable.[54] No state or city wants to be a "welfare magnet"; no state or city wants to alienate its own tax base. Without a nationally recognized normative floor, the states are driven to compete in a destructive race to the bottom.[55] Congress cannot be relied on to establish such a normative floor, because the Democrats and the Republicans are engaged in the same race to the bottom on the national level.[56]

Instead, the political process has produced frenzied cutbacks in public spending, attacks against legal as well as illegal immigrants, and threats to take children away from their mothers.[57] These are precisely the kinds of human rights violations, carried out by the government and unchecked by national law, contemplated by human rights law. The Economic Covenant is the law enacted thirty years ago to prevent them, or at least to soften their impact.[58] This is not to suggest that ratification would be easy or that it would not require substantial, concrete reform. Human rights advocates would have to develop effective strategies to deal with the current emphasis in the United States on individual responsibility at the expense of entitlements. They can begin by pointing out that "individual responsibility is not necessarily incompatible with the "progressive realization" of economic rights contemplated by the Economic Covenant. The issue becomes how to enable individuals willing to take responsibility for their own economic rights to do so effectively.

The current hostility to entitlements, moreover, may well have peaked. State governors have pointed out, for example, that provisions of the Welfare Reform Act are unconstitutional. Even conservatives, such as New York's mayor Rudy Giuliani, challenge the inconsistent and counterproductive burdens imposed on cities. Finally, it is widely agreed that the welfare system, as well as middle-class entitlement programs such as Social Security, need an overhaul. The Economic Covenant offers much to many — including politicians who want to express a rhetorical commitment to human dignity without committing themselves to specific programs or specific expenditures. The human rights community can serve an invaluable function by educating the aged, minorities, workers, and the growing ranks of the working poor about what the Economic Covenant offers them. As domestic groups learn how the Covenant can be used to support their specific agendas and how they can use it, support for ratification is likely to grow.

INTERNATIONAL INCENTIVES

Although Americans still agree with President Clinton that this is the "greatest country on earth," comparisons with other Western industrialized states proliferate as the holes in our own safety net become increasingly obvious. The American press constantly reminds us that this country consistently falls below other affluent states regarding health care and welfare reform. While we may respond to such comparisons defensively, we certainly want what everyone else has, the basic elements of the good life. Though we may respond to foreign criticism with resentment, moreover, we want the rest of the world to respect us and to look up to us.

American leaders, similarly, feel pressure to meet international standards when America participates in world conferences. We take national pride in our commitment to human rights, and we are offended when other states scoff at us. Just as Americans criticize states that violate the civil and political rights of their people, the rest of the world criticizes the United States for its neglect of economic rights. As Professor Henkin has pointed out, "Failure to adhere to [ICESCR] is seen the world over . . . as a blind confusion of ideological communism (which almost all are now prepared to reject), with commitment to the welfare of individual human beings, to which virtually all States are now committed in principle and in fact." [59]

American rejection of ICESCR has practical as well as ideological repercussions. Although ICESCR imposes no obligation on one state to aid another, American indifference to the welfare of its own people leaves those in developing states with little hope of American concern for theirs.[60] Rather, it confirms cynics', including those leading antidemocratic factions' views that American aid is merely a tool of foreign policy and that the end of the Cold War means the end of aid.[61] Indeed, American officials acknowledge that until the "Soviet Empire collapsed . . . the central purpose of foreign aid was to lure countries away from communism. Alleviating poverty and hunger was a secondary goal." [62]

Failure to ratify ICESCR, and to promote human rights generally, moreover, is perceived by many as part of a larger failure of U.S. leadership.[63] Ratification would not only reassure the rest of the world that we share its values and understand its needs, but it would also enhance our credibility and our image as "world leader" at a relatively low cost.[64]

Human rights law relies primarily on domestic adoption.[65] Therefore, domestic groups throughout the world have relied on international opinion to press for adoption by their own states.[66] The civil rights movement in the United States, for example, drew on international opinion in the 1950s. The spreading "human rights idea" that nations could not abrogate the rights of their own people was an important catalyst.[67] As Mary Dudziak has explained, "U.S. government officials realized that their ability to sell democracy to the Third World was seriously hampered by continuing racial injustice at home."[68] The Third World was appalled by media coverage of civil rights struggles in the South: "Those pictures of dogs and fire hoses were published in Europe, Africa, India, Japan. Photographs were especially powerful in countries where large parts of the population could not read."[69] The crucial leverage provided by international human rights helped the domestic civil rights movement obtain desperately needed federal support. Indeed, the Justice Department brief in *Brown v. Board of Education* explicitly described how segregation at home hurt the United States abroad.[70]

International opinion does not mean today what it did during the Cold War, when the Soviets sought to exploit racial tensions in the United States.[71] But it is still a significant factor in domestic politics, and domestic groups have become increasingly sophisticated about using it.[72] As during the civil rights movement in the 1950s, those seeking economic rights can draw on international opinion to obtain leverage at home.

The Economic Covenant provides a legal umbrella under which domestic groups dealing with homelessness, children's rights, hunger, and education can all find shelter.[73] When these groups mobilize separately, they spread their support thin and compete against each other in divisive ways. They can better address the wide-ranging and often overlapping needs of their respective constituencies by supporting broadly defined economic rights. Just as the civil rights movement relied on U.S. endorsement of civil and political rights in the 1950s, economic rights groups can rely on U.S. endorsement of economic and social rights in recent years. The United States recognized economic rights, for example, when it signed the Charter of Paris for a New Europe in 1990 and the Vienna Declaration in 1993.[74] Even if these economic rights groups never function as an effective political movement, they can surely muster enough support to push the Economic Covenant past an increasingly discredited Jesse Helms, chair of the Senate Foreign Relations Committee.[75]

At the same time, domestic economic rights groups can help shape a nascent but growing international economic rights jurisprudence. Fran Ansley, noting the internationalization of capital and the multiplying formal and informal networks among multinational corporations, has mapped some of the possibilities for such networks among workers.[76] Similar networks would be useful for those denied economic rights — especially, perhaps, those already falling through an increasingly diaphanous safety net.[77]

Why the Human Rights Community Should Make Ratification a Priority

Some in the human rights community regard any commitment beyond ratification as a distraction from civil and political rights — on which, they argue, all others depend.[78] They argue further that human rights rely on emerging consensus and there is no consensus on economic rights. Communism collapsed with the Soviet Union, and the social democracies of Western Europe are reassessing their generous welfare policies as their populations become increasingly diverse and the global economy resists quick fixes.[79] Even developing states have jettisoned the rhetoric of "economic rights" now that it serves no strategic purpose.[80] Indeed, it might be argued that ratification of ICESCR as a self-executing treaty would make the United States one of the only countries in the world where the Economic Covenant was actually being used as domestic law.[81]

Opponents might further point out that trying to use the Economic Covenant as a substitute for a coherent federal welfare policy would fatally politicize human rights. Human rights advocates would risk the land mines of domestic welfare politics, politics in which they have no experience and few friends. They risk backlash; the same "financialization of the economy" that makes social welfare programs so urgent makes taxpayers unwilling to pay for them.[82] They risk failure, the kind of failure that has plagued large-scale poverty programs.[83] Finally, they risk more focused efforts to implement economic rights, such as school desegregation.[84]

Although human rights advocates should proceed cautiously, these risks should not deter them. Implementation of human rights always requires domestic reform and participation in messy domestic politics.[85] The risk of backlash remains, but human rights advocates are not likely to be blacklisted or accused of "sympathizing with the Russians."[86] During the Cold War they might have been.[87] Domestic groups concerned with economic rights, moreover, represent a large and growing constituency.[88] Human rights advocates are likely to find invaluable "natural allies" among them.[89]

Though failure remains a real risk, it is precisely because of our historic ineptitude that ICESCR is so crucial.[90] Where we have failed because we lacked sustained commitment, ratification of ICESCR would represent a long-term promise. Where we have failed because of too much bureaucracy, the Covenant process could be used to generate more manageable, down-sized approaches to intractable problems.[91] Where we have failed because of our stubborn belief in the rhetoric of opportunity, the Covenant could help us develop the "kinder and gentler" aspects of that rhetoric, focusing our resourcefulness on communal improvement rather than on competitive advantage.[92]

International human rights law recognizes that all human beings are entitled to a bottom line of human dignity and that national governments cannot be depended on to assure it. Indeed, governments are often indifferent or even hostile to human rights. As the domestic human rights community has repeatedly pointed out, governments throughout Latin America, Africa, Asia, and the former Soviet bloc have callously denied the civil and political rights of their own people. The community has been conspicuously less vocal about the denial of economic rights here in the United States.

If there ever was an excuse for this silence, it ended with the Cold War. No longer can there be any claim that pressing for human rights at home plays into the hands of America's enemies abroad. On the contrary, ratification of the Economic Covenant can only reassure our friends abroad of the United States' commitment to human rights. At the same time, the need for economic rights, for "freedom from want," is increasingly urgent for growing numbers of Americans. Ratification of the Economic Covenant would be a crucial first step toward showing these Americans the practical value of international human rights law.

The domestic human rights community has been criticized for its idealism, for its distance from the practical problems of the real world.[93] Ratification of ICESCR would begin to bring domestic human rights down to earth. Human rights advocates have too often been like the angels in Wim Wenders's film, *Wings of Desire*.[94] Wenders's angels are passive observers in a black and white world, invisible to mortals. They hover nearby, thoughtfully and compassionately watching us suffer. Like the carefully worded reports of human rights advocates, the angels' interventions are subtle and often unnoticed. When one of the angels finally rejects ethereal abstraction to become a mortal, the screen bursts into color. Ratification of the Economic Covenant — along with the long, hard work of applying it in a multitude of domestic contexts — could bring domestic human rights to life in the same way.[95]

Notes

I am grateful to Fran Ansley, Hillary Charlesworth, Judy Cornett, Rosalyn Hackett, Glenn Harlan Reynolds, Shelley Wright, and the students in my international human rights classes for their helpful comments on earlier versions of this article. I also acknowledge the generous support of the University of Tennessee College of Law. Jeffrey Grimes, Benjamin Pressnell, Gabrielle Cowan, and Jeff Stephens provided outstanding research assistance.

1. President George Bush "broke the logjam." "Breaking the Logjam," *Georgia Journal of International and Comparative Law* 20 (1990): 299.

2. *United Nations Treaty Series* (*UNTS*) 999 (December 19, 1966): 171. Entered into force March 23, 1976. *UNTS* 660 (March 7, 1966): 195. Entered into force January 4, 1969. On June 24, 1994, the Senate ratified ICERD. Senate Executive Report No. 29, 103rd Congress, 2nd session, 1994. December 18, 1979, General Assembly Resolution 34/180; *UN General Assembly Official Reports Supplement* 34 (no. 46): 193; UN Document A/34/46 (1980). Entered into force September 3, 1981, reprinted in *International Legal Materials* (*ILM*) (1980): 33. Arvonne S. Fraser, "The Women's Human Rights Treaty," *American Society of International Law* (March–May 1995): 19.

3. *UNTS* 999 (Dec. 19, 1966): 3. Entered into force January 3, 1976. David B. Ottoway, "Universality of Rights Is Defended by U.S.," *Washington Post*, June 15, 1993.

4. The Economic Covenant has been ratified or acceded to by 133 states as of May 1996. Christina M. Cerna, "Human Rights Letters from Geneva," *ASIL Human Rights Interest Group Newsletter* (spring 1996): 11.

5. See notes 54–57.

6. The phrase appears in the Universal Declaration of Human Rights, G. A. Res. 217, UN GAOR, 3rd session, pt. 1: 71, UN Doc. A/810 (1948).

7. Franklin Roosevelt laid the groundwork in his famous "four freedoms" speech. Eighth Annual Message to Congress (January 6, 1941), in *The State of the Union Messages of the Presidents 1790–1966* (New York: Chelsea House, 1966), 3: 2855, 2860.

8. UN *Charter*, Articles 55 and 56; Universal Declaration, n.11. Eight Soviet bloc

states abstained. Louis Henkin et al., *Cases and Materials on International Law*, 3rd ed. (St. Paul: West, 1993), 606.

9. The Universal Declaration "is not in terms a treaty instrument." UN Secretary-General, *Survey of International Law* (1971): 85, UN Doc. A/Cn.4/245.

10. *Reports of the Commission to Study the Organization of Peace, Building Peace* 2 (1973): 641.

11. Most scholars agree that two Covenants evolved from the Universal Declaration, "because of the East/West split and a disagreement over the value of socioeconomic rights." David P. Forsythe, review of *International Cooperation for Social Justice* by A. Glenn Mower Jr., *Human Rights Quarterly* 8 (1986): 540. The bifurcation of rights into two Covenants was further justified by differences in "the nature of the legal obligation and the systems of supervision that could be imposed." D. J. Harris, *Cases and Materials on International Law*, 4th ed. (London: Sweet & Maxwell, 1991), 666.

12. Text of the Resolution of Ratification, *ILM* 31 (1992): 658.

13. See, e.g., *Dandridge v. Williams*, 397 U.S. 471 (1969) (no right to welfare); *Clark v. Community for Creative Non-Violence*, 468 U.S. 288 (1984) (no right to sleep in public places); *Harris v. McRae*, 448 U.S. 297 (1980) (no right to Medicaid funding for abortion); *Lindsay v. Normet*, 405 U.S. 56, 73–74 (1972) (no right to housing). Federal programs, such as Social Security, do not purport to meet a "minimum core obligation to ensure the satisfaction of, at the very least, minimum essential levels of each of the rights." *Manual on Human Rights Reporting*, UN Doc. H.R. Pub/91/1 45 (1991): 214 (text of general comment 3, para. 10).

14. Economic Covenant in Cerna, "Human Rights Letters," Articles 11–13.

15. Henkin, *Cases on International Law*, 596.

16. See "Indivisibility and Interdependence of Economic, Social, Cultural, Civil and Political Rights," G. A. Res. 44/130, UN GAOR, 44th session, suppl. no. 49: 209, UN Doc. A/Res/44/130 (1989) (accepted Dec. 15, 1989). Nadine Strossen, "What Constitutes Full Protection of Fundamental Freedoms?" *Harvard Journal of Law and Public Policy* 15 (1992): 43, 48–49.

17. *Building Peace*, 2: 641. Although the Economic Covenant is to be implemented through "progressive realization," this imposes a legal obligation on the state. See *Manual*, H.R. Pub/91.

18. *Building Peace*, 1: 176 n.16.

19. Forsythe, *The Internationalization of Human Rights* (Lexington MA: Lexington Books for D. C. Heath, 1991), 119; accord Richard Bilder, "An Overview of International Human Rights Law," in *Guide to Human Rights Practices*, ed. Hurst Hannum (Philadelphia: University of Pennsylvania Press, 1983).

20. Forsythe, *Internationalization*, 21.

21. See Mary L. Dudziak, "Desegregation as a Cold War Imperative," *Stanford Law Review* 41 (1986): 61.

22. See 81st Congress, 2nd session, 1950, 10–20, 22–52, 154–202, 205–208, cited in Louis Sohn and Thomas Buergenthal, *International Protection of Human Rights* (Indianapolis: Bobbs-Merrill, 1973). Bert B. Lockwood Jr., "The UN Charter and U.S. Civil Rights Litigation: 1946–1955," *Iowa Law Review* (1984): 901. The view that the United States could not be bound by treaties, especially human rights treaties, addressing "domestic issues" was "long ago refuted." Henkin et al., *Cases on International Law*, 626; *Restatement (Third)*, sec. 302, rep. note 2.

23. Paula Dobriansky, "U.S. Human Rights Policy: An Overview, U.S. Department of State," *Current Policy*, no. 1091 (1988): 2–3.

24. Senator McCarthy and his committee were suspicious of internationalism; see, e.g., Oscar Schachter, "Phillip Jessup's Life and Ideas," *American Journal of International Law* 80 (1986): 878, 887. They treated economic rights as a threat to national security. Ann F. Ginger, "Human Rights and Peace Law in the United States," *Temple International and Comparative Law Journal* 6 (1992): 25, 26. The civil rights movement, in contrast, was able to draw on international opinion. Human rights law was rightfully perceived as a threat by opponents of civil rights (see Hearings, 81st Congress) and as a powerful tool by civil rights lawyers (see Lockwood, "Civil Rights Litigation").

25. See, e.g., Oscar Schachter, "The Charter and the Constitution: The Human Rights Provisions and American Law," *Vanderbilt Law Review* 4 (1952): 643.

26. As with most states, the United States had generally been tolerant of human rights violations by foreign states, especially against their own nationals. Violations of American property rights by foreign states, in vivid contrast, outraged Congress. See, e.g., First Hickenlooper Amendment, 22 USCA 2370(e)(1) (prohibiting aid to state expropriating American assets). In *Banco National de Cuba v. Sabbatino*, 376 U.S. 398 (1964), the Supreme Court declined to rule on the validity of a Cuban expropriation of United States-owned sugar plantations, correctly observing that international law was unsettled on the issue. Id. at 428. Congress responded by enacting the Second Hickenlooper Amendment, 22 USCA 2370(e)(2) in 1964, which explicitly overruled *Sabbatino* and required courts to hear cases involving expropriations absent an executive directive to the contrary. Later, the human rights community was aided by a supportive President Jimmy Carter, who sent the Civil and Political Covenant, the Economic Covenant, the Race Convention, and the Women's Convention to the Senate in 1978. Transmittal Letter, *Weekly Compilation of Presidential Documents* 13 (February 23, 1978): 395.

27. Louis Henkin, *The Age of Rights* (New York: Columbia University Press, 1991), 9. The period from 1953 through 1974 has been described as a time of "outright neglect given Brickerism at home and Dullesism in foreign policy by 1953." Forsythe, *Internationalization*, 122.

28. See UNTS 999 (December 19, 1966).

29. See, e.g., Philip Alston, "U.S. Ratification of the Covenant on Economic, So-

cial and Cultural Rights: The Need for an Entirely New Strategy," *American Journal of International Law* 84 (1990): 366.

30. Henkin et al., *Cases on International Law*. For early arguments, see Symposium, "Should the Constitution Be Amended to Limit the Treaty-Making Power," *Southern California Law Review* 26 (1953): 347.

31. Instead, economic rights have been championed by loose and shifting coalitions of grassroots organizations. See, e.g., Thomas A. Krueger, *And Promises to Keep: The Southern Conference for Human Welfare* (Nashville: Vanderbilt University Press, 1967), 139–158 (postwar labor organizing in the South).

32. President Carter recommended that the Economic Covenant also be ratified as a nonself-executing treaty. Transmittal Letter, Doc. 13 (February 23, 1978). See Louis Henkin, "U.S. Ratification of Human Rights Conventions: The Ghost of Senator Bricker," *American Journal of International Law* 89 (1995): 341, 348.

33. Ottoway, "Universality of Rights." See, e.g., Secretary Christopher, "Democracy and Human Rights: Where America Stands," *U.S. Department of State Dispatch* 4 (June 21, 1993): 441, 442 (insisting on the "universality" of human rights).

34. See note 19.

35. The United States has made several reservations to the ICCPR and ICERD. See generally, Richard B. Lillich, ed., *U.S. Ratification of the Human Rights Treaties: With or Without Reservations?* (Charlottesville: University Press of Virginia, 1981). For a scathing critique, see Henkin "U.S. Ratification of Human Rights Conventions," n.40. See also the chapter by Schabas in this volume. There is considerably less normative consensus with respect to refugees or immigrants who are not protected by the U.S. Constitution. See, e.g., *Mathews v. Diaz*, 426 U.S. 67 (1976) (holding that Congress may condition aliens' eligibility to participate in federal medical insurance programs, noting narrow standard of review on immigration matters).

36. The debate, once virtually nonexistent, is now ubiquitous. See, e.g., "Welfare Surprises," *Business Week*, March 13, 1995, 44, (the first Census Bureau study of AFDC recipients shows that most AFDC mothers are or had been married); Celia W. Dugger, "Displaced by the Welfare Wars," *New York Times*, February 26, 1995, sec. 4, 1 (national welfare debate needs to address "moral and political question: What will happen to the children?"). Some in the domestic human rights community have already contributed substantially to this debate. See, e.g., Bert Lockwood, "The Economic Brown," in *World Justice: U.S. Courts and International Human Rights*, ed. Mark Gibney (Boulder CO: Westview, 1991), 149; and Constance de la Vega, "Protecting Economic, Social, and Cultural Rights," *Whittier Law Review* 15 (1994): 471.

37. See Francis Boyle et al., "International Lawlessness — Grenada," *American Journal of International Law* 78 (1984): 172; Christopher Joyner, "The United States' Action in Grenada," *American Journal of International Law* 78 (1984): 131; Agora, "U.S. Forces in Panama," *American Journal of International Law* 84 (1990): 494.

38. See, e.g., Philip Alston, "Economic and Social Rights," in *Human Rights: An*

Agenda for the Next Century, ed. Louis Henkin and John Lawrence Hargrove (Washington DC: American Society of International Law, 1994).

39. See text accompanying notes 67–71.

40. I refer here to the rhetoric of the American Dream, the idea that if you are poor in the "land of opportunity," it is your own fault. Barbara Stark, "Postmodern Rhetoric, Economic Rights and an International Text: 'A Miracle for Breakfast,'" *Virginia Journal of International Law* 33 (1993): 433, 437–450 (describing the impact of the rhetoric of "opportunity to enjoy a middle-class, American" standard of living.

41. Keith Bradsher, "Inequalities in Income Are Reported Widening," *New York Times*, October 29, 1995, 2.

42. See generally, "Talk of the Town," *New Yorker*, May 11, 1992, 27 (on the L.A. riots: "What, as a nation, did we really expect? The residents of our inner cities have for many years now been unable to lay claim to our national sense of common humanity and simple decency. On what basis can we expect to suddenly lay claim to theirs?").

43. Louis Uchitelle, "The Rise of the Losing Class," *New York Times*, November 20, 1994, E1 (opinion polls show that "Americans are increasingly angry about their economic insecurity"); Michael Wines, "Taxpayers Are Angry. They're Expensive, Too," *New York Times*, November 20, 1994, E5 ("Payments to the poor add up to less than the three largest tax breaks that benefit the middle class and wealthy: deductions for retirement plans, the deduction for home mortgage interest, and the exemption of health-insurance premiums that companies pay for their employees.")

44. Douglas Jehl, "Health, Crime, and Economy Top Clinton's Agenda for '94," *New York Times*, January 2, 1994, 1. President William Clinton, "We Must Forge a New Social Compact," State of the Union Address, 1995, in *Washington Post*, January 25, 1995, A30.

45. Henry G. Cisneros, "Focus On: Urban America—Introduction," *Yale Law and Policy Review* 12 (1994): 1; Robert Pear, "Poverty 1993: Bigger, Deeper, Younger, Getting Worse," *New York Times*, October 10, 1993, Week in Review section, 5 (citing Census Bureau Report of increase in poverty in spite of the end of the latest recession).

46. As Marian Wright Edelman, head of the Children's Defense Fund, recently noted, "No other industrialized nation has dreamed of letting its children go without basic levels of nutrition or medical care." Calvin Tomkins, "Children of a Lesser Country," *New Yorker*, January 15, 1996, 26.

47. *Building Peace*, H.R. Pub/91, 1: 127.

48. Thomas L. Friedman, "Foreign Aid Agency Shifts to Problems Back Home," *New York Times*, June 26, 1994, 1.

49. See, e.g., "Human Rights Watch Looks Within," *New Yorker*, December 13, 1993, 53.

50. This does not mean that the Economic Covenant is always effectively imple-

mented in these countries. See Alston, "Economic and Social Rights," 137 and n.93 (Western Europe reducing welfare benefits).

51. See, e.g., George A. Billias, ed., *American Constitutionalism Abroad* (New York: Greenwood, 1990).

52. See note 13. For powerful critiques of this line of decision, see Frank I. Michelman, "The Supreme Court, 1968 Term: On Protecting the Poor Through the 14th Amendment," *Harvard Law Review* 83 (1969): 7; Charles L. Black, "Further Reflections on the Constitutional Justice of Livelihood," *Columbia Law Review* 86 (1986): 1103, 1105 (discussing "the derivation of a constitutional right to a decent material basis for life").

53. Indeed, some commentators have suggested that the poor are effectively excluded from meaningful participation in that process. See, e.g., Stephen Loffredo, "Poverty, Democracy and Constitutional Law," *University of Pennsylvania Law Review* (1993): 1277, 1309. Only "insular minorities" are entitled to constitutional protection under Carolene Products' famous footnote 4. *U.S. v. Carolene Products Company*, 303 U.S. 144, 152–153 n.4 (1938). For an argument that heightened scrutiny would be better applied to "diffuse" groups such as the poor, see Bruce Ackerman, "Beyond Carolene Products," *Harvard Law Review* (1985): 713.

54. William Buckley's *National Review* viewed the November 1994 election as a popular rejection of Clinton, the Democrats, and liberalism in general. See, e.g., Rich Lowry, "Renovating the House," *National Review*, December 19, 1994, 37.

55. Paul E. Peterson and Mark C. Rom, *Welfare Magnets: A New Case for a National Standard* (Washington DC: Brookings Institution, 1990) (discussing state welfare systems and the establishment of a national welfare standard).

56. See notes 54 and 57. See also Judith Haveman, "Liberal Advocacy Groups Urge Veto of Welfare Bill," *Washington Post*, October 6, 1995, A11; Robert Pear, "A Welfare Revolution Hits Home, But Quietly," *New York Times*, August 13, 1995, sec. 4, 1.

57. See, e.g., Jonathan Alter, "Decoding the Contract," *Newsweek*, January 9, 1995, 26; Robert S. McIntyre, "Taxing the Poor," *New Republic*, January 30, 1995, 15; Jim Impoco and Mike Tharp, "California Tries to Give Back the Tired and the Poor," *U.S. News & World Report*, November 21, 1994, 42; Robert Pear, "Deciding Who Gets What in America," *New York Times*, November 27, 1994, E5; "The Orphanage," *Newsweek*, December 12, 1994 (a half million children are in "government funded substituted care, 75 percent in foster homes").

58. *Building Peace*, 1: 165, 181–182.

59. Louis Henkin, Foreword to *Human Rights: An Agenda for the Next Century*, xix–xx; accord Alston, "Economic and Social Rights," 141.

60. See generally, Craig N. Murphy, "What the Third World Wants: An Interpretation of the Development and Meaning of the New International Economic Order Ideology," in *The Politics of International Organizations*, ed. Paul F. Diehl (Chicago: Dorsey, 1989), 226, 228. Charter of Economic Rights and Duties of States, G. A. Res.

3201 (s-vi) (1974); UN Declaration on the Establishment of a New Economic Order, G. A. Res. 3281 (xxix, 1974).

61. "African Democracies Worry U.S. Aid Will Dry Up," *New York Times*, March 19, 1995, 1.

62. See Steven Greenhouse, "Foreign Aid: Under Siege in the Budget Wars," *New York Times*, April 30, 1995, E4.

63. Barbara Crossette, "Look Who Wants U.S. as a Leader," *New York Times*, February 12, 1995, E5.

64. Greenhouse, "Foreign Aid." Cf. Elaine Sciolino, "Call It Aid or a Bribe, It's the Price of Peace," *New York Times*, March 26, 1995, E3

65. See note 19.

66. See, e.g., Margareth Etienne, "Addressing Gender-Based Violence in an International Context," *Harvard Women's Law Journal* 18 (1995): 139 (rapes by both Serb and Croatian armies).

67. See Henkin, *The Age of Rights*.

68. Dudziak, "Desegregation as a Cold War Imperative," n.28, n.61; accord Forsythe, *Internationalization*, 122.

69. Vicki Goldberg, "Remembering the Faces in the Civil Rights Struggle," *New York Times*, July 17, 1994, H31.

70. Brief for the United States as amicus curiae at 4–6, *Brown v. Board of Education*, 347 U.S. 483 (1954). Many in the civil rights movement realized that economic rights were the obvious next step: "By 1963, the civil rights movement was attacking economic barriers keeping blacks in poverty. . . . There were 900 demonstrations in more than 100 cities. . . . On August 28, 1963, a quarter of a million people marched on Washington for social justice." "War on Poverty," PBS television broadcast, 1995.

71. The Soviet Union broadcasted 1,400 pictures of civil rights demonstrations abroad. Goldberg, "Remembering the Faces."

72. See, e.g., ESHRAN, letter of October 5, 1995, Meeting of the Working Group on Racial Discrimination; A. Borrus, "What the UN Women's Conference Can Do for Women," *Business Week*, September 4, 1995, 42.

73. Alston, "U.S. Ratification of the Covenant," 392.

74. Charter of Paris for a New Europe, November 21, 1990, ILM 30 (1991): 190, 194; Document of Copenhagen Meeting of the Conference on the Human Dimension of the Conference on Security and Cooperation in Europe (CSCE), ILM 29 (1991): 1306; and Human Rights: Vienna Declaration and Programme of Action, ILM 32 (1993): 1663.

75. See Elaine Sciolino, "Awaiting Call, Helms Puts Foreign Policy on Hold," *New York Times*, September 24, 1995, 1.

76. Fran Ansley, "Standing Rusty and Rolling Empty: Law, Poverty and America's Eroding Industrial Base," *Georgetown Law Journal* 81 (1993): 1757. Cf. John Humphrey, *Human Rights and the United Nations* (New York: Transnational, 1984), 141

(noting ILO opposition to inclusion of social and economic rights in the Covenant, "presumably because they felt this would impinge on their jurisdiction").

77. But see Mary Becker, "Politics, Differences and Economic Rights," *University of Chicago Legal Forum* (1989): 526–533 (American approach to rights is fundamentally at odds with the approach of those states that have adopted ICESCR).

78. There is sometimes surprising support for the proposition that democracy underlies other kinds of rights. Famine in China affected up to 30 million people during the Great Leap Forward because the government believed it had 100 million more metric tons of grain than it did. Sylvia Nasar, "It's Never Fair to Just Blame the Weather," *New York Times*, January 17, 1993, sec. 4, 1.

79. See, e.g., Patrick R. Ireland, *The Policy Challenge of Ethnic Diversity: Immigrant Politics in France and Switzerland* (Cambridge: Harvard University Press, 1994).

80. See generally, Barbara Crossette, "The 'Third-World' Is Dead, But Spirits Linger," *New York Times*, November 13, 1994, sec. 4, 1.

81. Portugal is another. Phillip Alston and Gerard Quinn, "The Nature and Scope of States Parties' Obligation under the International Covenant on Economic, Social and Culture Rights," *Human Rights Quarterly* 9 (1987): 156, 166.

82. The phrase is Kevin Phillip's, referring to the increasing concentration of wealth held by those whose incomes are already above the incomes of 99 percent of the population. Kevin Phillips, *Arrogant Capital: Washington, Wall Street, and the Frustration of American Politics* (Boston: Little, Brown and Co., 1994), n.52.

83. See Nicholas Lemann, "The Myth of Community Development," *New York Times*, January 9, 1994, sec. 6, 27 (listing federal programs since 1949).

84. See Symposium, "Brown v. Board of Education After Forty Years: Confronting the Promise," *William & Mary Law Review* 36 (1995): 337.

85. See Schachter, "The Charter and the Constitution."

86. It would be hard to accuse even the Russians of such sympathies at this point.

87. See text accompanying notes 22–24, 27, and 30, describing McCarthyism and Brickerism.

88. See text accompanying notes 72–74; Tomkins, "Children of a Lesser Country." See also Kevin Phillips, *The Politics of Rich and Poor: Wealth and the American Electorate in the Reagan Aftermath* (New York: Random House, 1990); Theodore R. Marmor et al., *America's Misunderstood Welfare State: Persistent Myths, Enduring Realities* (New York: Basic Books, 1990), 47–48 (noting widespread public support for the Medicare, food stamp, and social security programs). Paul M. Sniderman and Thomas Piaucca, *The Scar of Race* (Cambridge: Harvard University Press, Belknap, 1993) (white survey respondents say they support assistance for blacks who genuinely need it).

89. Alston, "U.S. Ratification of the Covenant," 392 (describing ICESCR's appeal to diverse groups).

90. See Symposium, "Poverty and the Law," *Harvard Civil Rights — Civil Liberties Law Review* 22 (1987): 1.

91. See, e.g., Theresa Funicello, *The Tyranny of Kindness: Dismantling the Welfare System to End Poverty in America* (New York: Grove Atlantic, 1993); see also, Barbara Stark, "Economic Rights in the U.S. and International Human Rights Law: Toward an 'Entirely New Strategy,'" *Hastings Law Journal* 44 (1992).

92. Former president George Bush coined the phrase in his speech accepting the Republican nomination for president on August 18, 1988, at the Republican Convention in New Orleans. "Republicans in New Orleans," *New York Times*, August 19, 1988, A14. The continuing evisceration of the public sector that followed Bush's election made the phrase ironic.

93. See, e.g., Ann Goldstein, Foreword to *Reconceiving Reality, Women and International Law*, ed. Dorinda G. Dallmeyer (Washington DC: American Society of International Law, 1993).

94. *Wings of Desire* (Argos Films, 1987).

95. See Peter Bailey, *Bringing Human Rights to Life* (Sydney: Federation Press, 1993), 192–213. Ann Fagan Ginger, "The Energizing Effect of Enforcing a Human Rights Treaty," *DePaul Law Review* 42 (1993): 1341, 1392.

5

The United States and the American Convention on Human Rights

•

Prospects and Problems of Ratification

•

CHRISTINA CERNA

The UN Charter established the blueprint for the new world order after the end of the Second World War. The inter-American system was reorganized as a "regional arrangement," pursuant to chapter 8 of the Charter, renamed the Organization of American States (OAS), and given the primary function of maintaining "international peace and security as are appropriate for regional action." To further peaceful and friendly relations among nations, the United Nations was mandated to promote "universal respect for, and observance of, human rights and fundamental freedoms for all without distinction as to race, sex, language, or religion."[1] All member states of the United Nations pledge themselves to take joint and separate action in cooperation with the organization for the achievement of these purposes.[2]

The United Nations today (May 1999) is composed of approximately 185 member states, and the Organization of American States is composed of 35.[3] The principal UN treaties for the international protection of human rights are the International Covenant on Civil and Political Rights, ratified by 144 states and the International Covenant on Economic, Social and Cultural Rights, ratified by 141 states. These two instruments, together with the Universal Declaration of Human Rights, are known as the "International Bill of Rights." The United States ratified the International Covenant on Civil and Political Rights in 1992. It has not yet ratified the International Covenant on Economic, Social and Cultural Rights or either of the optional protocols to the Civil and Political Rights Covenant. In March 1995, the United States presented its first report to the UN Human Rights Committee, the supervisory body that monitors compliance with the terms of the Covenant.[4]

The principal inter-American human rights treaty within the OAS framework is the American Convention on Human Rights (hereinafter "American

Convention"), which has been ratified by twenty-five of the thirty-five member States of the Organization. The American Convention entered into force on July 18, 1978, when Grenada, the requisite eleventh country, ratified it. Every Spanish-speaking state in the hemisphere (except Cuba) has become a party to the Convention, and the largest state in the Southern Hemisphere, Brazil, became a party in 1992.[5] Both the United States and Canada (which just joined the organization in 1990) have not become states parties. This paper addresses the problems and prospects related to U.S. ratification of the American Convention.

The American Convention on Human Rights is the regional equivalent to the [European] Convention for the Protection of Human Rights and Fundamental Freedoms of the Council of Europe. But whereas the European Convention was drafted in 1950 (and entered into force in 1953), the drafters of the American Convention (in 1969) had almost twenty years of experience to benefit from when drafting their convention, and as a result the American Convention is considered "somewhat more advanced."[6]

Both these regional conventions are comparable in scope to the UN's Covenant on Civil and Political Rights, and the drafters, recognizing the possibility of simultaneous overlap in the presentation of individual communications to the universal and the regional bodies, included in each treaty a prohibition on admitting a case if "the subject matter of the petition or communication is . . . pending in another international proceeding for settlement."[7]

The Complementary Regional Human Rights Regime

So why do we need a regional human rights regime if we already have a universal one? Since the inter-American system predates the creation of the United Nations, the states of our hemisphere feared domination of the UN system by the Great Powers and their increasing insignificance in world affairs. The states of the inter-American system, because of the bonds created by history, geography, language, and common culture, sought to preserve their own regional organization, which they viewed as complementary to the international organization.[8]

The rights protected in the American and European Conventions are, in general, the same as those protected in the UN's International Covenant on Civil and Political Rights and by the U.S. Bill of Rights, such as the right to life, the right to be free from torture, and cruel, inhuman, or degrading punishment or treatment, the right to be free from slavery and forced labor, the right to personal liberty and security, the right to a fair trial, the right to be free from ex post facto laws, the right to privacy, the right to compensation if one has been a victim of a miscarriage of justice, the right to freedom of conscience and of religion, the right to freedom of thought and expression, the right of reply if one is injured by inaccurate or offensive statements, the right to associate and the right of peaceful assembly, the right to participate in government, the right to equal protection before the law, and the right to judicial protection.

In my view, once the United States ratified the UN's Covenant on Civil and Political Rights, any substantive problem impeding it from ratifying the American Convention was eliminated, because the American Convention is but the regional equivalent of this Covenant.[9] In addition, the Clinton administration ostensibly intended to move forward on these treaties, and Secretary of State Warren Christopher declared at the UN World Conference on Human Rights in Vienna in 1993 that "we strongly support the general goals" of the American Convention and other treaties signed by the United States. They "will constitute important advances, and our Administration will turn to them as soon as the Senate has acted on the racism convention."[10]

U.S. Ratification of the International Covenant on Civil and Political Rights

President Carter signed the American Convention in 1977, and it was included as part of a package of four treaties sent to the Senate in 1978 for advice and consent.[11] The three other treaties in the package were the two Covenants and the racism convention.[12] In his letter of transmittal, President Carter stated that "United States' ratification of the [American] Convention will give us a unique opportunity to express our support for the cause of human rights in the Americas" and that "the great majority of the substantive provisions of these four treaties are entirely consistent with the letter and spirit of the United States Constitution and laws."[13]

All four treaties were submitted together for congressional action. Hearings were held before the Senate Foreign Relations Committee in November 1979, but "domestic and international events at the end of 1979, including the Soviet invasion of Afghanistan and the hostage crisis in Iran, prevented the Committee from moving to a vote. . . ."[14]

The Reagan administration did not show any interest in ratifying the Covenant on Civil and Political Rights.[15] In 1991, however, the Bush administration revived the Covenant, still pending before the Senate with the other three treaties, making ratification a matter of bipartisan consensus, and proposed the following five reservations:

1. that the Covenant's requirement to prohibit war propaganda and the advocacy of national, racial, or religious hatred must be read consistent with the U.S. Constitution;

2. that, contrary to the Covenant, the United States reserves the right to impose capital punishment on persons who were under eighteen at the time of their crimes;

3. that the Covenant language on cruel and degrading treatment or punishment is no broader than the concept as it appears in the U.S. Constitution;

4. that the United States will not comply with the Covenant provision that states that when new legislation reduces the penalty for crime, anyone currently under sentence for the crime shall benefit from the new legislation; and

5. that the United States reserves the right to treat juvenile offenders as adults, despite the language in the Covenant that calls for separate procedures and separate incarceration for juveniles.[16]

Hearings on the Civil and Political Rights Covenant were held in November 1991 on the recommendation of President Bush, who urged the Senate "to renew its consideration of the Covenant 'with a view to providing advice and consent to ratification.'"[17] In addition, the committee favorably reported the treaty to the Senate after a unanimous vote taken on March 4, 1992.[18] The Senate gave its advice and consent to ratification on April 2, 1992.[19]

Congressional Opposition to Legislating by Treaty

The key to ratification of the Covenant was the support of a democratic President (Carter) and a republican one (Bush). As President Carter had pointed out, the great majority of the substantive provisions of the four treaties is entirely consistent with the letter and spirit of the U.S. Constitution and laws. Any discrepancies between the Constitution and one of the treaties would be dealt with by the inclusion in the instrument of ratification of a reservation, declaration, or understanding to the conflicting provision of the treaty.

The Vienna Convention on the Law of Treaties defines a "reservation" as "a unilateral statement, however phrased or named, made by a State, when signing, ratifying, accepting, approving or acceding to a treaty, whereby it purports to exclude or to modify the legal effect of certain provisions of the treaty in their application to that State."[20] The Vienna Convention requires that reservations be compatible with the "object and purpose" of the treaty and that they not conflict with "a peremptory norm of general international law." States parties, however, even if they protest the reservations of another state party, rarely go so far as to seek to block the entry into force of the treaty for that state.[21]

According to one commentator, the "overriding concern of Senators like Jesse Helms, Orrin Hatch, and Richard Lugar," was that no treaty be supreme to the Constitution or the domestic laws of the United States."[22] The Senate Foreign Relations Committee Report stated that "The overwhelming majority of the provisions in the Covenant are compatible with existing U.S. domestic law. In those few areas where the two diverge, the Administration has proposed a reservation or other form of condition to clarify the nature of the obligation being undertaken by the United States."[23]

During consideration of the Covenant by the Senate, the Foreign Relations Committee accepted a proviso introduced by Senator Helms to be included in the resolution of ratification, to the effect that "the Covenant does not require any legislation or other action prohibited by the Constitution."[24]

For example, U.S. law differs from the international standard in the imposition of the death penalty "for crimes committed by persons below the age of eighteen but U.S. law allows it for juveniles between the ages of 16 and 18."[25] "In such areas as these," the committee suggests that "it may be appropriate and necessary to question whether changes in U.S. law should be made to bring the United States into full compliance at the international level." However, the committee anticipates that "changes in U.S. law in these areas *will occur through the normal legislative process*" (emphasis added).[26]

The U.S. position regarding the ratification of the Covenant was not to implement the provisions of the Covenant that were not in force in domestic law but rather to propose reservations thereto. The United States decided to opt out of implementing any provisions of the Covenant to bring U.S. law into compliance with the international standard *on the theory that the treaty power should not become a basis for changing domestic law*. The rationale for this was presented in the following terms:

The approach taken by the Administration and the Committee in its resolution of ratification will enable the United States to ratify the Covenant promptly and to participate with greater effectiveness in the process of shaping international norms and behavior in the area of human rights. *It does not preclude the United States from modifying its obligations under the Covenant in the future* if changes in U.S. law allow the United States to come into full compliance. In view of this situation, ratification with the Administration's proposed reservations, understandings, and declarations is supported by broad coalition of human rights and legal groups and scholars in the United States, notwithstanding concerns any of them may have with respect to particular conditions.[27]

Since the U.S. Senate, under the leadership of Senator Jesse Helms, has taken the position that human rights treaties should not drive changes in U.S. domestic law in the rights area, there is no outstanding substantive argument to impede the Senate from giving advice and consent to the American Convention, because Congress could simply attach the required reservations, declarations, and understandings to any provision that it considered incompatible with U.S. domestic law, as it did with the Covenant.

In the interest of perfection, the human rights community also has played a role in impeding U.S. ratification of the major human rights instruments; seeking U.S. ratification unburdened by reservations has become a greater good than seeking U.S. ratification at all. International law is neither well understood nor taken seriously in the United States, and part of the blame must fall on the international lawyers in this country. By fighting over the number and nature of the reservations attached to an instrument of ratification of a human rights treaty, the international lawyers give the impression that the treaty should change domestic law, and perhaps Senator Helms and his colleagues are not completely wrong.

The process of internalizing international standards on the domestic level is a slow one, especially when these standards involve matters of culture and religious belief, such as abortion, the death penalty, and freedom of expression and belief. No state, anywhere, is required to be in full compliance with all the international human rights treaty standards at the moment of becoming a state party to the treaty. If that were the case, international treaties would have no relevance as standard-setting instruments, and standard setting has been, perhaps, the most important contribution of the intergovernmental organizations in the human rights area over the past fifty years. It also defeats the purpose of the creation of supervisory bodies to demand perfection in state implementation of these standards at the moment of ratification.

Reasons for Ratification

If the United States did not seek to expand the human rights protection of its inhabitants by ratifying the Covenant, why then did it ratify this treaty? The Senate Foreign Relations Committee report provides some answers. We shall look at each of these considerations to determine whether the report could be used as a valid argument in favor of ratification of the American Convention.

LEADERSHIP IN THE INTERNATIONAL ARENA AND REGIONAL SOLIDARITY

In view of the leading role that the United States plays in the international struggle for human rights, the absence of U.S. ratification of the Covenant is conspicuous and, in the view of many, hypocritical. The Committee believes that ratification will remove doubts about the seriousness of the U.S. commitment to human rights and strengthen the impact of U.S. efforts in the human rights field. By ratifying the Covenant at this time, the United States can enhance its ability to promote democratic values and the rule of law, not only in Eastern Europe and the successor states of the Soviet Union but also in those countries in Africa and Asia which are beginning to move toward democratization.[28]

Clearly this same reasoning applies to U.S. influence in the Americas as much as it does in the rest of the world, perhaps more so, because the states of the Americas are our closest neighbors and for reasons of security we have historically been concerned about their form of government and general welfare. Today, the United States is engaged in promoting free and fair elections and democracy throughout the hemisphere, and it is considered hypocritical for not having ratified the American Convention, especially at a time when all the Spanish-speaking states (except Cuba) and Brazil have done so.

The United States seeks to be a leader in the Americas yet lags behind its neighbors in undertaking the same regional obligations. This undermines our ability to shape international norms and to move the system forward. Twenty years ago, one used to say that the system "did not apply to the large States" such as Mexico, Brazil, and the United States, whereas today, both Mexico and Brazil have ratified the American Convention and accepted the compulsory jurisdiction of the Inter-American Court. Most Latin Americans are incredulous to learn that the United States still has not ratified the Convention.

PARTICIPATION IN INTERGOVERNMENTAL SUPERVISORY BODIES

Ratification will enable the United States to participate in the work of the Human Rights Committee established by the Covenant to monitor compliance.[29]

This is a less significant argument in the inter-American system than in the United Nations. The United States already participates in the work of the Inter-American Commission on Human Rights simply by being a member state of the OAS. Mere membership in the OAS signifies that a state accepts the competence of the Inter-American Commission on Human Rights to examine and decide communications from individuals against OAS member states for violations of their human rights as set forth in the catalogue of human rights known as the American Declaration of the Rights and Duties of Man.[30]

If the United States were to ratify the American Convention on Human Rights and accept the jurisdiction of the Inter-American Court, pursuant to Article 62 of the American Convention, individuals who allege violations of their rights by the United States would have the possibility of having their cases heard by the Inter-American Court.[31] Even if the United States were to ratify the American Convention and not accept the jurisdiction of the Inter-American Court, the United States would be permitted to vote for judges on the court and could present U.S. candidates for these posts.[32]

The United States, as a member state of the OAS, consents to have the Inter-American Commission examine and decide individual communications presented against it for violations of the human rights set forth in the American Declaration. The United States has not consented to the UN Human Rights Committee's exercising a similar competence and consequently, because the United States has not ratified the Optional Protocol, by which states consent to grant individuals the right to present petitions against them to the UN Human Rights Committee.

It is a little known fact that the Inter-American Commission is the only intergovernmental human rights body to have found the United States in violation of internationally recognized human rights, in a case dealing with the death penalty. The case, known as the "Roach" case after the name of the juvenile, involved the imposition of the death penalty on a juvenile offender, which was held to be in violation of the American Declaration.[33] The American Declaration does not contain a specific prohibition on the execution of juveniles, as does the American Convention, and the United States, had it ratified the American Convention, could have reserved to this explicit provision in the Convention rather than having left itself open to condemnation by the commission based on an interpretation of the nonspecific language of the Declaration.[34]

One could question whether a reservation to Article 4(5) of the American Convention would be in accord with the "object and purpose" of the treaty, but the practice of states has been to object to reservations that are not recognized as valid while declaring that "the present reservation will not be deemed to be an obstacle to the entry into force of the treaty" between the objecting country and the reserving country.[35]

INTERSTATE COMPLAINTS

The Committee agrees with the Administration that the United States should accept the competence of the Human Rights Committee to hear complaints from one State Party about another State Party's failure to comply. This competence is critical to the Human Rights Committee's ability to monitor and enforce compliance. By accepting this competence, the United States will not only further enhance the effectiveness of the Human Rights Committee but also have an opportunity to play a more aggressive role in the process of enforcing compliance with the Covenant.[36]

The United States accepted the competence of the UN Human Rights Committee to receive and consider communications under Article 41 in which a state party claims that another state party is not fulfilling its obligations under the Covenant. A similar procedure exists under Article 45 of the American Convention, and clearly if the United States is willing to accept this competence on the part of the UN Human Rights Committee, it presumably would be willing to accept it on the part of the Inter-American Commission on Human Rights.[37]

It is worth noting that neither the Human Rights Committee nor the Inter-American Commission has ever received an interstate complaint, so acceptance of Article 45 of the American Convention does not appear to incur many obligations for the ratifying state.

PARTICIPATION IN SHAPING INTERNATIONAL HUMAN RIGHTS LAW

The Committee recognizes that [the Covenant Art. 19 and 20] restrictions are inconsistent with the guarantees of free speech in the U.S. Constitution . . . and therefore, strongly supports the Administration's proposed reservation to Article 20 and declaration on the limitation of rights. Ratification of the Covenant will allow the United States to seek revisions in Articles 19 and 20 and to help ensure that the limitations permitted under these articles are interpreted narrowly. . . .[38]

Ratification will enable the United States . . . to participate with greater effectiveness in the process of shaping international norms and behavior in the area of human rights.[39]

Ratification of the American Convention would afford the United States the opportunity to seek revision of any article of the Convention with which it is in disagreement. Currently, the Organization of American States is considering possible ways to "reform" the system, and, in particular, the commission's regulations, and it is clearly inappropriate for the United States to express itself regarding reforms of the commission's procedures under the Convention, or before the Court, as long as the United States is not a party to the Convention.

Ratification of the International Covenant on Civil and Political Rights provides the United States with the opportunity to participate fully in two important international human rights bodies, the universal and the regional system for the promotion and protection of human rights, should the U.S. Senate consent to ratification of the American Convention.[40] Ratification of the American Convention would also entitle the United States to ratify the additional protocols to the Convention, namely the Additional Protocol to the American Convention on Human Rights in the Area of Economic, Social and Cultural Rights ("Protocol of El Salvador") and the Additional Protocol to the American Convention on Human Rights to Abolish the Death Penalty in support of the international trend toward its abolition.[41]

The Purpose of the System

The regional and universal systems were designed to be complementary institutions. It makes no sense to interpret them as if they were in competition with each other or as if their norms were contradictory. For that reason, each of the intergovernmental human rights treaties prohibits consideration of a matter under examination by another intergovernmental body of a similar nature.

Much has been made of the "right to life" language of Article 4 of the American Convention as the prime example of why the U.S. Senate will not and cannot give consent to ratify the American Convention. Article 4(1) of the American Convention protects the right to life "in general, from the moment of conception." In fact, the Inter-American Commission, in a 1981 case dealing with the United States and the legality of abortion, held that the protection of the unborn could not be found in the American Declaration.[42] This issue has never been interpreted by the commission in a case brought pursuant to the American Convention, but there would be no justifiable reason to believe that the right to life would be interpreted under the Convention in a way that would contradict the interpretation under the American Declaration.[43]

In addition, the United States may resort to a reservation, declaration, or understanding with regard to Article 4, to reiterate its position that domestic law on the death penalty and abortion will not be subject to modification by the act of ratification of this treaty. These possibly minor discrepancies between U.S. law and international law should not constantly be held up as a red herring to prevent greater U.S. participation in the inter-American human rights system.

Further delay in U.S. ratification of the American Convention continues to erode our leadership position in the inter-American system and sends the message to our neighbors that we value the United Nations but do not value the Organization of American States.[44]

Notes

1. Article 55 of the UN Charter.
2. Article 56 of the UN Charter.
3. The thirty-five member states of the OAS are: Antigua and Barbuda, Argentina, the Bahamas (Commonwealth of), Barbados, Belize, Bolivia, Brazil, Canada, Chile, Colombia, Costa Rica, Cuba, Dominica (Commonwealth of), Dominican Republic, Ecuador, El Salvador, Grenada, Guatemala, Guyana, Haiti, Honduras, Jamaica, Mexico, Nicaragua, Panama, Paraguay, Peru, Saint Kitts and Nevis, Saint Lucia, Saint Vincent and the Grenadines, Suriname, Trinidad and Tobago, United States, Uruguay, and Venezuela.

4. U.S. Department of State, "Civil and Political Rights in the United States," *Initial Report of the United States of America to the UN Human Rights Committee under the International Covenant on Civil and Political Rights,* July 1994, 213 pp.

5. The twenty-five states parties to the American Convention are: Argentina, Barbados, Bolivia, Brazil, Chile, Colombia, Costa Rica, Dominica (Commonwealth of), Dominican Republic, Ecuador, El Salvador, Grenada, Guatemala, Haiti, Honduras, Jamaica, Mexico, Nicaragua, Panama, Paraguay, Peru, Suriname, Trinidad and Tobago, Uruguay, and Venezuela. The ten states that have not yet become states parties are: Antigua and Barbuda, the Bahamas (Commonwealth of), Belize, Canada, Cuba, Guyana, Saint Kitts and Nevis, Saint Lucia, Saint Vincent and the Grenadines, and the United States.

6. See William A. Schabas, "Substantive and Procedural Hurdles to Canada's Ratification of the American Convention on Human Rights" in *Human Rights Law Journal* 12 (1991): 405–407. Schabas cites as an example Article 4 of the American Convention, which clearly contemplates the abolition of the death penalty, whereas Article 2 of the European Convention "virtually endorses the maintenance of this barbarous form of punishment."

7. See Article 46(1)(c) of the *American Convention*, Article 27(1)(b) of *the European Convention*, and Article 5(2)(a) of the *Optional Protocol to the International Covenant on Civil and Political Rights.*

8. The inter-American system was created in 1890 and is the oldest regional organization in the world. The Latin American states are responsible for the introduction of "regional arrangements" into chapter 8 of the UN Charter and also the exception to the prohibition on the use of force, set forth in Article 51 of the charter, which allows for the exercise of collective self-defense and was designed to accommodate the inter-American reciprocal defense regime.

9. International Covenant on Civil and Political Rights, opened for signature December 16, 1966, *United Nations Treaty Series (UNTS)* 171 (vol. 999) (entered into force on March 23, 1976; ratified by the United States on June 8, 1992).

10. The International Convention on the Elimination of All Forms of Racial Discrimination (the "racism" convention) was ratified by the United States in October 1994 (International Convention on the Elimination of All Forms of Racial Discrimination, opened for signature December 21, 1965, UNTS 195 (vol. 660); entered into force January 4, 1969); Secretary W. Christopher, "Democracy and Human Rights: Where America Stands," Address at the UN World Conference on Human Rights, Vienna, Austria, June 14, 1993, in *U.S. Department of State Dispatch,* vol. 4, no. 25.

11. Message from the president of the United States transmitting "Four Treaties Pertaining to Human Rights," Senate Executives C, D, E, and F, 95th Congress, 2nd session (February 23, 1978), reprinted in *Weekly Compilation of Presidential Documents* 14 (February 23, 1978): 395. The American Convention on Human Rights,

opened for signature November 22, 1969, *UNTS* 123 (vol. 1144), reprinted in *International Legal Materials* (*ILM*) 9 (1970): 673 (signed by the United States on June 1, 1977; entered into force July 18, 1978).

12. The three treaties other than the American Convention were the International Convention on the Elimination of All Forms of Racial Discrimination, opened for signature December 21, 1965, *UNTS* 195 (vol. 660) (ratified by the United States October 21, 1994; entered into force January 4, 1969); the International Covenant on Economic, Social and Cultural Rights, opened for signature December 16, 1966, *UNTS* 3 (vol. 993), reprinted in *ILM* 6 (1967): 360 (entered into force January 3, 1976); and the International Covenant on Civil and Political Rights, *UNTS* 171.

13. See Letter of Transmittal of the "four treaties" by President Carter to the Senate of the United States, February 23, 1978, in Message from the President of the United States Transmitting "Four Treaties Pertaining to Human Rights," Senate Executives C, D, E, and F, 95th Congress, 2nd session (February 23, 1978), reprinted in *Weekly Compilation of Presidential Documents* 14 (February 23, 1978): 395.

14. See "International Human Rights Treaties," Hearings before the Senate Committee on Foreign Relations, 96th Congress, 1st session (1979). See also *Report on the International Covenant on Civil and Political Rights*, 102nd Congress, 2nd session (1992), reprinted in *ILM* 31 (1992): 645, 648.

15. See Senate Committee, *Report*, 645, 648.

16. As summarized by Prof. John Quigley; see Quigley, "The International Covenant on Civil and Political Rights and the Supremacy Clause," *Depaul Law Review* 42 (1993): 1287, 1289 n.15; see also Senate Committee, *Report*, 10–14, reprinted in *ILM* 31: 645, 652–653.

17. See Senate Committee, *Report*, 649. The Covenant did not have to be "resubmitted" to the Senate for advice and consent because it had been submitted originally during the Carter administration. Unlike legislation, which dies if it is not passed by Congress, a treaty remains before the Senate.

18. Senate Committee, *Report*.

19. 138th Congress Rec. s4781–84 (daily ed., April 2, 1992). In 1994 the "racism" Convention was ratified. Since then no action has been taken on either the American Convention or the Covenant on Economic, Social and Cultural Rights.

20. Convention on the Law of Treaties, opened for signature May 23, 1969, *UNTS* 331 (vol. 1155) (entered into force January 27, 1980). It is only a "reservation" (as distinguished from a declaration or an understanding), which prevents the reserved part of the treaty from entering into force for the reserving state.

21. In the author's view, much too much importance has been placed on the issue of reservations and whether or not the United States should ratify if the instrument of ratification is burdened with too many reservations. The UN Convention on the Rights of the Child, for example, is burdened by the blanket reservations of some Is-

lamic countries, which subject ratification to the treaty's compatibility with shari'ah, or Islamic law. The international human rights community is not calling for these ratifications to be declared invalid or for these states parties to be deprived of their status. The objective is to achieve universal ratification of the human rights treaties and then to peel away the reservations.

22. Article 6, sec. 2 of the U.S. Constitution provides that treaties are the "supreme law of the land," but the issue was whether a treaty rises above the Constitution. The Senate has replied in the negative by the use of these reservations, declarations, and understandings. See Cherif Bassiouni, "Reflections on the Ratification of the International Covenant on Civil and Political Rights by the United States Senate," *Depaul Law Review* 42 (1993): 1169, 1177.

23. See Senate Committee, *Report*, 650. The committee explained that "since this relationship is a matter of domestic U.S. law, the proviso is not included in the instrument of ratification. This approach eliminates the potential for confusion at the international level about the nature of the U.S. ratification." A similar proviso was adopted by the Senate in October 1990 during consideration of the resolution of ratification of the UN Convention against Torture and Other Cruel, Inhuman or Degrading Treatment or Punishment.

24. See David P. Stewart, "United States Ratification of the Covenant on Civil and Political Rights: The Significance of the Reservations, Understandings, and Declarations," *Depaul Law Review* 42 (1993): 1183, 1184–1185 n.5.

25. Stewart, U.S. Ratification.

26. Stewart, U.S. Ratification.

27. Stewart, U.S. Ratification.

28. Stewart, U.S. Ratification.

29. Stewart, U.S. Ratification.

30. On the functioning of the Inter-American Commission on Human Rights, see Christina M. Cerna, "The Inter-American Commission on Human Rights: Organization and Functioning," in *The Inter-American System for the Protection of Human Rights*, ed. David Harris (New York: Oxford University Press, 1998).

31. As of May 15, 1999, the twenty-one states parties to the American Convention that have recognized the compulsory jurisdiction of the Inter-American Court of Human Rights are: Argentina, Bolivia, Brazil, Chile, Colombia, Costa Rica, Dominican Republic, Ecuador, El Salvador, Guatemala, Haiti, Honduras, Mexico, Nicaragua, Panama, Paraguay, Peru, Suriname, Trinidad and Tobago, Uruguay, and Venezuela.

32. As of early May 1999 there is no U.S. national on the Inter-American Court of Human Rights. In the past a U.S. national has served on the Court but was nominated by a state other than the United States.

33. See Res. No. 3/87, Case 9647 (United States) in the Commission's *Annual Re-*

port 1986–1987, 147–184. See also, "Application of Death Penalty on Juveniles in the U.S./ Violation of Human Rights Obligation Within the Inter-American System," reported and accompanied with note by Dinah Shelton, *Human Rights Law Journal* 8 (1987): 344, 355; Dinah Shelton, "The Prohibition of Juvenile Executions in International Law," *Revue International de Droit Pénale* 58 (1987): 773; David Weissbrodt, "Execution of Juvenile Offenders by the United States Violates International Human Rights Law," *American University Journal of International Law and Policy* 3 (1988):339; Christina M. Cerna, "U.S. Death Penalty Tested before the Inter-American Commission on Human Rights," *Netherlands Quarterly of Human Rights* 10 (1992): 155.

34. Article 1 of the American Declaration provides: "Every human being has the right to life, liberty and the security of his person." Article 4(5) of the American Convention provides: "Capital punishment shall not be imposed upon persons who, at the time the crime was committed, were under 18 years of age."

35. See ICCPR, Reservations, Declarations, Notifications and Objections Relating to the International Covenant on Civil and Political Rights and the Optional Protocols Thereto. Note by the Secretary General, CCPR/C/2, Rev. 3, May 12, 1992.

36. See Senate Committee, *Report*, 650.

37. All member states of OAS are entitled to vote in elections at the General Assembly for the seven members of the commission. Currently, of the seven males who comprise the commission, one is a U.S. national.

38. See Senate Committee, *Report*, 650.

39. Senate Committee, *Report*.

40. In the inter-American system the following twenty-five states participate in both the Covenant system and have ratified the American Convention: Argentina, Barbados, Bolivia, Brazil, Chile, Colombia, Costa Rica, Dominica, the Dominican Republic, Ecuador, El Salvador, Grenada, Guatemala, Haiti, Honduras, Jamaica, Mexico, Nicaragua, Panama, Paraguay, Peru, Suriname, Trinidad and Tobago, Uruguay, and Venezuela.

41. Additional Protocol to the American Convention on Human Rights in the Area of Economic, Social and Cultural Rights opened for signature November 17, 1988, OAS, Treaty Series No. 69, reprinted in *ILM* 28: 156. See also Additional Protocol to the American Convention on Human Rights to Abolish the Death Penalty, opened for signature June 8, 1990, OAS, Treaty Series No. 73.

42. Res. No. 23/81, Case 2141 (United States), March 6, 1981, in the Commission's *Annual Report 1980–1981*, 25–54.

43. In the "Baby Boy" case cited above, the commission looked to the American Convention to serve as a gloss on the Declaration and stated that: "In the light of this history, it is clear that the . . . addition of the phrase 'in general, from the moment of conception' does not mean that the drafters of the Convention intended to modify the concept of the right to life that prevailed in Bogota, when they approved the American Declaration. The legal implications of the clause 'in general, from the mo-

ment of conception' are substantially different from the shorter clause 'from the moment of conception.'" See Res. No. 23/81 U.S. Commission, Case 2141, para. 30.

44. See Stephen S. Rosenfeld, "Taken with the OAS, Jesse Helms Finds an International Organization He Likes," *Washington Post*, August 2, 1996. If Senator Helms likes the OAS so much more than the UN, as this article alleges, ratification of the American Convention would be an appropriate way to begin to show it.

6

Spare the RUD or Spoil the Treaty

•

The United States Challenges the Human Rights Committee on Reservations

•

WILLIAM A. SCHABAS

The United States has come kicking and screaming into the modern world of international human rights treaties. Originally an active participant in the drafting process undertaken by the Commission on Human Rights in the late 1940s, the United States did a sudden about-face when Secretary of State Dulles announced, in 1953, that our country did not intend to ratify international human rights treaties.[1] Despite attempts by some presidents, notably Kennedy and Carter, to reverse the policy, U.S. aloofness from the treaties continued until the late 1980s, when the Convention on the Prevention and Punishment of the Crime of Genocide was ratified.[2] Three years later the United States ratified the International Covenant on Civil and Political Rights, and in 1994 it ratified the Convention for the Prevention of Torture and Other Cruel, Inhuman and Degrading Treatment or Punishment and the International Convention for the Prevention of All Forms of Racial Discrimination.[3] The ratification of the Convention for the Elimination of Discrimination against Women was recommended by the Senate Foreign Relations Committee, and the committee hoped that this would be done in time for the Beijing Conference, in September 1995, but the process has been stalled since then.[4] In February 1995, the Convention on the Rights of the Child was signed, but its ratification does not appear to be imminent.[5] The principal reason why the ratification of human rights treaties has now broken down is Washington's reaction to the position taken by treaty bodies, notably the Human Rights Committee, to the issue of reservations.

In each case, ratification was accompanied by a series of reservations, interpretative declarations, understandings, and provisos.[6] Although the practice of attaching such conditions to ratification is quite widespread, in recent years there has been growing concern about its abuse.[7] The Vienna Declaration and Plan of Action called for states to reduce the number of reservations to human rights treaties.[8] Some states parties have taken an increasingly aggressive stance toward abusive reservations, reviving the practice of objection, which had become almost obsolete. International tribunals such as the European Court of Human Rights have contributed to the debate.[9] The special rapporteur of the UN International Law Commission, Professor Alain Pellet, in his first report on reservations, referred to the "bold new stand" taken by the international tribunals and other bodies.[10] By 1984, the chairpersons of treaty bodies were recommending "that treaty bodies state clearly that certain reservations to international human rights instruments are contrary to the object and purpose of those instruments and consequently incompatible with treaty law."[11]

In November 1994, the Human Rights Committee adopted its general comment on reservations, wherein it addressed a number of highly controversial questions, including the role of the committee itself, the criteria for determining the legality of reservations, the role of objections, and the effect of invalidity of reservations.[12] It was an open secret that the committee had sought to clarify its position on the subject of reservations in anticipation of the presentation by the United States of its initial report under the Covenant, scheduled for its March–April 1995 session. After examining the American reservations, the committee adopted the following conclusion:

> The Committee regrets the extent of the State party's reservations, declarations and understandings to the Covenant. It believes that, taken together, they intended to ensure that the United States has accepted what is already the law of the United States. The Committee is also particularly concerned at reservations to Article 6, paragraph 5, and Article 7 of the Covenant, which it believes to be incompatible with the object and purpose of the Covenant.[13]

Immediately prior to the sittings of the committee, the United States issued its critical observations on General Comment 24.[14] Representatives of the United States also spoke to the issue during the committee sessions and renewed their arguments later in the year during the sessions of the Sixth Committee of the General Assembly, as it was considering a report of the International Law Commission. Subsequently, both the United Kingdom and France issued similar statements on the committee's general comment.[15]

Status of Reservations by the United States to Human Rights Treaties

Since 1988 the United States has ratified four international human rights treaties. In each case, ratification has been accompanied by various reservations, "understandings," and "declarations." Even if not formally labeled reservations, such statements may be so deemed to the extent that they seek to limit the obligations assumed by the ratifying state.[16] U.S. human rights jargon has collectively coined them "RUDS." Some of these are little more than international "boilerplates." Two such statements are part of the package filed at the time of ratification of the International Convention for the Prevention of All Forms of Racial Discrimination, the International Covenant on Civil and Political Rights, and the Convention Against Torture and Other Cruel, Inhuman and Degrading Treatment or Punishment. First, the United States affirms that the treaties are not self-executing, a matter that is essentially of interest to the courts of the United States.[17] The latter may take such a declaration of executive intent into consideration in refusing to give legal effect to the instruments.[18] Second, it sets out a standard concerning the difficulties of implementation of the treaties in a federal system: "That the United States understands that this Convention shall be implemented by the Federal Government to the extent that it exercises jurisdiction over the matters covered therein, and otherwise by the state and local governments. To the extent that state and local governments exercise jurisdiction over such matters, the Federal Government shall, as necessary, take appropriate measures to ensure the fulfillment of this Convention."

After ratification of the Convention on the Prevention and Punishment of the Crime of Genocide, in 1988 the United States made a reservation to Article 9, which provides that the International Court of Justice has jurisdiction in case of disputes between states parties. Several other states have made similar reservations, and the International Court of Justice appears to consider that such a reservation is not incompatible with the object and purpose of the Convention.[19] The United Kingdom, Mexico, and the Netherlands all formulated objections to this reservation by the United States. The second reservation by the United States to the Genocide Convention states, "That nothing in the Convention requires or authorizes legislation or other action by the United States of America prohibited by the Constitution of the United States as interpreted by the United States." The United States also produced several "understandings" concerning the Genocide Convention. Two of these address problems of interpretation of specific terms used in the Convention. The United States declares that the undertaking concerning extradition in Article 7 of the Convention extends only to acts that meet the double criminality rule of extradition law. The United States also declares that nothing in Article 6 affects the right of any state to bring to trial before its own tribunals any of its nationals for acts committed outside a state. Another understanding declares that "acts in the course of armed conflicts committed without the specific intent required by Article 2 are not sufficient to constitute genocide as defined by this Convention." Finally, in an understanding that is really a reservation, the United States reserves the right to participate in the international penal tribunal, described in Article 6 of the Convention, only by separate treaty.

The United States made five reservations to the provisions of the International Covenant on Civil and Political Rights on accession in 1992. One was to both paragraphs of Article 20 of the Covenant, which states that propaganda for war and advocacy of national racial or religious hatred shall be prohibited by law.

Another reservation was directed at a portion of Article 15(1), which offers an offender the benefit of the lesser penalty if sentencing provisions are changed since the commission of the offense. The United States further reserved application of Article 10, to the extent it requires separation or segregation of juvenile offenders. The heart of the controversy was the two reservations concerning the death penalty.[20] On the subject of implementation of the death penalty for crimes committed while under the age of eighteen, eleven objecting states affirmed that this was contrary to the object and purpose of Article 6 of the Covenant, or of the Covenant as a whole. In several cases, objections made reference to Article 4(2) of the Covenant, which deems Article 6 to be a nonderogable norm. Some of the objecting states appear to have misunderstood the scope of the U.S. reservation to Article 6, which goes well beyond the juvenile execution issue, as the comments of Conrad Harper, legal advisor to the Human Rights Committee, make quite clear.[21] Most of the objecting states also challenged the reservation to Article 7 of the Covenant, which prohibits torture and cruel, inhuman, or degrading treatment or punishment.

Several members of the Human Rights Committee, during presentation of the initial periodic report of the United States, contested the validity of the reservation to Articles 6 and 7. Cecilia Medina Quiroga "suggested that the reservation might, in fact, be unacceptable because of the consensus in international law against capital punishment of juveniles."[22] Fausto Pocar referred to "international standards" prohibiting juvenile executions, "which could be considered part of international customary law."[23] He made the same complaint with respect to the reservation to Article 7, a provision "which reflected international customary law in that area."[24] Both Pocar and Bhagwati referred to Article 6 as representing a "peremptory norm" of international law and not therefore subject to reservation.[25]

The U.S. accession to the Covenant was also accompanied by several "understandings." The first understanding deals with the nondiscrimination provisions of the Covenant and declares that, according to the United States, distinctions are permitted when they are, at minimum, rationally related to a legitimate governmental objective. Furthermore, the United States understands that the Covenant does not bar distinctions that may have a disproportionate effect on persons of a particular status. For both Sweden and Finland this constitutes a reservation to the Covenant's most essential provisions and is inadmissible. The other understandings seem to be uncontroversial and deal with the right to compensation in the case of unlawful arrest or a miscarriage of justice, criteria for punishment, certain due process guarantees, and problems of implementation in federal systems.

The United States made reservations on ratification of the International Convention for the Elimination of All Forms of Racial Discrimination in 1994, none of which has provoked any objection whatsoever by other states parties. The first referred to the protection of freedom of speech, expression, and association and stated that the Convention could not restrict these rights any more than they were already limited by the U.S. Constitution. The second affirmed the same principle with respect to the protection against discrimination in the private sphere and declared that to the extent that the Convention called for a broader regulation of private conduct, the United States did not assume any obligations requiring it to enact legislation or take other measures. The third reservation dealt with Article 22, providing for the compulsory jurisdiction of the International Court of Justice; it was essentially the same reservation as that formulated with respect to Article 9 of the Genocide Convention.

Also in 1994 the United States ratified the Convention for the Prevention of Torture and Other Cruel, Inhuman and Degrading Treatment or Punishment, making two reservations. The first states: "That the United States considers itself bound by the obligation under Article 16 to prevent 'cruel, inhuman or degrading treatment or punishment,' only insofar as the term 'cruel, inhuman or degrading treatment or punishment' means the cruel, unusual and inhumane treatment or punishment prohibited by the Fifth, Eighth, and/or Fourteenth Amendments to the Constitution of the United States." There have been no objections to this reservation, although Germany has transmitted a note stating "it is the understanding of the Government of the Federal Republic of Germany that [the said reservations and understandings] do not touch upon the obligations of the United States of America as State Party to the Convention." [26] The second reservation is specifically contemplated by the Convention and simply declares that the United States is not bound by an arbitration procedure that includes dispute settlement by the International Court of Justice. There are also several detailed understandings dealing with interpretation of various terms used in the Convention, including the scope of the word "torture." One of them, known as the "Soering understanding" because it responds to a celebrated judgment of the European Court of Human Rights, states that "the United States understands that international law does not prohibit the death penalty, and does not consider this Convention to restrict or prohibit the United States from applying the death penalty consistent with the Fifth, Eighth and/or Fourteenth Amendments to the Constitution of the United States, including any constitutional period of confinement prior to the imposition of the death penalty." [27]

General Comment 24 and Its Critics

The issue of reservations has stirred controversy in human rights circles for many years. Litigation concerning reservations has come before the Inter-American Court of Human Rights and the European Court of Human Rights, both of which have made important pronouncements on the subject. [28] The starting point, in the case of both bodies, has been an appreciation of the fact that human rights treaties have special features and that there are problems in the mechanical application of the customary legal rules developed over the years and codified in the Vienna Convention on the Law of Treaties. Probably the most important distinction is the fact that human rights treaties are not principally concerned with the creation of reciprocal rights and obligations between states parties, but rather with the promotion of rights in the interest of some third party, be it individual, group, minority, or people. In General Comment 24, although the Human Rights Committee concedes that the Vienna Convention "provides relevant guidance," it quite clearly considers certain of its principles to be of doubtful validity when human rights treaties are concerned.[29] In this respect, it is not innovating, because much of the ground has already been well worked over by the Inter-American and European Courts. The United States, the United Kingdom, and France clearly reject these efforts at innovation. As the United States says in its observations, this approach "while interesting, runs contrary to . . . international law."

In General Comment 24, the committee declares that it is "important to address which body has the legal authority to make determinations as to whether specific reservations are compatible with the object and purpose of the Covenant."[30] The committee concludes that it is indeed the appropriate body to determine whether or not reservations are consistent with the object and purpose of the Covenant and whether they are therefore legal or admissible.[31] The committee proposes several arguments in support of its position, of which the most important deal with the significance of objections. The Vienna Convention on the Law of Treaties, generally viewed as a codification of customary principles, contemplates a scheme whereby states that are already parties to a multilateral treaty may object to reservations. The Human Rights Committee notes that the Vienna Convention system is based on inter-state reciprocity, something that is "inappropriate" and that "has no place" in the Covenant system (and in human rights treaties in general).[32] The Human Rights Committee does not deny the fact that objections may have some significance but notes that limited use has been made of them and that the legal effects of them are far from clear. None of the arguments submitted by the three states parties, the United States, the United Kingdom, and France, effectively contests the committee's reasoning on this point.

In its observations, the United States says that "the Committee appears to dispense with the established procedures for determining the permissibility of reservations and to divest States parties of any role in determining the meaning of the Covenant." Later in the year, Legal Advisor Conrad Harper returned to this point in the Sixth Committee of the General Assembly, stating "The critical role of States — as opposed to the Human Rights Committee — in determining matters related to such treaties should be respected on both legal and practical grounds."[33] France was even more superficial, stating that the committee relied "on the poorly-supported supposition that States parties do not accord their full attention and discernment to their right to make objections to reservations." The most serious of the three critics, the United Kingdom, observed that the source of the Vienna Convention regime is the advisory opinion of the International Court of Justice on reservations to the Genocide Convention. The United Kingdom asks: If the very origin of the rules is a case dealing with a human rights treaty, how can the Human Rights Committee determine that the Vienna Convention system is inappropriate?

In its General Comment 24, the committee affirms that "It necessarily falls to the Committee to determine whether a specific reservation is compatible with the object and purpose of the Covenant."[34] According to the committee, this is partially because it is inappropriate for states parties to do so, using the objection mechanism — the only argument that is addressed by the United States — but there are also other grounds for this conclusion. The committee notes that its duties under Article 40 of the Covenant, in the examination of periodic reports of states parties, call upon the committee to assess the legality of reservations. The committee adds: "Because of the special character of a human rights treaty, the compatibility of a reservation with the object and purpose of the Covenant must be established objectively, by reference to legal principles, and the Committee is particularly well placed to perform this task."[35]

The United States presents no answer to this part of the committee's reasoning. France, in its observations, states: "As for the opinion by which the Committee is particularly well placed to address the compatibility of reservations with the object and purpose of the Covenant, France notes that the Committee, like any other jurisdictional or similar body created by agreement, owes its existence solely to the treaty and has no powers other than those that have been conferred upon it by the States parties; therefore they, and they alone, are empowered to rule on the incompatibility of reservations with the object and purpose of the treaty, unless the treaty otherwise provides."

But the silence of the treaty is really no argument at all, because the Covenant does not address the issue of reservations. What it does is create a body, the Human Rights Committee, which is charged with receiving periodic reports from states parties "on the measures they have adopted which give effect to the rights recognized herein and on the progress made in the enjoyment of those rights."[36] The committee is to "study the reports" and then "transmit its reports, and such General Comments as it may consider appropriate."[37] To fulfill its functions, the committee requires all the implicit powers necessary for this task.

The United Kingdom does not share the views of France, or the silence of the United States. It recognizes that "the Committee must necessarily be able to take a view of the status and effect of a reservation where this is required in order to permit the Committee to carry out its substantive functions under the Covenant." The United Kingdom agrees that the committee will need to assess reservations in examining periodic reports and adds that it "might find itself unable in particular cases to deliver a report under the special powers conferred upon it by Article 40 of the First Optional Protocol" [*sic*]. The United Kingdom has difficulty with General Comment 24 regarding the use of the verb "determine" to describe the committee's functions and with the fact that it excludes states parties from the process of assessing reservations by the traditional mechanism of objection.[38]

The Covenant establishes no particular test for the admissibility of reservations. However, the committee reaches the uncontroversial conclusion that the object and purpose test "governs the matter of interpretation and acceptability of reservations" to the Covenant.[39] With respect to the application of the test, the committee makes some important and innovative contributions. It suggests that reservations will be incompatible with the object and purpose of the Covenant if they offend peremptory norms and if they run counter to customary international law. To state that a reservation cannot be made to peremptory (*jus cogens*) norms is simply a logical deduction that flows from the terms of Article 53 of the Vienna Convention on the Law of Treaties. To state that it cannot be made to customary norms is an original proposition, one that finds little or no echo in either scholarly writing or case law. The committee then takes the even bolder step of listing several norms that it deems to be customary.[40]

The United States proposes its own description of the "object and purpose" of the Covenant: "The object and purpose was to protect human rights, with an understanding that there need not be immediate, universal implementation of all terms of the treaty." It adds: "A primary object and purpose of the Covenant was to secure the widest possible adherence, with the clear understanding that a relatively liberal regime on the permissibility of reservations should therefore be required." These remarks are correct but incomplete. They do help to focus attention on a genuine paradox: Reservations are tolerated and even at times encouraged to promote widespread ratification of human rights treaties; but abusive use of reservations only undermines the significance of the treaty. All three states take issue with the claim that reservations may not be made to customary norms. The United States' observations describe the committee's position as a "significant and sweeping premise" that is "wholly unsupported by and is in fact contrary to international law." Making reference to the committee's suggestion that there is a customary norm forbidding states "to permit the advocacy of national, racial or religious hatred," which is presumably codified by Article 20(2) of the Covenant, the United States argues that "It cannot be established on the basis of practice or other authority, for example, that the mere expression (albeit deplorable) of national, racial or religious hatred (unaccompanied by any overt action or preparation) is prohibited by customary international law." The United States also takes issue with the committee's position that the prohibition of execution for crimes committed under the age of eighteen is a customary norm. All eleven objecting states challenged the United States' reservation to Article 6(5) of the Covenant, which expresses the norm. Moreover, the Human Rights Committee, in its observations on the United States' initial report, concludes that the reservation to Article 6(5) is invalid, although without explaining why.

"The normal consequence of an unacceptable reservation is not that the Covenant will not be in effect at all for a reserving party," states the committee in General Comment 24. "Rather, such a reservation will generally be severable, in the sense that the Covenant will be operative for the reserving party without benefit of reservation." [41] In other words, the reserving state might find itself bound by an obligation that it had no intention of ever assuming. On this extremely significant point, the committee is regrettably rather laconic. If the reservation will "generally" be severable, what factors are to be considered? When will a reservation not be severable?

The severability issue is among the most sensitive, and the United States, France, and the United Kingdom all react vigorously on this point. The United States says: "Since this conclusion is so completely at odds with established legal practice and principles and even the express and clear terms of adherence by many States, it would be welcome if some helpful clarification could be made." [42] The United States adds that its reservations are "integral parts of its consent to be bound by the Covenant and are not severable. If it were to be determined that any one or more of them were ineffective, the ratification as a whole could thereby be nullified." The United States argues that "the general view of the academic literature" is that reservations are an essential part of a State's consent, and "cannot simply be erased. "A State which expressly withholds its consent from a provision cannot be presumed, on the basis of some legal fiction, to be bound by it."

Here the United States is on insecure ground, because the judicial authorities — and the academic literature, despite Washington's claim to the

contrary — support the view of the Human Rights Committee that reservations are indeed severable. As Professor R. St. John MacDonald has written
"to exclude the application of an obligation by reason of an invalid reservation is in effect to give full force and effect to the reservation."[43] The only solution, he suggests, is for the entire treaty to come into effect including the
impugned reservation. In its 1988 judgment in *Belilos v. Switzerland*, the European Court of Human Rights not only ruled that Switzerland's "reservation" (Switzerland had called it an "interpretative declaration") to Article 6(1) of the European Convention on Human Rights was invalid, it went
on to find that Switzerland was bound by the Convention as a whole including Article 6(1). The Court reached a similar conclusion when it ruled
illegal Turkey's "reservations" to Articles 25 and 46 of the European Convention of Human Rights in a judgment issued March 23, 1995, only a week
prior to presentation by the United States of its initial report to the Human
Rights Committee.[44] Given that the only judicial pronouncements on the issue of severability are two individual opinions of Judge Lauterpacht of the
International Court of Justice and the two European Court of Human Rights
cases, which tend to favor the severability thesis, the United States might
have explained why it considers the Human Rights Committee's support for
severability to be "completely at odds with established legal practice and
principles."[45]

In the Sixth Committee's discussion on the report of the International Law
Commission, in autumn of 1995, several representatives expressed the view
that the question of reservations had been adequately dealt with in the Vienna Convention on the Law of Treaties.[46] The views expressed by the United
States and the United Kingdom in their observations were expressly supported (without any comment on the contradictions between the two sets of
observations).[47] Yet the shortcomings of the Vienna Convention reservations regime seem unavoidable. Even Conrad Harper said that the scheme of
the Vienna Convention "was not perfect" and added only that it "should be
preserved as far as possible."[48] Others were more critical. Italy urged the
Commission on International Law to give the issue special attention, noting
that "The need to fill in the gaps in the Vienna Convention regime with respect to those treaties was particularly urgent."[49]

    There is a final argument, referred to only summarily in the observations
of the United Kingdom, the United States, and France, that invoked "practical considerations." It is alleged that the innovative approach to reservations

adopted by the Human Rights Committee will discourage ratifications of the Covenant and — it is the United Kingdom that uses the word — may even lead to denunciation by existing parties.[50] The Covenant makes no provision for denunciation, and it has been argued that denunciation is not possible.[51] But even assuming that international law permits a denunciation, practice indicates that this is a threat not to be taken too seriously. European jurists have heard it all before. The same suggestions were made when the European Court of Human Rights began taking a more aggressive stance on the matter of reservations. But no denunciations ever materialized.

The United States remained virtually aloof from international human rights treaties for several decades. It would not have been chagrined if the whole system had foundered and failed. But as ratifications steadily increased, and as the prestige of the Human Rights Committee and the other treaty bodies grew, participation in the systems became more inevitable. But the United States would like to ratify on its own terms. Its belated ratification or accession, accompanied by the subversive RUDS, is a last gasp of an opposition that traces its roots to a conservative State Department in the early years of the Cold War. Louis Henkin, in an editorial comment in the *American Journal of International Law*, wrote that "U.S. ratification practice threatens to undermine a half-century of effort to establish international human rights standards as international law."[52] The European states that filed objections, and the Human Rights Committee in its turn, have said that Washington's approach is inadmissible. In so doing, they give effect to a growing opposition to reservations, whose abuse threaten ultimately to discredit human rights treaties and undermine their effectiveness.

The three states parties that have chosen to submit observations on General Comment 24 — the United States, the United Kingdom and France — have undoubtedly done so to stall the momentum of progressive development of international law on the subject of reservations to human rights treaties. The arguments are frequently flawed and often quite superficial. It is not at all clear that they seek to engage in a serious debate on the subject but more simply to avoid any subsequent suggestions that "silence means consent" and that they have acquiesced in the views of the committee. But as the European Court pointed out in the Loizidou case, such protest may already be too late. Human rights treaty practice was still very undeveloped at the time of the International Court of Justice's advisory opinion, or for that matter at the time the Vienna Convention on the Law of Treaties was adopted, and as a result some of the difficulties with reservations that emerged only in the 1980s and 1990s could not have been fully contemplated. Human rights treaty organs, initially the Inter-American and European Courts of Human Rights, and more recently the Human Rights Committee, have fulfilled the important role entrusted to them by developing international law on this point.

Notes

1. Louis Henkin, "U.S. Ratification of Human Rights Conventions: The Ghost of Senator Bricker," *American Journal of International Law* 89 (April 1995): 341–350.

2. Richard B. Lillich, ed., *U.S. Ratification of the Human Rights Treaties: With or Without Reservations?* (Charlottesville: University Press of Virginia, 1981); David Weissbrodt, "United States Ratification of the Human Rights Covenants," *Minnesota Law Review* 63 (November 1978): 35–78. Convention for the Prevention and Punishment of the Crime of Genocide, *United Nations Treaty Series (UNTS)*, vol. 78.

3. *UNTS* 171 (vol. 999). For the Report of the Committee on Foreign Relations recommending accession to the Covenant, see "Senate Committee on Foreign Relations Report on the International Covenant on Civil and Political Rights," *International Legal Materials* (May 1992): 648. See also Dinah Shelton, "Issues Raised by the United States Reservations, Understandings and Declarations," in *United States Ratification of the International Covenants on Human Rights*, ed. Hurst Hannum and Dana D. Fischer (Washington DC: American Society of International Law, 1993), 269–289; David P. Stewart, "U.S. Ratification of the Covenant on Civil and Political Rights: The Significance of the Reservations, Understandings and Declarations," *Human Rights Law Journal* 14 (April 30, 1993): 77–83; Ved Nanda, "The U.S. Reservation to the Ban on the Death Penalty for Juvenile Offenders: An Appraisal under the International Covenant on Civil and Political Rights," *Depaul Law Review* 42 (summer 1993): 1311–1339. G. A. Res. 39/46, Annex (1985). *UNTS* 195 (vol. 660).

4. *UNTS* 13 (vol. 1249). The Committee on Foreign Relations of the United States Senate recommended that the Senate consent to ratification of the Convention: Senate Committee on Foreign Relations, *Report on Convention on the Elimination of All Forms of Discrimination Against Women*, S. Doc. No. 99–115, 103rd Congress, 2nd session (1994): 8–9. See Ann Elizabeth Mayer, "Reflections on the Proposed United States Reservations to CEDAW: Should the Constitution Be an Obstacle to Human Rights?," *Hastings Constitutional Law Journal* 23 (spring 1996): 727–823.

5. Convention on the Rights of the Child, G. A. Res. 44/25, Annex (1989).

6. *Multilateral Treaties Deposited with the Secretary-General*, 1996 (status as of December 31, 1995) UN Doc. ST/LEG/SER.E/14, UN Sales No. E.95.V.II. The texts of reservations, declaration, and objections to the four human rights treaties are also available on the Internet, at *http://www.un.org/Depts/Treaty/* [April 1999].

7. On reservations to multilateral treaties, see Kaye Holloway, *Les réserves dans les traités multilatéraux* (Paris: LGDJ, 1958); Pierre-Henri Imbert, *Les réserves aux traités multilatéraux* (Paris: Pédone, 1979); Frank Horn, *Reservations and Interpretative Declarations to Multilateral Treaties* (Amsterdam: Elsevier Science Publishers, 1988); William A. Schabas, "Reservations to International Human Rights Treaties," *Canadian Yearbook of International Law* 32 (1995): 39. Rebecca Cook, "Reservations to the Convention on the Elimination of All Forms of Discrimination Against Women," *Virginia Journal of International Law* 30 (spring 1990): 643–716; Belinda Clark, "The Vienna Convention Reservations Regime and the Convention on Discrimination Against Women," *American Journal of International Law* 85 (April 1991): 281–321.

8. "Vienna Declaration and Programme of Action," UN Doc. A/CONF.157/24 (part 1), chap. 3 (1993), *Human Rights Law Journal* 14 (1993): 352–363.

9. *Loizidou v. Turkey* (preliminary objections), 310 Eur. Ct. H.R. (ser. A) (1995).

10. "Report of the International Law Commission on the Work of Its Forty-Seventh Session," UN GAOR, Fiftieth session, suppl. no. 10, at 241, UN Doc. A/50/10 (1995).

11. "Effective implementation of international instruments on human rights, including reporting obligations under international instruments on human rights," UN Doc. A/49/537 at 30. Also see UN Doc. A/47/628 (1992), 36, 60–65.

12. UN Doc. CCPR/C/21/Rev.1/Add.6, *Human Rights Law Journal* (1994): 464.

13. "Consideration of Reports Submitted by States Parties under Article 40 of the Covenant, Comments of the Human Rights Committee," UN Doc. CCPR/C/79/Add.50 (1995), 14.

14. "Observation by the United States of America on General Comment No. 24 (52)," UN Doc. A/40/40, *Human Rights Law Journal* 16 (1995): 422–424.

15. "Observations by the United Kingdom on General Comment No. 24," UN Doc. A/50/40, *Human Rights Law Journal* 16 (1995): 424–426; UN Doc. A/51/40.

16. *Belilos v. Switzerland*, 132 Eur. Ct. H.R. (ser. A) (1988).

17. According to Senate report, "the intent is to clarify that the Covenant will not create a private cause of action in U.S. courts." "United States: Senate Committee on Foreign Relations Report on the International Covenant on Civil and Political Rights," *U.S. Senate Executive Report*, 102–123 (102nd Congress, 2nd session), January 30, 1992, 19, reprinted in *International Legal Materials* (May 1992): 645. However, Louis Henkin suggests that such a declaration may run counter to the obligation assumed under Article 3 of the Covenant: Henkin, U.S. Ratification, 348 n.1. See also Carlos Manuel Vasquez, "The Four Doctrines of Self-Executing Treaties," *American Journal of International Law* 89 (October 1995): 695–723; Lori F. Damrosch, "The Role of the United States Senate Concerning 'Self-Executing' and 'Non-Self-Executing' Treaties," *Chicago-Kent Law Review* 67 (summer 1991): 515–532; Yuji Iwasawa, "The Doctrine of Self-Executing Treaties in the United States: A Critical Analysis," *Virginia Journal of International Law* 26 (spring 1986): 627–692.

18. See *Power Authority of New York v. Federal Power Commission*, 247 F. 2nd 538,

540 (App. D. C. 1957) (vacated on remand), holding that such a declaration is not binding, and is only hortatory; *United States v. Stuart*, 109 S. Ct. 1183 (1989).

19. *Reservations to the Convention on Genocide, Advisory Opinion*, 1951 ICJ 15. The Court's opinion was accepted by the General Assembly, G. A. Res. 598 (5).

20. See William A. Schabas, "Invalid Reservations to the International Covenant on Civil and Political Rights: Is the United States Still a Party?," *Brooklyn Journal of International Law* 21 (1995): 277–325.

21. UN Doc. CCPR/C/SR.1405 (12).

22. UN Doc. CCPR/C/SR.1401 (52). Also see Prado Vallejo, UN Doc. CCPR/C/SR.1402 (44).

23. UN Doc. CCPR/C/SR.1402 (34).

24. UN Doc. CCPR/C/SR.1402 (34).

25. UN Doc. CCPR/C/SR.1406 (11); UN Doc. CCPR/C/SR.1406 (39).

26. This approach, which appears to be rather uniquely German, was also taken in statements produced in response to U.S. reservations to the Covenant.

27. *Soering v. United Kingdom*, 161 Eur. Ct. H.R. (ser. A) (1989). See Richard Lillich, "The Soering Case," *American Journal of International Law* 128 (January 1991).

28. *Restrictions to the Death Penalty* (Arts. 42 and 44, American Convention on Human Rights), Advisory Opinion OC-3/83, 3 Inter-Am. Ct. H.R. (ser. A) (1983); *Belilos v. Switzerland, 132 Eur. Ct.*; *Loizidou v. Turkey* (preliminary objections), *310 Eur. Ct.*

29. See *Human Rights Law Journal* 16: 464 (6).

30. See *Human Rights Law Journal* 16: 464 (16).

31. See *Human Rights Law Journal* 16: 464 (18).

32. See *Human Rights Law Journal* 16: 464 (17).

33. UN Doc. A/C.6/50/SR.18 (51).

34. See *Human Rights Journal* 16: 464 (18).

35. See *Human Rights Journal* 16: 464 (18).

36. *International Covenant on Civil and Political Rights*, Article 40 (1).

37. *International Covenant on Civil and Political Rights*, Article 40 (4).

38. The United Kingdom observations refer to paragraph 20 of the General Comment, but the verb "determine" does not appear there. Presumably, the reference should be to paragraph 18.

39. See *Human Rights Journal* 16: 464 (6).

40. See *Human Rights Journal* 16: 464 (8). In the past, the Human Rights Committee has overlooked reservations to such customary provisions, which it now says are illegal. For example, in *C. L. D. v. France* (Case 228/1987), UN Doc. A/43/40, 257, it applied the French "declaration" (really, a reservation) to Article 27 of the *International Covenant on Civil and Political Rights*, which ensures the right of minorities to enjoy their own culture, to profess their own religion, or to use their own language.

41. See *Human Rights Journal* 16: 464 (18).

42. See also the comments of the legal advisor, Conrad Harper, to the Sixth Committee: UN Doc. A/C.6/50/SR.13 (1995), 52.

43. Ronald St. John Macdonald, "Reservations Under the European Convention on Human Rights," *Revue belge de droit international* 21 (1988): 428–450.

44. *Loizidou v. Turkey* (preliminary objections), *310 Eur. Ct.*

45. *Norwegian Loans Case (France v. Norway)*, 1957 ICJ 9: 43–66; *Interhandel Case (Switzerland v. United States)*, 1959 ICJ 6: 117.

46. UN Doc. A/C.6/50/SR.18 (62) (Pakistan); UN Doc. A/C.6/50/SR.23 (46) (Czech Republic); UN Doc. A/C.6/50/SR.23 (15) (Israel).

47. UN Doc. A/C.6/50/SR.18 (62).

48. UN Doc. A/C.6/50/SR.13 (48).

49. UN Doc. A/C.6/50/SR.23 (71).

50. See the comments of Conrad Harper before the Sixth Committee: "The United States could not accept the Human Rights Committee's views in its General Comment No. 24 (52), since it did not believe that the classic rules on reservations were inadequate for human rights treaties. On the contrary, they had helped to advance the fundamental objective of broad participation by states. The critical role of states — as opposed to the Human Rights Committee — in determining matters related to such treaties should be respected on both legal and practical grounds." UN Doc. A/C.6/50/SR.13 (51); also see para. 53.

51. Manfred Nowak, CCPR *Commentary* (Kehl: Engel, 1993), xxvii–xxviii.

52. Henkin, *U.S. Ratification*, 349.

PART 2

Looking Outward on U.S. Foreign Policy

SECTION 1
Public Opinion and Private Action

7

Public Opinion on Human Rights in American Foreign Policy

•

OLE HOLSTI

The Vietnam War had a significant impact on American thinking about foreign policy, the processes by which it should be formulated, and the values
that should be reflected in the country's external relations. Among the many
debates stimulated by that conflict were two that are central to this chapter.
First, the conflict in Southeast Asia revived interest in an issue — the role of
public opinion in foreign policy making — that had become rather passé for
most foreign policy analysts. As a result of the Vietnam conflict, even the
distinguished journalist Walter Lippmann, author of several books on the
thesis that the public is inherently incapable of playing the role demanded by
classical democratic theory, questioned his prescription that only strong executive leadership, insulated from the vagaries of public opinion, could ensure the survival of democracies in a dangerous world.[1] The Vietnam War
also contributed to a heightened interest in the role that human rights values
should play in America's relations with both allies and adversaries. A combination of the civil rights movement at home, revelations of gross human
rights abuses by some American allies — including the South Vietnamese
regime on whose behalf the United States was expending vast treasure and
lives — and reactions to the stark *realpolitik* foreign policies of the Nixon-
Kissinger period combined to kindle interest in human rights foreign policy
goals that had rarely played more than a secondary role during the height of
the Cold War.[2]

The links between controversies about the appropriate roles of public
opinion and human rights are not, however, merely a coincidental result of
having been stimulated by the same event. These issues were also central
points of contention in the heated post-Vietnam debates, both in academic
and policymaking circles, between proponents of two important and enduring perspectives on international affairs — realism and liberalism.

I will begin with a brief review of the realist and liberal positions on public opinion and foreign policy, on human rights and foreign policy, and on

the linkages between the two topics. These two schools of thought lend themselves to some competing hypotheses, discussed in the next section, about public opinion on human rights. The third section describes the data and analyzes some evidence relating to these hypotheses. The conclusion addresses some policy implications of the findings.

Liberals versus Realists on Public Opinion and Foreign Policy

At first glance it might appear that this discussion really addresses two quite distinct issues: The role of public opinion in foreign policy making and human rights as a foreign policy goal. In fact, they are linked in several ways. Both issues are at the core of the venerable debates between advocates of realism and liberalism, the two dominant theories on the conduct of foreign affairs. These two schools of thought generally hold sharply divergent views on the appropriate role of public opinion and the weight that should be accorded to human rights in relations with other countries.

The first issue centers on the role of public opinion and its ability to make a useful contribution to the quality of foreign policy and diplomacy. A long liberal tradition, dating back to Immanuel Kant and Jeremy Bentham and continuing through Woodrow Wilson, asserts that democracies are more peaceful at least in part because the public can play a constructive role in constraining policy makers. Elihu Root, a distinguished Republican foreign policy leader, effectively summarized the case for democratizing foreign policy in the initial issue of *Foreign Affairs*: "When foreign affairs were ruled by autocracies or oligarchies the danger of war was in sinister purpose. When foreign affairs are ruled by democracies the danger of war will be in mistaken beliefs. The world will be the gainer by the change, for, while there is no human way to prevent a king from having a bad heart, there is a human way to prevent a people from having an erroneous opinion."[3]

In contrast, Alexis de Tocqueville, Walter Lippmann, E. H. Carr, Hans J. Morgenthau, George F. Kennan, and other realists are intensely skeptical of the public because the effective conduct of diplomacy requires long-term strategic visions of the national interest, combined with the ability to pursue those interests with speed, secrecy, and flexibility. These requirements would often be jeopardized were the public, whose preferences are allegedly driven by emotions and short-term considerations, to have a significant role in foreign affairs. Lippmann's indictment of the public would gain the support of many realists: "The unhappy truth is that the prevailing public opinion has been destructively wrong at the critical junctures. . . . Mass opinion has acquired mounting power in this country. It has shown itself to be a dangerous master of decision when the stakes are life and death."[4] Fears expressed by Lippmann and other realists notwithstanding, by the late 1960s or early 1970s a near consensus had developed on three points: public opinion is *volatile*, *lacks in any coherent structure*, and is largely *irrelevant* in the conduct of foreign affairs. Were these three propositions generally valid, it would scarcely be of more than modest academic interest to devote much effort to analyzing public attitudes toward human rights. However, during the past quarter century some powerful challenges have been mounted against all three of them. Although the debate about the nature and impact of public opinion is far from over, we now have a growing body of evidence that public attitudes are quite stable, have at least a moderate degree of structure, and are often a significant factor in foreign policy decisions.[5]

Realists and Liberals on Human Rights

Realists and liberals also disagree about the extent to which human rights and humanitarian concerns abroad are proper objectives of foreign policy. The realist thesis is grounded in three propositions. First, an effective foreign policy requires that national interests be pursued with a sound understanding of the balance between risks and rewards, on the one hand, and relevant resources on the other. It is necessary and sufficient that such policies be focused on the demanding task of influencing the international behavior of other states, without taking on the added and extraneous burden of judging and seeking to reform their domestic institutions and practices as well.

The doctrines of state sovereignty and noninterference in the internal affairs of other countries constitute the second pillar in the realist argument against a human rights priority in foreign affairs. In an imperfect world, these norms are essential to avoid constant conflict. Without them, the international system would more closely approximate a state of perpetual war, because no injustice — real or perceived — would lie beyond the reach of external powers that might be tempted to redress them. Although realists are generally not among the staunchest defenders of international institutions, they frequently remind their liberal critics that Article 2(7) of the UN Charter explicitly endorses the doctrine of noninterference: "Nothing contained in the present Charter shall authorize the United Nations to intervene in matters which are essentially within the domestic jurisdiction of any state or shall require Members to submit such matters to settlement under the present Charter."

Realists often cite the absence of internationally accepted standards of human rights as a third important reason for skepticism. Even if there were such a consensus, because the multiplicity of national interests makes it impossible to be consistent in the pursuit of human rights goals, to do so selectively is merely to invite charges of hypocrisy.[6]

Although the conventional realist position, described above, opposes giving weight to human rights considerations in foreign affairs, some realists argue that although "morality should not drive foreign policy," there is no tradeoff to be faced, because the diligent pursuit of American security interests automatically promotes global human rights: "Typically, of course, human rights and morality are advanced around the globe as a happy byproduct of specific American policies."[7]

Liberals bring forth a number of responses to the realist brief against a human rights priority in foreign affairs. They can muster evidence about the emergence of at least some international consensus on the definition of human rights. The 1926 international agreement to abolish slavery constitutes a pre–World War II example. The UN Declaration on Human Rights and additional international and regional treaties and institutions created in the wake of the Nazi Holocaust constitute further indications of widening agreement that the doctrines of sovereignty and noninterference in internal affairs are not absolute barriers against international concern with egregious violations of basic human rights.[8] Although events in Cambodia, Somalia, Burundi, Rwanda, Bosnia, Chechnya, Kosovo, and elsewhere provide ample evidence that progress on protecting human rights is at best slow and uneven, there is a discernible international trend in the direction of more, rather than less, concern for such rights. Thus, according to liberals, it is in its national interest for the United States to be a leader rather than a laggard in the undertaking.[9]

The Links between Public Opinion and Human Rights

The role of public opinion in the policy process and the priority to be assigned human rights concerns in foreign policy are intimately linked in the liberal-realist debate. The fear that the public will give undue weight to human rights and humanitarian goals — what Michael Mandelbaum has derisively called "foreign policy as social work" — is not the least reason for realist skepticism about public opinion.[10] Indeed, one of the worst realist nightmares is that the public, aroused by vivid television presentations about gross human rights violations in some country of no vital national interest, will press Washington to undertake a costly and ill-fated intervention at the risk of major losses while achieving little more than salving the American national conscience. Moreover, should the undertaking result in even modest casualties, the public may then clamor for immediate withdrawal, further damaging America's credibility and reputation for mature international leadership.[11]

The liberal rebuttal to the realist case begins with the proposition that promoting human rights constitutes the "right thing" and that doing so is consistent with the most basic American values, including those articulated in the Declaration of Independence and the Bill of Rights. Liberals further assert that their concerns for public opinion and human rights are not merely a reflection of dedication to fundamental democratic values but also that they are grounded in a sober appreciation of two important political realities. First, long-term domestic support, a prerequisite for success in any significant international undertaking, can only be sustained when the public is persuaded that the ends and means of foreign policy are consistent with basic American values — including human rights. As Jimmy Carter put it in his May 1977 speech at Notre Dame: "I believe that we can have a foreign policy that is democratic, that is based on fundamental values, and that uses power and influence for humane purposes. We can also have a foreign policy that the American people both support and understand."[12] Moreover, although the public may not be sufficiently informed or sophisticated to understand all the nuances of international affairs, it correctly believes that regimes which consistently mistreat their own citizens cannot be trusted to behave responsibly toward other countries, much less to carry out their international agreements.

Some survey data will be analyzed in the next section to assess three pairs of competing hypotheses about public and elite opinions on the appropriate role of human rights considerations in the conduct of American foreign relations. The hypotheses focus initially on the impact of the end of the Cold War, secondly on differences in the attitudes of leaders as compared to those of the general public, and, finally, on the extent to which attitudes toward human rights issues are embedded within broader political ideologies.

The End of the Cold War

The quarter century for which survey data on human rights are available has been a period of almost unprecedented international change. It spans the waxing and waning of détente during the Nixon, Ford, and Carter years; the inception of Cold War II during the first Reagan administration; the onset of another period of détente during the late 1980s; the end of the Cold War and disintegration of the USSR; and, during the early years of the post–Cold War era, the outbreak of numerous intrastate conflicts that have often been marked by massive violations of human rights. Although the euphoria that attended the end of the Cold War — for example, the "end of history" thesis — has been replaced by a recognition that the growth of democratic values and institutions is neither inevitable nor irreversible, there are nevertheless reasons for thinking that these developments have not been irrelevant to public thinking about human rights. More specifically, it is possible to develop plausible arguments in support of diametrically opposite hypotheses about how the end of the Cold War has affected American attitudes on human rights. According to one line of reasoning:

1a. *The end of the Cold war has triggered a decline of interest in the state of human rights abroad as a vital concern for American foreign policy.*

This hypothesis is grounded in the view that the end of the Cold War has generally eroded American interest in international affairs while also providing sustenance for the belief that the United States has neither compelling interests nor sufficient resources to permit it to assume either the role of policeman or nanny of the world.[13] For example, Tonelson has argued that in the absence of a powerful ideological Cold War rival, "the state of human rights around the world does not have, and never has had, any demonstrable effect on U.S. national security."[14] Many holding this view also assert that a long list of domestic problems, many of which were neglected during four decades of Cold War, provide an ample agenda for America's attention, energies, and resources. More specifically, the argument is that although the end of the Cold War has not, unfortunately, abated massive violations of human rights, after a half century of very active international leadership during the period between Pearl Harbor and the collapse of the Soviet Union, Americans are experiencing an acute case of "compassion fatigue."

The alternative hypothesis takes a very different view of post–Cold War attitudes on human rights.

1b. The end of the Cold War has increased American willingness to apply human rights criteria in the conduct of U.S. foreign relations.

According to this position, the end of the Cold War has freed the public from any compelling need to view human rights issues through the lenses of its rivalry with the Soviet Union. Americans are no longer constrained by the argument, for example, that it is expedient to turn a blind eye toward human rights violations by friends and allies — especially if the victims of such abuse can be depicted as "communists" or "communist sympathizers" — because the imperatives of the global competition with the Soviet Union must be given a priority that overrides undue fussiness about the domestic policies of those on the free world side of a bipolar world.[15] Or, as John F. Kennedy reportedly said of Dominican dictator and human rights abuser par excellence Raphael Trujillo, "Sure, he's a bastard, but at least he's our bastard." Even some of those who earlier may have been persuaded by Jeane Kirkpatrick's apologies for support of some less-than-democratic Cold War allies, based on a distinction between authoritarian and totalitarian regimes, may now be more likely to question whether her thesis provides a compelling rationale for overlooking systematic human rights violations.[16] Finally, in contrast to the earlier period, the pursuit of human rights goals in the contemporary world runs less risk of triggering a major power crisis — a confrontation with China is perhaps an exception — than would have been the case during the Cold War.

Leaders and the General Public

A second pair of competing hypotheses centers on differences between leaders and the general public on the appropriate weight to be accorded to human rights in the formulation of American foreign policy. The first hypothesis is closely linked to a realist perspective.

2a. Compared to leaders, the general public is likely to assign a higher priority to human rights goals in the conduct of American foreign affairs.

Although there are some important distinctions among the various realist approaches to international affairs, adherents to this school of thought share a highly skeptical view about whether the public can make a constructive contribution to foreign policy.[17] Because the average citizen is less sophisticated than leaders in his factual and conceptual understanding of international affairs, he is less capable of appreciating the distinction between core and peripheral national interests. Thus, members of the general public are more likely to indulge in emotional rather than reasoned and hardheaded appraisals of what is generally desirable and feasible in the international arena, as well as in any specific situation. Especially in an era when CNN can bring into every home graphic evidence of such human rights violations as deliberate starvation of populations, ethnic cleansing, extrajudicial punishment of dissidents, and other abuses, members of the general public are more prone to fall prey to the belief that for each such outrage there is an effective American remedy. In contrast, leaders are more likely to appreciate that in the real world, as distinct from some hypothetical ideal one, assigning a high foreign policy priority to human rights abroad is neither feasible nor desirable in most cases.

In contrast, the alternative hypothesis posits a quite different relationship in the human rights attitudes of leaders and the general public.

2b. Leaders are more likely than members of the general public to ascribe importance to promoting and defending human rights abroad.

One of the most widely supported generalizations about American public opinion is that, compared to the general public, leaders are consistently more internationalist in their general orientations to foreign policy as well as on a broad range of more specific issues.[18] Hypothesis 2b assumes that a greater propensity to support active involvement abroad will include a greater concern for human rights. Further, it is based on the reasoning that leaders have a better appreciation that such vital long-range national interests as a stable and sustainable world order are linked to the state of human rights and the growth of democracy abroad. Moreover, governments that respect human rights "are likely to be more stable and reliable strategic allies."[19] In contrast, members of the general public are more inclined to accord primacy to short-term goals and domestic problems, on the one hand, and, on the other, to experience "compassion fatigue" about the plight of human rights victims abroad.

Human Rights Views: Pragmatism or Ideology?

The third pair of hypotheses yields divergent expectations about the extent to which views about human rights in foreign policy are narrowly circumscribed or, alternatively, are embedded within a broader political ideology. The first hypothesis adopts the former view:

3a. *Positions of support for or opposition to a human rights focus in American foreign policy are specifically and narrowly grounded in pragmatic assessments of the feasibility and desirability of permitting national interests—and the strategies used to pursue them—to be defined and constrained by the human rights policies, practices, and preferences of other nations.*

According to this hypothesis, skeptics agree with the classical realist thesis that a priority on human rights is neither desirable, because it may run counter to more compelling national interests as well as the principles of sovereignty and noninterference in the internal affairs of other states, nor feasible, because it is rarely possible to extend effective American protection to victims of human rights violations abroad. According to this hypothesis, such views are quite independent of other policy preferences, for example, on domestic human rights issues. A concern for human rights must be situational, and opponents argue that foreign affairs generally constitute the wrong situation, especially because the fiat of American values and preferences does not extend beyond the country's frontiers. Moreover, if human rights criteria are to be invoked in any specific circumstances, they should reflect a sober appreciation of power considerations; it is more prudent to invoke them, for example, against Grenada or Panama than against China. Consequently, positions on human rights in foreign affairs are not correlated with general preferences on a broader political agenda, including domestic issues bearing on human rights. According to this hypothesis, a pragmatic skepticism about a human rights emphasis in foreign policy should also be independent of partisanship and ideology.

The competing hypothesis stipulates that attitudes in support or opposition to a human rights focus in American foreign policy are part of a broader political ideology.

3b. *Attitudes toward the priority that should be accorded to human rights in the conduct of foreign affairs are likely to be embedded within a broader cluster of policy preferences—an ideology—that includes attitudes on domestic human rights issues.*

The reasoning behind this hypothesis is that supporters of a strong human rights focus are likely to believe that concern for such values should be circumscribed by neither geography nor political boundaries; concern for human rights is a core or terminal value rather than an instrumental one. Or, to paraphrase Lincoln, these supporters might argue that the world cannot — and should not — endure a situation in which half the people enjoy human rights that are systematically denied to the other half.[20] Thus, according to this hypothesis, there should be a strong correlation between attitudes toward human rights issues at home and abroad. Moreover, these attitudes are likely to be embedded in wider ideological differences and, to the extent that party and ideology are correlated, in partisan ones as well.

Data

Although many efforts to put human rights on the international agenda arose from the horrifying experiences of World War II, especially but not limited to the Nazi Holocaust, until the early 1970s human rights concerns played a limited role in the conduct of American foreign relations. As noted earlier, the conjunction of the domestic civil rights movement, the costly but failed effort to preserve the independence of South Vietnam, and a backlash against the *realpolitik* foreign policy strategies of the Nixon-Kissinger period stimulated various congressional actions in 1973 aimed at injecting a human rights component into American foreign policy.

It is therefore not surprising that there are relatively few public opinion survey questions about human rights prior to the 1970s. Scarcer still are standard questions using identical wording that have been repeated with sufficient frequency to offer the possibility of reliable trend analyses. The situation described by Geyer and Shapiro — "Strikingly few questions about human rights have been repeated verbatim in national surveys, making it extremely difficult to track opinion trends" — has not changed materially during the past decade.[21] Even for the period since 1973 we have nothing that comes close to approximating the almost monthly surveys assessing presidential approval and performance ratings. There are, however, two continuing survey projects, both initiated during the mid-1970s and continuing into the 1990s, that provide some evidence about American attitudes toward human rights.

In 1974 the Chicago Council on Foreign Relations (CCFR) undertook a major survey project on attitudes toward foreign affairs. Subsequent replications of that study have been conducted at four-year intervals.[22] Those taking part in the six CCFR studies include both the general public and much smaller samples of leaders. The Foreign Policy Leadership Project (FPLP) surveys of opinion leaders, initiated in 1976, have also included follow-up studies at four-year intervals (1980, 1984, 1988, 1992, 1996). The analysis to be undertaken here is based on a broad, rather than restrictive, view of human rights. It thus goes beyond a narrow definition wherein human rights are limited to such civil and political "freedom of" rights as conscience, speech, assembly, and competitive elections, and "freedom from" rights against arbitrary arrest, excessive punishment, and the like. Evidence will also be presented about two economic aspects of human rights as well as protection of the global environment. Thus, in terms of the classification scheme for human rights proposed by Scott Davidson, the following analysis encompasses two core or first generation civil and political human rights, two second generation or economic-social-cultural human rights (hunger, the standard of living in less developed countries), and one third generation human right (protecting the global environment).[23]

The first pair of hypotheses introduced above provides divergent assessments about how the end of the Cold War may have affected attitudes toward human rights, whereas the second pair focuses on possible differences between the attitudes of leaders and those of the general public. As noted earlier, few surveys have repeated identical questions about human rights, making it difficult to undertake extensive trend analyses with confidence. The two exceptions are the CCFR and FPLP surveys, both of which have included some relevant questions asking respondents to indicate how much importance should be attached to a series of possible foreign policy goals. Several of these items were also included in a 1993 Times-Mirror survey of both leaders and the general public.

Beginning in 1978, those taking part in the CCFR and FPLP surveys were asked to rate "promoting and defending human rights in other countries" as a foreign policy goal, with response options ranging from "very important" to "not important at all." The results for both leaders and the general public, summarized in table 7.1, yield several conclusions. First, with one exception, in none of the surveys did human rights abroad emerge as a top priority goal for either leaders or the general public. The high point occurred in 1990, just a year after the Berlin Wall had come down, when 58 percent of the general public rated human rights abroad as a "very important" goal, but even then it ranked only sixth, placing it behind such economic and security goals as protecting the jobs of American workers, protecting the interests of American business abroad, securing adequate supplies of energy, defending our allies' security, and preventing the spread of nuclear weapons. Second, even though human rights abroad never ranked among the top priorities during the 1970s and 1980s, the period since the end of the Cold War has nevertheless witnessed an erosion of enthusiasm for this foreign policy goal among both leaders and the general public. The evidence in table 7.1 thus appears to provide greater support for hypothesis 1a than for hypothesis 1b.[24] Indeed, the more salient pattern is that responses of the two groups have generally moved in tandem. Finally, differences between leaders and the general public are rather muted, with the single exception of the responses to the 1990 CCFR survey.[25] Consequently, the evidence does not provide a clear verdict in favor of either hypothesis 2a or 2b.

A second human rights–related question asked respondents to rate the importance of "helping to bring a democratic form of government to other nations." The correlation between democracy and respect for human rights is far from perfect. A government may be voted into office in "fair" elections on a platform of suppressing some minority; for a century after the American Civil War, for example, countless Southern Democrats won office by promising to maintain segregation and otherwise preventing black Americans from enjoying the status of first-class citizens. Nevertheless, the human rights records of democracies are, on balance, far better than those of most authoritarian regimes. Thus, one reason respondents might attach importance to promoting democracy abroad is precisely because of a belief that doing so might also improve the state of human rights.

Although Presidents Bush and Clinton have assigned a high priority to promoting democracy abroad, they have not been able to kindle widespread public support for that undertaking.[26] Indeed, more often than not it has been the foreign goal that was assigned the fewest "very important" ratings by both leaders and the general public (table 7.2).[27] Although some observers have criticized American diplomacy for misguided zeal in attempting to propagate the country's values and institutions abroad, there is little evidence of public enthusiasm for such undertakings in the post-Vietnam era. Nor do the data in table 7.2 indicate that the end of the Cold War and the disintegration of the Soviet Union have kindled — or rekindled, as the case may be — any burning desires to promote the spread of democracy, even though the risks of igniting a superpower confrontation with Moscow by doing so have virtually vanished. Starting from a very low baseline, the 1980s witnessed a modest increase in the number of leaders who assigned a "very important" rating to the goal of promoting democracy abroad, but the most recent surveys reveal that by the mid-1990s that support had waned. In contrast, the opinions of the general public have remained stable during the past two decades. Thus, the evidence would not appear to provide compelling support for either hypothesis 1a or 1b.

Finally, compared to leaders, the general public has been somewhat more inclined to support the promotion of democracy abroad, but the differences between the two groups, most pronounced during the 1970s, have diminished. In conclusion, the figures in the right-hand column of table 7.2 offer further evidence exonerating the public against the charge that its opinions on foreign affairs are afflicted by a high degree of volatility.

Although the United States has been involved in a broad range of economic assistance programs since the end of World War II, American officials have usually resisted any efforts to include economic-social "needs" as an integral part of human "rights," preferring to confine the latter term to civil-political rights. But as noted earlier, this analysis adopts a broader view of human rights, wherein appraisals of "helping to improve the standard of living in less developed countries" as a foreign policy goal are germane. Assessments of that goal by leaders and the general public are summarized in table 7.3. The data reveal a rather consistent erosion of support for attempting to improve the standard of living in poor countries. The evidence from both the CCFR and FPLP surveys shows that among leaders support for this goal peaked well before the end of the Cold War and has declined steadily since the mid-1980s, whereas assessments among the general public remained quite stable through 1990. The sharp decline among both groups in 1994, the first CCFR survey following the disintegration of the Soviet Union, provides support for hypothesis 1a and runs counter to hypothesis 1b.

The data in table 7.3 also indicate that, compared to the general public, leaders have consistently accorded more "very important" ratings to the goal of improving living standards in the LDCs, thus providing some support for hypothesis 2b. But those differences, which were quite pronounced through the mid-1980s, have diminished more recently as respondents in both groups have expressed reduced interest in this goal. These results are consistent with other survey data that have shown a steady decline in public support for international economic assistance programs. But the public has spoken with a clear voice on one aspect of foreign aid — by very strong majorities it approves linking international assistance to the recipient's performance on human rights, and it is critical of aid to countries with poor human rights records.[28]

A second question that bears on the economic aspects of human rights asked respondents to rate the importance of "combatting world hunger" as a foreign policy goal. Their appraisals, summarized in table 7.4, reveal considerably greater support for coping with hunger than for the more general goal of raising the standard of living in the Third World. Two possible reasons come to mind. First, hunger represents a deprivation of the most basic human need. A second possible reason is that the means for dealing with hunger, at least in the short run, are more obvious and readily available, especially for a country such as the United States that consistently produces massive agricultural surpluses. In contrast, raising the standard of living in poor countries may appear to be an open-ended goal without a clearly defined end for which there are fewer ready and uncontroversial solutions.

There has been considerable erosion in the importance ascribed to coping with hunger as a foreign policy goal among leaders taking part in both the CCFR and FPLP surveys; the evidence in table 7.4 thus provides support for hypothesis 1a concerning the impact of the end of the Cold War. The views of the general public, in contrast, have remained quite steady through the two decades covered by the CCFR surveys, as each study found that clear majorities rated combatting world hunger as a "very important" foreign policy goal. However, the evidence does not yield a clear-cut verdict with respect to hypotheses 2a and 2b. With the single exception of the 1994 CCFR survey, the differences between leaders and the general public have not been of a striking magnitude. Through the early 1980s, leaders were somewhat more inclined to rate the goal of combatting hunger as "very important," but since then the direction of the gap between the two groups has been reversed.

Advocates of third generation human rights include a safe environment. Evidence on this foreign policy goal—"protecting the global environment"—is even sketchier than for the other four issues, because the question did not appear in the CCFR surveys until 1990. We thus lack a Cold War era baseline against which to assess the more recent responses of the general public. There might be no special reason to suspect that the end of the Cold War would have a direct impact on attitudes toward environmental protection, but the collapse of communist governments in Eastern Europe and the disintegration of the USSR did result in much fuller information about massive environmental depredations in many of those countries. The limited evidence summarized in table 7.5 provides little basis on which to assess the relative merits of the competing hypotheses on the impact of the end of the Cold War. Attitudes among the general public have remained quite stable, with more than half the respondents consistently rating environmental protection as "very important." In contrast, leaders' views have been more variable, with increasing interest among those taking part in the FPLP surveys through 1992, followed by a sharp drop in 1996, as well as declining "very important" ratings among the leaders surveyed by the CCFR. These results do not give rise to any clear verdict about the validity of hypotheses 2a or 2b.

The third pair of hypotheses presented above posited quite different answers to the question of whether attitudes toward incorporating human rights concerns into foreign relations are narrowly circumscribed or, alternatively, whether such views are embedded within broader political ideologies. Table 7.6 summarizes the relationship between leadership attitudes toward "promoting and defending human rights abroad" and the other four human rights goals questions. For leaders taking part in the FPLP surveys the correlations are consistently very high, averaging well over .60. The comparable CCFR survey figures for leaders and the general public are somewhat lower, averaging .31 and .35, respectively. These correlations indicate consistently strong links between attitudes toward various aspects of human rights abroad. Weak or negative, correlations would have provided strong evidence against the hypothesis (3b) that attitudes toward human rights are part of a broader belief system, but by themselves they are not sufficient to sustain that hypothesis.

To assess the relative merits of hypotheses 3a and 3b, the analysis will proceed in three stages. The first will examine the relationship between appraisals of the human rights "goal" question and respondents' political party and ideology, as well as two other attributes of opinion leaders — foreign policy orientations and domestic policy orientations. A second step will examine the relationship between these respondent attributes and assessments of American foreign policy issues and decisions with significant human rights implications. The final step will analyze the correlation between attributes of leaders and their answers to questions about several domestic human rights issues. Assessments by both leaders and the general public of "promoting and defending human rights in other countries" are drawn from the Chicago Council and Times-Mirror surveys; the FPLP surveys provide additional evidence about the human rights views of opinion leaders.

Whereas table 7.1 provided aggregate summaries of responses to the human rights goal question in several studies, table 7.7 reports assessments of that goal according to the party affiliation and ideological self-description by both leaders and members of the general public who took part in the CCFR and Times-Mirror surveys. Table 7.8 classifies opinion leaders who responded to the FPLP surveys according to four attributes: political party, ideology, foreign policy orientation, and domestic policy orientation.

The results summarized in table 7.7 yield several conclusions. First, Democrats have generally accorded higher importance to the goal of defending and promoting human rights abroad, although partisan differences among the general public were quite small during the peak years of support for human rights — 1986 and 1990. In the latter survey, the partisan gap was only 4 percent, as a majority of Republicans, Democrats, and independents assigned the highest rating to that goal. Second, compared to the general public, partisan gaps have consistently been much wider among leaders. Differences between Republicans and Democrats reached a peak of 37 percent in 1994, when only 9 percent of the GOP leaders rated human rights abroad as a "very important" foreign policy goal. Further evidence of partisan differences among leaders emerges in table 7.8. Compared to Republicans, more Democrats gave the goal of human rights abroad the top rating in each of the five FPLP surveys. Although promoting human rights abroad has not ranked near the top as a foreign policy goal among opinion leaders, the gap between Democrats and Republicans has been quite high, ranging between 21 and 38 percent. The data in tables 7.7 and 7.8 are consistent with ample evidence that the political views of leaders are characterized by greater coherence and consistency than are those of the general public.

When respondents are classified according to ideology, the range of opinions about human rights as a foreign policy goal has generally been even wider than partisan differences, and there is little evidence that the gaps have been narrowing with the end of the Cold War. Both the CCFR and Times-Mirror surveys found that liberals have consistently given a higher priority to human rights goals (see table 7.7). As was true of partisan gaps, the ideological differences are more pronounced among leaders than among the general public. Evidence of wide gaps in assessments of the human rights goal among leaders also emerges from the FPLP surveys (see table 7.8). In each of these surveys support for human rights increases steadily as one moves from the conservative to the liberal end of the scale. Whereas the assessments by self-described conservative leaders have remained rather stable during the 1980–92 period, support for human rights as a foreign policy goal has increased among moderates and liberals. By 1996, however, the importance attributed to human rights declined across the entire ideological spectrum, among liberals as well as conservatives.

The "foreign policy orientation" categories are constructed from responses to seven questions that deal with various aspects of "militant internationalism" (MI) and seven others that focus on "cooperative internationalism" (CI). Respondents who support MI but oppose CI are *hard-liners*; the other three groups are *isolationists* (oppose both MI and CI), *internationalists* (support both MI and CI), and *accommodationists* (oppose MI, support CI).[29] Table 7.8 reveals sharp differences among opinion leaders in the four groups in their appraisals of human rights as a foreign policy goal. Hard-liners and isolationists have consistently been the least inclined to accord importance to human rights, although probably for different reasons; whereas the former generally take a *realpolitik* stance that places little premium on human rights, the latter are wary of goals that may imply widespread American commitments abroad. In contrast, respondents in the two groups that support cooperative internationalism — the internationalists and accommodationists — have assigned greater importance to human rights as a foreign policy goal. The gaps between the hard-liners and accommodationists are especially wide, ranging between 25 and 42 percent. These results parallel David Forsythe's finding that in congressional voting, "How one votes on a general series of foreign and military issues is thus an excellent predictor of how one will vote on more specific human rights issues."[30]

In the final part of table 7.8 respondents are classified into four domestic policy orientation groups according to their answers to six questions on economic issues and to six others on social-value issues. These questions were first included in the 1984 survey, and, thus, there are no data under the 1980 column of table 7.8. According to this classification scheme, *conservatives* are leaders who express conservative policy preferences on both economic and social-value questions; the other three groups are *libertarians* (economic conservatives, social-value liberals), *populists* (economic liberals, social-value conservatives), and *liberals* (liberals on both sets of issues).[31] The evidence reveals strong differences on human rights among respondents in the four groups. Not surprisingly, the widest gaps are between the conservatives and liberals, with the libertarians and populists in the middle.[32] Support for human rights declined among all groups in 1996.

To this point the analysis has focused on a set of questions asking respondents to assess foreign policy goals. Although these questions have the virtue of having been asked over a span of more than two decades with precisely the same wording, they have the disadvantage of being rather abstract and removed from the specific context of actual decisions and policies. Stated differently, the "goals" questions may provide evidence about what respondents believe to be *desirable*, but they tell us little about what they regard as *feasible* in given circumstances, or about how they may assess *trade-offs* between goals. Two of the most difficult and controversial issues touching on the trade-offs between human rights and other foreign policy goals have involved the former Soviet Union and China: To what extent should the United States press for better treatment of Jews and other minorities in the USSR if doing so might endanger negotiations on arms control and other strategic issues? Should the United States insist on improvement of China's human rights record as a condition for better relations, including normalized trade, with Beijing?[33]

The next step in assessing hypotheses 3a and 3b is an effort to overcome the limits of the goals questions by analyzing assessments of actual U.S. foreign policy decisions and actions on issues that have a significant human rights element. Table 7.9 summarizes responses by Republicans, Democrats, and independents among the general public to several human rights questions posed in the Chicago Council surveys; comparable results for the CCFR leadership samples are presented in table 7.10. Several points emerge from these data. First, compared to the general public, leaders generally expressed more support for pro-human rights positions. This was most notably the case on questions dealing with South Africa and, to a lesser extent, on Soviet treatment of its minorities. In contrast, leaders and the general public had quite similar views on dealing with friendly tyrants; both agreed that it is "morally wrong" to back such regimes, but they also accepted the proposition that it may be necessary to do so if they are "friendly toward us and opposed to the Communists." Second, some partisan gaps existed among the general public, but they were generally much smaller than those in the CCFR leadership sample, wherein Democrats were consistently stronger supporters of human rights positions.

Further evidence on the impact of partisanship emerges from responses by opinion leaders taking part in the FPLP surveys to a series of foreign policy decisions with human rights dimensions. Specifically, these include three decisions concerning the application of economic sanctions against South Africa (the Reagan administration's decision not to invoke them, congressional action imposing sanctions on Pretoria by overriding a Reagan veto, and the lifting of sanctions by the Bush administration after steps by South Africa to abandon apartheid); the imposition of economic sanctions on Poland following the institution of martial law by the Polish government as a response to the Solidarity reform movement; the decision to return refugees to Haiti; the level of Iraqi casualties in the Persian Gulf War; the relative weights to be assigned to stability and self-determination in post–Cold War policies for dealing with civil wars; the grant of most favored nation (MFN) status to China in the wake of its violent crackdown on protesters in 1989; and the general proposition that, "The United States should avoid using economic sanctions to promote and defend human rights."

Responses by Republicans, Democrats, and independents to these issues, all but two of which were taken by the administrations of Republican Presidents Reagan and Bush, are presented in table 7.11. The imposition of economic sanctions on Poland was supported by moderate majorities among members of both major parties as well independents, with a rather modest 10 percent gap between the more enthusiastic Republicans (64 percent) and Democrats (54 percent), and by 1996 partisan differences on China's trade status had all but disappeared. In contrast, wide partisan gaps characterized responses to the remaining issues, with Democrats taking the stronger pro–human rights position on all of them. Five of the issues found a majority of Republicans on one side and a majority of Democrats on the other. The gap between members of the two political parties ranges between 13 percent and 44 percent, and the responses of the independents are in all cases approximately midway between those of the Republicans and Democrats. Because most of these decisions and actions were undertaken by Republican administrations, the evidence does not enable us to answer one key question: Do these results merely reflect partisan support or opposition to administration policies, or are they expressions of more fundamental beliefs about the appropriateness of applying human rights criteria to foreign affairs?[34] Responses to the issue of China's trade status illustrate the point. In 1992, Republicans were almost evenly divided on President Bush's decision to grant MFN status to the Beijing regime, whereas Democrats were strongly opposed. Four years later, after President Clinton had in essence adopted his predecessor's policy on the issue, in spite of a campaign pledge to the contrary, differences between Democratic and Republican opinion leaders were insignificant.

When members of the general public and leaders taking part in the CCFR surveys are classified according to ideological self-identification, their responses to these questions reveal quite substantial differences between liberals and conservatives except on the proposition that "The U.S. should put pressure on countries which systematically violate basic human rights." The differences are generally wider than those between Republicans and Democrats, as summarized in tables 7.9 and 7.10. Moreover, as was true in the analysis of partisanship, the gaps between conservative and liberal leaders are much wider than the comparable differences among the general public; those among leaders exceed 20 percent in every case except one and are greater than 35 percent on questions relating to support of anti-communist friendly tyrants (1982) and opposition to apartheid (1974, 1978).

Further evidence of ideological differences among leaders emerges from the FPLP surveys. Table 7.12 presents assessments of the ten foreign policy issues with human rights implications by respondents when they are classified according to their self-placements on a standard "very conservative-to-very liberal" ideology scale. Liberals have expressed the strongest pro–human rights views on the preponderance of issues, and gaps between the most liberal and most conservative opinion leaders are typically huge, ranging from 25 percent to 73 percent on the question whether "too many Iraqis were killed in the Persian Gulf War." There is, moreover, a steady increase or decline in support for the human rights positions as one moves from one end of the ideology scale to the other. As was the case in the analysis of partisanship on these issues (table 7.11), however, questions about economic sanctions against Poland and China are noteworthy exceptions to this pattern. The imposition of sanctions on Poland was an issue with strong Cold War implications for which a punitive American policy would be expected to gain the strongest support from conservatives, and, indeed, it did so. Responses to China's trade status reveal a striking change between 1992 and 1996. Whereas in the earlier survey liberals were most critical of the decision to grant MFN to the Beijing regime, four years later the strongest dissent was to be found among both the most conservative and most liberal opinion leaders, while those in the middle of the ideological spectrum expressed much greater support.

When leaders taking part in the FPLP surveys are classified according to their general foreign policy orientations, their assessments of all but one of the foreign policy decisions once again reveal substantial differences. The decision to grant China MFN status is the exception; only a third of the leaders expressed approval of President Bush's action, and differences across the four groups are not significant. The China MFN case aside, there are wide ranges of assessments, exceeding 20 percent, on all the issues. The hardliners supported the imposition of economic sanctions on Poland but were consistently the least enthusiastic about allowing human rights criteria to govern policies toward South Africa, Haitian refugees, the Gulf War, and the maintenance of international stability. On the other hand, the accommodationists were the strongest supporters of human rights except on the issues of economic sanctions on Poland and China's trade status in 1996. The isolationists and internationalists generally took positions in between the other two groups, except that the former were by far the strongest in agreement with the dictum that the United States should *avoid* using economic sanctions in support of its human rights policies.

One of the key differences between hypotheses 3a and 3b is the extent to which human rights attitudes on domestic issues carry over to foreign affairs issues, and vice versa. According to hypothesis 3a, assessments of the eight foreign policy decisions should differ little, if at all, among leaders in the four groups. Hypothesis 3b, on the other hand, stipulates that there should be significant differences among them.

The results are generally consistent with the latter hypothesis. Leaders in all four groups defined by domestic policy preferences —*liberals, populists, libertarians,* and *conservatives*— expressed moderate support for the imposition of economic sanctions on Poland, with somewhat stronger approval from the conservatives, and in 1996 differences among the four groups on granting MFN trade status to China were not significant. Assessments of the remaining issues gave rise to a consistent pattern wherein liberals took the strongest position in support of human rights emphasis, the conservatives were the most skeptical, and the populists and libertarians were arrayed in between. The range of responses among the leaders in the four groups was uniformly large, ranging between 16 and 46 percent. Unfortunately, the Chicago Council surveys did not pose the kinds of domestic questions that would have permitted a comparable analysis of linkages between attitudes on foreign and domestic issues among members of the general public.

The final stage of the analysis related to hypotheses 3a and 3b focuses on a

number of domestic issues with a human rights dimension, including freedom of dissent, busing for purposes of school integration, the death penalty
the Equal Rights Amendment, and discrimination against homosexuals
Each of these questions was posed in the four most recent FPLP surveys. A
noted above, the CCFR surveys have not included questions on domestic issues. The analyses are initially aimed at discovering whether the background
attributes that have already been shown to be strongly correlated with posi
tions on the use of human rights criteria in the conduct of foreign affairs –
party, ideology, and foreign policy orientation – are also associated with
preferences on the domestic issues.[35]

The relationship of party affiliation to the five domestic human rights issues is summarized in table 7.13. With one exception – the policy of "barring
homosexuals from teaching in public schools," which steadily lost suppor
between 1984 and 1996 – aggregate opinions on these issues have been re
markably stable, varying by only slight amounts over twelve year period. Partisan differences also have remained consistently large. In each case, Democrats expressed far stronger support for the right to dissent, school busing
abolition of the death penalty, and the Equal Rights Amendment, while Republicans were the stronger advocates of preventing homosexuals from
teaching in public schools. Except on the latter issue, the policy preferences
of both Democrats and Republicans remained quite stable across the three
surveys. In all instances, independents as a group expressed views that placed
them between members of the two major political parties.

When leaders taking part in the FPLP surveys are classified according to
their self-placements on the ideology scale, the range of responses to the
domestic human rights issues can only be described as huge (table 7.14). Although fewer than a third of the leaders judged that the right to dissent damages American foreign policy, differences between liberals and conservative
on that question are consistently very large. For all the other issues, the gap
between the most conservative and most liberal leaders exceed 60 percent
in each of the four surveys. But wide differences are not merely confined to
those at the endpoints of the ideology scale; even those who describe themselves as "somewhat conservative" hold sharply different views from leaders who regard themselves as "somewhat liberal"; the gaps between them
are typically 40 percent and higher. Nor is there much evidence that the
stark ideological differences of the earlier surveys are being bridged in the
later ones.

The final step in this analysis examines the relationship between foreign policy orientations and the domestic human rights issues. On each issue, the hard-liners are the strongest advocates of preventing homosexuals from teaching in public schools and are most critical of the freedom of dissent; they are also the strongest critics of school busing, abolition of the death penalty, and the Equal Rights Amendment. Responses of the accommodationists, as a group, are precisely the reverse on all five issues. In each case, the isolationists and internationalists expressed views that placed them between the hard-liners and accommodationists.

The correlations between leadership opinions toward human rights abroad and at home are reported in table 7.15. They provide further support for the hypothesis that views about human rights are in fact embedded within a broader political ideology.

The opinion surveys reviewed here suggest, on balance, that the end of the Cold War has not served as an impetus to greater support for a human rights emphasis in American foreign policy. To the extent that we can discern any trends, the data offer greater support for hypothesis 1a — that the end of the Cold War has seen an erosion of interest in human rights — than for the competing hypothesis 1b. The evidence on the hypothesized differences between leaders and the general public is less conclusive. However, the data point to this conclusion: The opinions of both leaders and the general public on human rights have tended to be rather similar, and during the past two decades they have generally moved in the same direction. Evidence supporting this conclusion appears most clearly in tables 7.1–.5 and 7.7.

More broadly, the data presented here point rather dramatically to the persisting — and perhaps growing — gap between the rhetoric of "American exceptionalism," and the relatively low priority attached to human rights, especially when promotion and protection of such rights might entail significant costs or trade-offs. A gap between lofty rhetoric and behavior is not, of course, a uniquely American quality, but its real world consequences may be greater than in the case of most other countries. For example, archival evidence recently made available has established beyond doubt that in 1956 Hungarian nationalists were encouraged to take up arms against the Soviets in the expectation that American rhetoric about a "rollback of the Iron Curtain" would be followed by material assistance from the United States. A much clearer conclusion emerges on the relative merits of the third pair of hypotheses (3a or 3b). Attitudes toward incorporating human rights considerations into the conduct of American foreign policy are embedded within broader political belief systems that also encompass attitudes on domestic issues, and they are strongly associated with partisanship and ideological preferences. There is little evidence to support the contrary hypothesis that skeptics are merely isolating foreign relations as a special domain that should be exempt from human rights concerns. But some caution is warranted even with respect to these hypotheses, because the data are stronger for leaders than for the general public. Indeed, there are strong indications that, as in most aspects of political thinking, there is substantially greater ideological coherence in the views of leaders than in those of the general public.

President Jimmy Carter had hoped that a concern for human rights abroad might provide one of the foundations for restoring at least some semblance of a bipartisan foreign policy consensus in the wake of the disastrous war in Vietnam. For many reasons — not the least of which is that even the most ardent advocate of human rights will concede that in the formulation of foreign policy this goal must compete with other national interests — President Carter was not more successful in this endeavor than his predecessors had been in promoting détente as a basis for a post-Vietnam consensus or his successor was to be in creating a greater degree of unity by means of a massive arms buildup and a more confrontational stance toward the Soviet Union.

But that was then and now is now. Has the end of the Cold War created a more benign environment within which to attempt, once again, to place human rights concerns near the top of the foreign policy agenda? Specifically, have the dramatic international changes of the almost two decades since the Carter era reflected attitudes that would provide domestic support for foreign policies that accord somewhat stronger weight to human rights criteria?

The evidence reviewed here falls short of the ideal. Nevertheless, it appears to point toward some rather sober conclusions. First, there are few indications of a vast increase in Americans — either among leaders or the general public — who regard the post–Cold War international system as a more inviting arena for expressing human rights concerns. To the contrary, the evidence suggests a discernible erosion of support for a human rights emphasis on American foreign policy among both leaders and the general public. As was the case during the Cold War, when faced with trade-offs in relations with other major powers, Americans are rarely inclined to place human rights concerns ahead of such issues as arms control negotiations. The evidence thus does not provide much sustenance for the fears expressed by Henry Kissinger and other realists that a misguided public will endanger efforts to stabilize relations with major adversaries. Yet if human rights is not a top priority among the public, it is nevertheless a source of division. Heated controversies about appropriate American responses to events in Somalia, Haiti, Bosnia, Rwanda, and Kosovo, as well as China's trade status, reflect at least in part the state of a very divided public.

More importantly, the data reviewed above indicate that human rights attitudes are deeply embedded in partisan and ideological differences that also encompass a broader range of questions about the proper American role in the post–Cold War international arena, the scope of the country's global obligations—including to international organizations with human rights missions—and the resources that the United States can call on in operating within that international system.[36] Although liberals are more supportive of human rights, both in the abstract and in most specific situations, there are issues on which conservatives can be expected to express greater enthusiasm for human rights. They generally did so on the state of human rights in the Soviet Union during the Cold War and currently are more ardent advocates of steps to dislodge Fidel Castro from power in Cuba. In quite specific situations it may even be possible to forge a bipartisan coalition for action that is, ostensibly, directed at improving the state of human rights abroad. The Helms-Burton Act of 1996, an effort to attack the Castro dictatorship for its many human rights violations by punishing Canada, Mexico, and European nations that trade with Cuba, is an example. Although Helms-Burton is a wholly misguided action that violates trade treaties to which the United States is a party, it sailed through the Republican 104th Congress and received President Clinton's signature. To oppose it in an election year was apparently perceived as an act of political suicide.

Such anomalies aside, most of the evidence reviewed here provides strong support for David Forsythe's conclusion that, "Human rights voting in Congress is largely but not completely a partisan and ideological matter, a prospect that cannot be viewed with optimism by the victims of politics in various foreign nations."[37] In this respect, congressional cleavages appear to reflect rather faithfully those in the country at large. That these differences also overlap with, rather than cut across, cleavages on some of the most contentious domestic issues is further reason for a cautious appraisal of the prospects for American leadership on human rights issues.

Appendix

Table 7.1. Assessments of "Promoting and Defending Human Rights in Other Countries" as a Foreign Policy Goal for the United States: Leaders and the General Public, 1978–96

(% "very important")

Below is a list of foreign policy goals that the United States might have. Please indicate how much importance you think should be attached to each goal.

		Leaders			
Year	Survey	CCFR	FPLP	T-M	General public
1974	CCFR	NA	—	—	NA
1976	FPLP	—	NA	—	—
1978	CCFR	36	—	—	39
1980	FPLP	—	27	—	—
1982	CCFR	41	—	—	43
1984	FPLP	—	33	—	—
1986	CCFR	44	—	—	42
1988	FPLP	—	39	—	—
1990	CCFR	45	—	—	58
1992	FPLP	—	38	—	—
1993	T-M*	—	—	22	28
1994	CCFR	26	—	—	34
1996	FPLP	—	23	—	—

*Response options different from other surveys. Reported percentages are for "top priority" rather than "very important."

NA = question not asked; CCFR = Chicago Council on Foreign Relations; FPLP = Foreign Policy Leadership Project; T-M = Times-Mirror Center for People and the Press.

Table 7.2. Assessments of "Helping to Bring a Democratic Form of Government to Other Countries" as a Foreign Policy Goal for the United States: Leaders and the General Public, 1974–96

(% "very important")

Here is a list of foreign policy goals that the United States might have. Please indicate how much importance you think should be attached to each goal.

| Year | Survey | Leaders | | | General public |
		CCFR	FPLP	T-M	
1974	CCFR	13	—	—	28
1976	FPLP	—	8	—	—
1978	CCFR	15	—	—	26
1980	FPLP	—	9	—	—
1982	CCFR	23	—	—	29
1984	FPLP	—	18	—	—
1986	CCFR	29	—	—	30
1988	FPLP	—	24	—	—
1990	CCFR	26	—	—	28
1992	FPLP	—	23	—	—
1993	T-M*	—	—	21	22
1994	CCFR	21	—	—	25
1996	FPLP	—	15	—	—

*Response options different from other surveys. Reported percentages are for "top priority" rather than "very important."

CCFR = Chicago Council on Foreign Relations; FPLP = Foreign Policy Leadership Project; T-M = Times-Mirror Center for People and the Press.

Table 7.3. Assessments of "Helping to Improve the Standard of Living in Less Developed Countries" as a Foreign Policy Goal for the United States: Leaders and the General Public, 1974–96

(% "very important")

Here is a list of foreign policy goals that the United States might have. Please indicate how much importance you think should be attached to each goal.

		Leaders			
Year	Survey	CCFR	FPLP	T-M	General public
1974	CCFR	62	—	—	39
1976	FPLP	—	39	—	—
1978	CCFR	64	—	—	35
1980	FPLP	—	44	—	—
1982	CCFR	55	—	—	35
1984	FPLP	—	59	—	—
1986	CCFR	46	—	—	37
1988	FPLP	—	51	—	—
1990	CCFR	42	—	—	41
1992	FPLP	—	43	—	—
1993	T-M*	—	—	23	18
1994	CCFR	28	—	—	22
1996	FPLP	—	28	—	—

*Response options different from other surveys. Reported percentages are for "top priority" rather than "very important."

CCFR = Chicago Council on Foreign Relations; FPLP = Foreign Policy Leadership Project; T-M = Times-Mirror Center for People and the Press.

Table 7.4. Assessments of "Combating World Hunger" as a Foreign Policy Goal for the United States: Leaders and the General Public, 1974–96

(% "very important")

Here is a list of foreign policy goals that the United States might have. Please indicate how much importance you think should be attached to each goal.

| Year | Survey | Leaders | | | General public |
		CCFR	FPLP	T-M	
1974	CCFR	76	—	—	61
1976	FPLP	—	52	—	—
1978	CCFR	67	—	—	59
1980	FPLP	—	51	—	—
1982	CCFR	64	—	—	58
1984	FPLP	—	56	—	—
1986	CCFR	60	—	—	63
1988	FPLP	—	57	—	—
1990	CCFR	NA	—	—	NA
1992	FPLP	—	54	—	—
1993	T-M	NA	—	NA	NA
1994	CCFR	41	—	—	56
1996	FPLP	—	35	—	—

NA = Question not asked; CCFR = Chicago Council on Foreign Relations; FPLP = Foreign Policy Leadership Project; T-M = Times-Mirror Center for People and the Press.

Table 7.5. Assessments of "Protecting the Global Environment" as a Foreign Policy Goal for the United States: Leaders and the General Public, 1974–96

(% "very important")

Here is a list of foreign policy goals that the United States might have. Please indicate how much importance you think should be attached to each goal.

Year	Survey	Leaders			General public
		CCFR	FPLP	T-M	
1974	CCFR	NA	—	—	NA
1976	FPLP	—	NA	—	—
1978	CCFR	NA	—	—	NA
1980	FPLP	—	48	—	—
1982	CCFR	NA	—	—	NA
1984	FPLP	—	54	—	—
1986	CCFR	NA	—	—	NA
1988	FPLP	—	69	—	—
1990	CCFR	72	—	—	58
1992	FPLP	—	66	—	—
1993	T-M*	—	—	45	56
1994	CCFR	49	—	—	58
1996	FPLP	—	47	—	—

Note: The CCFR and T-M survey wording was: "Improving the global environment."

*Response options different from other surveys. Reported percentages are for "top priority" rather than "very important."

NA = Question not asked; CCFR = Chicago Council on Foreign Relations; FPLP = Foreign Policy Leadership Project; T-M = Times-Mirror Center for People and the Press.

Table 7.6. Correlation between Assessments of "Promoting and Defending Human Rights in Other Countries" and Four Other Human Rights Goals in the Foreign Policy Leadership Project and Chicago Council on Foreign Relations Surveys, 1978–96

Correlations between the importance attached to the goal of "Promoting and defending human rights in other countries" and:

Year	Spreading democracy abroad	Improving standards of living	Combatting world hunger	Protecting the global environment
		FPLP		
1980	.58	.58	.70	.56
1984	.46	.62	.78	.63
1988	.50	.61	.78	.55
1992	.62	.65	.75	.62
1996	.67	.65	.73	.57
		CCFR—leaders		
1978	.41	.23	.36	—
1982	.21	.36	.32	—
1986	.32	.27	.43	—
1990	.26	.25	—	.22
1994	.23	.52	.38	.26
		CCFR—general public		
1978	.38	.44	.43	—
1982	.37	.43	.47	—
1986	.26	.36	.42	—
1990	.22	.32	—	.10
1994	.36	.39	.36	.27

Table 7.7. Assessment of Promoting and Defending Human Rights Abroad: Leaders and the General Public, 1978–94

(% "very important")

	1978 CCFR	1982 CCFR	1986 CCFR	1990 CCFR	1993 T-M*	1994 CCFR
	General public					
All respondents	39	43	42	58	28	34
By party**						
Republicans	34	35	43	57	20	23
Democrats	44	48	42	61	26	37
Independents	39	42	41	56	21	34
By ideology**						
Conservatives	38	41	37	57	NA	29
Middle-of-the-road	36	46	41	56	NA	34
Liberals	47	44	52	64	NA	43
	Leaders					
All respondents	36	41	44	45	22	26
By party						
Republicans	20	18	24	23	14	9
Democrats	37	46	54	48	36	46
Independents	46	32	42	47	26	24
By ideology						
Conservatives	16	15	26	27	12	NA
Middle-of-the road	24	25	35	40	23	NA
Liberals	55	53	59	54	42	NA

*Reported percentages are for "top priority" responses.

**Not all respondents were asked about party and ideology in the 1978–94 CCFR surveys.

CCFR = Chicago Council on Foreign Relations; NA = Question not asked; T-M = Times-Mirror Center for the People and Press survey.

Table 7.8. Assessment by U.S. Opinion Leaders of Promoting and Defending Human Rights as a U.S. Foreign Policy Goal: FPLP Surveys of U.S. Opinion Leaders, 1980–96

(% "very important")

	1980 (N = 2,502)	1984 (N = 2,515)	1988 (N = 2,226)	1992 (N = 2,312)	1996 (N = 2,141)
All respondents	27	33	39	38	23
By party					
Republicans	15	16	25	25	12
Democrats	36	47	53	52	34
Independents	26	35	36	35	23
By ideology					
Very conservative	14	10	21	17	11
Somewhat conservative	17	17	24	22	11
Moderate	26	30	36	38	22
Somewhat liberal	41	53	55	52	36
Very liberal	48	61	67	70	48
By foreign policy orientation					
Hard-liners	6	9	16	6	4
Isolationists	5	7	15	6	2
Internationalists	29	29	37	37	30
Accommodationists	38	47	51	48	29
By domestic policy orientation					
Conservatives	NA	13	19	18	11
Libertarians	NA	23	33	40	16
Populists	NA	28	31	33	24
Liberals	NA	51	55	52	35

NA = Questions used to develop the domestic policy orientation scale not asked.

Table 7.9. Attitudes toward Human Rights Issues in the Chicago Council on Foreign Relations Surveys of the General Public, 1974–86: The Impact of Party

(% "agree strongly" or "agree somewhat")

	Year	All respondents	Republicans	Independents	Democrats
It is morally wrong to back military dictatorships that deny basic rights, even if we have military bases in those countries.	1974*	74	75	77	72
The United States may have to support some dictators because they are friendly toward us and opposed to Communists.	1982	63	72	60 .	60
We should take a more active role in opposing the policy of apartheid—that is,racial segregation—in South Africa.	1974 1978 1982	34 40 45	28 31 37	34 43 44	36 44 49
Support total or partial economic sanctions on South Africa	1986*	57	55	56	59
How the Soviet Union handles the treatment of Jews or other minority groups is a matter of internal Soviet politics and none of our business.	1974 1978	41 49	37 54	42 47	42 49
The United States should put pressure on countries which systematically violate basic human rights.	1974* 1978*	68 67	70 66	70 70	67 70

Note: Differences significant at the .001 level unless indicated otherwise by asterisk (*).

Table 7.10. Attitudes toward Human Rights Issues in the Chicago Council on Foreign Relations Surveys of Leaders, 1974–86: The Impact of Party

(% "agree strongly" or "agree somewhat")

	Year	All respondents	Republicans	Independents	Democrats
It is morally wrong to back military dictatorships that deny basic rights, even if we have military bases in those countries.	1974	72	57	73	80
The United States may have to support some dictators because they are friendly toward us and opposed to Communists.	1978	63	83	54	59
	1982	65	84	60	52
We should take a more active role in opposing the policy of apartheid — that is, racial segregation — in South Africa.	1974	59	31	61	72
	1978	66	48	77	68
	1982	79	62	75	89
Support total or partial economic sanctions on South Africa.	1986	79	65	73	95
How the Soviet Union handles the treatment of Jews or other minority groups is a matter of internal Soviet politics and none of our business	1974	34	45	41	22
	1978	30	48	22	34
The United States should put pressure on countries which systematically violate basic human rights.	1974*	87	84	89	88
	1978	78	57	87	76

Note: Differences significant at the .001 level unless indicated otherwise by asterisk (*).

Table 7.11. Assessments of U.S. Foreign Policy Decisions by Republicans, Democrats, and Independents in the Foreign Policy Leadership Project Surveys of U.S. Opinion Leaders, 1984–96

(% "agree strongly" or "agree somewhat")

	Year	All respondents	Republicans	Democrats	Independents
Failing to impose economic sanctions on South Africa	1984	44	60	30	47
Placing sanctions on Poland after the imposition of martial law	1984	58	64	54	58
Imposing economic sanctions on South Africa for its policy of apartheid	1988	62	41	80	63
Lifting the economic sanctions that had been imposed on South Africa	1992	70	83	57	74
Returning refugees to Haiti	1992	50	71	31	53
Too many Iraqis were killed in the Persian Gulf War.	1992	38	15	59	35
The United States should exercise its power in such a way as to assure continuing stability in world affairs even at the cost of denying self-determination to some groups.	1992	52	63	43	52
Granting Most Favored Nation trade status to China	1992	34	46	24	35
	1996	46	48	46	46
The United States should avoid using economic sanctions to promote and defend human rights.	1996	25	31	18	27

Note: Differences significant at the .001 level for all items except MFN to China in 1996.

Table 7.12. Attitudes toward Human Rights Issues in the Chicago Council on Foreign Relations Surveys of General Public, 1974–86: The Impact of Ideology

(% "agree strongly" or "agree somewhat")

	Year	All respondents	Conservatives	Middle-of the-road	Liberals
It is morally wrong to back military dictatorships that deny basic rights, even if we have military bases in those countries.	1974	74	69	75	80
The United States may have to support some dictators because they are friendlytoward us and opposed to the Communists.	1982	63	68	65	58
We should take a more active role in opposing the policy of apartheid—that is, racial segregation—in South Africa.	1974 1978 1982	34 40 45	28 32 40	31 42 47	52 53 56
Support total or partial economic sanctions on South Africa	1986	57	54	56	67
How the Soviet Union handles the treatment of Jews or other minority groups is a matter of internal Soviet politics and none of our business.	1974* 1978	41 49	47 56	38 45	41 49
The United States should put pressure on countries which systematically violate human rights.	1974* 1978*	68 67	65 63	71 71	71 73

Note: Differences significant at the .001 level unless indicated otherwise by asterisk (*).

Table 7.13. Assessment of Domestic Policy Issues by Republicans, Democrats, and Independents in the FPLP Surveys of U.S. Opinion Leaders, 1976–96

(% "agree strongly" or "agree somewhat")

	Year	All respondents	Repub- licans	Demo- crats	Inde- pendents
The freedom to dissent at home	1976	28	40	19	40
inhibits the effective conduct of	1980	27	35	20	16
U.S. foreign policy.	1984	27	40	26	28
Busing children in order to	1984	37	12	59	36
achieve school integration	1988	40	17	62	36
	1992	38	16	69	34
	1996	34	15	55	27
Banning the death penalty	1984	33	11	54	31
	1988	35	13	55	31
	1992	33	10	55	28
	1996	34	14	54	31
Reviving the Equal Rights	1984	56	29	77	56
Amendment	1988	55	31	75	54
	1992	53	31	74	50
	1996	49	26	70	46
Barring homosexuals from	1984	38	60	22	37
teaching in public schools	1988	33	55	15	33
	1992	28	48	14	27
	1996	25	46	10	22

Note: Differences significant at the .001 level for all items.

Table 7.14. Assessments of U.S. Foreign Policy Decisions by Self-Identified Ideological Preferences in the FPLP Surveys of U.S. Opinion Leaders, 1984–96

(% "agree strongly" or "agree somewhat")

	Year	All respondents	Conservative		Moderate	Liberal	
			Very	Somewhat		Somewhat	Very
Failing to impose economic sanctions on South Africa	1984	44	70	61	44	26	16
Placing sanctions on Poland after the imposition of martial law	1984	58	73	62	55	57	45
Imposing economic sanctions on South Africa for its policy of apartheid	1988	62	28	44	64	83	95
Lifting the economic sanctions that had been imposed on South Africa	1992	70	86	86	69	61	37
Returning refugees to Haiti	1992	50	76	71	51	32	17
Too many Iraqis were killed in the Persian Gulf War.	1992	38	9	17	34	60	82
The United States should exercise its power in such way as to assure continuing stability in world affairs even at the cost of denying self-determination to some groups.	1992	52	73	62	52	44	28
Granting Most Favored Nation trade status to China	1992	34	48	41	35	26	20
The United States should avoid using economic sanctions to promote and defend human rights.	1996	25	35	32	23	20	10

Note: Differences significant at the .001 level for all items.

Table 7.15. Correlations between Assessment of "Promoting and Defending Human Rights in Other Countries" and Four Domestic Issues with a Human Rights Dimension in the 1984–96 FPLP Surveys of U.S. Opinion Leaders

Correlations between the importance attached to the goal of "promoting and defending human rights in other countries" and support for:

Year	School busing	Equal rights amendment	Barring homosexual teachers	Banning the death penalty
1984	.46	.43	-.35	.50
1988	.38	.40	-.35	.44
1992	.40	.40	-.37	.45
1996	.36	.35	-.31	.37

Note: Coefficients are gamma. Domestic policy questions were not included in the 1980 FPLP survey; therefore, correlations are not reported for that year.

Notes

I am indebted to the National Science Foundation for five grants that supported the Foreign Policy Leadership Project surveys of American opinion leaders; to Eugene R. Wittkopf for sharing some of his data from the Chicago Council on Foreign Relations and Times-Mirror surveys; to Robert Jackson for obtaining data on human rights issues from the Roper Center; to Peter Feaver, David Forsythe, and Robert Keohane for helpful comments on an earlier draft; to Daniel F. Harkins for programming assistance; to David Priess for research assistance; and to Rita Dowling for secretarial assistance.

1. Walter Lippmann, *Public Opinion* (New York: Macmillan, 1922); Lippmann, *The Phantom Public* (New York: Harcourt Brace, 1925); and Lippmann, *Essays in the Public Philosophy* (Boston: Little Brown, 1955).

2. For good discussions of the concept of human rights and the development of American human rights policy, see Jack Donnelly, *The Concept of Human Rights* (New York: St. Martin's, 1985); David P. Forsythe, *Human Rights and U.S. Foreign Policy: Congress Reconsidered* (Gainesville: University of Florida Press, 1988); Forsythe, "Human Rights in U.S. Foreign Policy: Retrospect and Prospect," *Political Science Quarterly* 105 (1990): 435–454; Forsythe, "Human Rights in a Post–Cold War

World," *Fletcher Forum of World Affairs* 15 (summer 1991): 55–69; Forsythe, "Human Rights and U.S. Foreign Policy: Two Levels, Two Worlds," *Political Studies* 43 (1995): 111–130; Forsythe, "The UN and Human Rights at Fifty: An Incremental but Incomplete Revolution," *Global Governance* 1 (1995): 297–318; Stanley Hoffmann, *Duties Beyond Borders* (Syracuse NY: Syracuse University Press, 1981); Tamar Jacoby, "Reagan's Turnaround on Human Rights," *Foreign Affairs* 64 (summer 1986): 1066–1086; Kathryn Sikkink, "The Power of Principled Ideas: Human Rights Policies in the United States and Western Europe," in *Ideas and Foreign Policy: Beliefs, Institutions, and Political Change*, ed. Judith Goldstein and Robert O. Keohane (Ithaca NY: Cornell University Press, 1993); and Sara Steinmetz, *Democratic Transition and Human Rights* (Albany: State University of New York Press, 1994).

3. Elihu Root, "A Requisite for the Success of Popular Diplomacy," *Foreign Affairs* 1 (1922): 5.

4. Lippmann, *Essays in the Public Philosophy*, 20.

5. Ole R. Holsti, *Public Opinion and American Foreign Policy* (Ann Arbor: University of Michigan Press, 1996).

6. Hans J. Morgenthau, *Politics among Nations*, 5th ed. (New York: Knopf, 1978); and George F. Kennan, "Morality and Foreign Policy," *Foreign Affairs* 64 (1985–86). According to James N. Billington, a human rights focus can serve to provide both the needed idealism or vision and realism for American foreign policy. However, he appeared to view it primarily as a Cold War weapon. After asserting that neither internal democratization nor imperial disintegration is likely to reduce the Soviet threat, he stated that, "Human rights provides a valuable vehicle for peaceful, evolutionary democratization throughout the communist world." James N. Billington, "Realism and Vision in American Foreign Policy," *Foreign Affairs* 66 (1987): 630–652.

7. Burton Yale Pines, "A Primer for Conservatives," *National Interest*, no. 23 (spring 1991): 61–68; Billington, "Realism and Vision," 630–652; Samuel P. Huntington, "American Ideals versus American Institutions," in *American Foreign Policy: Theoretical Essays*, ed. G. John Ikenberry, (Glenview IL: Scott Foresman & Co. 1989), 223–258; Walter Laqueur, "The Issue of Human Rights," *Commentary* 63 (May 1977): 29–35; and Daniel Patrick Moynihan, "The Politics of Human Rights," *Commentary* 64 (August 1977): 19–26.

8. For critiques of cultural relativism on human rights, see Rupert Emerson, "The Fate of Human Rights in the Third World," *World Politics* 27 (1975): 201–226; Sam McFarland, A Defense of Universal Human Rights against Cultural Relativism and Other Philosophical Challenges. Paper prepared for the Annual Conference of the International Society of Political Psychology, Vancouver, Canada, July 1996; and Morton E. Winston, "The Case for Universality: Human Rights Standards Apply to All Cultures," *Amnesty Action* 19 (summer 1996): 10.

9. See, for example, William G. Hyland, "America's New Course," *Foreign Affairs* 69 (spring 1990): 1–12; Paul M. Kattenberg, "Moral Dilemmas in the Development

of United States Human Rights Policies," in *The Dynamics of Human Rights in U.S. Foreign Policy*, ed. Natalie Kaufman Hevener (New Brunswick NJ: Transaction Books, 1981); Charles William Maynes, "A Workable Clinton Doctrine," *Foreign Policy*, no. 93 (winter 1993–94): 3–21; Michael Posner, "Rally Round Human Rights," *Foreign Policy*, no. 97 (winter 1994–95): 133–139; and Cyrus R. Vance, "The Human Rights Imperative," *Foreign Policy*, no. 63 (summer 1986): 3–19.

10. Michael Mandelbaum, "Foreign Policy as Social Work," *Foreign Affairs* 75 (January–February 1996): 16–32.

11. See, for example, George F. Kennan, "Somalia, through a Glass Darkly," *New York Times*, September 30, 1993, A25.

12. Jimmy Carter, "Text of President's Address at Notre Dame on Foreign Policy," *New York Times*, May 23, 1977, sec. 12, 1.

13. James Schlesinger, "New Instabilities, New Priorities," *Foreign Policy*, no. 85 (winter 1991–92): 3–24.

14. Alan Tonelson, "Jettison the Policy," *Foreign Policy*, no. 97 (winter 1994–95): 127.

15. William G. Hyland, "The Case for Pragmatism," *Foreign Affairs* 71 (1991–1992): 38–52.

16. Jeane Kirkpatrick, "Dictatorships and Double Standards," *Commentary* 68 (November 1979): 34–45; and Kirkpatrick, "U.S. Security and Latin America," *Commentary* 71 (January 1981): 29–40.

17. Kenneth Waltz, the leading proponent of structural realism, is an exception. Waltz, "Electoral Punishment and Foreign Policy Crises," in *Domestic Sources of Foreign Policy*, ed. James N. Rosenau, (New York: Free Press, 1967).

18. For a review of the extensive evidence on this point, see Holsti, *Public Opinion and American Foreign Policy*, chp. 4.

19. Michael Posner, "Rally Round Human Rights," *Foreign Policy*, no. 97 (winter 1994–95): 136.

20. Critics of a human rights emphasis in foreign affairs also cite Lincoln and his impatience with those who claim to be acting in accord with the will of Providence: "These are not, however, days of miracles, and I suppose it will be granted that I am not to expect a divine revelation. I must study the plain physical facts of the case, and ascertain what is possible and learn what appears to be wise and right." Quoted in Morgenthau, *Politics among Nations*, 263.

21. Anne E. Geyer and Robert Y. Shapiro, "The Polls — A Report: Human Rights," *Public Opinion Quarterly* 52 (1988): 388.

22. John E. Rielly, ed., *American Public Opinion and U.S. Foreign Policy, 1975* (Chicago: Chicago Council on Foreign Relations, 1975); also similarly titled monographs for 1979, 1983, 1987, 1991, and 1995.

23. Scott Davidson, *Human Rights* (Philadelphia: Open University Press, 1993).

24. The 1993 Times-Mirror surveys were conducted July 7–August 16 (leaders) and September 9–15 (general public), prior to the fire fight in Somalia that resulted in the

deaths of eighteen American troops. Thus, the results in tables 1–3 and 5 could not have been affected by that event.

25. The CCFR and FPLP samples of leaders differ in several respects, most notably in the inclusion of senior military officers in the latter. This difference, as well as the two-year time gap between them, may account at least in part for some of the differences in responses by leaders to identical items.

26. For further evidence on this point, see Holsti, Promotion of Democracy as Popular Demand, paper prepared for a conference on U.S. Promotion of Democracy, Washington, January 12–13, 1998.

27. Specifically, in the six CCFR surveys leaders ranked this goal lowest three times, second to lowest twice, and third to lowest once. It was ranked lowest four times by the general public, second to lowest once, and third to lowest once.

28. Most surveys indicate strong support for reducing the level of foreign aid, but there is also strong evidence that Americans are poorly informed about the actual costs of such programs. When asked what would be a fair or reasonable level of foreign aid, they typically propose figures that are far greater than actual U.S. international assistance expenditures. For evidence on this point, see Steven Kull, *Americans and Foreign Aid: A Study of American Public Attitudes* (College Park MD: Center for International and Security Studies 1995). In 1981 two Yankelovich, Skelly, and White surveys found that, by a margin of 76 to 15 percent, the public disapproved of "giving economic and military support to anti-communist allies even if they violate human rights," and almost as large a majority expressed the same view when the question specifically mentioned South Korea. Five years later a survey for the Overseas Development Council revealed that a very large majority — 76 to 18 percent — agreed that the United States should require recipients of foreign aid to make human rights reforms. Data from the Roper Center. On linking foreign aid to human rights, also see Kull, *Americans and Foreign Aid.*

29. For fuller descriptions of the MI/CI scheme, see Eugene R. Wittkopf, "On the Foreign Policy Beliefs of the American People: A Critique and Some Evidence," *International Studies Quarterly* 30 (1986): 425–445; Eugene R. Wittkopf, *Faces of Internationalism: Public Opinion and American Foreign Policy* (Durham NC: Duke University Press, 1990); Ole R. Holsti and James N. Rosenau, "The Structure of Foreign Policy Attitudes among American Leaders," *Journal of Politics* 52 (1990): 94–125; and Holsti and Rosenau, "The Structure of Foreign Policy Beliefs among American Opinion Leaders — After the Cold War," *Millennium* 22 (1993): 235–278

30. Forsythe, *Human Rights and U.S. Foreign Policy*, 41.

31. The domestic policy classification scheme is described in more detail in Ole R. Holsti and James N. Rosenau, "Liberals, Populists, Libertarians, and Conservatives: The Link Between Domestic and International Affairs," *International Political Science Review* 17 (1996): 29–54.

32. Table 8 reports findings for only one of the "goals" questions. Analyses of the

other four human rights goals questions (tables 2–5) yielded very similar findings about the impact of party, ideology, foreign policy orientations, and domestic policy orientations. The tables are not reported here in order to save space.

33. For a discussion of surveys on China and human rights, see Wynne Pomeroy Waller and Marianne E. Ide, "The Polls — Poll Trends: China and Human Rights," *Public Opinion Quarterly* 59 (1995): 133–143.

34. Multivariate analyses indicate that ideology dominates party identification as a source of variance in responses to human rights goal question. That is, once self-placement on a standard ideology scale is introduced into the analysis, the impact of party is significantly eroded.

35. There is no comparable analysis to assess how the four domestic policy groups —*liberals, libertarians, populists,* and *conservatives*— appraised the domestic policy issues, because responses to several of those are also used to define the four groups.

36. There is ample other evidence that human rights policy is intensely partisan and ideological. See, for example, the *Commentary* symposium on "Human Rights and American Foreign Policy," *Commentary* 72 (November 1981): 25–63. The eighteen contributors, heavily weighted toward such conservatives and neo-conservatives such as William Barrett, Midge Decter, Sidney Hook, Jeane Kirkpatrick, Robert Nisbet, and Michael Novak, predictably fired salvo after salvo at the alleged failings of the Carter administration's human rights policy. See also Ernest W. Lefever, "The Trivialization of Human Rights," *Policy Review* (winter 1978): 11–26; and T. E. Utley, "A Reappraisal of the Human Rights Doctrine," *Policy Review* (winter 1978): 27–34. Critiques of the Reagan administration's human rights policies include Charles Maechling Jr., "Human Rights Dehumanized," *Foreign Policy*, no. 52 (fall 1983): 118–135; and Tamar Jacoby, "Reagan's Turnaround on Human Rights," *Foreign Affairs* (summer 1986): 1066–1086; they are defended by Jeane J. Kirkpatrick and Allan Gerson, "The Reagan Doctrine, Human Rights, and International Law," in *Right v. Might: International Law and the Use of Force* (New York: Council on Foreign Relations Press, 1989). Post–Cold War debates on such issues as Bosnia, China's trade status, and Cuba are hardly less passionate.

37. Forsythe, *Human Rights and U.S. Foreign Policy*, 50.

8

U.S. Foreign Policy and the Human Rights Movement

•

New Strategies for a Global Era

•

ELLEN DORSEY

By the mid-1990s human rights nongovernmental organization (NGO) activists critiqued the Clinton administration for jettisoning the human rights component of U.S. foreign policy and selling out the human rights ideal to the promotion of market democracies and a flourishing arms trade worldwide. U.S. policy was lambasted as inconsistent at best, consistently contradictory in its political sophistication and cynical, unethical, and weak spirited at worst.

These critiques mark more than the errors of one administration; they identify the strategic challenges posed by increasing globalization. The critiques are driven, more often than not, by an NGO community grappling with tremendous change and pained by its own sense of inefficacy in the face of continued disappointments. A publicly sympathetic administration, a Congress unencumbered by the security imperative of the Cold War, and a depoliticized public discourse on U.S. global policy objectives should have produced more than rhetorical legitimization of the human rights ideal. Activists predicted that the 1990s would present the most conducive environment to date for strong U.S. leadership in the promotion of human rights worldwide. Yet a more sophisticated, highly specialized human rights community, savvy in its access to and manipulation of international institutions and U.S. decision-making processes, has been unable to translate its leverage into real influence over policies in areas with the greatest significance for human rights.

Is there a human rights movement in the West able to deliver a political punch when necessary and perceived as a coherent constituency with sufficient strength to set foreign policy priorities? Is the aggregate sum of interconnected, specialized human rights NGOs greater than its parts? Does it represent a mass movement that can be mobilized? Can a new imperative be articulated that reflects the complexity of the challenges presented by the global era, yet delivers a simple, powerful vision that inspires and moves citizen activists? Without strong and committed political leadership from the administration or Congress, how can the political pressure be intensified to ensure that the foreign policy elite apply a consistent set of human rights guidelines while pursuing economic growth and unfettered trade?

This paper explores these questions and addresses the impact of the human rights movement on U.S. foreign policy in a global era. It first traces the historic impact of the human rights movement in shaping Cold War foreign policy. It outlines the new challenges presented and the movement's adaptation to those challenges. It then examines how globalization has changed the environment for promoting human rights in the hierarchy of U.S. foreign policy objectives. Finally, it assesses the current weakened state of the human rights movement in the United States and sketches some important trends toward a renewal of the grassroots activist base of the movement.

A Historical Perspective

It is well known that Western reactions to fascism and militarism in the 1930s and 1940s led to human rights norms being written into the UN Charter, and widespread knowledge of the Holocaust gave the human rights movement a further push. Western states sought to blend their national security concerns with standards of individual rights. It is also well known that the emerging Cold War, and especially the contest between wars of national liberation and counter-insurgency strategy, pushed concern for individual rights far into the background for both Superpowers. The communist East was said to be interested in human liberation from imperialism and colonialism, and the capitalist West was said to be interested in freedom and democracy. But in reality each side supported gross violations of human rights in a power struggle.

The clash between East and West in Vietnam became a watershed in international relations, with important consequences for human rights developments. Western individuals, supported especially by liberal churches, challenged the drift of U.S. security policy. Given the weaknesses of U.S. policy, these private actors were able to more easily build transnational networks, tapping into widespread discontent with the global status quo. At the

United Nations a deal was struck between those states wishing to focus on South Africa, Israel, Portugal, and other alleged manifestations of imperialism, neo-colonialism, and racism on the one hand and on the other hand those progressive Western states that were willing to examine the fate of human rights in countries such as Greece under military rule and Haiti under perennial repression.

It was at this time that the earliest human rights organizations began to channel popular, public concern for human rights, peace, and social justice into policy recommendations and grassroots activism derived from international standards of human rights. While a small number of organizations had already been monitoring and exposing the human rights violations of the Cold War proxy states, little connection had been made with a grass roots constituency, and policy recommendation bore virtually no weight in foreign policy decision making. With the important exception of Amnesty International, cross-national citizen action on human rights had previously occurred primarily through the efforts of religious institutions and labor organizations. The combined actions of the growing membership of Amnesty International and the ecumenical movements further amplified the human rights message in public discourse and the mainstream media.

What is important to note is that, even if inconsistently applied, the very inclusion of human rights rhetoric reflected tremendous growth and unprecedented impact for social movements concerned with the global advancement of human dignity. And it demonstrated the rapidly growing power of NGOs to channel citizen advocacy into real leverage over the policy process. In the 1970s and the 1980s, NGOs became both a player in the foreign policy process and the messengers of a vision of a global order.

The collapse of the Berlin Wall and the end of the Cold War was greeted with euphoria by the transnational human rights community. Yet new challenges to human rights, centering around the concept of globalization, have emerged in the 1990s. The characteristics of globalization are the focus of rich intellectual and political discourse, where a general consensus about its contours matches profound difference of opinion in its origins.[1] The debates are mirrored in a human rights community struggling to analyze how globalization has produced a paradigm shift for human rights. One could summarize these debates into four paradoxes posed to the advancement of the human rights ideal and methodologies in a global era.[2]

The Weakened State

There is much debate about whether all states have been weakened in contemporary international relations.[3] Clearly, some states are weak, even to the point of disintegration, and this weakness raises important issues for human rights.

Paradoxically, some weakened states are no less repressive. Their only means of control may be coercion when economic and national identity needs can no longer be satisfied by the government. Nigeria under military rule comes to mind as example.

In the extreme, in some parts of the world the weakening of the state has shifted power onto increasingly autonomous and anarchic forces. The disintegration of Somalia and Liberia have become symbols of the autonomous power warring factions can gain and the profound inefficacy of the international community to exert pressure on them. In these cases, human rights advocates have increasingly begun to monitor and target nonstate actors for their abuses. But their leverage over these actors is greatly diminished, if it exists at all. The weakened state in extremis goes right to the heart of the human rights methodology. This human rights methodology emerged out of the Westphalian system, where state to state leverage is applied to demand an accounting of internal practices. The erosion of state authority is felt, therefore, in the inability of human rights advocates to mobilize bilateral and multilateral pressure between states and against nonstate actors. This is the most important methodological challenge of human rights in a global era.

Ironically, in an age of presumed state weakness, stable and consistent state actors are essential to the extent that they can still exert real leverage over economic actors, strengthen international institutions, and demand accountability of other states. For foreign states seeking to shape human rights through the traditional levers of foreign policy, the erosion of state authority can ultimately result in a diminished capacity to build societal support for an assertive focus on rights. A strong liberal state, guided by the imperatives set by its citizenry, is still the most powerful weapon for upholding human rights norms — whether through domestic or foreign policy.

Globalization and the Fragmentation of Identity

It has been noted frequently that global markets and other global processes — such as the development of universal human rights standards — have been accompanied by personal identification with increasingly smaller social groups. This situation in turn has given rise to concern about the tyranny of mass and illiberal democracy, which runs roughshod over minority rights. Democracy pure and simple, empowering a numerical majority, may indeed prove disrespectful of certain groups within its jurisdiction. This has been all too evident in the new European democracies after the Cold War, with numerous examples from Croatia to Serbia to Ukraine to Georgia to Bulgaria, and so forth. The absence of liberal democracy, characterized not just by political participation through relatively free and fair elections but by protection of a wide variety of civil rights including minority rights, is a situation leading to much mischief and not a little misery.

Whether universal or even regional notions of human rights, stemming as they do from liberal political philosophy, can alter illiberal political cultures over time is a perplexing question. Elites in illiberal states tend to argue for cultural relativism and national particularism. All the states at the 1993 Vienna Conference on Human Rights, sponsored by the United Nations that championed cultural relativism, national particularism, and "Asian values" were illiberal states. It remains to be seen if universal human rights can take hold in these countries. In Indonesia there has been a shift in that direction as of 1998, and even China seems to be inching in the same direction.

Global Markets and Multinationals

The ascending power of transnational capital is neither a new nor unique challenge for the promotion of human rights. For the past twenty years or more, rights activists have grappled with the long-term impact of structural adjustment policies and the spread of private international investment on the political, social, and economic environment in countries where spiraling rights abuses have occurred. They have increasingly begun to document the link between austerity and repression while struggling to find mechanisms to exert influence over the nontransparent decision-making processes of the International Financial Institutions. Similarly, in the past ten years rights advocates have also turned their attention to the link between private, transnational investment and the repression of environmental, labor, and development activists globally.

Important gains have been made in monitoring and exposing the correlation between the transnationalization of capital and human (and labor) rights abuses. Although little ground has been gained in countering the speed and magnitude of transnational capital flows, the impact of consumer power and the harnessing of cross-national resistance to labor exploitation has already been felt. The move by an international coalition of rights, environmental, and labor organizations toward the creation of a transnational code of corporate conduct, while in its nascent stages, will only grow in strength in the future. Campaigns such as those against Pepsico in Burma, Nike in Indonesia, and Shell in Nigeria have reinforced the drive toward "corporate responsibility," demonstrating to concerned citizens that these economic actors are both accountable for the human costs of their actions and their vulnerability to concerted political action.

Transnational Civil Society

In human rights terms, the most dynamic and promising dimension of globalization is the consolidation of networks of activists, the convergence of strategies, and the global sharing of information and resources. This has created a power base exponentially greater than that which can be harnessed in any one national context. Once dismissed as academic reification of a complex convergence of political, social, and economic forces, there is now a generalized acceptance that a new political force has emerged on the world stage. The conscious transnational development of human rights activism both reflected and precipitated the shift to a new global paradigm. The recent and rapid global coordination of human rights activism has created new and interesting challenges for rights promotion. Increasingly, activists are asking if such global formations can transcend the differences in visions of a just and fair world system, economic attainment, cultural differences, political realities, and the imperatives set by mobilized activists. Will northern NGOs respond to the challenges of their southern counterparts to channel real resources for capacity building; to simultaneously step back from leadership of the global movement, while opening the corridors to political power in international institutions; and to fully commit to the advancement of social and economic rights, when their Western constituents are hostile to and threatened by their very appearance in domestic debates? And can northern NGOs translate the mandate of the global movement into a political strategy that has real influence over foreign policy and in a way that will inspire and mobilize activists in the West? This challenge is not an esoteric one; rather, it defines the political and ideological environment in which human rights NGOs are building their post–Cold War strategies.

After the power of transnational organizing illustrated in the recent spate of UN world conferences for the environment, social development, population, and women's human rights, it can no longer be argued that the idea of a global social movement is a reification. Yet there is still a hopeful quality to labeling this activity "global civil society." The strength of transnational organizing exists in paradoxical tension with the state system. Transnational connections and global solidarity, emerging as a byproduct of the failures of the state, are carried forth by the preeminent international institution, the United Nations. Can these connections be sustained without a renewed commitment to strengthening the institutions of global governance? The human rights community depends now more than ever on a strong United Nations and regional institutions to uphold both the rights norms and to secure a political space to organize cross-nationally. The human rights community needs the support of national governments to sustain these institutions financially and politically, in a period of deepening distrust and questioning of their utility.

Responding to the New Global Dynamics

The Clinton administration's record is a prism of the challenges the human rights movement is facing and a test case for the obstacles that even a sympathetic U.S. government will confront in implementing a foreign policy responsive to human rights in the global era. Candidate Clinton campaigned on the promise that human rights would be a cornerstone of U.S. foreign policy. The new administration took a strong stand, initially, on the failure of Clinton's predecessors to be resolute in the face of competing policy interests, particularly regarding economic interests in China and domestic political considerations in the treatment of Haitian refugees. Former human rights activists, friends of the human rights NGO community and ideologically driven academics, were given high priority in political appointments and placed in positions of real influence over foreign policy decision making.

But the concrete results of such commitment are mixed, at best. The contours of the administration's policy resulted in the de-prioritization of human rights in the face of concern for promotion of economic interests. National Security Adviser Anthony Lake has made statements regarding the shift in the hierarchy of the administration's foreign policy concern, moving from citing human rights as an equal and autonomous objective to one that is subsumed under the primacy of promoting market democracies abroad. In the early days of the administration, Lake cited the goals as "the expansion of democracy and free trade, defending democracy from its foes, quarantining repressive and pariah states, and protecting and promoting human rights."[4] This hierarchy was quickly eclipsed into a simple formula: the development, support, and strengthening of market democracies.

Increasingly, U.S. foreign policy was being driven by both bureaucratic vested interests and the push to enhance trade worldwide. A coalition of business and government interests had come to define the character of relations with those countries that may be egregious violators of their citizen's fundamental rights. And the Clinton administration waffled, in the face of congressional criticism, to vigorously push a multilateral approach to human rights, either with its allies or through international institutions.

Human rights advocates within the government have often been marginalized, ignored, or rebuffed when pushing for a stronger rights responsive policy.[5] The general impression from the perspective of human rights NGO activists is that although there were very smart and talented people in the administration, it was questionable whether they could influence the bottom line. Given its access to the decision-making process and its relationship with allies in the administration, human rights NGOs have been at great pains to depersonalize the failures of the Clinton administration, citing instead telling actions. A short summary of bilateral and multilateral considerations is illustrative.

Bilateral Relations

U.S. bilateral relations with China and Russia show the difficulty of interjecting human rights considerations, to the satisfaction of human rights NGOs, into foreign relations manifesting strong economic and security dimensions.

This is nowhere more obvious than the de-linking of human rights from granting most favored nation (MFN) status to China. As detailed in the statement by the administration's press secretary upon announcement of MFN renewal, the hierarchy of priorities in Washington's constructive engagement policy were clear:

> Substantial U.S. interests are at stake and renewal of the MFN best advances those interests. Revoking MFN would raise average tariffs on Chinese imports from 5 percent to 45 percent. It would effectively sever our economic relation-

ship with China, undermining our capacity to influence China in a broad range of areas, including human rights, nonproliferation, trade, Taiwan relations and others. It is a clumsy and unproductive instrument that would set us down the wrong path.

Virtually every NGO official interviewed cited this case as the single most damaging action taken by a U.S. president for human rights in recent years. As one official said, "The de-linking of trade from human rights set back the overall integration of rights into U.S. foreign policy by light years." The 1996 annual U.S. government human rights report on China, and subsequent reports, showed that constructive engagement, with an emphasis on continued trade, did not lead to more political freedom. Moreover, it was not always clear that China was cooperating with the goals of U.S. security policy as it played out in countries such as Iran, Pakistan, and North Korea. It was clear that U.S. economic objectives were mostly well received by China.[6]

The Clinton administration became increasingly convinced that the way to advance human rights in China was through long-term engagement leading to incremental improvements. Thus at the time of the president's visit to China in 1998, the administration had essentially given up on pushing for democratic rights in the short term. Rather, it stressed such improvements as improved attention to the rule of law, steps against copyright violations and thus in defense of property rights, increased moderation in Chinese statements about Tibet and the Dali Lama, ratification of the International Covenant on Economic, Social, and Cultural Rights, and promises to ratify the companion Covenant on Civil and Political Rights, inter alia. During Clinton's visit there was unprecedented open discussion in China of sensitive subjects such as personal freedom and repression at Tiananmen Square. President Clinton had his critics, both in the Republican party and among human rights NGOs. But the policy, and the president himself, were clearly popular with the American people.

The Clinton administration's policy toward Russia regarding the Chechen affair reflects a parallel dynamic. The administration remained mostly silent in the face of egregious violations of rights and Russia's blatant disregard for international standards of access for humanitarian and relief organizations in conflict areas. Amnesty International, throughout the course of the conflict, had consistently documented gross violations of human rights by Russian forces in Chechyna, including 30,000 civilian deaths, extrajudicial executions, torture, and hostage taking.

Similarly, Amnesty International condemned the silence of the Clinton administration as contributing to an atmosphere of impunity for Russian violations. When Russian troops returned to the bombardment of densely populated civilian areas, their own warning for civilian evacuation was ignored. After giving forty-eight hours notice, within twenty-four hours they began shelling corridors established for civilian flight. Throughout, the strongest U.S. public statements regarding Yeltsin's record was that the Chechen affair is an internal one. While quiet internal pressure was clearly being applied, the public face of U.S. commitment to the international law of human rights and humanitarian affairs was again tarnished.

In many ways, Russia is the primary test case of the market democracy strategy of the Clinton administration. With Russia's communist-controlled legislature and radical nationalists lurking in the wings, the Clinton team has seen little alternative but to economically prop up the Yeltsin regime despite its many shortcomings. Given that reasonably free and fair elections are held, despite the fact that President Yeltsin subsequently governs by decree, the real thrust of policy has been to push for a strong free market economy. Although the administration has indeed invested resources in democracy building in the former Soviet Union, most resources have gone to market restructuring. Even the most sympathetic of analysts would have great difficulty naming Yeltsin as a liberal democrat; the regime's human rights record has been quite poor relative to European standards. But a U.S. emphasis on a free market is clear.[7] Thus in 1998 the Clinton team supported a new International Monetary Fund (IMF) loan to Russia and stated publicly that the terms should not be too severe.

The administration also has security interests at stake. It has taken financial and other steps to make more secure nuclear weapons in Russia, has sought the help of Moscow in dealing with the situation in former Yugoslavia and Iraq, inter alia, and has pressured Russia regarding military exports to countries such as India and Iran.

In both Russia and China, human rights NGOs have been unsuccessful in getting the Clinton administration to focus on numerous specific human rights concerns in the short run. The private groups have fared better when a country, Burma/Myanmar, for example, is on the margins of the global economy or lacks a strategic position.

Real gains have been evidenced in bilateral relations when economic, political, and ideological concerns are aligned. For example, in the case of U.S. relations with El Salvador and South Africa, as well as with other regimes in transition to a new system of rule, the Clinton administration has expended financial resources for capacity building in civil society, enterprise opportunities for the historically disenfranchised, and human rights education for the larger population.

Multilateralism

Within the human rights community, a strong American multilateral policy on human rights is, perhaps, the ideal prescription for the global era. Multilateralism ensures that an assertive human rights policy will not be perceived as a cover for alternative motives by the United States, exponentially expand the political leverage that can be brought to bear on any one human rights crisis, and concurrently strengthen the international norms. Similarly, when American interest wanes in a particular crisis, multilateralism is an insurance policy for sustained attention to the human rights crisis at hand.

For human rights NGOS, U.S. support for the United Nations is an integral component to an effective international response to rights violations. As such, NGOS have worked closely to pressure the Clinton administration to strengthen UN human rights capacity, while enhancing its overall public support for the United Nations. The Clinton administration's record of general support for the United Nations is well known, but on specific issues in the area of human rights, its record is again mixed.

In its early days the administration played a pivotal role in the creation of the new office of the High Commissioner for Human Rights. Subsequently, in the international forums, the Clinton administration's profile has been much lower. In the 1996 session of the UN Human Rights Commission, China lobbied hard to ensure that the resolution condemning its violations of human rights would be defeated. The U.S. did not counter with an equally substantial lobbying effort. In the 1997 session the United States was unable to hold the Western group together in support of a similar resolution.

In other areas of multilateral concern, the administration has again pursued a policy of supporting specific institutional development for rights but lacked the political will to infuse them with real power. It has typically provided strong endorsement but wielded little leverage over the political processes necessary to ensure effective action. For instance, the United States has strongly supported the establishment of the War Crimes Tribunals for the former Yugoslavia and Rwanda, where our country has provided considerable financial support for the investigations and prosecution.[8] The Clinton administration was much more hesitant when it came to putting U.S. troops in possible harm's way to arrest those indicted from the former Yugoslavia despite heavy lobbying by NGOs. In the case of establishing a permanent International Criminal Court, Clinton differed from human rights NGOs and the so-called like minded states in pursuit of a court that, except for charges of genocide, would be constrained by the traditional operation of the principle of state sovereignty. The United States wanted a court that could only function on the basis of state consent regarding war crimes and crimes against humanity, even if this approach meant that the Iraq and other illiberal states would also benefit from the same principles. NGO efforts to effectuate a change in this restrictive approach failed. On the other side of the issue was the Pentagon, fearful of international prosecution of U.S. military personnel, and important forces in the Senate ideologically opposed to international review of U.S. policies and personnel.

The record was equally mixed when it came to enforcement and peacekeeping actions through the United Nations. The Clinton administration followed the Bush administration's lead in expanding the scope of chapter 7 of the UN Charter to deal with the security of persons inside states. But it cut and ran in Somalia while directing unwarranted criticism to UN personnel after U.S. forces, under U.S. command, made faulty decisions that cost lives in the fall of 1993. The United States then blocked deployment of UN forces in both Rwanda in 1994 and in what was then Zaire in 1995 and 1996, while genocide and other violence was in process. Likewise, the Clinton team was supportive of complex or second generation peacekeeping, entailing numerous human rights activities, under chapter 6 of the charter in places such as Cambodia, but it deferred to Japan in that situation and refused to make major commitments of U.S. resources. NGOs published many critiques of these UN field operations and tried to nudge U.S. policy toward more sustained and extensive support but without much success.

NGO efforts were largely ineffective in altering Clinton's multilateral policy on rights for several basic reasons. As the preceding chapter showed, American public opinion did not demand a foreign policy reflecting moral or liberal internationalism. Indeed, in Somalia, Haiti, and Bosnia it was clear that the public was not supportive of foreign involvements that cost American lives but that seemed remote from U.S. expediential interests. Similarly, the Republican-controlled Congress was more isolationist than internationalist, and more unilateralist than multilateralist. It was particularly unimpressed with the United Nations. Senator Helms was a major roadblock toward any multilateral policy involving the United Nations. Finally, the Pentagon was still affected by the Vietnam syndrome, accentuated by events in Somalia. It continued to be hesitant about deployment of U.S. military personnel in low-level intensity conflicts where the full might of U.S. industrial and technological power could not easily be brought to bear. Parts of the Pentagon were profoundly suspicious of "operations other than war," such as policing and peacekeeping, that might sap U.S. combat ability.

Emerging Challenges for the Human Rights Movement

The new imperative for human rights NGOs and the broader human rights movement is both to influence the *content* of U.S. policy and thus to contest the unmitigated dominance of market concerns, and *to revitalize* a public constituency for human rights in an era of neo-isolationism. Interviews with representatives of the largest human rights organizations based in the United States led to two basic themes: (1) human rights NGOs in the current era will only be effective if they can build sustainable coalitions with other NGOs from the environment, development, and democracy fields; and, (2) they must develop new and effective strategies to revitalize and mobilize a grass-roots constituency.[9]

Over the last few years, new coalitions of NGO activists from the historically fragmented worlds of "development," "the environment," "peace," and "human rights" have begun to develop coordinated strategies to lobby, mobilize constituencies, and demand accountability. While in the nascent stages of collaboration, already there is strong evidence that these coalitions have served an important function. Not only are they vehicles for dialogue about effective policy response, allowing for the influx of current information from the regions where the crisis is looming, but they have generated an intensified level of pressure on the administration to respond to this disparate community of mobilized interest groups.

Beyond the information human rights organizations provide and prescriptions they develop, the political capital that they have over the foreign policy process is the power of the grassroots base of the human rights movement. In the United States the perception is that support is seriously eroding. Many human rights organizations are witnessing a shortfall in membership and resources.[10] Although a constituency for human rights may still exist, it is not readily mobilized as a political force, as evidenced by the failure to mount a sufficient challenge to Clinton's China policy or respond to the genocide in Rwanda.

Various factors account for the erosion of support and the steady demobilization. Though the reasons may differ by individual activists, together they include: (a) the perception of success — namely, that the demise of the Cold War made the world safe for human rights, at least the type of human rights violation associated with the formerly communist regimes; (b) the perceived distance between the U.S. government and egregious violators of human rights characteristic of the Cold War — namely, that those motivated by a feeling of shame for U.S. policies in the past no longer feel a sense of culpability; (c) the declining sense of efficacy in the face of rapid genocidal violations of rights, humanitarian emergencies, refugee flows, and poverty; and, (d) the lack of new organizing principles and mandates for human rights action, as articulated by the NGOs that typically harness and channel grassroots concerns.

The human rights NGO community is grappling with the implications of these changes and the meaning of grassroots politics in the contemporary era. Some maintain it is unlikely that a long-term sustained campaign could be mounted today around any human rights crisis. The models of the past are unlikely to work in the current era, given the changing nature of rights violations. The model of the Anti-Apartheid Movement was unique both in the conditions in South Africa that it was responding to, the length of time that it took to build the movement globally, and the interface of concern with domestic political and social concerns in the United States. The divestment campaign required a long-term strategy with a strong, broad-based level of public support. Most of the human rights strategies of the future will be crisis oriented (such as ethnic conflict) or will occur in the conditions of the breakdown of the states or will directly incorporate socioeconomic issues that do not typically generate public support for government action in the United States. Instead, it is most likely that movements will crop up episodically, reflecting concern over a particular issue and the advocacy of organizations whose work is salient to that issue.

Some have argued that the natural foundation for a renewed movement is that which would reflect the changing face of human rights globally. Making the issues salient and accessible to people's daily lives and experiences is critical to building the base of the movement. The key to mobilizing a constituency here is to demonstrate commonalties in the social fabric of this socity with societies around the world: inner-city problems, violence against women, the decline in education, the impact of racism, and so forth.[11]

Rebuilding the Grassroots Movement

Given the different bases from which a new constituency can be mobilized, three different strategies may be employed, each with differing messages designed to inspire and mobilize. One target population is the tired, frayed core of the historic human rights movement: its traditional, latent constituency. Another target population is the attentive public, both historically concerned with global affairs and self-identifying as liberal, even if not active on human rights issues. A third target is one traditionally untapped: activists drawn from the ranks of the civil rights movement, the women's movement, labor, social, and economic justice movements in the United States. Different strategies and messages must be developed to engage these target communities in ways appropriate to their concerns and inspiring their sense of efficacy.

Target 1

The first step to revitalizing the activist base of the movement necessitates redefining the global challenges and the possibilities for real impact. The main objective is to rebuild a sense of efficacy. If the main challenge facing the international community today is responding to intrastate conflict, it must be demonstrated that human rights work is essential for prevention of crises and building a human rights culture once violence has occurred.

On prevention, the human rights community has begun to develop more effective strategies and monitoring methodologies to track discrimination and patterns of violence as they lead to full-scale conflict. These monitoring and policy efforts will become more sophisticated with time, but there is a breakdown between these new and appropriate methods and how we convey the role of grassroots activism. For individuals to be compelled to continue their traditional human rights activism they must be guided by the perception that their work is at the front line of sending out early warning signals. The idea that the work they do creates an imperative for international action has, by and large, been lost.

And as the world moves to focus on the complex roots of conflict, similarly it must be demonstrated that human rights violations are the window into patterns of discrimination. The tracking of violations amplifies the trends showing where there are shifts in political power between and among social forces and governments and their citizens. These shifts in power presage the full-scale crises that leave one of two options: military intervention or whole-scale genocide. Human rights activism and monitoring act as fire walls.

Another message that can be conveyed to the traditional base of the human rights movement and liberal peace and justice activists is that sustainable, postcrisis reconstruction demands the building of a human rights culture. To ensure that the backward slide into renewed violence does not occur, human rights activists must continue to remain vigilant in their efforts to focus international attention. A human rights culture requires accountability for violations, an effective and functioning rule of law, and the strengthening of civil society. Human rights activism is about capacity building, and again the strength of U.S. government commitment can be instrumental to the success of indigenous efforts at reconstruction. Human rights activism is also about ensuring U.S. resources for that capacity building and international pressure for accountability. The link between these goals and to foreign assistance is essential.

Target 2

A clear and solid strengthening of the traditional activist base of the human rights movement alone is probably inadequate to shape the contours of U.S. foreign policy in a global era. The perception of the lack of citizen concern is too great, the power of mobilized economic interests too determining. Can the human rights imperative once again capture the imagination of a broader public, drawing new supporters into the activist ranks and mobilizing others to vote with a rights agenda? Is there still a latent constituency for "liberal internationalism," and what messages can inspire its response to human rights crises and new patterns of violations? Hoffmann argues that a compelling case for a new liberal internationalism as the basis for foreign policy can be fostered. Human rights is at once the articulation of a common value system by which competing identities must be measured, it is the floor by which economic changes must be assessed, it is the gauge of success for efforts to broker peace and resolve disputes, and it is the only common imperative for international action that can withstand the test of a global civil society.[12]

The compelling logic of human rights in a global era is the hope of a new liberal internationalism. But is liberal internationalism the force that can mobilize a segment of the politically attentive public to engage in renewed human rights activism? Human rights NGOs have begun experimenting with new messages that resonate with their latent constituencies' concerns about the "new world order." Most of these messages evoke the need for international stability and dance within the fears of a mainstream society concerned that chaos equals a threat to American life that costs others lives. New messages also link human rights to the preventive dimension of conflict. For example, if action is taken in the early stages, then the decision for full-scale military intervention will never have to be made. No empirical tests have been made on the effectiveness of these messages for converting latent support to mobilization for political action.

In addition to developing new messages, human rights NGOs have also begun experimenting with new methods of organizing: at the places where people work and across communities of people with similar ethnic, racial, sexual, and gender-based identities. They are also attempting to link people according to specific issue concerns and regional orientations.[13]

New messages and methodologies are certainly essential to building a political constituency for human rights, but the chasm between compelling logic and organizing principles that effectively mobilize is huge. Even if we assume a real public concern for human rights and a commitment to seeing a strong U.S. role in the global arena, the challenge to converting a latent constituency into human rights activism is the one most troubling to human rights NGOs today.[14]

Target 3

One of the most lively and contentious debates in the human rights community today is whether the dramatic changes in the world both mandate and offer the possibility of forging a fundamentally different base for a grassroots human rights movement in the United States. Often, the debate itself reflects completely different underlying philosophical and ideological assumptions about the human rights framework and the scope of its application.

The transnational development of the human rights movement, coupled with the shift from military security to economic security as the defining characteristic of the global system, has brought a new salience to social and economic rights issues in the United States. For many years, human rights NGOs have tried to reach into diverse communities of social and economic justice activists in the United States to broaden the base of support for international solidarity work. More often than not, they were stymied both by those questioning the priority that should be attached to global concerns when there is profound injustice in the United States and by those questioning the place of social and economic rights in the advocacy of international human rights activism.

But the political and social terrain has shifted, creating a wide-open space for building connections through human rights language. Globalization demands new coordinated strategies. And community activists are looking for new organizing principles to link their struggles and offer a new face for a progressive movement. Whether brought together in preparation for UN World Conferences or born out of necessity, labor activists, women's rights advocates, housing, and welfare rights coalitions are beginning to use international standards in their education, outreach, and advocacy strategies. Local, community-based hearings have been held assessing the status of women and minorities using the international covenants on race and the rights of women as the standard of evaluation.

As one human rights activist is fond of saying, the traditional human rights organizations "risk becoming accidental tourists in their own movement."[15] With the spread of the networks associated with the Global Women's Movement and the power of the label that women's rights are human rights, with the growing use of the human rights language to describe hate crimes in the United States, and with new grassroots educational campaigns to draw community organizers together around the common theme of human rights, a new human rights movement *is* being built.

Whether this constituency can be mobilized equally around social and economic justice issues in the United States and genocidal conditions in sub-Saharan Africa remains to be seen. There can only be a positive gain in the efforts made to enhance American understanding of the human rights framework. But many in traditional human rights organizations express fear that the elasticization of human rights language will become the fad of the 1990s, legitimating any individual's or group's claim to self-entitlement. Will the American public come to associate human rights with the gripes of disenfranchised minorities, or will these new applications of international standards infuse new meaning, build new support, and result in the deepening of commitment for global activism among citizens who will claim the human rights framework for their own?

Increasingly, traditional human rights NGOs have responded to the explosion of interest and activity. They have expanded their monitoring and reports of abuses in the United States, ranging from police brutality to prison conditions to rape in custody. Similarly, much attention has been placed on grassroots educational campaigns, linking international principles of rights to domestic public policy debates.

It is too early to tell whether or not the move to define "your rights as human rights," taken together with efforts to revitalize the traditional base of the human rights movement, will be shaped into a new force with real political leverage over U.S. policy. The messages are still being tested, and the methods are still experimental. These efforts certainly seem to be appropriate responses to the challenges globalization has laid at the foot of human rights NGOs. Are they sufficient to sustain America's critical role in upholding the international system of rights, or will they further fragment efforts across disparate NGOs peddling uphill with little support or resources?

What is clear is that without renewed attention to the grassroots base of the movement and without creative strategies to build that base, a strong U.S. role in the world is unlikely to emerge. Without visionary political leadership, human rights activism is the essential ingredient to demand responsive policies, both globally and nationally.

It was citizen action that breathed life into the human rights framework, challenging the Cold War practices that had shaped the framework and the methods used to advance it. Grassroots movements utilized the instruments and called on the norms to erode the base of the Cold War and unleash the dynamic that brought down the repressive regimes and shook the foundation of the international system. Globalization is characterized by and was brought into being with grassroots action — transnational citizen action, demanding responsiveness to the human rights ideal and harnessing political power exponentially greater than that which could be generated subnationally. Yet today a new global paradox has emerged. Without the political imperative set by the grassroots campaign, human rights will be subsumed under the force of the global markets and the disaffection marked by increasingly parochial identities.

The new modern, human rights paradox is twofold for the human rights community. First, NGOs must lead to redefining, revitalizing, and breathing life into their historical base of citizen activism. And second, they must lay the gauntlet at the feet of today's international leaders: to develop new and visionary strategies to respond to the global paradigm shift or retreat into the parochialism and neo-isolationism of those that came before the human rights revolution.

Notes

1. See for instance, Samuel Huntington, *The Third Wave: Democratization in the Late 20th Century* (Norman: University of Oklahoma Press, 1991); Immanuel Wallerstein, *After Liberalism* (New York: New Press, 1995); Benjamin Barber, *Jihad Versus McWorld: How Globalism and Tribalism Are Reshaping the World* (New York: Ballantine Books, 1995); and Joel Kotkin, *Tribes: How Race, Religion, and Identity Determine Success in the New Global Economy* (New York: Random House, 1992).

2. E. Kaufmann, "The Relevance of the International Protection of Human Rights to Democratization and Peace," Occasional Paper Series, the Joan B. Kroc Institute for International Peace Studies, University of Notre Dame.

3. For the classic treatment on the subject of the erosion of state legitimacy, see Juergen Habermas, *The Legitimization Crises* (Boston: Beacon Press, 1975), and *Life World and System: A Critique of Functionalist Reason*, vol. 2 of *The Theory of Communicative Action* (Boston: Beacon Press, 1987).

4. Stanley Hoffmann, "The Crises of Liberal Internationalism," *Foreign Policy*, no. 98 (spring 1995): 159–179.

5. The case of John Shattuck, assistant secretary of state, bureau of democracy, human rights, and labor, is illustrative. After questioning U.S. policy toward Haiti, he was publicly sanctioned by Secretary of State Warren Christopher. Shattuck, a strong ally of the human rights community, has had many hard-fought battles within the administration, the most notable with regard to policy in the Bosnian conflict and over concerns for Haitian refugees.

6. For a sampling of the debate that occurred at the time of de-linking in 1994, see "Christopher Is Drawing Fire in Washington on China Visit," *New York Times*, March 18, 1994; "New Tack on China," *New York Times*, January 23, 1995; and "The Wolf and the Lamb," *New York Times*, November 18, 1995.

7. See the two chapters in this volume dealing the with the Middle East.

8. As of July 1995, the U.S. government had given $6 million in cash contributions and detailed twenty-five USG personnel full time to the tribunals. Interview with Secretary Shattuck by H. Gereostathos, July 6, 1995.

9. Some of these interviews were conducted in the summer of 1996 as primary research for this paper. Others were conducted as background information in the author's preparation for convening several policy conferences on the subject of the current state of the US human rights movement. And some of the cited information comes directly from discussions in conference sessions. As cited above, the proceedings of the conference were later published by the Stanley Foundation, the text of

which was solely the author's interpretation and reflected a compilation of primary research and conference discussions. Interviews from both 1994 and 1996 were undertaken with the understanding that there would be no individual attribution.

10. Amnesty International has witnessed a 25 percent drop in both its donor and activist membership base from 1990 to 1996. Other membership and grassroots organizations concerned with global affairs have witnessed similar shortfalls.

11. See Ellen Dorsey, "Human Rights and U.S. Foreign Policy: Who Controls the Agenda?," Strategy for Peace Conference, October 1993, a Stanley Foundation Report.

12. Hoffmann, "Crises."

13. Amnesty International has used to great effect a complex and comprehensive set of structures that links highly focused communities of activists nationally. But it has had greater difficulty in drawing an expanded constituency into these structures.

14. "An Emerging Consensus: A Study of American Public Opinion on America's Role in the World," Steven Kull and I. M. Destler, principle investigators, July 1996.

15. Loretta Ross, executive director, Center for Human Rights Education, Atlanta.

SECTION 2
Democracy Abroad

9

Democracy and U.S. Foreign Policy

•

Concepts and Complexities

•

JACK DONNELLY

Americans commonly see democracy and human rights as inextricably linked. For example, Secretary of State Warren Christopher argued at the 1993 Vienna World Human Rights Conference that "democracy is the best means not just to gain — but to guarantee — human rights," that "democracy will build safeguards for human rights in every nation." Americans also commonly view the political system established under their Constitution and Bill of Rights as the model for realizing these ideals. Without denying a link between human rights and democracy, I will emphasize their differences and argue that the failure to appreciate the complexities of their relationships has contributed to major failings in U.S. international human rights policies.

In many contemporary discussions, there is also an implicit assumption of historical inevitability. Democracy and human rights today seem almost natural, obvious, or necessary. Without denying the contemporary hegemony of these ideas, I will emphasize their historical particularity. A broad historical perspective reveals democracy and human rights to be exceptions rather than the rule and only contingently linked. This too, I will argue, has important implications for U.S. international human rights policy.

Democracy

THE DEMOCRATIC IDEA

The term democracy is derived from the ancient Greek *demokratia*, literally, rule (*kratos*) of the *demos*. Although most often (and properly) translated as "the people," the heavy class connotations of *demos* suggest that a more accurate rendering would be "the masses;" *hoi polloi*, literally, the many. Democracy, like aristocracy (rule of "the best"), was a form of class rule.

In the ancient world, the democratic classes advanced their claim to rule in a hostile social and political environment in which the inherent superiority of the wellborn was largely unquestioned (at least among the elite).[1] Members of the *demos* were generally seen, especially by the "best" elements of society, as not merely socially but also morally inferior, lacking in virtue (*arete*). Democratic rule thus rested on "lower," crass considerations; not quality or even equality, but the power of mere numbers.

Not surprisingly, then, democracy received little praise in the dominant traditions of Western political theory and practice of the ancient, medieval, and early modern periods. Rule by the many cannot be desirable when the few are seen as having important political virtues or skills largely inaccessible to the masses. For democracy to be attractive there must be an egalitarian political ethic, which did not become a regular part of mainstream political debate in the West until the eighteenth century. Praise of democracy is thus largely a nineteenth- and twentieth-century phenomenon.

Although Americans today unreflectively think of their polity as "democratic," this is not reflected in our founding political traditions. Most of the founding fathers looked to the *republican* ideal of self-government and citizen participation rather than the democratic idea of mass, egalitarian politics. Madison's argument in Federalist No. 10 for an extended republic is primarily a device to check the excesses and enthusiasms of mass (democratic) politics. Indirect election of the Senate was intended to add aristocratic checks to the more democratic House. Consider also the intense controversy over "Jacksonian democracy," where the very idea of democracy was at the core of the controversy. And although they are today merely historical artifacts, the names of our two principal political parties reflect a fundamental ambivalence toward democracy even in mid-nineteenth-century America.

Hard as it would be for most Americans to accept, one of the few major traditions of Western political thought to place democracy at the center of its political ideal has been Marxism. The dictatorship of the proletariat is explicitly class rule by the many; democracy in a strong, classical sense of the term. But with the proletariat conceived as a universal class whose (class) interests are those of society as a whole, the few over whom they would exercise dictatorial power, far from being the best elements of society, are seen as those who would tyrannize the many to achieve their selfish material interests. Although the fortunes of regimes that claim to represent such political ideals have declined precipitously, it would be a serious error to ignore either the historical power or the democratic credentials of the underlying ideas — and thus the possibility of deep conflict between human rights and democracy.[2]

Marxist conceptions are examples of the broader idea of substantive democracy. A substantively democratic regime is measured by its aims and outputs. "Democracy is a matter of the interests rule serves rather than of the procedures for selecting rulers."[3] The standard is whether goods, services, and real opportunities are enjoyed "democratically," that is, by the masses on an egalitarian basis. The people may or may not do the work of ruling, but they are beneficiaries of a regime that rules both in their name and in their interest.

Substantive democracy is typically contrasted to procedural democracy. Procedural democrats emphasize representative political institutions filled through fair and open periodic elections with universal suffrage. Such polities may or may not pursue egalitarian (substantively democratic) policies. Their democratic credentials rest on the people ruling, on the fact that the authority of the government derives from the sovereign choice of the people.

Regimes that claim to be substantively but not procedurally democratic would seem to face insurmountable practical problems, especially in the medium and long run, in sustaining plausibly democratic rule. For example, the claims of real-world Leninist/Stalinist regimes to be governments of and for the people (by a vanguard party) have not been believable. A relatively sophisticated Chinese defense of the Tienanmen massacre claimed that "the fact that our people become the actual masters of the state . . . cannot be denied."[4] Precisely because this claim is incredible, the democratic credentials of the regime do not stand up to scrutiny.

Nonetheless, the theoretical distinction is important, especially in light of the naive faith in elections common across much of the American political spectrum. In fact, because elections are not an end in themselves, procedural conceptions of democracy must rest on some underlying substantive values. Any set of allegedly democratic procedures thus can legitimately be subjected to a substantive "test." For example, to determine whether an election was really (substantively) fair and open, we can measure the outputs of the resulting government against an independent measure of the will or interests of the people. Jefferson's familiar formula can be used to draw a similar distinction. All democratic governments must be governments *of* the people. Some (procedural) conceptions of democracy, however, emphasize government *by* the people. Other (substantive) conceptions stress government *for* the people.

WHAT DEMOCRACY IS NOT

However we define democracy, it is essential that we not confuse it with particular practices or values that exist in many "democratic" polities. For example, democratic governments seek to realize the interests of the people. But most political systems claim to protect and foster the interests of the people. Aristocratic and royal governments often have claimed to act in the interest of all of society (the people, understood in the broadest sense of the term), including the masses (the people understood in class terms). Such systems, however, cannot be called democratic in any useful sense of the term. Democratic polities are those in which the people rule. The people must be sovereign, not merely the beneficiaries of the rule of others. Democracy is about who rules, not who benefits.

Consider also political participation. Most political systems provide some mechanism for the people to participate in government. For example, kings in medieval and early modern Europe often allowed (some) subjects to petition for redress of grievances. Riots and rebellions have been a important recurrent form of "irregular" political participation in many areas of the world. But popular participation alone does not make a regime democratic. The question is not whether the people participate but the grounds and mechanisms of their participation. In a democracy the people participate as a ruling power and by right of the fact that political authority derives from them.

Democracy must also be distinguished from limited government. Government may be limited in a great variety of ways: for example, tradition, divine injunction, moral code, constitution, statute, the threat of rebellion, or simple lack of capacity, none of which has any necessary connection with democracy. Quite the contrary, the only theoretical limit on democracies is the people's will — which in practice has often been vicious, intrusive, and intolerant. Thucydides's account of the revolutions in Corcyra, in which the victorious democrats devoted themselves to "butchering those of their fellow-citizens whom they regarded as their enemies" (III.81.4), and Socrates's execution by the newly restored Athenian democracy are classical examples. Consider also the aggressive intolerance of modern radical substantive democrats during the French Terror or the persecution and even extermination of class enemies in the Soviet and Chinese peoples' democracies.

The rule of law is another idea typically embodied in the practice of modern Western "democracies" that has no necessary relation to democracy in its root sense. The people may choose to rule through known standing laws, by direct decree, or by some other means. Conversely, the rule of law can be implemented in royal and oligarchic regimes. South Africa in the 1950s and 1960s is a good example of massive repression largely through the careful and "correct" use of (discriminatory) law.

It is too easy, for Americans in particular, to think that democracy means the way *we* do things. Even if one's polity is at its core democratic in some important sense of that term, there may be different political practices that are no less democratic. And any particular practice in that polity may have only a contingent connection to democracy, or even no connection at all. I will return to these points below.

Human Rights

Human rights are literally the rights one has simply because one is human. They are rights, entitlements in strict and strong sense. And because they rest only on one's humanity, they are universal, equal, and inalienable rights. They are held by all human beings, universally. One either is or is not human and thus has or does not have human rights, equally. And one cannot lose these rights, because one cannot stop being a human being.

As I have argued elsewhere, human rights thus understood rest on and seek to realize a particular conception of human nature, dignity, or flourishing.[5] Human beings are seen as equal and autonomous individuals. This gives them an irreducible worth that entitles them to equal concern and respect from the state and the opportunity to make choices about what constitutes the good life (for them), who they associate with, and how.

Such a conception of human dignity or flourishing is, in a broad cross-cultural and historical perspective, extremely unusual.[6] Although many cultures and societies across time and space have shared values such as equity, fairness, compassion, and respect for one's fellows, very few have sought to realize these values through equal and inalienable universal rights.

In most premodern societies, both Western and non-Western, persons were seen not as equal and autonomous individuals but as differentiated occupants of social roles defined by ascriptive characteristics such as birth, sex, age, and occupation. For example, ancient Greeks distinguished between Hellenes and barbarians (non-Greeks), who were seen as congenitally inferior. The Romans recognized rights based on birth, citizenship, and achievement, not mere humanity. Medieval Christians discriminated against Jews, infidels, and heretics and never seriously considered extending the idea of the equality of all believers into politics. The idea that shared humanity grounds basic social and political rights is almost completely absent from the mainstream of classical and medieval Western political theory, let alone practice.

The duties of premodern Western rulers to govern wisely and for the common good arose from divine commandment, natural law, tradition, or contingent political arrangements, not the rights of human beings to be ruled justly. In a well-ordered society the people were to benefit from the political obligations of the rulers. But they had no (human) rights that could be exercised against unjust rulers.[7]

Natural (human) rights entered the political mainstream in late seventeenth-century Europe (especially Britain) in response to the social disruptions and transformations of modernity. Political and economic centralization and the growing penetration of markets created (relatively) autonomous individuals and families in place of members of traditional local communities occupying ascriptive roles. These new modern individuals and families were left (relatively) alone to face both the growing coercive powers of ever more intrusive states and the new indignities of market capitalism. These same forces supported the political rise of the middle classes, who found in natural rights a powerful argument against aristocratic privilege.

Although early formulations reflected the class interests of their advocates — for example, Locke's list of natural rights includes only life, liberty, and estates, and he further restricts (natural) rights to propertied European males — the evolution of contemporary notions of internationally recognized human rights can be seen as an unfolding of the theoretical logic of human rights. In effect, racist, bourgeois patriarchs found the same natural rights arguments they had used against aristocratic privilege turned against them. The result has been a gradual expansion of the recognized subjects of human rights toward the ideal of including all members of the species on an equal basis.[8] Gender, race, property, and religion have been formally eliminated as legitimate grounds for denying the full enjoyment of natural or human rights in almost all realms of public life in nearly all Western countries. Sexual orientation and disability are increasingly contested grounds for discrimination.

As the range of subjects with recognized natural rights expanded, the substance of those rights underwent a parallel revision. For example, the political left argued that existing private property rights were incompatible with true liberty, equality, and security for working men (and, later, women). After much struggle, this led to social insurance schemes, regulations on working conditions, and an extended range of recognized economic and social rights, culminating in the welfare state societies of late twentieth-century Europe.

Social change and learning have also altered dominant human rights ideas and practices. The increasing reach and coercive capacity of the state have made protecting space for autonomous public and private action a growing priority. New legal rights have thus been recognized, and a greater emphasis has been placed on an expanded understanding of such rights as freedom of religion, expression, and association. The reshaping of families and communities by market forces has led to new mechanisms to assure subsistence and social welfare. New economic and social rights have also come from our growing recognition of the destructive unintended consequences of private property rights and a growing appreciation of alternative, rights-based means for realizing economic security and participation in a world of industrial capitalism.

The current culmination of this process has been the global codification of these rights in authoritative international documents such as the 1948 Universal Declaration of Human Rights and the 1966 International Human Rights Covenants. They represent the dominant contemporary international understanding of the minimum prerequisites for individual dignity, a life worthy of a human being.

Human rights, like democracy, must be distinguished from related ideas and practices. Values such as the rule of law, political participation, or social security are only human rights values if they are pursued through the equal and inalienable rights of all human beings. For example, protection against arbitrary execution is today recognized internationally as a human right. But the fact that people are not executed arbitrarily may reflect only a government's lack of desire or capacity. Even active protection against arbitrary execution may have nothing to do with a right not to be executed. For example, a divine injunction to rulers need not endow subjects with any rights. And a right not to be arbitrarily executed need not be a human right. It may, for example, be granted by the state or arise from one's social status.

Such distinctions are not mere scholastic niceties. When subjects lack a right (title), they are protected differently. There is an important difference between denying something to someone that it would *be* right for her to enjoy in a just world and denying her something she is entitled (*has* a right) to enjoy. Violations of rights are a particular kind of injustice, with a distinctive force and remedial logic.[9] Furthermore, whether the right is merely a legal right granted by the state or a human right will dramatically alter the relationship between states and subjects and the character of the injury suffered.

What the state owes to those it rules, and what subjects can legitimately demand from the state, are perennial questions of politics. Human rights, however, provide but one way of answering these questions. Divine right monarchy is another. The dictatorship of the proletariat, the principle of utility, aristocracy, theocracy, class, ethnicity, and gender provide still different answers. As with democracy, we must preserve a conceptually clear, historically distinctive, and theoretically strong conception of human rights. If human rights means whatever we take to be politically good and democracy whatever political system realizes that good, then "human rights" and "democracy" lose most of their analytical value.

The Liberal Democratic Welfare State

If democracy and human rights are such different bases of political organization, why are they so intimately linked in contemporary popular discourse? The answer lies in the liberal democratic welfare state, the hegemonic form of political organization in the contemporary world. This particular and contingent linkage of democratic and human rights ideas is mistaken as "natural" and essential. Furthermore, the tendency to refer to this form of government as "democracy" obscures the central place of human rights as a political ordering principle.

The very idea of human rights sets limits on the potentially legitimate forms of political regimes. Any substantive set of human rights limits the range of legitimate political choice. As Rhoda Howard and I have argued elsewhere, internationally recognized human rights envision a liberal democratic (or social democratic) welfare state.[10]

The legitimate state, as specified by internationally recognized human rights norms, is liberal: the state is seen as an institution to create the conditions needed to realize the rights of its citizens.[11] It is democratic: political authority arises from the sovereignty of the people. It is a welfare state: economic and social rights extend well beyond the right to property. And all three elements are rooted in the overriding and irreducible moral equality of all members of society and in the political equality and autonomy of all citizens.

This particular linkage of human rights and democracy arose in large measure from the impact of egalitarian human rights ideas on conceptions of "the people." Rather than a rabble separate from and inferior to the best elements of society, "the people" today are seen to encompass the whole of society. Locke's *Second Treatise* was seminal in establishing this link between democracy and human rights. The democratic core of Locke's theory is the controlling role he gives citizens in shaping state policies through the legislature. Its liberal core rests in a conception of politics and society that emphasizes the pursuit of interests by politically autonomous individuals, whose natural rights define a sphere of personal autonomy.

As I noted previously, Locke's own conceptions of both the subjects and the objects of human rights may appear to late twentieth-century eyes as undemocratic and illiberal. Nonetheless, today's Western European states, with their competitive electoral systems, robust civil societies, comprehensive social welfare systems, and extensive personal liberties, represent the fruits of long and difficult struggles to create societies that fuse liberal and democratic ideals in this "Lockean" fashion.[12] Precisely because this linkage is so pervasive today, it is essential to emphasize that democracy and human rights have very different, and often competing, theoretical and moral foundations.

Democracy answers the question who should rule. Furthermore, it rests on a fundamentally collectivist conception of politics. Democracy empowers the people and seeks to realize the collective good of the people.

Human rights addresses how governments should rule. And they ground an individualistic political ethic. Human rights empower the individual. They seek to assure that personal and societal goals are pursued within the confines of guaranteeing every individual certain minimum goods, services, and opportunities.

The rule of the people need not mean respect for the human rights of all people (citizens). Quite the contrary, "the people" often want to do some very nasty things to some of their "fellow" citizens, especially those they see as dangerously different. Thus in liberal democratic polities a (or the) principal function of human rights is to limit democratic decision making. Human rights prohibit the people from inflicting certain harms on any citizen. They also require the people to provide every citizen certain goods, services, and opportunities. Contemporary "democracies" are indeed limited governments. But they are limited by human rights, not by the will or the interest of the people.

Human rights ordinarily take precedence over the wishes of the people, no matter how intensely even the vast majority of society desires to harm some individual or group. Consider the standard complaint about American civil libertarians that they frustrate the will of the people. That is precisely the point of human rights in democratic societies — when the popular will targets basic rights. Human rights, especially when legally entrenched as constitutional rights, protect those who would be victimized by the majority. The politically weak or despised need their human rights as a practical political matter. The majority, and those with independent economic or political power, usually can protect themselves and pursue their interests without appealing to their human rights.

This mixed *liberal* democratic conception is reflected in the standard civics text formula "majority rule with minority rights." There is nothing distinctively "democratic" about minority rights. Quite the contrary, "minority rights" are prior and superior to the democratic rights of the majority. And since this "minority" is constantly shifting from issue to issue, the actual referent of "minority rights" is the individual human rights of every citizen. They define the range within which democratic decision making is allowed to operate.

But human rights also seem to demand (procedural) democracy. Rule of the people, understood as the whole of society, does seem almost "natural" when politics are built on a foundation of the equal and inalienable rights of all citizens. Although democracies need not protect a robust range of human rights, human rights would seem to demand a democratic polity.

The common label "liberal democracy" thus inverts adjective and noun. Contemporary Western liberal democracies are liberal states first. The rights of the citizenry provide the authority of the government and the standard by which its achievements are to be judged. The sovereignty of the people derives from the individual rights of each person. And the scope of democratic politics is defined by the human rights of every citizen.

Popular sovereignty, the idea that legitimate political authority derives from the people, today is rarely questioned. Democratic control over government is also taken for granted: legitimate government is assumed to be government of, for, and by the people. But "pure" democracy continues to be frowned on. Popular sovereignty and democratic control, as commonly understood today, are founded on human rights. The political ideal embodied in both theory and practice in contemporary Western Europe and North America is the liberal democratic welfare state, a type of regime that is primarily liberal (rights-based) and only derivatively democratic. This is the referent of "democracy" in many contemporary policy discussions.

In the rest of this chapter, I will try to show that a failure to understand the complexity of this hegemonic political ideal underlies some shortcomings in contemporary U.S. international human rights policy. In particular, I will argue that American policy has in several ways been undermined by inappropriate disaggregations of the liberal democratic ideal.

Human Rights, Democracy, and Cold War U.S. Foreign Policy

American failures in pursuing human rights and democracy abroad have been numerous and often tragic. Competing national interests, Cold War conceptions of national security, and plain disinterest have been at the root of most of these failures. Although not my principal concern here, we must start with these (all too familiar) factors. In this section, I will restrict myself to the Cold War era.

Electoral democracy was central to American Cold War rhetoric. Practice, however, was governed by material and ideological interests. The United States, other things being equal, probably preferred dealing with anticommunist regimes installed through fair and open elections. But anticommunism took undoubted priority over democratic elections. Client regimes regularly held elections marked by corruption, intimidation, and even outright fraud. And when the United States did not like the results of fair and open elections, as in Guatemala in 1954 or Chile in the early 1970s, it resorted to subversion and violent overthrow of the government.

A difficult to untangle mixture of cynical manipulation, incompetence, and wishful thinking underlay the often implausible, even ludicrous, claims of democratic credentials for repressive American "friends." To the extent that American rhetoric was merely convenient ideological cover, it was culpable but obviously not worth taking seriously. To the extent that it reflected a subordination of concern for democracy to competing ideological, security, and economic interests, it raised familiar problems of trade-offs between foreign policy objectives. Other than illustrating the low value American policy placed on democracy abroad, this dimension is not particularly interesting either. My concern here instead is with the way in which conceptual confusion contributed to some of these failures.

Consider U.S. policy toward Central America in the 1980s. Some support for the "democratic" credentials of repressive American allies was rooted in, or could draw cover from, misguided proceduralism. A standard refrain in the second Reagan administration's support for El Salvador and Guatemala, despite their deplorable human rights records, was that Presidents Duarte and Cerezo had been "freely elected." Even granting this claim — although the elections in El Salvador in 1984 and in Guatemala in 1986 were relatively fair, parties of the left were both formally and informally excluded in both countries — its force rests largely on two interrelated conceptual errors.

First, it assumes that elections are equivalent to "democratic" control of the state. But in El Salvador, and especially in Guatemala, the military was a semi-autonomous political actor. The Salvadoran and Guatemalan governments also had limited control over the social and political elites of their countries, as illustrated by the difficulties faced in land reform. The government held office, but did not fully rule; it was a well-positioned, but not clearly dominant, competitor for political authority and power. Furthermore, the party and electoral systems made the link between the will of the people and the outcome of elections unusually tenuous.

Second, the appeal to free elections rested on an implicit assumption that elections would eliminate the gross and persistent human rights violations that had made Central America a subject of such controversy in U.S. foreign policy. But in El Salvador in 1985, the year after Duarte's election, the government estimated that death squads were killing "only" about thirty people a month; Americas Watch put the number at five or six times that figure. Torture continued. The number of political prisoners even increased, apparently because of the decline in political murders. Things were as bad in Guatemala after the return of "elected civilian rule."[13]

These mistaken assumptions are rooted in disaggregations of the liberal democratic ideal. A part — elections — is mistaken as a sign of the whole. In El Salvador and Guatemala, elections had only a loose connection with respect for human rights. And this loose connection was not primarily due to flaws in the design or operation of the electoral process. Rather, it reflected the particular way elections were embedded in the social and political systems.

In Western liberal democracies, elections usually do set the terms for solving basic political conflicts. But they "solve" problems because they effectively convey authority and the power to rule. The respect of competing political actors and forces for the will of the people is essential to effective democracy. This respect simply was not present in El Salvador and Guatemala in the 1980s. And it is missing, to a greater or lesser extent, in many countries today.

Elected governments in established liberal democracies refrain from systematic direct political violence against their people. But this has less to do with elections than with separation of powers and a system of checks and balances. In El Salvador and Guatemala, however, the judiciary was completely subordinated to the executive, and the legislature was weak and ineffective. The only real political checks and balances were between elected officials and the military, which were effectively the two "branches" of government. In addition, tight controls on freedoms of speech, press, association, and assembly prevented popular control of the state by civil society.

Elections are central to "democratic" political life, as Americans use that term. They play a central role, however, only because of attitudes and institutions that assure that elected governments respect the sovereignty of the people and the rights of all citizens. In nearby Costa Rica, these supporting attitudes and institutions were present. In Guatemala and El Salvador they were not.[14] Therefore, elections simply could not "work their magic." In fact, it would have required magic for elections to have had the political effects the Reagan administration hoped for and claimed.

Conceptual confusion was not the principal source of American support for these quasi-democratic, rights-abusive regimes, as was illustrated by the Reagan administration's refusal to recognize the (no more defective) elections in Nicaragua in 1984. These policies, however, were facilitated by such confusions. At least some Americans who backed these governments did so (at least in part) because of a sincere overestimation of the significance and power of elections. At least some critics or potential critics, especially in the political "center," were (at least partly) disarmed by a mistaken faith in the transforming political power of elections.

U.S. appeals to substantive conceptions of democracy revealed very different conceptual problems. For example, electoral systems that exclude parties of the left might be defended as necessary to protect democracy from those who would impose dictatorship. The procedural ideal of fully open elections could be argued to be legitimately subordinated to the higher substantive goal of protecting a generally "democratic" system. An appeal to a substantive democracy — the true will and long-run interest of the people — was available, although hardly convincing, even in extreme cases such as Guatemala and Chile. The Kirkpatrick Doctrine was the most sustained official effort to press such arguments.

Much of this rhetoric was cynical. Rather than leftist dictatorial wolves in electoral sheep's clothing, right-wing American clients (for example, Marcos in the Philippines and Park in South Korea) dispensed with the constitution when their term of office expired. And claims that, say, Pinochet in Chile represented the popular will or interest would be laughable were the situation not so tragic.

Such arguments, however, are not implausible in the abstract. Procedural democracy is always subject to "testing" against a substantive conception of democracy or some other substantive standard (such as human rights). The problem was the nature of the test applied. Here too, inappropriate disaggregation of the liberal democratic ideal played a part.

Human rights, the liberal element of liberal democracy, were largely absent from this discourse. From the mid-1950s until the mid-1970s the language of human rights receded dramatically in American international rhetoric, replaced by freedom and democracy. Even after the return of the language of human rights to U.S. foreign policy, loose and ideological conceptions of freedom and democracy continued to be preferred when defending governments with suspect electoral credentials.

Once more, a part — a substantive conception of "democracy" — was mistaken for the whole. And selectivity in choosing that part attempted to obscure broader shortcomings in the practices of these American "friends." Seen in this light, the language of freedom, because of its vagueness, was particularly dangerous. (One might also speculate on the convenient linguistic link between "freedom" and "free elections.") Even more dangerous was anticommunism, which focused on a single negative attribute of liberal democracy, to the exclusion of all positive substantive standards and values.

El Salvador again provides a good example. This line of argument would suggest interpreting the debates of 1982 and 1983, when appeals to elections were not available, as a struggle between competing conceptions of democracy. The Reagan administration in effect advanced a disaggregated, minimalist understanding restricted to Kirkpatrick's tests of anticommunism and geopolitical support for the United States. Human rights advocates in effect advanced a more robust liberal democratic vision. They stressed elections and respect for civil and political rights. Their support for land reform and trade unions included a broader welfare component as well. The same competing tests — Cold War orientation versus elections, personal security and civil liberties, and welfare — framed the debate over Nicaragua.

Had the Reagan administration been forced to justify its policies in terms of a comprehensive liberal democratic model, its task would have been much more difficult. Only selective disaggregation allowed presenting the pursuit of ideological and security objectives as a defense of democracy. Interestingly, the greater moderation of the Reagan administration's second term coincided with a growing use of the language of human rights. The shift to a human rights justification reflected both political cleverness and the end of the worst of the killing in El Salvador and Guatemala. But adopting the language of human rights also reflected, and I would suggest contributed to, "better" (less bad) U.S. human rights policies.

Democratization and Human Rights in the Post–Cold War World

The end of the Cold War removed the corrupting influence of anticommunism from American international human rights policies. Now that Third World allies seem to matter very little, the (weak) American preference for democracy and human rights abroad has more space to express itself. The emergence of liberal democracy from a regional political ideal in the West to a position approaching global hegemony has also opened space.[15] This convergence of local desires with American preferences has encouraged a striking upsurge in initiatives that reflect a genuine commitment to human rights or democracy, and even a willingness to accept costs in their pursuit.

Consider, for example, UN-sponsored elections in Cambodia (and the preceding political transition); the restoration of Haiti's elected government; and humanitarian and political initiatives in Bosnia culminating in the Dayton agreements (and the ensuing work to implement them). At a more ordinary diplomatic level, consider American pressure on the military governments of Nigeria and Burma and quieter but fairly sustained efforts to prevent backsliding in countries as diverse as Peru, Albania, Thailand, and Kenya. Some economically or strategically important countries, such as North Korea, remain insulated from U.S. human rights pressures. In a growing number of cases, though, the United States has genuinely pursued its interests in human rights and democracy.

No less important, the worst of the pretense and convenient self-delusions discussed have receded. For example, Clinton's May 1994 announcement of his decision to delink human rights from most favored nation trading privileges for China made no pretense about the state of human rights or democracy in China: Clinton admitted that China had failed to meet even the limited human rights conditions he had laid down a year earlier. As did Bush before him, Clinton chose a strategy of active engagement rather than punitive sanctions and bowed to very substantial competing economic and security concerns.

But even when competing interests can be overcome, U.S. support for democracy and human rights abroad can be undermined by superficial understandings of the nature of these goals and the means necessary for their achievement. The following sections consider economic and social rights. In the remainder of this section, I will look briefly at democratization.

Many Americans have an optimistic, teleological view of democratization. They see the current "wave" of democratization as almost inescapable. There is a widespread belief that democratization, once commenced, unavoidably deepens (although not necessarily without temporary reverses).

Self-righteous satisfaction — we "won" the Cold War — underlies this view. So does the American belief in (and desire for) the political "quick fix." But so do conceptions of liberal democracy and the political process that sustain it.

Expectations of inescapable deepening fail to distinguish between liberalization, understood as increased tolerance for independent political activity, and democratization, understood as establishing a political system that reliably transfers authority and effective power through fair and open periodic elections. El Salvador and Guatemala illustrate the fact that although liberalization may increase the pressure for democratization, it is no guarantee. And electoral democracy, as noted previously, can be a long distance from a rights-protective liberal democratic polity.

Just getting the bad guys out, whether right-wing generals or Stalinist bureaucrats, is only a start. Abolishing the apparatus of a totalitarian police state or gaining control over national security institutions is only a beginning. One danger facing U.S. post–Cold War international human rights policy is the failure to appreciate just how much work remains to be done. A related danger is the failure to appreciate the changing nature of post–Cold War struggles for human rights. Consider Central America again.

After being elected in Nicaragua in 1990, President Violetta Chamorro tried, with some success, to heal the wounds of the contra war and restore the ravaged economy. In October 1996 Sandinista leader Daniel Ortega again ran for the presidency and lost again, this time to Arnoldo Aleman. The glib headline in The Economist was "Democracy 2, Sandinists 0."[16] But as the story went on to recount, this "victory" for democracy came at the cost of a vicious and polarizing electoral campaign. And while the enjoyment of basic economic rights by the poor stagnates or declines, Aleman seems much more concerned with restoring property nationalized during the revolution to its "rightful" owners (who supported his campaign).

Compared to Somoza's kleptocratic dictatorial rule, this is substantial progress. But the distance from the liberal democratic ideal, particularly in the areas of welfare and tolerance, remains great and troubling. And the situation in Nicaragua is probably equal to or slightly better than the Latin American average. Compared to much of Africa, where open and fair multiparty elections still are not the norm, Nicaraguan democratization seems well advanced.

In Guatemala issues of economic privilege and unequal power have begun to be addressed. But trade unions and peasant organizations remain under assault. The price of freedom of association today rarely is death. It may, however, be harassment; political opponents may bomb an office or beat up an activist with almost no risk of prosecution. For all the progress, underlying structures of domination and control have changed little. Guatemala thus remains a long way from even equal enjoyment of most basic civil and political liberties, let alone widespread enjoyment of economic and social rights and basic social equity.

The changing nature of the struggle for human rights in Guatemala and many other countries poses special problems for U.S. foreign policy. In the 1980s it was in many ways *relatively* "easy" for the United States to pursue its human rights concerns. When death squads and the army were massacring thousands, or even just assassinating dozens, the target was clear and the offense evoked a visceral response. But today's more subtle techniques of repressing, intimidating, and controlling those who would use their human rights to bring about real social change do not provoke such a response.

Human rights abuses in a country such as Guatemala have become more "ordinary." But the international community, and the United States in particular, has responded particularly ineffectively to such violations. Just as famine but not malnutrition provokes (relatively) strong international responses, torture and politicide provoke (relatively) strong responses, but more subtle violations of civil and political liberties do not. If suspending aid over mass murders was difficult, what chance is there of doing so, even now that the Cold War is over, because of nonlethal violence against peasant activists, or judicial corruption that protects the wealthy and powerful and denies justice to the poor and weak?

But even where motivation exists, neither public criticism nor reductions in foreign aid, the two principal instruments of U.S. Cold War international human rights policy, seems suited to these new realities. Verbal policies attempt to mobilize shame to undermine a country's reputation. But intimidating union activists just isn't shockingly shameful. Nor, sadly, is consigning a large proportion of one's citizens to a life of grinding, debilitating poverty. This may reflect a lack of political understanding or a tragic failure o moral imagination, but earlier progress has made the remaining tasks of international human rights policy more difficult by reducing the effectiveness of one of our major policy instruments.

Reducing foreign aid is also likely to miss the mark. What seems needed instead is more aid but of a different sort: for example, support for victimized groups and organizations. Such a strategy, however, would require long-term support of a slow and incremental human rights struggle, whereas U.S policy typically prefers the grand gesture of an electoral quick fix.

More generally, many of today's central human rights problems call for small-scale local strategies of positive support of progressive elements in society, rather than broad negative strategies of punishing governments.[17] The United States has not ignored such initiatives entirely. Consider, for example economic assistance to peasant cooperatives or efforts by the National Endowment for Democracy to foster understanding of the liberal democratic rules of the game in new political parties in countries without a civic culture of electoral politics. But the level of attention to such efforts has been low And the efforts have been curiously detached from broader American human rights diplomacy.

The picture is not quite as bleak as this account suggests. The Clinton administration's unwillingness to go to the mat for international human rights in some high-profile cases such as China has rightly drawn much attention But its record on a day to day basis, where Secretary of State Christopher's strength seemed to lie, has been somewhat better. More than in any previous administration, expressions of concern for human rights and electoral democracy have become a standard, and by all indications often a sincere and real part of U.S. diplomacy. But the gap between these aspirations and values and the policies and practices to realize them remains great.

The American public's lack of concern with this gap reflects preoccupation, disinterest, and an unwillingness to accept the costs of more effective action. I believe, however, that it also reflects a shallow understanding of the politics of implementing human rights and democracy. For example, Clinton's reference in his 1996 victory speech to the fact that for the first time in history more than half the world's population now lives in democracies reflects three problems that I have already identified. The count itself relies on a narrow proceduralism. The celebratory context and tone misleadingly suggest a continuing, triumphal march of democracy through the rest of the world. And the glib self-satisfaction suggests that the United States has been doing all that it should in support.

This latest American conceit is preferable to the active involvement in the brutal deprivation of the human rights of tens of millions of people that arose from anticommunism. Simplistic (mis)understandings of democracy are not all equally dangerous. But as Henry Shue so clearly reminded us, beyond duties not to deprive, human rights also impose duties to prevent deprivations and to aid victims.[18] Here U.S. policies continue to fall seriously short, in part, I have argued, because of failure to appreciate the richness and complexity of rights — protective liberal democratic rule. And these misunderstandings are particularly tragic, because they undermine U.S. foreign policy even when there is a real inclination, as has too rarely been the case, to act on the best of America's intentions.

Markets, Democracy, and Economic and Social Rights

The decline in the grossest abuses of civil and political rights, coupled with a resurgence of belief in the virtues of markets, has created space for greater attention to economic and social rights. American policy, however, has failed to meet these new human rights opportunities and challenges because of deeply rooted ideas about human rights and their relationship to markets. In this section I will focus on American divergences from international human rights standards and their underlying liberal democratic political model. The following section addresses inconsistency between U.S. national and international policies toward economic and social rights.

The United States regularly, and loudly, presents itself as a champion of the universality of human rights. In fact, however, the U.S. operates both nationally and internationally with a narrow, idiosyncratic conception that systematically denigrates economic and social rights. Perhaps the clearest evidence of the stunning deviance of the American position is the fact that of the 144 parties to the International Covenant on Civil and Political Rights the United States is one of a handful that is not also a party to the International Covenant on Economic, Social and Cultural Rights.

Other Western liberal democracies strive to take seriously the UN formula of the interdependence and indivisibility of civil and political and economic, social, and cultural rights.[19] The United States, by contrast, has avoided even talk of interdependence and indivisibility — except in attacks on its Cold War adversaries for denigrating civil and political rights. And American practice systematically denigrates economic and social rights.

At least half a million Americans, and perhaps several times that number are homeless. Twenty-five or thirty million lack access to nonemergency health care — and the issue is of such low priority that the numbers can be estimated only give or take a few million people. Some areas have infant mortality rates characteristic of countries with a per capita income one-tenth that of the United States. Recent welfare "reform" legislation even intends to refuse food to starving people who have received public assistance for more than a fixed period, as well as to aliens, and even legal immigrants who have not yet qualified for or have become citizens.

The most prominent international manifestation of the American disregard for economic and social rights has been its aggressive support for structural adjustment programs in the Third World and the former Soviet bloc. The sad state of command economies in these areas certainly supports a strong preference for more market-oriented economies. But the reforms demanded by the United States–led International Monetary Fund typically require dismantling social programs, such as food subsidies, that help the poor and vulnerable. People whose governments in the 1970s and 1980s told them that they could not enjoy civil and political rights because of the demands o development are now being told by international financial institutions that development requires that they sacrifice their economic and social rights.

This American tolerance of massive preventable suffering at home and abroad is tied to a refusal to see such suffering as a matter of human rights. The United States professes to see no human rights problem if people are "merely" dying, disabled, or maimed by readily preventable diseases, starving, malnourished, or hungry, without access to clean water or sanitation uneducated, unemployed, or living under a sheet of salvaged plastic. Such suffering is lamentable but a matter for private charity and public development assistance — an issue of compassion, not rights and obligations.

This illustrates a general theoretical point noted above: the difference it makes when a value or objective is conceived of in terms of (human) rights. People suffering in this way are considered "disadvantaged;" in an older (no longer politically correct) idiom, "poor unfortunates." But in the dominant American view, their plight is *merely* unfortunate. They are not entitled to something better. Because they may only ask for assistance, not claim or demand it, political tolerance of their continued suffering is facilitated.

Homelessness, for example, in the dominant American view reflects a failure to live up to high moral ideals. But that is all. Should the state fail to intervene if someone is prohibited from obtaining a place to live because she is black, female, or Muslim, Americans see this as a serious and culpable failure that involves the special harm of not protecting basic human rights. But if that same person cannot obtain a place to live because of economic misfortune, Americans see no political obligation to intervene. The homeless are victims of "circumstances." They suffer no harm from the state.

These attitudes are rooted in distinctively American views of the relationship between markets, personal worth, and individual rights. The high value Americans place on economic achievement often verges on equating a person's material wealth and moral worth. Particularly problematic from a human rights perspective is the moral suspicion of those who do not "make it" on their own.

Markets, for all the American bravado about individual initiative, ground a collectivist, "utilitarian" political theory. Similar to (pure) democracy, (free) markets are justified by arguments of collective good and aggregate benefit, not individual rights (other than, perhaps, the right to economic accumulation). Markets foster efficiency, not social equity or the enjoyment of individual rights *for all*. Markets simply are not designed to ensure that everyone is treated with a certain degree of economic concern and respect. Quite the contrary, when left alone markets systematically deprive some individuals to achieve the collective benefits of efficiency.

Efficient markets produce economic growth, an increase in the total supply of goods and services available within an economy. But markets will *necessarily* distribute that growth unequally and without regard for individual needs, interests, and rights. The sole basis of market distributions is contribution to economic value added, which varies sharply and systematically across individuals and social groups. The poor tend to be "less efficient;" that is, as a class, they have fewer of the skills valued highly by markets.

A large gap between rich and poor is inherent in capitalist market systems. Market economies allow, and even foster, social mobility. But this only changes the identities of the privileged and the deprived. The weakest suffer systematic relative deprivation. In the short and medium run, they may even become absolutely worse off as the economy grows all around them.

All this is well known, despite the inattention it receives from most contemporary market advocates. It is one of the underlying reasons for the government controls that are now being dismantled across the globe. And in

Western liberal democracies, the need to compensate those who fare less well in the market is a central justification for the welfare state.

Individuals who are harmed by the operation of social institutions that benefit the whole — markets and private property rights — have a *right* to a fair share of the social product their participation helped to produce. If markets produce more for all, the collectivity that benefits has an obligation to look after individual members who are disadvantaged in or harmed by those markets. The welfare state is a device to assure that *every* individual is guaranteed certain economic and social goods, services, and opportunities irrespective of the market value of their labor.

Advocates of market reforms admit that some are harmed in the pursuit of collective gain. But, they argue, everyone benefits in the long run from the greater supply of goods and services. "Everyone," however, does not mean every individual. The referent is the *average* individual, an abstract collective entity. And even "he" is assured of significant gain only at some point in the future. In the here and now, and the near future, many real, flesh and blood individual human beings and families suffer.

Market-oriented reforms simply are *not* Pareto optimal. Efficient markets improve the lot of some (ideally the many) only at the cost of increased suffering by others. And that suffering is concentrated among society's weakest, poorest, and most vulnerable elements.

Even more troubling, those who suffer now have no reason to expect full recompense in the long run. Markets distribute the long-term collective benefits of growth entirely without regard to short-term deprivations. Those who suffer "adjustment costs" — the loss of a job, higher food prices, reduced pensions, worse or no healthcare or education — do not acquire any special claim to a share of the collective benefits that efficient markets produce. One's "fair share" is a function solely of efficiency, of monetary value added. The human value of suffering, the human costs of deprivation, and the claims they justify do not enter the accounting of markets.

Assuaging short-term suffering and assuring long-term recompense are the work of the state, not the market. These are matters of justice, rights, and obligations, not efficiency. They raise issues of individual rights. Markets simply cannot address them — because they are not designed to.

I do not want to belittle the problems faced in implementing economic and social rights. Nor would I deny that efficient markets may provide a foundation for implementing economic and social rights. But markets alone annot achieve that goal. To use a slightly different metaphor, markets may provide the bricks, but the welfare state assures that everyone has a house.

I do not even want to deny the possibility of tragic choices between growth and equity. The economic success of Taiwan and Korea while pursuing aggressive policies to implement economic and social rights (especially in education, health, housing, farm income, and rural social services) suggests to me more choice than necessity in these trade-offs. But even where victims of market-driven growth truly cannot be prevented (at a reasonable cost), they must be acknowledged and mourned. This is almost completely absent from American foreign policy. In their enthusiasm for sweeping away the old, Americans seems not to see, let alone be troubled by, the problems in the new — an attitude with eerie similarities to Reagan-era attitudes toward the homeless.

There is a disturbing parallel with Cold War anticommunism. Excessive focus on the "problem" (communism; command economies) yields inattention to the "unintended" consequences of the "solution" (dictators; markets). And detached from the political vision that justified the initial critique, these "solutions" often become inconsistent with that vision. Similar to yesterday's anticommunist political arguments, today's antigovernment economic arguments too easily lose sight of, and even become a threat to, individual rights.

Free markets are an economic analog to a political system of majority rule without minority rights. The welfare state, from this perspective, is a device to assure that a minority that is disadvantaged in or deprived by markets still is treated with minimum economic concern and respect. And because this minority is shifting and indeterminate — much like the minority that would engage in unpopular political speech or be subject to arbitrary arrest — these "minority rights" are actually individual rights for all. We hold them not because we are members of a "minority group" but simply because we are human (or, somewhat more precisely, citizens).

If human rights are what civilizes democracy, the welfare state is what civilizes markets. If civil and political rights keep democracy within proper limits, economic and social rights set the proper limits of markets. Free market, similar to pure democracy, sacrifices individuals and their rights to a "higher" collective good. Only when the pursuit of prosperity is tamed by economic and social rights — when markets are embedded in a welfare state — does a political economy merit our respect.

"To get rich is glorious." These words of the butchers of Beijing are perilously close to the social and economic policies that the United States presses on others and practices at home. Such shameless flouting of international human rights norms, leading to the pursuit of prosperity without concern for the victims of that pursuit, cannot but weaken American international human rights policies.

Human Rights versus Market Democracy

Other major economic powers also support structural adjustment. Therefore, one might suggest that the deeper international policy problem is double standards: one for home (at least in the case of the other OECD [Organization for Economic Co-Operation and Development] countries) and one for abroad. In this light, there may even be a certain respectability to the consistency of the United States position; it appears principled in an important sense of that term. This apparent consistency, however, rests largely on a one-sided view of the American welfare state. A more nuanced picture reveals deep inconsistency between American national and international policies toward economic and social rights.

For all the gaps in its coverage, the United States has a sizable welfare state. A substantial portion of the working population is covered by unemployment and worker's compensation insurance. Health and safety regulations, both in and outside the workplace, are extensive. Primary and secondary education are free and compulsory. And market distributions are treated only as a starting point for substantial state redistributions. Social security is nearly universal. Millions of Americans receive food subsidies. The disabled are eligible for government assistance. There are large programs of housing subsidies, job training, and cash assistance to the destitute. More than one-third of total American health care spending is by the government.

From this angle, the American problem with economic and social rights is an excessive preference to realize them through civil society — George Bush's thousand points of light — and the family. Health care is provided primarily through employers. Care for the aged and infirm is seen primarily as the responsibility of families. The needy should be assisted wherever possible by churches and private charities. The state is only a provider of last resort. Government, Americans feel, should provide a safety net, not a security blanket.

In practice, the American safety net is not merely tattered but torn. I think that there are serious factual and analytical problems with associated argu ments about individual initiative and other alleged virtues of keeping the government as far as possible outside society and the economy. Furthermore, most proponents of such arguments adopt logically inconsistent positions in other areas of economic and social rights, most notably social security and Medicare, which provide blanket, rather than safety, net coverage. But even in this kinder and gentler account, the United States is a liberal democratic *welfare* state, and a massive one at that. For example, workers and employers are taxed almost one sixth of an employee's salary to cover old age and disability pensions. Education drives taxation in most municipalities and, along with police and fire services, is a central function of most local governments.

Despite the corruption of the language of welfare in American political discourse and a reticence to speak of economic and social rights, Americans see their welfare state as essential to a decent life and part of what makes their government worthy of respect. Even the moral legitimacy of the American government today rests in part on the safety net. Although it may come relatively far down on the list of immediate American priorities, the welfare state is an essential part of the contemporary American political ideal.

In American foreign policy, however, all one hears about is markets. Yet it is hard to see any good justification for discouraging others, through a combination of bilateral and multilateral policies, from pursuing the sorts of protections that Americans at home see as a matter of basic decency.

Consider the new buzz term "market democracy." For example, National Security Advisor Anthony Lake has even argued that "the successor to a doctrine of containment must be a strategy of enlargement — enlargement of the world's free community of market democracies." [20] Notice again the disaggregation of the ideal of the liberal democratic welfare state. Not only are human rights left out of the rhetoric, but markets are separated from their welfare state context.

Markets are indeed central to the welfare state political economy. But what distinguishes twentieth-century liberal democracies from "classical liberalism" or "free market capitalism" is their redistributive policies aimed at protecting individual rights and achieving social justice. The language of market democracy is simply inconsistent with the liberal democratic ideal, because it leaves out the central redistributive role of the welfare state demanded by individual human rights.

Consider the right of everyone to "a standard of living adequate for the health and well-being of himself and his family, including food, clothing, housing and medical care" (Universal Declaration of Human Rights, Article 25). As with other human rights, this sets minimum standards; to use still another housing metaphor, a floor beneath which none must be allowed to fall. The proper role of the market is to distribute resources above this floor. The proper role of the (welfare) state is to guarantee that no one falls through, let alone becomes trapped under, the floor.

Efficient markets may leave more to be distributed in the upper stories. Efficient markets may even be essential to producing enough to allow the floor to be repaired, or even raised over time. These are important tasks. But so is the state's task of guaranteeing a social minimum to every person, assuring that everyone has a firm and decent place to stand. And it is only the particular combination of market and state that produces the welfare state political economy that meets international human rights standards and is worthy of contemporary respect and emulation.

"Market democracy" once more mistakes part of the liberal democratic ideal for the whole, with consequences that for some are, literally, deadly. Markets, similar to elections, are a means, not an end. Both must be evaluated by their contribution to realizing human rights. The language of market democracy, however, removes them from the liberal democratic context that gives them their value.

The conceptual problems I have focused on here, as I noted several times, probably are not the most important shortcomings in American international human rights policy. Even "market democracy" can be read as pointing to the priority of competing interests: market economies as trading partners and electoral democracies as peaceful neighbors. Nonetheless, I think that I have shown that the failure to grasp clearly the multiple dimensions of the liberal democratic ideal, and the complexity of the task of implementing it, has contributed to failings of American policy. And it seems set to continue to bedevil even the best of American intentions.

Notes

1. For a good, brief introduction to this value system, see A. W. H. Adkins, *Moral Values and Political Behavior in Ancient Greece: From Homer to the End of the Fifth Century* (New York: W. W. Norton, 1972).

2. The failings of actual communist party-state regimes were practical, not theoretical, in a way similar to that in which many ostensibly procedurally democratic regimes have been little more than covers for elite domination. Marxist theory, in

sharp contrast to most other Western traditions of political thought, is radically democratic. For a useful discussion, which also considers related human rights issues, see Joseph V. Femia, *Marxism and Democracy* (Oxford: Clarendon Press, 1993). See also Alan Gilbert, *Democratic Individuality* (Oxford: Oxford University Press, 1990). Francis J. Kase, *People's Democracy: A Contribution to the Study of the Communist Theory of State and Revolution* (Leyden: A. W. Sijthoff, 1968) provides a relatively neutral discussion of the ideological basis of people's democracy.

3. This quote is from Andrew J. Nathan, describing the official Chinese conception, in "Sources of Chinese Rights Thinking," in *Human Rights in Contemporary China*, ed. R. Randle Edwards, Louis Henkin, and Andrew J. Nathan (New York: Columbia University Press, 1986), 146.

4. Zhang Lin, "What Kind of Democracy Do We Need?" *World Affairs* 152, 3 (winter 1989–90): 168.

5. Jack Donnelly, *Universal Human Rights in Theory and Practice* (Ithaca: Cornell University Press, 1989), 18–19 and pt. 2.

6. For extended and extensively illustrated arguments to this conclusion, focusing on non-Western societies, see Donnelly, *Universal Human Rights*, chs. 3 and 8; Rhoda E. Howard, *Human Rights in Commonwealth Africa* (Totowa NJ: Rowman and Littlefield, 1986), ch. 2; and Jack Donnelly, "Human Rights and Asian Values." For ease of exposition, and to further emphasize the contingency of human rights, the examples used below (as with the examples on democracy above) will be Western.

7. For an extended argument to this conclusion in the case of Aquinas, see Jack Donnelly, "Natural Law and Right in Aquinas' Political Thought," *Western Political Quarterly* 33 (December 1980): 520–535.

8. The principal exceptions today, beyond the persistence in practice of discrimination on already outlawed grounds, are age (children) and nationality (aliens).

9. For a more extended discussion of the special character of rights-based protections, see Donnelly, *Universal Human Rights*, 9–16. See also Joel Feinberg, "The Nature and Value of Rights," *Journal of Value Inquiry* 4 (1970): 243–251, reprinted in Morton E. Winston, *The Philosophy of Human Rights* (Belmont CA: Wadsworth, 1989).

10. Rhoda E. Howard and Jack Donnelly, "Human Rights, Human Dignity, and Political Regimes," *American Political Science Review* 80 (September 1986): 801–817, reprinted in Donnelly, *Universal Human Rights*, ch. 4. Compare also Jack Donnelly and Rhoda E. Howard, "Assessing National Human Rights Performance: A Theoretical Framework," *Human Rights Quarterly* 10 (May 1988): 214–248.

11. My conception of "liberalism" is very close to that outlined in Ronald Dworkin, *A Matter of Principle* (Cambridge: Harvard University Press, 1985), ch. 8. The heart of political liberalism, as I am using that term, is the view that the principal task of government is to realize the (natural or human) rights of its citizens. *Economic* liberalism, understood either as a theory emphasizing the virtues of markets or a the-

ory that restricts economic and social rights to the right to private property, has no necessary theoretical connection with political liberalism thus understood. In fact, most "classic" nineteenth-century British liberals were utilitarians and thus justified political decisions on the basis of a collective good (social utility) rather than on individual rights.

12. For a more extended argument for the Lockean pedigree of contemporary liberal democratic welfare state, see Donnelly, *Universal Human Rights*, ch. 5.

13. For a brief overview of the human rights situation in the region, with an emphasis on El Salvador and Nicaragua, see Jack Donnelly, *International Human Rights* (Boulder CO: Westview Press, 1993), 105–110. The U.S. response is reviewed on pp. 110–117.

14. For an account of Costa Rica's difference from Guatemala, emphasizing its control over the security forces, inclusionary social ideology, and political framework of compromise, see Hilde Hey, *Gross Human Rights Violations: A Search for Causes* (The Hague: Martinus Nijhoff, 1995).

15. The principal exception to this rule, namely, the recent growth of arguments asserting a distinctive set of Asian values that justify or require systematic deviations from international human rights norms, is only a partial exception. These arguments were decisively defeated at the 1993 Vienna World Conference on Human Rights. And at the Bangkok preparatory meeting, where they received their most sustained multilateral expression, they were strongly challenged by Asian states such as Japan and South Korea. The resulting Bangkok Declaration is thus marked by a diplomatic compromise that reflects a fundamentally incoherent combination of universalist and relativist positions.

16. *The Economist* 341 (October 26, 1996): 54.

17. There is, however, the danger of backing away from negative sanctions without aggressively pursuing more positive initiatives. There is an analogy here with the Reagan administrations' practice of constructive engagement with South Africa, where Carter-era criticisms were muted and sanctions eased, but only symbolic or token steps were taken to utilize other channels of influence.

18. Henry Shue, *Basic Rights: Subsistence, Affluence and U.S. Foreign Policy* (Princeton: Princeton University Press, 1980), 52–60.

19. See, for example, paragraph 5 of the Vienna Declaration and Programme of Action of the 1993 World Human Rights Conference.

20. Speech at Johns Hopkins University, September 21, 1993, quoted in David M. Lampton, "America's China Policy in the Age of the Finance Minister: Clinton Ends Linkage," *China Quarterly* (1994): 615.

10

U.S. Foreign Policy, Democracy, and Human Rights

•

Barriers to Action in the Middle East

•

STEPHEN ZUNES

Human rights violations by foreign governments and their lack of democratic institutions generally get the most attention in the United States when a given administration has called attention to such situations to mobilize domestic and international opinion in support of a U.S. policy against such governments. However, every administration in recent years has also had to address, at least to some degree, the less expedient phenomenon of public and Congressional pressure regarding the lack of democracy and human rights in allied countries. Oftentimes, such official responses would constitute little more than lip service and damage control, but — since the 1970s — it has been difficult to ignore completely. Most of the pressure has stemmed from grassroots movements, sometimes amplified by sympathetic segments of the media and members of Congress. The resulting debates have covered world regions ranging from East and Southeast Asia, to Eastern Europe, to Latin America, and to Africa, and have been particularly vehement regarding regimes that directly receive arms and foreign assistance from the U.S. government. However, human rights in the Middle East — the area that receives the largest amount of American arms and foreign aid — has been notably absent from the public debate. Not only has there been mostly silence from traditional human rights advocates in Congress, but there has not been much in the way of grassroots pressure, either. This relatively docile response is particularly striking, because a large majority of countries in that region lack democratic institutions and engage in a pattern of gross and systematic human rights violations. In addition, three major recipients of U.S. aid — Morocco, Israel, and Turkey — have conquered parts of neighboring countries by force, engaged in ethnic cleansing, and continue to subjugate the population of these occupied territories in defiance of the Geneva Convention and the United Nations.

In other parts of the world, the United States has insisted that competitive elections and other legal structures were an adequate indicator of democracy.[1] The Middle East is more problematic, however, because some of America's closest allies are absolute monarchies without even the pretense of democratic institutions. As a result, successive administrations and the media have frequently labeled such governments as "moderate," even if there was nothing particularly moderate in their level of despotism. The term is used primarily in reference to governments that have been relatively friendly to the United States and its foreign policy goals in the Middle East; there is virtually no correlation with their record on democracy and human rights.

In any case, Western-style elections are not as important a test for freedom as is a just and equitable social and economic system, which is a rarity in the Middle East. Most Middle Eastern states have elections, but they are usually formalities, the primary purpose of which is to ratify the existing leadership. The monarchies of the Gulf, which generally eschew any kind of formal elections, traditionally maintained legitimacy through the majlis system, providing for the direct petitioning of grievances. In addition, monarchical succession was not automatic to the eldest son or any single member of the royal family; the successor was chosen by a consensus of tribal elders based on his qualifications. The British helped ossify the sheikly system to a largely inherited position, which — with American assistance in subsequent years — has led to the evolution of several Middle Eastern monarchies to resemble less these relatively open traditional governing structures to models more closely resembling modern bureaucratic authoritarianism.[2] As a result, human rights abuses by these regimes are mostly on the increase, and their legitimacy is being challenged to a growing degree from within.

As with other parts of the world, the U.S. government will often cover up for the abuses of its allies and exaggerate the abuses of its adversaries. To cite some recent examples: in the State Department's annual human rights report, the description of the Sultanate of Oman was changed, as a result of pressure from superiors, to downplay the authoritarian nature of the monarchy.[3] The State Department has allowed Israeli officials to review and edit its human rights report on Israeli practices in the occupied territories prior to publication, substantially toning down the original remarks.[4] There have been efforts by U.S. officials to block articles in American publications critical of Saudi Arabia's lack of freedoms. Iraq's lack of democracy and human rights was downplayed during its invasion of Iran and subsequent war only to be raised to prominence after its invasion of Kuwait.

One of the more striking examples of the Clinton's administration's lack of concern for human rights regards the Universal Declaration of Human Rights, which is recognized in U.S. courts (and elsewhere) as "customary international law" and as the authoritative definition of standards of human rights. For example, Article 13 of the Universal Declaration, perhaps the most famous part of the declaration, guarantees the right of everyone to leave and return to their own country. The Clinton administration, in a break with previous administrations, no longer supports its application, such as in UN General Assembly Resolution 194 guaranteeing the return of Palestinian refugees (or compensation if they refused return). Even before the United States reversed its stance, American officials rarely mentioned it, emphasizing only the first part (the right to leave) regarding Soviet Jews or other victims of oppression in communist countries while not mentioning, and even notably omitting when it involved allied governments, the right of return.[5]

Double standards are rampant as well. Iraqi repression of its Kurdish minority has been condemned by U.S. officials — at least since the 1990 Iraqi invasion of Kuwait — while, just to the north, Turkish repression of its Kurdish minority has been defended. Strict enforcement of reactionary interpretations of Islamic law in Iran are condemned as human rights violations, while even more draconian measures in the name of Islam taking place in Saudi Arabia are rationalized as inherently part of its culture and should therefore not be subjected to criticism. Kuwaiti Arabs, it is argued, have the right to national self-determination, but Palestinian Arabs or Sahrawi Arabs do not. Martial law in NATO ally Turkey during the 1980s was justifiable, according to U.S. officials, while martial law in the Warsaw Pact nation of Poland during that same period was not. Such hypocrisy is not unique to U.S. policy toward the Middle East nor to the foreign policy of virtually any government. What makes the Middle East stand out is that, while such official American rationalizations for allies and such double standards are at least sometimes challenged in op-ed columns, in academia, and in the halls of Congress, they generally do not get as much attention when they involve Middle Eastern countries.[6]

Over the past decade, the United States — once tolerant and even supportive of dictatorial rule in much of the world — has come to encourage at least some trappings of democracy in many countries. Although this may come less from greater moral sensitivity on the part of American leaders as it does from a realization that at least limited democracy is a more stabilizing force that can encourage greater global economic liberalization, this still marks a shift from the height of the Cold War. In some countries the human rights situation has improved only marginally — and social and economic rights have, in many cases, actually declined — but the United States in recent years has at times played a progressive role in ways that were previously unthinkable. Once again, however, there has not been such a shift when it comes to the Middle East.

Rather than encourage democratization in the Middle East, the United States has reduced — or maintained at low levels — its economic, military, and diplomatic support to Arab countries that have experienced substantial liberalization in recent years while increasing support for dictatorial regimes such as Saudi Arabia, Kuwait, and Morocco. Indeed, the Saudis — recipients of billions of dollars worth of armaments from the United States and the hosts of thousands of U.S. troops dispatched to keep the regime in power — have shown outright hostility regarding democratic trends in neighboring Yemen as well as toward the exiled democratic opposition to Saddam Hussein's regime in Iraq, without apparent U.S. objections. Similarly, Jordan received large-scale U.S. support in the 1970s and 1980s despite widespread repression and authoritarian rule. Now that Jordan has become, arguably, the most democratic country in the Arab world, with a relatively free press, opposition political parties, and lively debate in a parliament that wields real political power, the United States has substantially reduced — and, for a time, suspended — foreign aid.[7] Aid to Yemen was cut off within months of the newly unified country's first democratic election in 1990.[8] U.S. aid to Israel has often increased as the Israeli government's repression in the occupied territories has also increased.[9] In addition, American occupation forces failed to stop widespread repression, even lynchings, of Palestinian residents of Kuwait immediately after liberation from Iraq.[10] Aid to Morocco increased as that country's repression in occupied Western Sahara and even within Morocco itself continued unabated.[11] The United States largely welcomed the 1992 military coup in Algeria, which nullified that country's first democratic elections.[12] The United States has pressed Syria, an authoritarian government undergoing some gradual liberalization, to crack down even harder on left-wing Palestinian groups based in Damascus critical of the U.S.-led peace process. The Clinton administration has also pressured the Palestine National Authority to engage in active suppression against both Islamic and secular opposition groups within areas of their administrative jurisdiction.

The Clinton administration has also defended and aided dictatorial regimes in the Central Asian republics of the former Soviet Union, some under the same authoritarian leaders who were in charge under Communism.[13] The message to Middle Eastern countries appears to be that democracy is not important to the United States.

Given this record, it becomes all the more striking that U.S. policy in the region, which is often at odds with efforts toward greater democracy and human rights, has not become a more pressing issue of political debate and why it has not been given the same sense of priority by advocates of democracy and human rights as have other regions. The major reasons appear to be threefold: the strategic importance of the region, prejudicial attitudes toward the religion and culture of the Middle East, and the ideological divisions stemming from the Arab-Israeli conflict.

Strategic Importance

Among American policymakers, there is widespread bipartisan agreement on the strategic importance of Middle Eastern allies of the United States, a direct consequence of the strategic importance of the region as a whole. For more than four thousand years, the Middle East has been contested by competing great powers. As the intersection of three continents and the source of most of the world's petroleum reserves, there is perhaps no region that the United States considers more important. The State Department has described the Middle East as "a stupendous source of strategic power, and one of the greatest material prizes in world history, . . . probably the richest economic prize in the world in the field of foreign investment."[14] President Dwight Eisenhower described the Middle East as the most "strategically important area in the world."[15] U.S. officials are no longer concerned that the region might fall to Soviet influence, yet the United States has also had a longstanding concern about the influence of indigenous movements that could also challenge U.S. interests. There is an ongoing perceived threat from radical secular or radical Islamic forces, as well as concern over the instability that could result from any major challenges to the rule of pro-Western regimes, even if led by potentially democratic movements.[16] This has led to a policy in which the United States has generally supported maintaining the status quo regardless of a given regime's lack of commitment to democracy or human rights.

Indeed, attention to human rights by successive American administrations has always been relative to the perceived strategic importance of the country in question; Middle Eastern countries have always been considered of great strategic value.

Israel is perhaps America's most important military ally in the world today, and U.S. policy has historically opposed Palestinian statehood, even under democratic rule, as contrary to U.S. strategic interests. Turkey, Egypt, and Morocco are populous, strategically located, and traditionally sympathetic to U.S. interests in the region. The Gulf monarchies are guardians of valuable oil reserves for which the United States seeks access, not just to supplement American reserves but as a means of maintaining a degree of leverage over the import-dependent European and Japanese markets.[17]

In addition, the Middle East is the destination of the majority of American arms exports, creating enormous profits for politically influential arms manufacturers.[18] Joe Stork, in a survey for the Middle East Research and Information Project, argues that the ongoing Middle Eastern arms race continues for three reasons:

1. arms sales are an important component of building political alliances, particularly with the military leadership of recipient countries;

2. there is a strategic benefit coming from interoperability, of having U.S.-manufactured systems on the ground in the event of a direct U.S. military intervention; and,

3. arms sales are a means of supporting military industries faced with declining demand in Western countries.[19]

One revealing episode was a 1993 off-the-record seminar with assistant Secretary of State Richard Murphy, top Saudi officials, and the vice chairman of the board of Morgan Guaranty (the bank that organized the financing of Saudi Arabia's 1991 war effort), in which it was acknowledged that arms transfers had little to do with the objective security needs for the kingdom.[20]

To link arms transfers with human rights records would lead to the probable loss of tens of billions of dollars of annual sales for American arms manufacturers, which are among the most powerful special interest groups in Washington.

With the exception of Israel, none of America's allies in the region could really be considered democracies, yet none requires democratic institutions to fulfill American strategic objectives. Indeed, the opposite may be true: the Middle Eastern countries that most vigorously opposed the U.S. war against Iraq in 1991 — Jordan and Yemen — were the two Arab states with the most open political systems. Most observers acknowledge that close strategic cooperation with the United States tends to be unpopular in Arab countries, as are government policies that devote large amounts of government expenditures toward the acquisition of weapons, most of which are of U.S. origin. Were these leaders subjected to the will of the majority, they would likely be forced to greatly reduce arms purchases from and strategic cooperation with the United States. As the British journalist and author Dilip Hiro describes it, the United States does not actually support democracy in the Middle East, because "it is much simpler to manipulate a few ruling families — to secure fat orders for arms and ensure that oil price remains low — than a wide variety of personalities and policies bound to be thrown up by a democratic system," as elected governments might reflect the popular sentiment for "self-reliance and Islamic fellowship."[21]

Given the strong economic and strategic interests in the Middle East, it is not surprising that human rights issues in the region are rarely a topic of debate in Washington, even by liberal Democrats. As a result, many advocacy groups believe that it would be virtually impossible to affect a change in U.S. policy regarding such important allies and that these organizations' limited resources would best be placed on more winnable political battles.

Lack of Awareness of Human Rights Struggles

Another major factor inhibiting greater awareness of struggles for democracy and human rights in the Middle East may be based on assumptions, which at times harbor somewhat racist overtones, that minimize the importance of democracy and human rights to Middle Eastern peoples or the desire of Middle Eastern peoples to encourage democratization and improve the human rights records of their governments. For example, widespread misunderstandings in the West of Islamic principles regarding human rights have minimized popular sympathy with victims of human rights abuses in many Middle Eastern countries. A crude kind of structural-functionalism and pseudo-sensitivity appears to underline the belief that the lack of better human rights records by Middle Eastern governments is somehow a cultural phenomenon that no policy shift by the United States could alter. Claims that Arabs "did not have word for freedom" are untrue; the word has been found in literature going back for centuries.[22] Even some otherwise reputable scholars will go to some lengths to dismiss the potential for democracy in the Islamic world.[23] Indeed, while there has been arguably a greater tolerance for

autocratic rule in the Islamic world than in the West, there is a strong belief
in a social contract between ruler and subject that gives the people the right
to resist if the rule is unjust.[24]

It is undeniable that democracy and universally recognized human rights
are not common in the Arab-Islamic world. Yet the emphasis in the West on
cultural or religious explanations tends to minimize other factors that are arguably more salient, including the legacy of colonialism, high levels of mili-
tarization, and uneven economic development, much of which can be linked
in part to the policies of Western governments, including the United States.
There is a tragic irony in a U.S. policy that sells arms, and often sends direct
military aid, to repressive Arab regimes that suppress their own people and
crush incipient human rights movements, only to then claim that the lack of
democracy and human rights is evidence that the people do not want them.
In reality, these arms transfers and diplomatic and economic support systems play an important role in keeping these regimes in power by strengthening the hand of the state and supporting internal repression.

A further irony is that the dictatorial orientation of these Arab regimes is
then used by American political leaders as an excuse for supporting the government of Israel, which also suppresses Arab peoples demanding democracy and human rights. Indeed, domestic political groups allied with Israel
in the United States have — along with sympathetic individuals in politics,
academia, and the media — frequently played on stereotypes of the "authoritarian nature" of Arab societies as reasons why the United States should continue large-scale military and economic support of Israel and should not
pressure the Israeli government to compromise further in the peace process
or improve its human rights record.[25]

There also appears to be a kind of self-righteousness regarding Western
concepts of individual liberty, which has only exacerbated such misunderstandings. An example is the reaction over the 1989 Iranian order to murder
Indian-British author Salman Rushdie as a result of offensive passages in his
novel *Satanic Verses*.[26] The death sentence by Iran got lots of coverage in the
West, but few of those familiar with the episode realized that the government
of Iran was the only government in the entire Muslim world to support the
fatwa. Similarly, there was also widespread support of Rushdie by Muslim
authorities, who argued that he had the right to offend anybody and Muslims
had a right to be upset and that a death sentence was beyond the jurisdiction
of temporal authorities.[27] Rushdie's previous and arguably better works had
been largely ignored in the West, but *Satanic Verses* became a bestseller. Al-

though public readings of texts offensive to Jews and Christians would not be considered appropriate in the United States, such readings of *Satanic Verses*, which was offensive to Muslims, were widespread.

For many Middle Easterners, the concern was not that the fatwa by Iranian authorities was appropriate but that Western governments and intellectuals would so vigorously defend Rushdie while ignoring the thousands of prisoners of conscience being detained, tortured, and murdered by Western-backed governments in the Middle East as well as the growing demand for greater political liberalization and democracy in these countries. Indeed, a survey of media coverage in the United States shows far more attention on the Rushdie episode than all other issues of human rights and democracy in the region for the preceding several years.[28]

Part of the problem is that the human rights and pro-democracy movement from within the Middle East has been relatively weak. Many of the outspoken critics of human rights violations in Middle Eastern countries have been radical Islamic groups whose own commitment to human rights and democracy is highly questionable; once elected, many Islamic groups would likely establish a new form of authoritarian rule. It is noteworthy, however, that in countries which have allowed Islamic groups to participate fully in the democratic process, such as Jordan, Turkey, and Yemen, the Islamists have played a responsible, albeit somewhat conservative, role in parliamentary politics. It has only been in countries where democratic rights are seriously curtailed that the Islamists have taken on the more reactionary anti-democratic form that the West finds so disturbing. Many of these Islamic movements, such as those in Egypt, Palestine, and Algeria, include many diverse elements that would span the ideological spectrum if they were allowed to function in an open democratic system. The more reactionary Islamic movements also appear to grow to prominence in countries where there has been major social dislocation of the population through war or uneven economic development and where there is widespread official corruption.[29] In a response that bears striking similarity to the perceived Communist threat during the Cold War, the U.S. reaction to radical Islamic movements appears to be to support authoritarian regimes in imposing military solutions to what are essentially political, economic, and social problems, thereby creating a reaction that encourages the very extremist forces they seek to curtail.[30]

During the Cold War, however, there were active grassroots movements in the United States supporting an end to U.S. aid to such authoritarian regimes as well as efforts to establish links to pro-democracy and other opposition groups in these countries. This has generally not been the case regarding the Middle East. Part of the problem is the lack of awareness in the United States of such indigenous human rights movements. These movements for human rights in most Middle Eastern countries operate in a variety of conditions. Some function in the open, others are banned and suppressed, while some, as in Egypt, are neither recognized nor banned and must operate in a legal limbo that makes them aware that the state could crack down if they went too far out of line. One of the more prominent regional groups is the Arab Organization for Human Rights (AOHR), based in Cairo and Geneva. It has separate country groups in Egypt, Kuwait, Algeria, Lebanon, Morocco, Tunisia, and Jordan. There are also national human rights groups: Tunisia's League for Human Rights, since banned by the government, was established in 1977, and other groups were active in Algeria prior to the 1992 coup. In 1989 the AOHR joined with the Tunisian government, the Tunisian League for Human Rights, the Arab Lawyers Union, and the UN Center for Human Rights to establish the region's first Arab Institute for Human Rights to train human rights workers and disseminate information. Other associations engage in human rights work along with more general programs, such as the Arab Lawyers Union, a regional organization founded in 1956 and based in Egypt. Human rights groups also work with local media, bar associations, trade unions, university groups, and women's and children's groups, which often set up separate human rights committees. The General Federation of Labor's Section on Education has organized conferences on teaching human rights. These groups have set up important logistical and intellectual support from academic and quasi-academic institutions, including the Arab Thought Forum in Amman, the Center for Arab Unity Studies in Beirut and Cairo, the Thought and Dialogue Forum in Morocco, and the Third World Forum in Cairo. These groups and their concerns, in turn, are often supported by outside nongovernmental organizations such as Amnesty International, Middle East Watch, the Adenauer Institute, the International Commission of Jurists, Article 19, and the Minority Rights Group. In addition, the Ford Foundation and other groups support human rights centers and programs for concerned Arabs in both Europe and in the Middle East.[31]

Yet outside certain intellectual circles and the most active elements of human rights work, there is little interest in the Middle East. These struggles have not captured the imagination of the grassroots organizations in recent decades to the extent of human rights movements in Latin America, southern Africa, the Philippines, or even East Timor. Though established human rights groups such as Amnesty International, Human Rights Watch, and others have generally given a proportional amount of attention to human rights abuses in the Middle East, it has not prompted the level of popular concern that might influence government decision making comparable to other parts of the world.

Polarization around the Arab-Israeli Conflict

The ideologically divisive Arab-Israeli conflict, which taints discussion of human rights as a universal principle, has also made debate on the subject problematic. This takes on several forms: many partisans of Israel or of particular Arab states or movements have used human rights as an excuse for attacking the other side while ignoring human rights abuses on "their" side. For example, many UN reports and resolutions critical of Israeli human rights violations, while in the most part valid, lacked credibility given support of such efforts by some of the world's most tyrannical states.[32] Criticisms of human rights abuses in Arab countries have been used to rationalize denying Palestinians their right to statehood or opposing Israeli withdrawal from its occupied territories, while criticisms of human rights abuses by Israel are often simply used as excuses to attack the world's only Jewish state. In addition, while I have argued elsewhere that the role of the pro-Israel lobby and its allied PACs in the actual formulation of U.S. Middle East policy has been greatly exaggerated, it has effectively neutralized congressional opposition to Israeli human rights abuses from liberal Democrats who have been outspoken on human rights issues elsewhere, a tendency reinforced by the rather idealistic view of Israel traditionally held by many American liberals.[33] Indeed, human rights violations by the Israeli government are generally not spoken about publicly in the halls of Congress. Many elected officials, particularly in the Democratic Party, are dependent on individuals and political action committees sympathetic with the Israeli government for a substantial amount of money for their election campaigns. A number of peace and human rights organizations with a strong universal commitment to democracy and human rights have been subjected to attacks and reduced funding when they have raised the issue of human rights violations in Israel or the subject of democratic rights for Palestinians.[34]

Many other peace groups avoid the issue altogether. For example, from its founding in 1973 until its demise in 1988, the Coalition for a New Foreign Policy was the peace and human rights movement's leading lobbying group on Capitol Hill. However, it consistently refused to address the issues of Palestinian rights or U.S. aid for Israel. A 1981 Coalition statement re-affirmed the group's support of the "sovereignty, territorial integrity, and political independence" of Middle Eastern states but explicitly stated that this principle "does not necessarily apply" to lands seized by Israel in the 1967 war. The Coalition also explicitly refused to include Israel in its otherwise strict standards of linking human rights and nuclear nonproliferation issues with U.S. military aid.[35] Similarly, Gretchen Eick, a former Coalition leader who became leader of National Impact, a progressive lobbying coalition that claimed to provide "leadership of peace and justice issues," declared, soon after the group's founding, that the Coalition also considered the Israeli-Palestinian conflict "off limits."[36] The Human Rights Political Action Committee, which raised funds for candidates based on their support of a human rights agenda in U.S. foreign policy, also made an exception regarding Israel.[37] There need not be a particularly powerful "pro-Israel lobby" if there is virtually no pro–human rights or pro-democracy lobby to counter it.

Perhaps the member of Congress with the strongest reputation regarding human rights has been Senator Tom Harkin, the liberal Iowa Democrat who has led several major human rights crusades since joining the House of Representatives in 1974. However, when it comes to Israel, he has been a staunch defender of Israeli policies in the occupied territories, a strident opponent of tying U.S. aid to Israel to concerns over human rights, and even attacked the Bush administration from the right as being overly concerned about Palestinian rights. A strong backer of the right-wing Likud governments of Menachem Begin, Yitzhak Shamir, and Benjamin Netanyahu, the normally receptive Harkin has refused to take calls or even respond to letters from those concerned with human rights cases involving Palestinians. During the 1992 campaign for the Democratic presidential nomination, he positioned himself as the most right-wing of the six major candidates regarding Palestinian human rights, yet — despite such a position — he received the endorsement of prominent human rights activists throughout the United States, once again highlighting how little concern there is when the victims of human rights abuses are Middle Eastern.

One problem facing human rights activists is the perception that — because U.S. policy is perceived to be pro-Israel — criticism of U.S. policy appears to some like criticism of Israel itself. Many on the Israeli left, however, have argued that U.S. policy is ultimately anti-Israel, because it discourages the Israeli government from making necessary compromises that would ensure peace, isolates Israel further from its Arab neighbors and the international community, and increasingly militarizes its economy at the expense of sustainable economic development. As a result, these Israelis argue that the American human rights activists must emphasize that their opposition to U.S. support of the Israeli occupation is not just pro-Palestinian but ultimately pro-Israel as well. Still, many peace activists oppose raising the issue of U.S. aid to Israel because, though most strategic analysts recognize that Israel — unlike some periods earlier in its history — is not under immediate military threat, there is still a widespread perception that Israel is under siege. As a result, those who oppose military aid to Israel, even out of legitimate concern for human rights, are easily depicted as advocating the military destruction of the Jewish state and are thus relegated to the fringe of U.S. public opinion along with anti-Jewish bigots.

As a result, critics of Israel's human rights record and U.S. complicity in that country's repression of those under its military occupation are much more on the margins than are critics of Arab countries' record when it comes to U.S. policy. Groups that do raise the issue are often further marginalized by their notable failure to criticize Arab regimes that violate human rights. The Center for the National Interest, the National Association of Arab Americans, the American Educational Trust, the American-Arab Anti-Discrimination Committee, and even the respected Middle East Policy Council are or have been dependent on money from Gulf Arabs to the degree to which they have felt compelled to limit their criticism of human rights violations of most Arab governments.[38] Another problem is that some of these organizations have often attracted followers who do not carry a universal concern for human rights and carry a hidden — and sometimes not-so-hidden — anti-Israel or even anti-Semitic agenda.

As a result, there is a concern that even legitimate criticisms of Israel's human rights record and its denial of full democratic rights of Palestinians may in some ways encourage anti-Semitism. Another complicating factor is that Israel's leadership has publicly endorsed Western values regarding democracy and human rights and has created exemplary democratic institutions for its Jewish citizens that surpass any other Middle Eastern country. In addition, though there are certainly widespread Israeli violations of the Universal Declaration of Human Rights against Arab populations under its control, Israel's most egregious violations of human rights generally fall under the Geneva Conventions, which are generally less likely to be cited by those raising issues of human rights. In addition, Israel's pivotal role as a strategic ally of the United States makes criticism of its human rights record all the more difficult.

Finally, the relative silence of human rights advocates regarding Israel may be related to the awareness that the refusal by members of Congress and the Clinton administration to address the issues of Israeli human rights violations is so categorical that activists simply choose to apply their limited resources to causes that are potentially more winnable. Thus, reluctance by grassroots movements to more vigorously address Israeli human rights abuses may be more tactical than ideological.

In many respects, there is a conspiracy of silence between partisans of Israel and various Arab governments. Both sides know that to raise the issue of human rights of any Middle Eastern country too much to the forefront would lead to inevitable questions about human rights elsewhere in the region. Generally speaking, it has only been groups whose agenda is worldwide, such as Amnesty International and Human Rights Watch, that carry any real credibility on this issue. However, such findings are rarely cited outside their small core constituency except when individuals with a clear ideological agenda find it expedient to utilize them.

The work of Amnesty International, Human Rights Watch, and other non-ideological human rights organizations with a global agenda has generally been quite solid and consistent regarding the Middle East, particularly in more recent years. However, such efforts make little difference regarding U.S. policy as long as the broader circle of human rights activists and sympathetic allies in academia, the media, and Congress do not give Middle Eastern countries the kind of attention that has often been given to other countries and regions. This chapter has reviewed how the strategic importance of the region, the lack of awareness of ongoing human rights struggles in the region, and the sensitivity of the Arab-Israeli conflict have made this problematic.

At the same time, each of these issues may also provide an opening for those concerned with human rights and democratization. For example, on the strategic imperative, one can make a case that it is in the strategic interest of the United States to support democratization and human rights. The experience of Iran could provide an opening: in the twenty-five years after the United States facilitated the overthrow of that country's constitutional government in 1953, our country gave extensive backing to the authoritarian regime of the Shah. His secret police — organized, armed, and trained by

U.S. agencies — essentially eliminated Iran's democratic opposition.[39] When the Shah's regime finally collapsed in 1978–79, what organized opposition remained became dominated by a stridently anti-American, reactionary Islamic movement based in the country's mosques (largely out of reach from the state) and was thereby able to take power, resulting in one of the worst strategic setbacks in modern U.S. foreign policy.

The lesson is that unrestricted military and diplomatic support of such unpopular and corrupt monarchies creates a situation where the opposition links the abuses of the regime with the United States, an attitude that is likely to remain if and when such opposition groups come to power. Such governments would also find themselves in possession of vast quantities of U.S. arms sent to the former regime, which could eventually be used against American soldiers or civilians. Similarly, whenever legitimate opposition is suppressed, such opposition tends to coalesce underground, often giving rise to more authoritarian and violent elements. Such a scenario may now be unfolding in Saudi Arabia, in the other Gulf monarchies, and in Morocco, where unconditional U.S. support of the ruling families has creating enormous resentment amid increasingly radicalized opposition forces. Similarly, the enormous amount of military and economic aid sent annually to the Egyptian government to prop up the increasingly corrupt and authoritarian rule of Hosni Mubarak may also backfire against American interests in this large and pivotal country. Therefore, even putting aside moral arguments for the backing of such regimes, one can make a case that it would be in the best strategic interests of the United States to cease its unconditional support of these kinds of authoritarian regimes in the Middle East.

Regarding Islamic movements, there may also be an opening. As the world's fastest-growing major religion and as a faith that encourages strong political manifestations, there is growing awareness of the importance in government and intellectual circles for a better understanding of Islam. Even within the United States, there are more than 4 million Muslims, some of whom are starting to organize politically. Inevitably, there will be growing interaction between Muslims and mainstream America, which should break down the stereotypes and lead to recognition that Muslims of the Middle East — as with Christians or secular individuals in the West — do not like to be tortured, jailed for political offenses, or suffer under dictatorial and arbitrary rule.

Finally, it is extremely unlikely that there will be real stability in the Middle East until the Israeli-Arab dispute is resolved. The core of that conflict has long been the Arab states' refusal to recognize Israel and the Israeli refusal to recognize Palestine and withdraw from its occupied territories. Most Arab states have now either recognized Israel or are ready to do so once Israel withdraws from Arab land. The main stumbling block, then, appears to be Israeli refusal to grant Palestinians their full statehood, withdraw their illegal settlements, share Jerusalem, and withdraw from remaining parts of the West Bank, southern Lebanon, and Syria's Golan. U.S. policy thus far has failed to pressure Israel to change these policies and at times has explicitly supported some of them. Ultimately, however, there could be a recognition that Israeli security and Palestinian rights are not mutually exclusive but mutually dependent on the other. Similarly, democracy and human rights can be a wedge for those interested in broader issues of peace and justice in the Middle East. Taking a consistent position for democracy and human rights, which challenged the policies of both Israel and the Arab states, as well as other Middle Eastern countries, gives a level of credibility to advocates that might otherwise be difficult to achieve.

In conclusion, the possibility of establishing a U.S. policy in the Middle East supporting democracy and human rights is bleak but not hopeless. The combination of the strong moral imperative of taking such action combined with enlightened self-interest could conceivably create the momentum that could successfully challenge even the very powerful interests that currently support the status quo. In the meantime, those who support democracy and human rights worldwide may need to focus additional attention on the Middle East to give those in the region struggling for freer societies any chance to gain the freedoms they deserve.

Notes

1. Under such a criterion, even El Salvador in the 1980s, where government-backed death squads were murdering tens of thousands of dissidents, was labeled a democracy by successive U.S. administrations and the mainstream media.

2. It is somewhat revealing that the Omani Sultan Qabus bin Said's speeches justifying his country's lack of democracy are written in English by his Western advisers and only then translated into Arabic.

3. Background briefing, Department of State, July 1995. In the 1991 report, Oman is described as "an absolute monarchy." A more recent report simply refers to the sultanate as "a monarchy without popularly elected representative institutions." (Source: "Country Reports on Human Rights Practices," report submitted to the

Committee on International Relations, U.S. House of Representatives and the Committee on Foreign Relations, U.S. Senate, by the Department of State, 1991 and 1995.)

4. Background briefing, U.S. Consular Offices, East Jerusalem, May 1993.

5. Jules Kagian, *Middle East International*, December 17, 1993. See Thomas and Sally Mallison, *The Palestine Problem in International Law* (New York and London: Longman, 1986), ch. 4. See also Noam Chomsky, *World Orders Old and New* (New York: Columbia University Press, 1995), 219.

6. Noam Chomsky has analyzed these double standards in a number of his writings, including *Necessary Illusions: Thought Control in Democratic Societies* (Boston: South End Press, 1989).

7. Congressional Research Service, "Jordan-U.S. Relations and Bilateral Issues," June 13, 1993.

8. Cited in Phyllis Bennis, *Calling the Shots: How Washington Dominates Today's UN* (New York: Olive Branch Press, 1996), 33.

9. See Stephen Zunes, "The Strategic Function of U.S. Aid to Israel," *Middle East Policy* 4 (October 1996).

10. "The Vengeful Ones," *The Economist* 318 (March 9, 1991): 39.

11. See Stephen Zunes, "The United States in the Sahara War: A Case of Low-Intensity Intervention," in *International Dimensions of the Western Sahara Conflict*, ed. Daniel Volman and Yahia Zoubir (Westport CT: Greenwood Press 1993), 53–92.

12. See Stephen Zunes, "Behind the Fundamentalist Upsurge in Algeria," *In These Times* 16 (January 29, 1992): 6.

13. Background briefing, Department of State, July 1995.

14. Department of State, *Foreign Relations of the United States*, 8 (1945), cited in Joyce and Gabriel Kolko, *The Limits of Power* (New York: Harper and Row, 1972), 45.

15. Steven Spiegel, *The Other Arab-Israeli Conflict* (Chicago: University of Chicago Press, 1985), 51.

16. Noam Chomsky argues that this has been a prevailing theme of U.S. policy, particularly in the Gulf region, for several decades, a view shared by the British when they were the dominant outside power. He quotes British Prime Minister Harold Macmillan, who stated in his memoirs that he found it "rather sad that circumstances compel us to support reactionary and really rather outmoded regimes, because we know that the new forces, even if they begin with moderate opinions, always seem to drift into violent revolutionary and strongly anti-Western positions." Chomsky, *World Orders Old and New*, 198–200; the Macmillan quote originated from his *At the End of the Day* (New York: Harper and Row, 1973).

17. See Stephen Zunes, "The United States and the Gulf Cooperation Council: Its Rise and Potential Fall," *Middle East Policy* 2 (summer 1993): 103–112.

18. See Stephen Zunes, "How Pax Americana Threatens Peace and Development in the Middle East," in *Economic Impediments to Middle East Peace*, ed. J. W. Wright (New York: Macmillan, 1997).

19. Joe Stork, "The Middle East Arms Bazaar after the Gulf War," *Middle East Report* 25 (November–December 1995): 14–19.

20. Robert Vitalis, "Gun Belt in the Beltway," *Middle East Report* 25 (November–December 1995): 6.

21. Dilip Hiro, "The Gulf Between the Rulers and the Ruled," *New Statesman and Society* 16 (February 26, 1993): 18–20.

22. See John L. Esposito and Joyhn O. Voll, *Islam and Democracy* (New York: Oxford University Press, 1996).

23. See Samuel Huntington, "Clash of Civilizations," *Foreign Affairs* 72 (summer 1993): 22–49.

24. See Khalid Kishtainy, "Violent and Nonviolent Struggle in Arab History," in *Arab Nonviolent Political Struggle in the Middle East*, ed. Ralph E. Crow, Philip Grant, and Saad E. Ibrahim (Boulder CO: Lynne Rienner Publishers, 1990).

25. See, for example, Israeli Prime Minister Benjamin Netanyahu's address before a joint session of the U.S. Congress in July 1996. See also Thomas Dine of the American-Israel Public Affairs Committee, "Testimony before the House Appropriations Subcommittee on Foreign Operations," March 1, 1993.

26. Salman Rushdie, *The Satanic Verses* (New York: Viking, 1989).

27. See Anouar Abdallah, *For Rushdie: A Collection of Essays by 100 Arab and Muslim Writers* (New York: George Braziller, 1994).

28. For example, the expanded academic index backfile 1980–90 showed nearly 300 citations about the Rushdie affair as compared with less than fifty dealing with human rights violations by Middle Eastern governments allied with the United States.

It is noteworthy that during the thick of the international reaction to the Rushdie affair, the Saudi government executed a man for alleged apostasy with scarcely a murmur of protest.

29. See Stephen Zunes, "The Roots of Radical Islam," *Peace Review* 7 (1995): 23–30.

30. See John Esposito, *The Islamic Threat: Myth or Reality* (New York: Oxford University Press, 1995).

31. See Jill Crystal, "The Human Rights Movement in the Middle East: The Arab Organization for Human Rights," *Human Rights Quarterly* 16 (August 1994): 435–454, and "The Emerging Human Rights Environment in the Arab World," in *Conflict and Its Solution in World Society*, ed. Volker Bornschier and Peter Lengyel, World Society Studies, vol. 3 (Frankfort: Campus Verlag, 1994).

See also Ann Mayer, *Islam and Human Rights: Tradition and Politics* (Boulder: Westview, 1991); Kevin Dwyer, *Arab Voices: The Human Rights Debate* (Berkeley: University of California Press, 1991); and Abdullahi Naim, ed., *Human Rights in Cross-Cultural Perspectives* (Philadelphia: University of Pennsylvania Press, 1992).

32. This is certainly not a unique phenomenon. During the Cold War, repressive

right-wing dictatorships would often join the U.S.-led efforts to condemn human rights violations by communist governments and, likewise, various left-wing dictatorships would join the Soviet Union in condemnation of rightist regimes.

33. See Stephen Zunes, "Factors Shaping the U.S.-Israeli Alliance," *New Political Science*, nos. 21–22 (spring–summer 1992): 91–116.

34. See Stephen Zunes, "Israel's Blank Check: Why Congressional Liberals Underwrite Human Rights Abuses," *The Progressive* 53 (November 1989): 20–25.

35. "Middle East Policy Statement," Coalition for a New Foreign Policy, spring 1981.

36. Telephone interview, May 1989.

37. Interview at headquarters, Washington DC, November 1982.

38. In the course of my research and activism on U.S. Middle East policy, I have interacted with a number of principals in these organizations and have heard a number of off-the-record stories about such financial dependence and its impact.

39. See James Bill, *The Eagle and the Lion: The Tragedy of U.S.-Iranian Relations* (New Haven: Yale University Press, 1989).

11

U.S. Foreign Policy, Democracy, and the Islamic World

•

CHRISTOPHER JOYNER

Democracy won the ideological contest of the Cold War. The collapse of global communism brought with it a widespread acceptance of democracy as the legitimate basis for political order, especially throughout Eastern Europe, Asia, and Latin America, as well as in Russia and South Africa. Tendencies toward democracy since 1990 have been less evident in the Middle East and North Africa, however. This study thus examines why democratization and the civil rights and liberties implicit in that transition have encountered such great difficulty in being accepted by Middle Eastern societies. Special attention focuses on how and why the United States introduces democratic principles and practices to the region, albeit as set against the manifest reluctance of U.S. policy to publicly address human rights concerns in key Arab countries, in particular, "friends" of the United States.

The Nature of Democratization

Democratization is a process in which an authoritarian society becomes increasingly open to popular political participation. Various factors and circumstances contribute to this process, among them periodic elections of candidates to representative bodies, the accountability of public officials, a transparent public administration, an independent judiciary, and a free press. Democratization does not lead either automatically or immediately to a fully integrated democratic society. That goal comes gradually, only in steps, with its pace determined by the susceptibility of a society to change various political, economic, social, and cultural factors.

Democratization takes hold in a society only when certain conditions are met. First and foremost, the political will must exist both at the government level and among the people to accept a more democratic approach to government. Second, citizens must be able to participate democratically in the decision-making process of the society. Minimum preconditions for this include: the ability to participate in free and fair elections; the opportunity to associate freely and form several political parties; and the ability to enjoy full access to information, including an independent media. Third, although necessary, these basic requirements in themselves are insufficient. Democracy can not be forged on forms alone. For democracy to function effectively, a developed and articulate society, as well as political cultures involving participation and consultation, must be present. U.S. policy actions can assist Middle Eastern governments to erect institutions needed for a more democratic system to evolve. But that is not enough. A government's leaders and the people must genuinely want to attain the values and principles of democracy as a political culture.[1]

Transformation of an independent state through a process of popular participation provides the foundation for a culture sympathetic to democratization.[2] Free and responsible communications media are essential for effective democratization. Independent media that report impartially to the public help to guarantee freedom of thought and the unimpeded flow of ideas and debate among the people. Media provide a means to expose policies of corruption, mismanagement, discrimination, and injustice in a society. In this sense, media contribute to building a political culture through civic education.[3] Similarly, elections must be conducted in a credible and transparent manner, with secrecy of the ballot an essential precondition. For successful elections to occur, it remains critical that voters have confidence in the credibility of the voting process and its institutions.[4]

Liberalization and democratization are distinct concepts. Liberalization precedes democratization and refers to the extension of rights that enhance opportunities for public participation in the governing process. Political liberalism involves recognition and protection of civil rights and liberties, especially those that enable citizens to engage in meaningful political discourse and to organize freely in pursuit of common interests.[5]

Democratization refers to changes in rules and procedures that ensure public accountability on rulers. Political democratization involves expansion of political participation such that citizens are provided with real and meaningful collective control over public policy. Without the context of political freedom, citizens are unable to effectively participate, organize, or freely choose among political alternatives. Elections supply the most common means for expanding political participation in government decision making.[6] Democratization, then, involves demands for increased popular political participation and empowerment in government and politics.[7] This con-

ception of the democratic process stems mainly from the political tradition
of Western Europe, and more recently, from that of the United States.

U.S. Interests and Middle East Democratization

Why should the United States promote democracy in Middle Eastern states?
Simply put, it is in the national security interest of the United States to do so.

U.S. policy toward the Middle East has been recently described as "active
and sustained engagement." Military security is a vital interest of the United
States. Reducing proliferation of weapons of mass destruction, controlling
the spread of dangerous technologies, preventing or curtailing violent regional conflicts, and countering international terrorism are all facets of protecting U.S. national security. So, too, is maintenance of economic security.
Preserving unrestricted access to natural resources and sea lanes for international trade is essential for the United States to prosper in today's interdependent international economy. The Middle East figures prominently in that
regard.[8]

Democratic governments pose far less threat today to U.S. national security than do despots and other authoritarian regimes. While fiercely competitive economically, democratic regimes tend to be more politically stable,
more diplomatically cooperative, and more peace inclined. In fact, the experience of this century suggests that democratic states do not go to war with
one another, do not threaten each other militarily with weapons of mass destruction, are more reliable as trading partners, and are more likely to respect
international agreements and legal obligations with one another. The infer-
ence is that because democracies respect civil liberties, rights of property, and
the rule of law within their own boundaries, they are similarly inclined to respect those patterns of conduct internationally. Democratic governments
thus supply a more reliable foundation on which to construct a world order
of peace and prosperity.[9]

Belief in a "Democratic Cycle" of peace and security supplies the theoretical underpinning for U.S. policy aimed at promoting democratization
within Middle Eastern states. This cycle begins with the premise that peace
and security in the region are good for the people in those countries and
good for the United States as well. Less conflict and violence allows for
greater possibilities to turn attention to social and economic needs. Maintaining peace and security permits greater economic development and op-

portunities to attain higher standards of living for people in those societies and to engage in more active international commerce. These societal conditions, largely produced by private free enterprise capitalism, permit greater opportunities for political pluralism and popular participation to develop in those societies, which in turn generate liberal values and institutions necessary for democratic government. Finally, attainment of democratic forms of government by states in the Middle East will contribute to peace and stability in the region, a conclusion sustained by belief in "the democratic peace," that is, the notion borne out by historical experience that democracies do not fight other democracies.[10] Thus, if all states in the Middle East are transformed into democratic political systems, then interstate peace in the region will be perpetrated, human rights and civil liberties for peoples in each state will be protected, and long-term U.S. interests will be enhanced by the resultant stable, more cooperative interdependent regional situation.

U.S. policy supports establishment of democratic governments around the world, inclusive of the Middle East. Still, to promote democracy should not be to export it. Democracy rarely functions well when foreign models are imposed. The American democratic model is not suited for all societies or cultures, especially those in economically poor, politically unstable, or ethnically divided countries. This realization should not be lost on how U.S. government efforts are conceived and implemented to promote democracy throughout the Middle East.[11]

Obstacles to Democratization

Major forces and factors complicate the acceptability of democratic principles and practices in the Middle East. These obstacles are ideological, historical, economic, political, and cultural. Moreover, they can be neither easily nor quickly overcome by American influence. Outstanding among these complications is the prevailing influence of Islam as a socio-religious force.

Islam embodies a monotheistic religion of beliefs, worship, doctrine, ideas, and ideals. Yet it is much more than that. Islam also connotes the whole civilization that has grown up under the authority of that religion. Historically throughout the Middle East Arab Islamic world, the most prevalent political system by far has been autocracy, undergirded by a political tradition of command and obedience. This is not to say oppression by despotism but rather submission to authoritarianism. In short, Islam has traditions of radical authoritarianism.

It is often asserted that Islamic political values are incompatible with, or at least in tension with, fundamental principles of democratic practice. Islamic emphasis is viewed in terms of divine rather than popular sovereignty, with the former set in a body of established law resistant to change, generally by an elite of religious scholars. This situation pushes much of public policy beyond the realm of public, participatory decision making. The lack of fundamental equality within Islam for various groups, notably women and religious minorities, is often noted as well.[12]

In Arab Islamic societies, an important historical and cultural fact is the absence of any real notion of citizenship. There is no word in Arabic, Persian or Turkish for "citizen." The cognate term in each language actually translates to countryman, or "compatriot." Absent, too, is the critical notion of one who participates in the affairs of the community, of the person as citizen-participant, and of citizenship as participation in civic and political affairs.[13]

Critical for democratization of a society are the twin philosophical pillars of sovereignty of the individual and freedom of opinion. Middle Eastern Muslim societies have not inherited either of these foundations for civil society as experienced in the West. Middle Eastern Islamic societies suffer from a lack of access to humanistic ideas, including the freedom of thought, sovereignty of the individual, right to freedom of action, tolerance as a principle and practice. Muslim societies in general have lacked true commitment to teaching and encouraging individual initiative.

Another obstacle for democratization is the general nature of political cultures in Islamic Arab societies. Arab Islamic cultures are grounded in traditions of and affinity for winner-take-all politics, rather than the more democratically sympathetic pluralist perspective.[14] The group, family, or tribe retains greater importance than the individual. Politics tends to focus on gaining and retaining power, under the family group banner, rather than presenting public policies approved by the citizenry.

The winner-take-all brand of politics can be seen in the claim by Islamists to represent the one true interpretation of Islam. To disagree with that claim is to repudiate oneself as a true Muslim. This theme arises in Egyptian and Algerian politics of the past decade, as assaults have been made against foreigners, non-Muslims, and secular Muslims. This situation presents a harsh dilemma for U.S. policy. Free and fair elections may bring radical fundamentalist leaders to power who will reject democracy. That "one man, one vote, one time" could occur is a genuine concern, especially in Arab states today having forms of participatory government, such as Morocco and Jordan.[15] The necessary cultural and civic infrastructure in Arab states for promoting and sustaining democratic processes, including a strong commitment among citizens and elites to democracy as the governing system of choice, a variety of public associations and interest groups autonomous from the state or Islam, and an independent mass media to inform the people about national events and governmental policies are also absent. In Middle Eastern Islamic countries, legislatures are weak, poorly financed, and understaffed. Legal systems lack resources and authority to protect human rights and ensure due process. Political parties lack organization, resources, grassroots constituencies, and general popular acceptance.

Profoundly different forms of government further complicate the task of introducing democracy to political cultures in the region. States in the Middle East have disparate systems of government and political cultures. All are sovereign, and all are free from external domination. Yet, most Arab states lack attributes of democracy, and their peoples live under internal subjugation.[16] Even so, clear differences are apparent between them in the degree and substance of that political subjugation. At least four types of governing systems earmark states in the Middle East, each of which has features unique to its political cultures.[17]

Some governments such as Saudi Arabia and the other Gulf sheikdoms can be classified as traditional autocracies with established dynastic regimes. Though firmly authoritarian in nature, these societies have their legitimacy grounded in popular acceptance of the regime. As a consequence, excessive repression presumably could prompt popular rejection of that legitimacy.[18]

A second type of political system in the Arab Middle East can be described as a "modernizing autocracy." Jordan, Egypt, and Morocco, for example, have their roots in traditional autocracy but have taken noteworthy steps toward modernization and democratization of their political institutions. Though neither full liberal democracies nor total autocracies, these governments today represent political systems in voluntary transition toward civil societies.

Still a third form of Middle Eastern government is the fascist-like dictatorship. Both Iraq and Syria are one-party Ba'athist governments, ruled by charismatic strong men — Saddam Hussein in the former and Hafiz al-Assad in the latter. Both regimes follow the fascist model of Benito Mussolini's Italy and Adolf Hitler's Germany during the 1930s and use brutal political repression, secret police, and authoritarian means to maintain control over their societies.

Fourth, there are radical Islamic regimes. The most fervent among these, Iran, Sudan, and Libya, appear bent on spreading political Islam as an anti-Western instrument throughout the region. The threat does not merely come from theological proselytizing, however. These militant regimes resort to and actively support international terrorist violence directed against Western persons and property, purportedly to preserve the nature of Islamic culture from such secular influences.[19]

Only a few Islamic countries have made significant strides toward establishing democratic systems in the Middle East, namely, Jordan, Lebanon, and Turkey. None has yet achieved a full, stable, mature democracy. Hence, this question arises: Is Islamic culture inherently incompatible with democratic values and processes? The temptation at first blush is to assert yes. But that would be misguided. The resistance to political change often associated with Islam is not necessarily a function of the Islamic faith. The rulers in some notoriously antidemocratic regimes in the Islamic Middle East are actually secular autocrats who refuse to share power — witness Saddam Hussein in Iraq and Hafez al-Assad in Syria. Nonreligious obstacles to political pluralism in the Middle East also persist, such as the secular ideologies of Ba'athism in Iraq and Syria. Strict government controls in some states such as Saudi Arabia isolate the people from democratic ideas and debate on political empowerment. Within the largest Islamic countries in the Middle East, moreover, acute problems of economic development, that is, illiteracy, disease, and poverty, make subsistence a priority over attaining the luxury of democratic politics.[20]

Arab societies have had no local history of democracy on which to draw conceptual inspiration or political resolve. This fact suggests that neither Islam nor its culture is perforce an insurmountable obstacle to political modernity in the Middle East, even if at times undemocratic rulers use Islam as an excuse. The basic tenets of Islam also preach principles of freedom, equality, justice, human dignity, governance by contract, popular sovereignty, and the rule of law. These principles embody the same ideals that fueled revolution in Western civilization in the eighteenth century and are compatible with, if not identical to, cognate principles underpinning liberal democracy. Further, Islam is not wanting for constructs and practices that are compatible with pluralism. Among these are traditions of itihad (interpretation), ijma (consensus), and shura (consultation).[21]

Similarly, attributes in Islamic law and tradition could facilitate development of democracy in the Middle East Islamic world. For instance, a rich political literature of Islam exists. Careful study has been devoted to the nature of political power in society and how power is to be secured and forfeited. Islamic scholars have long examined critically the duties and responsibilities, as well as the rights and privileges, of the powerful in their society. At the same time, Islamic tradition staunchly disapproves of arbitrary rule. The exercise of political power is conceived and presented as a social contract that creates mutual bonds between the rulers and the ruled. Subjects are obligated to obey the ruler, and the ruler is obligated to protect the ruled. Islamic scholars have also produced a wealth of theological, philosophical, and juridical literature on virtually every aspect of the state.

Finally, a fundamental paradox complicates successful democratization in Middle East Islamic countries. Serious concern exists among Western governments that elections in Arab states will bring fundamental Muslims to power. If free, fair, and open elections are held, and all eligible citizens are allowed to participate, then radical Islamists might gain considerable representation in national parliaments or consultative councils. Such electoral success would in turn endow these extremist elements with greater legitimacy and influence in national political processes. These Islamists, it is suggested, will then use democratic political reform to gain power, such as nearly happened in the Algerian elections in 1991, and then go on to instigate policies fostering Islamic revivalism while curtailing Western influence in the region.[22]

Such concerns present a real and disturbing conundrum for true democrats: To exclude hardline fundamentalists works strategically for the U.S. national interest. Clearly, it is not desirable for "another Iran" to gain power in the Middle East, particularly one committed to inciting politically radical, anti-Western views throughout the region. Yet to deny political Islamic elements the opportunity to participate in national democratic elections is overtly antidemocratic and blatantly hypocritical. Not only does it undercut the credibility of the democratic process symbolized by elections, but it also further radicalizes popular Islamic movements antithetical to U.S. policy objectives in the region.

Reflections on Arab Democracy

Can contemporary Muslim societies develop authentically Islamic programs of democracy? In the Islamic Middle East, the emergence and acceptance of democratic values, principles, institutions, and practices involves a complex process of redefining and combining democratic and at times antidemocratic traditions with existing democratic customs. Acceptance of democratic values must be cast in terms of reformulating new perceptions of social religious and political rights and obligations in society.

The suggestion also is made that, in the view of U.S. policymakers, there persists the presupposition of a working, effective American model of democracy, having specific features that can be transplanted to foreign political cultures. American leaders perceive democratic institutions as things that can be exported from the United States to strengthen opportunities for democracy abroad. These modern Western models of democracy, with specific concrete standards, could and should be adapted by governments in the Middle East.

If these perceptions are accurate, the problem here is obvious. Such policies make the United States appear in Arab eyes to be engaging in cultural imperialism, to be advocating imposition of its foreign political system on Islamic culture, rather than supporting local political reform in a gradual manner. Bluntly put, U.S. advocacy of Western democracy becomes viewed from the Arab perspective as cultural aggression that denies the validity of Islam as a way of life, and which in turn enhances the appeal of extremist Muslim revivalists and weakens the position of Muslim reformers striving to create a more democratic political system.[23]

If positive support is to arise for democratization in the Middle East, U.S. policymakers will have to transcend their narrow, ethnocentric conceptualization of democracy. American officials must recognize "the authentic roots for Islamic democracy that might create effective systems of popular participation, though unlike the Westminster model or the American system."[24] True, the United States can serve as an engine for promoting and publicizing the advantages of democracy worldwide. But the primary responsibility for choosing democratic rather than authoritarian-based regimes within Arab Middle Eastern states must rest with the peoples in those states. Democracy is premised on popular legitimacy. That legitimacy can only derive from those peoples' voluntary consent to such a political transformation of government.

U.S. Democratization Strategies

FOREIGN AID AND ECONOMIC ASSISTANCE

To the extent that liberalization has attained worldwide reach, it has done so largely by regimes to cope with economic and social crises. Regimes have responded with reforms to entice local elites into sharing responsibility for improving austerity measures. Many Middle Eastern regimes have thus viewed political liberalization as a vehicle for re-establishing their legitimacy that since the later 1960s had rested mainly on petro-revenues.[25]

Consequently, a potent policy instrument for the United States promoting democracy in the Arab Middle East is economic assistance. External economic factors alone can not effect change in Arab governments; but they can contribute to the cumulative impact of international pressures for reform, particularly along the lines of economic liberalization and eventually democratization. The premise here is that U.S. economic aid can encourage Arab elites to practice more economic pluralist participation, participation that can spill over into fostering greater political pluralist participation. Such logic suggests that greater economic privatization, when tied to genuine economic freedom, can foster the evolution of a strong, pro-democratic middle class and the formation of pluralist centers of political power.[26] Obviously, such a diffusion of economic and political power in turn facilitates the transition to a more civil society.

Public diplomacy and foreign aid programs comprise important facets of suasion used by the United States to influence governments in the Middle East. The U.S. government engages in efforts to persuade public opinion in the Middle East to encourage the process of democratic change in the region. The Agency for International Development (AID) is responsible for administering U.S. economic assistance programs, which come in three forms — economic support funds, development assistance, and Food for Peace aid. Additional U.S. influence is wielded through multilateral lending agencies, especially in U.S. voting decisions for assistance given out by the International Monetary Fund, the World Bank, and the International Development Association.[27]

Economic support funds are dollars loaned or granted to certain states considered to have particular security and political interests for the United States, such as enhancing political stability in a region, promoting economic reforms for market-based economies, or providing access to military bases on their territory. In the Middle East, such funds have gone to secure the

Middle East peace process; indeed, Egypt and Israel have been the two largest recipients of American economic aid since the Camp David agreement of 1978.

Development assistance provides loans and grants for social and economic development. Aid is allocated through designated projects for education, health, agriculture, and rural development. Development assistance aims at long-term objectives for American foreign policy, ostensibly to demonstrate the efficacy of free market capitalism in a political climate of democratic rule.[28]

Food aid, furnished through the Food for Peace Plan (PL 480), sells agricultural commodities on credit terms and makes grants for emergency relief and economic development. Importantly, the United States can designate relief under this program to reward governments that take notable steps toward democratization.[29]

MILITARY ASSISTANCE

If democratization is to have a reasonable chance for taking hold in Middle Eastern countries, the region must remain relatively stable and free of interstate conflict. Maintaining the balance of power among states is seen as key to regional stability, with the United States playing the role of equalizer.

The Middle East is the largest single regional market for weapons sales, with two main arenas for purchases: the states historically involved in the Arab-Israeli conflict and countries along the Persian/Arabian Gulf. The United States is the major arms supplier for countries supporting the peace process, with Jordan and Egypt being the greatest beneficiaries.[30] Happily, with Israel now formally at peace with both Jordan and Egypt, the likelihood for conventional military conflict in the Arab-Israeli arena has diminished substantially.

Concerning Gulf states, American arms sales are linked to efforts to contain Iraq and deter Iran from disruptive regional adventures. The Gulf remains a volatile region. The area contains the world's largest proven oil reserves and most of its excess productive capacity, which are in the possession of small, weak states having small populations. The United States in effect has assumed the role of Gulf policeman, without formally proclaiming it. This role is premised on human rights considerations, as the United States and its allies patrol no-fly zones over southern Iraq (Operation Southern watch to protect Shiite Muslims) and over northern Iraq (Operation Provide Comfort to protect Kurdish peoples).

The United States thus maintains a vital national interest in promoting stability in the Gulf. The security and prosperity of the international community is seen as inextricably linked to the free flow of oil at reasonable prices from the Gulf. This interest demands that the United States take the lead in dissuading and preventing any government — especially Iran or Iraq — from attempting to dominate this tremendously wealthy and strategic area. Dual containment of Iran and Iraq therefore is seen by the United States as a key strategic consideration in the Gulf.

NONGOVERNMENTAL MEANS OF INFLUENCE

Political culture remains an important and necessary consideration in trying to understand national politics. Cultural values shape perceptions of and attitudes toward desired sociopolitical goals, notions of political community, and criteria for legitimacy. If U.S.-sponsored activities can introduce democratic norms, or facilitate democratic practices, or sponsor democratic studies within Arab societies, the presumption is that indigenous peoples will come to realize the benefits associated with democratic liberalism and move gradually but surely to integrate them into their political cultures.

In the past, the United States believed that development aid could achieve the kind of economic growth and social opportunities that lead to societal stability and peaceful competition. In recent years, however, U.S. policymakers have realized that such a strategy was not effective, largely because problems in developing countries exceeded the reach of traditional economic assistance. These developmental problems were not fundamentally economic but were political in nature. Real economic development solutions required real democratic developmental changes, particularly in terms of cultural values, institutions, and organizations of democratic pluralism.

The U.S. government sets national priorities and designates foreign aid resources for democratic development abroad. Even so, much of the real work underpinning American-sponsored democratization policies in the Arab Middle East is performed by nongovernmental organizations.[31]

With communism's collapse and the decline of the Third World as a stage for ideological superpower rivalry, new opportunities arose for the United States to promote democratization. Channels for doing so have been indirect. One prominent channel has been the National Endowment for Democracy (NED), an independent agency not formally part of the U.S. government but dependent on it for funding. NED's mission is straightforward: to facilitate advancement of democracy worldwide.

Created in 1983, NED is a nonprofit, bipartisan grant-making organization that aims to strengthen democratic institutions around the world, including the Arab world, through nongovernmental efforts. In the Middle East, the NED's grants program assists organizations such as political parties and business, civic education, labor, media, and human rights groups in the Middle East that are working to attain democratic goals.[32]

NED supports a variety of pro-democratic activities in Middle Eastern countries. The Palestinian Center for Democracy and Elections (PCDE), founded in 1994, operates to assist Palestinians in the West Bank and Gaza for democratic governance. The center's first workshop brought together Palestinian political factions to ensure that principles would be included in various party platforms. The center distributed computers to democratically minded leaders to enable them to spread their message more efficiently. Further, the PCDE assists in developing programs for political parties and in organizing town meetings in remote villages near Hebron and Ramallah. Such gatherings expose people to democratic processes of discussion and debate, provide for leaders to dialogue with people on issues of local concern, and generally contribute to grassroots civil society activities.[33]

In Lebanon, NED funded the Lebanese Foundation for Permanent Civil Peace (LFPCP) to introduce the Lebanese people to notions of human rights, democracy, and citizenship. The LFPCP published a three-volume textbook, *Citizens for Tomorrow*, for adoption by schools and use by youth organizations.[34]

NED also supports the Free Iraqi Foundation and the Iraqi Research and Documentation Project for producing and distributing thousands of pamphlets into the country that promote ideas of democracy, tolerance, secularism, and human rights — concepts long denied the public under the regime of Saddam Hussein. NED also funds women's organizations throughout the Arab world. The Women's Union of Jordan functions to increase legal literacy and political participation of women in that state. Similarly, in Morocco, the Democratic Association of Moroccan Women sponsors seminars on women's issues at the University of Rabat to counter discriminatory practices and diatribes against women aggravated by Islamic extremist rhetoric. The hope is that seminar participants will act as multiplier effects in their own communities by spreading the message of social equality and discouraging discrimination on the basis of gender. In the West Bank and Gaza, NED assistance to the Women's Affairs Technical Committee has contributed to promoting the role of women in various institutions of a democratic Palestinian Authority. Intensive training sessions for women are designed to teach communication, mobilization, negotiation, and organization skills, which in turn participants can transmit throughout their respective communities.[35] NED also funds grant programs in Middle East countries. The Free Iraq Foundation promotes the notion of liberal democracy among Iraqis living inside Iraq and abroad. In Jordan funds enable the Al-Urdun Al Jadid Research Center to publish works on civil society and political life within the state. In Lebanon NED supports the International Peace Research Association to train Lebanese in conflict resolution, peace negotiation, human rights norms, and democratic values. Funds are also allocated for the Rene Maowad Foundation to support its Center on Research and Education on Democracy. Several programs for democratic activities have been undertaken in the West Bank and Gaza. The Israel-Palestine Center for Research and Information is funded to create a legal infrastructure that fosters private sector development and economic cooperation. The Jerusalem Fund/Center for Policy Analysis on Palestine holds teacher-training workshops in democracy education and has produced a teaching manual/workbook on democratic issues for teachers in secondary schools. Nonviolence International has been funded to study the reorganization and restructuring of Palestinian political movements, while support also goes for a "Pluralism in Action" project by the Panorama Center for the Dissemination of Alternative Information, which brings public leaders from prominent political factions to secondary schools for weekly roundtable debates with students.[36]

Under NED are four grantee, nonprofit organizations, of which the National Democratic Institute for International Affairs (NDI) and the International Republican Institute (IRI) have been especially active in supporting democratic-oriented activities throughout the Arab world. The National Democratic Institute for International Affairs, an independent organization affiliated with the Democratic Party, was established to promote democratic training programs and democratic institution building abroad.[37] The catalytic belief behind NDI is that the United States must include democratic development as an essential component of foreign assistance. Working democracies require working democratic institutions, for example, legislatures that represent the people and oversee the executive, as well as elections in which voters actually choose their leaders and judiciaries independent of external influences. Moreover, for a democracy to operate successfully there must exist a system of checks and balances, as well as leaders who are accountable to the public. NDI thus seeks to consolidate existing democratic institutions and engender peaceful transitions to democracy.

NDI funds programs to develop civic organizations, enhance political participation by women, and promote election processes in the Middle East. For example, the National Endowment for Democracy funded NDI to study the 1995 municipal elections in Jordan and to support the long-term institutional development of the New Jordan Research Center in Amman. In Lebanon NDI supports Lebanese civic organizations working for a more transparent parliamentary electoral process, and in the West Bank and Gaza a program on democratic elections was launched, which included sending two international missions to the region before the February 1996 elections and producing a report that assessed the regions' pre-election political environment.[38]

Also associated with NED, the International Republican Institute aims to foster greater freedoms around the world by supporting grassroots political instruction about political parties and election campaigning, assisting in legislative training, monitoring elections to facilitate free and fair multiparty elections, and promoting civic education that encourages citizen participation in governmental affairs.[39]

Fundamental to a successful Arab-Israeli peace is self-rule for Palestinians in the West Bank and Gaza. Concomitant is the need to narrow the communication gap between the Palestinian people — who have had little input into policy affecting their future — and their leadership in the National Authority, which has never actually governed anybody. To remedy this, the IRI funds the Center for Palestinian Research and Studies to conduct survey opinion polls of political events in the West Bank and Gaza. The specific democracy-related objectives of this program are: (1) to increase the availability of information concerning popular Palestinian attitudes on political, social, and economic issues in the transition period to self-rule; and (2) to heighten the level of popular discussion and cooperation about democratic values and practices within the Palestinian community. To a large degree, this program has provided a meaningful civic and useful public service.[40]

Besides furnishing more accurate information on Palestinian political attitudes relative to elections, these polls also supply valuable data about economic indicators, such as unemployment, the status of refugee camps, the status of the middle class, education levels, and attitudes toward various gender issues. In addition, CPRS polling provides an opportunity for the Palestinians to evaluate the performance of the Palestinian National Authority and thus acts as a channel of communication between the people and their leaders.[41]

Two other aspects of the IRI's West Bank and Gaza Strip program stand out. One is the institute's sponsorship of "community outreach workshops" for promoting popular dialogue about political attitudes, democratic participation, and public awareness.[42] Second, CPRS has been funded to conduct election-day exit polling of voters to determine Palestinian voting patterns, turnout, issue orientation, leadership criteria, and voter priorities. Such information about the Palestinian electorate could be useful in gauging the impact of issues and personalities affecting regional voting behavior.[43]

In Morocco IRI supports a project for improving the research and staff of the Moroccan parliament. IRI also sponsors programs to train local officials and conduct workshops on democratic governance.[44]

In Kuwait the IRI assisted pro-democratic groups in political techniques for the October 1993 elections. Since then IRI has supported a parliamentary assistance program to further the National Assembly's professional involvement in affairs of state, including insights into the separation of powers and emphasis on the rule of law as evidenced in the U.S. government system.[45]

As nongovernmental organizations, the National Endowment for Democracy, the National Democratic Institute for International Affairs, and the International Republican Institute are funded annually by U.S. congressional appropriation and are all specifically designed to support local groups abroad working for democratic goals. Grant programs for the Middle East are funded to support civic education, labor, political parties, business, media, and human rights groups involved in democratic institution building. These programs are clearly designed to facilitate acceptance of democratization at the grassroots level — to educate people about the democratic process, to establish the seed bed for developing democratic institutions, and to enhance the prospects for a more pluralist political culture in which competing groups vie through free and fair elections for legitimate authority to govern their society. Though this grassroots, sociological approach is undoubtedly slow, cumbersome, and piecemeal, its impacts promise to be more lasting with the general public — the very force allocated the ultimate say in the democratic process.

Democracy and Double Standards

In Freedom House's 1996 survey of "The Map of Freedom," the only Middle Eastern state that qualifies as being "free" (for example, having a democratically elected government) is Israel. Jordan, Kuwait, and Morocco are designated "partially free," primarily because of political reforms made in those countries during the past five years. But Algeria, Bahrain, Egypt, Iran, Iraq, Lebanon, Libya, Qatar, Saudi Arabia, Syria, Tunisia, and the United Arab Emirates are all categorized as "not free." Their governments cannot be changed by the people democratically, and serious human rights violations there are well documented. Such conditions seem especially regrettable for American foreign policy, given that several of these governments are considered "friends" of the United States and are even dependent on U.S. military and economic assistance. One might infer from this aid dependency that the United States could exercise influence on these governments to promote democratic reforms in their states, at least by pressuring them to be more diligent about protecting fundamental human rights of their citizens. This, however, has not been the case.

Five Arab states hold particular relevance for U.S. policy and the promotion of democratic values in the region: Morocco, Egypt, Jordan, Kuwait, and Saudi Arabia, as well as the Israeli-occupied territory of the West Bank and Gaza. But a cursory survey of the human rights situation in Arab states considered "U.S. friends in the region" quickly suggests that the United States puts little or no political or diplomatic pressure on these governments to adopt liberal reforms. The U.S. government's view is to treat democratization as a gradual, piecemeal process that must be internalized incrementally, rather than be imposed by outside pressures. Human rights organizations consequently are neither impressed by official U.S. policy statements advocating democratization in the Middle East, nor by the slow, subtle means applied to achieve that end. The political rhetoric of democratization sounds high-minded but has not measured up to the expectations of advocacy groups for changed human rights conditions in Arab countries viewed as friends of the United States.

Kuwait is a notable case in point. Several improvements in Kuwait's political structure suggest that democratic trends are under way. For example, Kuwait's parliament is functioning anew. Press censorship has been abolished, restrictions on public meetings by religious and professional associations have been lifted, and the first parliamentary committee on human rights in the Arab world now actively works to promote reforms in police practices. In 1995, the right to vote was granted to naturalized male citizens (albeit only twenty years after being naturalized!). More significantly, in 1995 Kuwait abolished its State Security Court, which had handed out death penalties and other harsh sentences in proceedings widely viewed by human rights groups as unfair, often using coerced confessions and denying legal counsel to the accused. Finally, in October 1996, Kuwait held its second national parliamentary election since the Gulf War.[46]

But official practices in Kuwait still contravene democratic ways. Women still cannot vote, nor can they hold public office. Political parties are banned. The Bedoons — native Kuwaitis denied nationality — and Palestinian inhabitants have been subjected to arbitrary arrests, harassment, and torture by security police. This abusive treatment has come in reaction to beliefs of collusion by these groups with Iraq during the Gulf War and the government's unmistakable intent to compel them to leave Kuwait.

Jordan, another close friend of the United States, has moved closer toward democracy over the last decade. In 1989 the king lifted restrictions on freedom of expression, and the official ban was lifted on party activity. Peaceful public demonstrations are permitted. In 1992 martial law was lifted, and in November 1993 Jordan had its first multiparty elections in nearly four decades. Public criticism of government policies freely occurs, although the king retains broad executive powers and must approve all laws.

Human rights abuses nevertheless do occur. Scores of people are annually arrested on political grounds. Allegations of torture by officers of the General Intelligence Department are often made, as is the practice of arresting persons without charges and detaining them incommunicado up to nine months. Women are discriminated against in inheritance and divorce matters and are not able to travel abroad without permission from a male guardian.

In recent years Morocco's human rights record has significantly improved. The number of abuses during detention has been reduced, although torture and mistreatment persist. The press enjoys a more open climate for political discourse, although criticism of King Hassan or challenges to Morocco's claim to the Western Sahara can prompt recriminations against journalists. Laws still discriminate against women, and few avenues are available for seeking redress in crimes of family violence.

In Egypt the Arab world's most populous country, the government pays short shrift to human rights considerations in its domestic battle with Islamic extremists, as nonviolent opposition groups are often mistreated as well. Security forces operate with near impunity. Arbitrary arrests, prolonged detention, torture, several prisoner deaths, hostage taking, and executions of civilians condemned to death by military courts are clear failures of Egypt's human rights record in recent years. In 1995 more than forty opposition lawyers were imprisoned, many after being tortured; political parties were banned, and a number of opposition candidates for parliamentary elections were imprisoned. Regrettably, the United States has done little publicly to condemn or penalize Hosni Mubarak's government for resorting to such abusive, antidemocratic tactics. The United States remains Egypt's largest donor and military supplier. In fact, Egypt still enjoys special status as the second largest recipient of U.S. foreign aid, after Israel. This aid — $1.3 billion from the Foreign Military Financing Program and $815 million from Economic Support Funds — flows as a reward for Egypt's maintaining peace with Israel under the Camp David accords. But it comes absent the United States imposing conditions for improving human rights or for ending egregious abuses committed by government security forces.

A close friend of the United States in the Gulf is Saudi Arabia. Paradoxically, that kingdom has one of the poorest human rights records in the Middle East. Arbitrary arrest, detention without trials, and mistreatment of prisoners is commonplace, and executions of opposition dissidents are well known. The government bans free speech, assembly, and association. Political participation is severely curtailed. There are no elections, nor are independent public expressions permitted. Restrictions are placed on the rights, movement, and employment of women, and non-Muslims are openly harassed. Furthermore, the government's recent crackdown on peaceful dissent by Islamist groups has led to holding hundreds of detainees without trial, coercing confessions and convening secret tribunals to try suspected opposition leaders, often without legal counsel, for subversion, rebellion, and heresy — capital offenses in Saudi Arabia.

U.S. policy interests in the Gulf subordinate human rights principles fundamental to making a democratic civil society and instead emphasize geostrategic, military, and commercial ties with the Saudi government. To these ends, U.S. government officials steadfastly refrain from commenting publicly on the human rights record in Saudi Arabia, presumably to avoid offending the royal family and to deny propaganda that might be used by militant Islamist opposition elements against the regime.

Human rights issues also cloud the legitimacy of the Middle East peace process. The Palestinian Authority's partial self-rule has not pleased either champions of human rights or advocates of democratization. Security forces of the Palestinian Authority have arrested, tortured, and abused opposition suspects, intimidated journalists critical of the Israeli-PLO accord, and imprisoned suspected members of opposition groups without formal charges for months. Israel continues to exercise security policies that restrict the freedom of Palestinians to enter or leave the occupied territories. In the West Bank areas where Israeli forces still exercise direct control, human rights abuses such as arbitrary arrest, collective punishment, and torture continue as in the past. The three suicide bombings by Hamas that killed fifty-nine Israelis in early 1996 provoked severe abridgments of Palestinian rights, as well as the change of party leadership in Israel's government.

The United States has mainly reacted to violations of fundamental human rights and freedoms in Gaza and on the West Bank with silence. The United States continues to furnish Israel with some $3 billion in economic and military assistance annually, making it the largest beneficiary of U.S. foreign aid. The United States now also qualifies as the largest donor to the Palestinian Authority, with some $500 million pledged in 1993 for development assistance and loan guarantees through 1998, including $24 million for a "democracy-building" program. These aid packages are used by the United States more as inducements for Israel and the Palestinian Authority to cooperate in the peace process, rather than as political instruments to promote further human rights and democratic freedoms for peoples in the region.

Since 1991 international attention has focused mainly on the Middle East peace process and the means for making that process happen for all the participants. Ostensibly, the objective here is for a successful peace process that can transform regional political cultures into more tolerant societies and more effectively integrate fundamental human rights considerations into democratic practice. But that has not happened. Instead, national interests as perceived by Western governments, especially the United States, have produced a double standard toward accountability. In the process, policies reflecting this double standard have politicized human rights issues, undercut the willingness of friendly Arab governments to respect the rule of law, and generally stalled progress for improving human rights conditions in the Middle East.

While certain governments openly hostile to the United States are publicly criticized, censured, and pressured by economic sanctions — Libya, Iraq, and Iran — abuses by governments considered friendly or valuable to competing U.S. interests in the region are seldom noted, much less condemned. Arab governments that support the peace process — Egypt, Morocco, and Jordan — or confront Islamist militants with nondemocratic means (especially Egypt and Saudi Arabia) are rarely criticized for their human rights abuses. However, governments or organizations perceived by the United States as threats to the peace process, as well as Islamic opposition groups, are held to a strict standard and are harshly condemned.[47]

The U.S. government also remains apprehensive that the horrendous violence that has consumed Algeria since 1991 might spread to neighboring countries, especially Egypt, Morocco, or Saudi Arabia. This fear has muted public expressions of concern by U.S. officials over those governments' abuse of fundamental human rights. The message of this double standard no doubt rings out loud and clear for Arab governments considered friends of the United States. In the domestic war against political Islam, the ends justify the means: brutal, arbitrary, and abusive actions will be tolerated to prevent other Irans from taking root in Middle Eastern countries.

The Balance Sheet

Although the U.S. government might champion promoting democracy for Middle East Arab states, its rhetoric far exceeds the reality of action for producing liberal reform in those countries. The United States asserts the high road when it comes to talking about advocating democracy in the Middle East. But U.S. policy demonstrates that it is actually the low road — the subtle, indirect, slow course — that most often is taken. U.S. policy, moreover, gives priority to regional political considerations over genuine incentives that would persuade Arab governments to reform human rights abuses and adopt democratic principles. The fact is this: The United States usually refrains from criticizing "friendly" Arab governments who compromise democratic values and abuse human rights of their own citizenry.

For U.S. policy, promoting democracy in Middle Eastern countries actually comes down to offering moral, political, diplomatic, and financial aid and support to individuals and organizations that are struggling to liberalize authoritarian regimes. People trying to institutionalize democratic governments in Middle Eastern states must receive aid so that they can attain economic reforms and acquire training and technical support necessary for institutionalizing democratic ways and means. Similarly, special assistance must be furnished so that certain nongovernmental elements essential to the democratic process — political parties, civic groups, trade unions, and the mass media — can take root and grow in those societies. Demands for instant democratization in the Middle East Islamic world are neither plausible nor desirable. Such a development would be revolutionary in its social and cultural impacts, bringing with it profound (and likely violent) political and legal upheavals in those societies. A preferable strategy is for the United States to pursue a policy of "democratic incrementalism." Democracy must be proffered to regimes and peoples in the Arab world gradually, in bits and pieces. Democratic practices and principles must be introduced carefully, patiently, and with genuine sensitivity for the region's Islamic-based political culture. The advantages of democracy must be demonstrated, not from the American vantage point but for the Arab peoples themselves. This must not be done in terms of the United States' experiences with democracy or the avowed progressive conceptions in the West of human rights and civil liberties. Rather, Arab peoples must be educated over time to realize the real practical advantages for all citizens that derive from democratic liberalism, as opposed to an authoritarian regime that rewards a few at the expense of the many.

Progress toward the acceptance of democratic values and institutions takes time, patience, and political will. Liberal democracies in the West did not appear overnight. U.S. policymakers must remain mindful of the history of slavery in the United States and the intentional disfranchisement, until this century, of women throughout most of the Western world. It will be no less true for Islamic societies in the Arab world as they enter their Enlightenment period in the twenty-first century. Maintaining the necessary patience by American foreign policymakers as Arab peoples gradually accumulate the political will to accept democratic values and principles may prove to be the greatest challenge for U.S. policy in promoting liberal democracy in the Middle East.

Notes

1. "Support by the United Nations of the Efforts of Governments to Promote and Consolidate New or Restored Democracies: Report of the Secretary-General," UN Doc. A/50/332 (August 7, 1995), paras. 11–13. Also see generally, the study by David P. Forsythe, with Garry Baker and Michele Leonard, "U.S. Foreign Policy and Enlarging the Democracy Community," paper for the Center for Migration, New School (August 1996).

2. See Michael C. Hudson, "The Political Culture Approach to Arab Democratization: The Case for Bringing It Back In, Carefully," in *Political Liberalization & Democratization in the Arab World*, ed. Rex Brynen, Bahgat Korany, and Paul Noble, vol. 1 (Boulder CO: Lynne Rienner, 1996), 61–76. But compare Lisa Anderson, "Democracy in the Arab World: A Critique of the Political Culture Approach," in *Political Liberalization*, 77–92.

3. See Lise Garon, "The Press and Democratic Transition in Arab Societies: The Algerian Case," in *Political Liberalization*, 149–166.

4. See generally, Saad Eddin Ibrahim, "Liberalization and Democratization in the Arab World: An Overview," in *Political Liberalization*, 29–60.

5. See Rex Brynen, Bahgat Korany, and Paul Noble, "Introduction: Theoretical Perspectives on Arab Liberalization and Democratization," in *Political Liberalization*, 3–29.

6. Brynen, Korany, and Noble, "Theoretical Perspectives," in *Political Liberalization*, 3. See also Mustapha Kamel al-Sayyid, "The Concept of Civil Society in the Arab World," in *Political Liberalization*, 31–148.

7. John Esposito and John O. Voll, *Islam and Democracy* (Oxford: Oxford University Press, 1996), 13–14.

8. Robert H. Pelletreau, "Update on Developments in the Middle East," *U.S. Department of State Dispatch* 7 (February 12, 1996): 42–44.

9. See generally, Larry Diamond, "Promoting Democracy," *Foreign Policy*, no. 87 (summer 1992): 25–46.

10. The "democratic peace" theory is not without controversy or conjecture, however. For a useful compendium of agreements in this debate, see Michael E. Brown, Sean M. Lynn-Jones, and Steven E. Miller, eds., *Debating the Democratic Peace* (Cambridge: MIT Press, 1995).

11. See generally the thoughtful contributions in Daniel Brumberg, ed., *Arab-American Relations: A New Beginning?* (Washington DC: Foundation on Democratization and Political Change in the Middle East, 1995).

12. See, e.g., Daniel Pipes, *In the Path of God: Islam and Political Power* (New York: Basic Books, 1983), 144–147; Al Colder, *Democracy and Arab Political Culture* (Washington DC: Washington Institute for Near East Policy, 1992), 5–8; and Mervat F. Hatem, "Political Liberalism, Gender and the State," in *Political Liberalization*, 187–211.

13. See Bernard Lewis, "A Historical Overview," *Journal of Democracy* 7 (April 1996): 53–63.

14. Mohammad Al Rumaihi, "Kuwait: Oasis of Liberalism?," *Middle East Quarterly* 1 (September 1994): 31–35.

15. Rumaihi, "Kuwait," 32.

16. See generally, Daniel Brumberg, "Authoritarian Legacies and Reform Strategies in the Arab World," in *Political Liberalization*, 229–260.

17. The following taxonomy is drawn from Bernard Lewis, "A Historical Over-view," 59–60.

18. This might be the motive behind terrorist attacks against U.S. military personnel in Saudi Arabia. See Thomas W. Lippman, "Mission to Bolster Saudi Security Also Provokes Rulers' Enemies," *Washington Post*, June 27 1996, A24.

19. Lippman, "Mission," A24. See also John Lancaster, "Few See Saudi Stability Threatened by Militants," *Washington Post*, June 27, 1996, A24. On the contemporary threat of terrorism to U.S. interests, see generally, Christopher C. Joyner and Tamara Cofman Wittes, "The United States and International Terrorism: Policy and Response," *International Issues* 39 (August 1996): 27–50.

20. See generally, Giacomo Luciani, "Resources, Revenues, and Authoritarianism in the Arab World: Beyond the Rentier State?," in *Political Liberalization*, 211–228.

21. Robin Wright, "Islam and Liberal Democracy: Two Visions of Reformation," *Journal of Democracy* 7 (April 1996): 64–75. Compare John Esposito and John O. Voll, *Islam and Democracy* (Oxford: Oxford University Press, 1996), 27–32; and Fazlur Rahman, "The Principle of Shura and the Role of Ummah in Islam," in *State, Politics and Islam*, ed. Mumtaz Ahmad (Indianapolis: American Trust Publications, 1986), 90–91.

22. See, e.g., James Phillips, "The Rising Threat of Revolutionary Islam in Algeria," *Heritage Foundation Backgrounder*, no. 1060 (November 9, 1995); and Andrew Pierre and William Quandt, "Algeria's War on Itself," *Foreign Policy*, no. 99 (summer 1995), 131–148.

23. John O. Voll and John L. Esposito, "Islam's Democratic Essence," *Middle East Quarterly* 1 (September 1994): 11.

24. Voll and Esposito, "Essence."

25. See "The Democracy Agenda in the Arab World" (editorial), *Middle East Report* 22 (January–February 1992): 3–6.

26. Pete Moore, "The International Context of Liberalization and Democratization in the Arab World," *Arab Studies Quarterly* 16 (summer 1994): 55–56.

27. Charles W. Kegley Jr. and Eugene R. Wittkopf, *American Foreign Policy: Pattern and Process*, 5th ed. (New York: St. Martin's, 1996), 138–139.

28. Kegley and Wittkopf, *Pattern and Process*, 138.

29. Presumably, such aid might also be denied to governments that are antidemocratic or even lethargic in accepting or implementing democratic practices. See generally, Robert F. Zimmerman, *Dollars, Diplomacy, and Dependency: Dilemmas of U.S. Economic Aid* (Boulder CO: Lynne Rienner, 1993).

30. See Michael Collins Dunn, "Settling Sands After Desert Storm," *Armed Forces Journal* (August 1996): 22–26.

31. "The Government vs. NGOs in Democratic Development," in "What Is the National Democratic Institute for International Affairs"? (May 1996), http://www.ndi.org [April 25, 1999].

32. National Endowment for Democracy (statement of purpose page, cover, n.d.).

33. National Endowment for Democracy, *Annual Report* (Washington DC, 1995), 61.

34. National Endowment for Democracy, *Annual Report*, 61.

35. National Endowment for Democracy, *Annual Report*, 62.

36. National Endowment for Democracy, *Annual Report*, 63–65.

37. "What Is the National Democratic Institute for International Affairs?" (May 1996), *http://www.ndi.org* [April 25, 1999], 2.

38. NED, Annual Report 1995, 63–65.

39. International Republican Institute 1995, IRI (pamphlet, May 1996), 1 (IRI Mission).

40. International Republican Institute, "International Republican Institute West Bank and Gaza Strip Program Mid-Term Report PDC-0023-A-00-1089-00" (Washington DC, 1996), tab 1.

41. See, e.g., "[Results of] Public Opinion Polls May 1995, March 1995, February 1995," in IRI, "West Bank and Gaza Strip Program Mid-Term Report," tab 3.

42. IRI, "Mid-Term Report," at tab 6.

43. IRI, "Mid-Term Report," at tab 8.

44. "Morocco" (Program Summaries, May 1996) (mimeographed sheet from IRI), on file with the author.

45. NED, Annual Report 1995, 63.

46. See John Lancaster, "Hot Winds of Democracy Rustle the Gulf," *Washington Post*, October 4, 1996, A25.

47. It is true that the Department of State's annual *Country Reports on Human Rights Practices* extensively documents, catalogues, and severely criticizes human rights violations in Egypt, Kuwait, Saudi Arabia, Morocco, Algeria, and the Israeli-Occupied West Bank and Gaza Strip. Regrettably, however, this criticism remains relegated to print; it is not translated into public policy commitments aimed at improving human rights conditions in these countries.

SECTION 3
Multilateralism

12

The United States, the IMF, and Human Rights

•

A Policy-Relevant Approach

•

LINDA CAMP KEITH AND STEVEN C. POE

Recent empirical research has improved our understanding of why some of the most serious human rights abuses occur. Studies using quantitative methods to analyze global cross-national data sets have sought to explain the occurrence of abuses of those human rights that pertain to integrity of the person — the rights not to be imprisoned, tortured, or killed either arbitrarily or for one's political views.[1]

Studies of this kind, and their conclusions in the form of general explanatory statements, are of interest to academicians who concern themselves mainly with the development of theory explaining why repression occurs. Unfortunately, the academic's enthusiasm for this line of research has not yet been shared by practitioners who tend to be more concerned with promoting human rights practices in a particular region or country. In this chapter we will first address the question of what might be done to make this research more relevant to the practitioners who make U.S. foreign policy. We will come to some conclusions on this issue and then will present an example of a study we think should be of some interest to policymakers — International Monetary Fund (IMF) stabilization loan programs (over which U.S. foreign policymakers have great influence) and their impact on human rights.

The Professor and the Policymaker: A Dialogue and a Dilemma

As a way to arrive directly at the crux of the problem with the quantitative research on human rights from the perspective of the foreign policy practitioner, let us imagine a discussion between a make-believe professor and a hypothetical foreign policymaker. Let us assume that the professor's occupation is to conduct quantitative, empirical research on human rights abuses and that the policymaker is truly interested in promoting human rights, when it is both in her power and consistent with her charge to do so.

"Why don't you read my work?" we can imagine the professor asking somewhat indignantly.

"That's easy—because it's not very relevant to what I do," would be the likely reply. "Your research may be an interesting theoretical exercise, but it doesn't tell me much of use about the real world. And it tells me even less about how to better human rights conditions in particular countries. Take Jordan for example. . . ."

"But my research is relevant to your policymaking. Studies published by myself and others in my subfield would undoubtedly be of some help, if you'd only take the time to read them!"

(The professor would say this and in the next instant realize that each of his pieces contain extended, jargon-laden, and generally inaccessible discussions of statistical methodology. If our policymaker were to actually read the professor's writings she would need considerable statistical expertise or a very strong will—or perhaps better yet, the prudence to read them en passim.)

The professor pauses for a moment while he considers this point. Choosing to dismiss it for the moment, he continues, "My studies provide a necessary background for people like you who wish to promote human rights. To be able to promote human rights, you have to understand why they are realized in some countries but not in others. If you read my work you might even find that it suggests paths the United States could take to improve human rights conditions around the world, Jordan included."

"How's that?"

"I'll give you a few examples. My findings uniformly indicate that countries with democratic political institutions tend to violate human rights less. They also indicate quite clearly that greater economic development leads to fewer human rights abuse and that international wars and civil threats lead to greater human rights abuses. So, what you need to do to further the cause of human rights is to increase the countries' economic standing or get them to adopt democratic political institutions. Or you can work to settle international and civil threats when they occur."

"And how would you suggest I do that?" she would ask with a bemused smile on her face.

A very long pause would follow as the professor considers the quandary presented by her question. Having arrived at the heart of the dilemma, we can close the curtain on this dialogue, for now.

The professor conveniently offered as his examples of relevant findings some of the conclusions from our ongoing research program on personal integrity abuses.[2] Though the main purpose proposed at the outset of this research program was to develop and test theories that help us to understand why decision makers choose to abuse these human rights, we held out the hope that this line of research might someday assist foreign policymakers and practitioners working for human rights IGOs and NGOs. Causal models of human rights abuse, such as the ones that we build and test, could conceivably inform their efforts, helping them to allocate scarce resources more effectively. However, the dilemma that was illustrated in the hypothetical dialogue we sketched above is a very real one. Thus far our findings indicate that to effectively improve human rights practices around the world necessitates dealing with "root causes," such as poverty, internal and external threat of violence, or nondemocratic regimes. Unfortunately, as even the most casual observers of international politics must realize, attacking problems of such vast proportion is an extremely difficult matter. "Root causes" defy easy solutions — and frequently more difficult ones, too. Each of the variables linked with human rights abuses mentioned previously has generated a considerable literature in its own right, and though each literature might imply some ways that the respective problems can be rectified, the "solutions" that would be necessary to manipulate those variables are also very difficult because they, too, often deal with root causes that are not easily manipulated.[3]

We stand by the professor's contention that the literature on the determinants of countries' human rights practices would provide a useful theoretical background to U.S. foreign policymakers were they to take the time to read it, but we concede the policymaker's point that such studies have not yet done a very good job of suggesting roads that policymakers wishing to further the cause of human rights might travel. We conclude from this dialogue that one way to be more relevant to policymakers is, after obtaining some confidence in our "root cause" explanations, to turn some of our attention to hypothesized determinants of human rights abuse that practitioners can more easily manipulate. If such variables are shown to influence variations in the abuse of human rights, then our research might make a difference to practitioners' efforts, if only at the margins.[4] A reasonable place to begin, if we care about making our research more relevant to U.S. foreign policymakers, is with the question, "What options are available to the U.S. government in its efforts to promote international human rights?"

Identification of U.S. Policy Opportunities

Guided by our desire to say something relevant and worthwhile to policymakers, we first set out to identify options that could actually be used by the U.S. government if it were interested in promoting improved human rights conditions abroad.[5] Our thinking quickly yielded a very long list of foreign policy outputs that could be used for this purpose. To narrow our search we sought next to identify options that had explicitly been linked by legislation to global human rights practices. Though other outputs might also be investigated, this was a good place to begin our inquiry, for if the U.S. government had expressed the willingness to tie a foreign policy output to human rights conditions, it would be more apt to manipulate that output than others where no such willingness has ever been evident.

A willingness, on the part of the U.S. government, to link certain foreign policy outputs with human rights criteria began to be in evidence in legislation passed in the early 1970s. In 1974 Congress passed the Harkin Amendment, which amended the Foreign Assistance Act of 1961 to require that:

> No assistance may be provided under subchapter I of this chapter to the government of any country which engages in a consistent pattern of gross violations of internationally recognized human rights, including torture or cruel, inhuman, or degrading treatment or punishment, prolonged detention without charges, causing the disappearance or persons by abduction and clandestine detention of those persons or other flagrant denial of the right to life, liberty, and the security of the person, unless such assistance will directly benefit the needy people in the country.[6]

Later, in 1978, Section 502B of the Foreign Assistance Act of 1961 was amended to deny security assistance to "any country the government of which engages in a consistent pattern of gross violations of internationally recognized human rights."[7]

The linkage between foreign policy and human rights was extended to U.S. actions in international financial institutions, such as the International Monetary Fund, through Section 701 of the International Financial Assistance Act of 1977, which declared that:

The United States Government, in connection with its voice and vote in the International Bank for Reconstruction and Development, the International Development Association, the International Finance Corporation, the Inter-American Development Bank, the African Development Fund, the Asian Development Bank, the African Development Bank, the European Bank for Reconstruction and Development, and the International Monetary Fund, shall advance the cause of human rights, including by seeking to channel assistance towards countries other than those whose governments engage in — a pattern of gross violations of internationally recognized human rights, such as torture or cruel, inhumane, or degrading treatment or punishment, prolonged detention without charges, or other flagrant denial to life, liberty, and the security of person.[8]

So our reading of human rights legislation indicates that, at least in theory, the United States is willing to manipulate its bilateral foreign aid allocations and loans from international financial institutions based on human rights related criteria. The impact of U.S. foreign aid allocations on human rights conditions in recipient countries was addressed recently by Regan, who concluded that foreign aid had little impact on human rights practices.[9] Therefore, we chose in this chapter to turn our attention to the United States and its participation in the IMF. Next we will examine the IMF and its conditional loan programs, as well as the position of the United States in that international financial institution.

The IMF, Balance of Payments Support, and U.S. Foreign Policy

In 1944, under the leadership of the United States and the United Kingdom, a conference was held in Bretton Woods, New Hampshire. There representatives from forty-five nations met to create an international system for economic development and currency stabilization in the post-war world. The meeting culminated in the signing of the Articles of Agreement, which would eventually establish the International Monetary Fund, in December of 1945.[10] The first of these articles outlines six purposes which that new institution was to fulfill. IMF has interpreted this article as giving it responsibility for: "surveillance of the world economy; provision of temporary balance of payments support; and maintenance of a system of multilateral trade and payments."[11] It is the second of these purposes, the provision of temporary balance of payments support, which is relevant to this study.

Balance of payments is the statistical record of all economic transactions of a country's residents with residents of other countries, during a given year These transactions include the exchange of resources (such as labor and capital) across countries, changes in foreign assets and liabilities, and transfer payments.[12] A country is said to have a balance of payments problem when "the country is spending (absorbing) more than the total of what it produces and can borrow from abroad."[13] IMF, under its charge to provide temporary balance of payments support, provides financial resources to help member countries correct payment imbalances. It assesses the borrowing country's imbalance and prescribes measures to correct the imbalance (a stabilization program), which the country must agree to follow. Some conditions usually must be satisfied before the loan is approved, and others must be met during the agreement period for the country to continue drawing against the account.[14] Three IMF adjustment programs that entail a degree of conditionality are the standby agreement; the Extended Fund Facility (EFF), which was introduced in 1974; and the Structural Adjustment Facility (SAF), which was introduced in 1986. Typically, if a certain set of conditions is not met, then no loan is given. If further conditions are not met after the loan period begins, the country becomes ineligible to draw further sums on IMF accounts unless a new agreement can be reached.[15]

For an examination of IMF balance of payments support to fit well with the goal of this study — to say something worthwhile to policymakers — there must first be a very good reason to believe that this support is related to human rights practices in recipient countries. Secondly, these programs must be manipulable by the U.S. government.

With regard to the first standard, we can imagine two distinct arguments as to why we should think IMF stabilization programs affect levels of personal integrity abuse. Our expectation is that the economic austerity programs connected with IMF conditions will, in many cases, lead to political unrest in the form of protests, riots, and other violent and nonviolent acts of political opposition. There are in fact numerous examples that lend support to this expectation. In 1986 the Zambian government implemented elements of an IMF austerity program, which included the removal of the subsidy on refined maize. This action, which resulted in a 120 percent price increase, led to serious food riots.[16] In April 1984 the Dominican Republic experienced three days of food riots following its implementation of an IMF program, which resulted in large increases in food prices. These riots resulted in sixty deaths, hundreds of injuries, and over one thousand persons being imprisoned.[17] In late 1983 and early 1984 Tunisia also experienced rioting over the removal of ood subsidies on grain. Over one hundred people died in the riots before he subsidies were restored by the government.[18] We hypothesize that such cts would bring regimes to perceive an increased threat to their rule, which night lead them to resort to repression as a means to decrease the threat.[19] uch visible forms of opposition are not a necessary condition for the decision makers to perceive a threat to their rule, however, because as Pion-Berlin points out, leaders may choose to strike preemptively.[20] In doing so hey would increase repressive measures prior to the appearance of an outward manifestation of threat, if their expectation is that threats will arise and endanger their rule in the future.

Conversely, if IMF stabilization programs are successful in achieving their designed purpose to improve the economic well-being of participating countries, we might expect them to be linked to less repression. Past empirical studies on repression have hypothesized, and the results have tended to how, that as countries have improved their economic positions, less repression is used.[21]

Our expectation in this study is that IMF programs are positively related to or lead to more) personal integrity abuses. This expectation is due in part o the nature of the tests that we will perform. The tests we conduct in this tudy will necessarily focus on only the short-term impacts of IMF programs because of data limitations. Our pooled cross-sectional time series data set overs a global sample of 153 countries but only for an eight-year period panning 1980–87, which unfortunately is much too short for meaningful analyses investigating possible long-term impacts.

On our second requirement, that the activity be manipulable by U.S. foreign policymakers, we again find IMF loans to be appropriate for our study. The evidence demonstrates convincingly that the United States is unquestionably the major factor in the International Monetary Fund. Benjamin Cohen argues that the United States has "substantial leverage" in the IMF that amounts to "unparalleled influence over IMF decision making."[22] Similar arguments have been made by such practitioners as former Secretary of State George Schultz.[23] The reasons for American dominance become clear upon examination of the weighted, majority voting system used in IMF decision making.[24] As Ferguson points out "the funds votes are weighed overwhelmingly on the basis of the quotas allotted to each member."[25] Each member state receives 250 basic votes plus one additional vote for each 100,000 Special Drawing Rights contributed to the IMF.[26] As a result of this quota system, he United States has traditionally exercised a great influence over IMF decision making. Since 85 percent of the votes are required to take action, and the United States has maintained at least 15.1 percent of the voting power since the Fund's beginnings, it has effectively exercised a veto over IMF decisions throughout the institution's history.[27] In 1996 the United States held 18.25 percent of the votes.

Clearly, this structure gives the United States the opportunity to use the IMF as a tool to implement its policy goals. Cohen suggests that:

> Washington might be able to supplement its power resources by pursuing policy objectives through the intermediation of a multilateral agency such as the International Monetary Fund — in effect, to deploy the Fund as part of the government's broader linkage strategies. Because of the global debt problem, the IMF has gained considerable leverage over the behavior of both debtor governments and banks. . . . In effect, therefore, an opportunity seems to have been created for U.S. policymakers to accomplish directly, via the IMF, what they cannot accomplish (or can accomplish only at a higher economic or political cost) on a direct, bilateral basis.[28]

There are many clear examples in which the United States has apparently used its influence in IMF decision making to achieve its own foreign policy goals. Forsythe found that during the first Reagan administration the United States' policy in the multilateral banks was "voting for loans to right wing allies while voting against loans to certain left wing developing countries," such as Angola, South Yemen, and Laos.[29] More recently, the United States (and Japan) have blocked IMF loans to Vietnam, insisting that Vietnam must first withdraw its troops from Cambodia and settle the MIA question to the United States' satisfaction.[30] In 1991 Senator Connie Mack of Florida argued for such a link to IMF loans to the Soviet Union, declaring, "Not one dime from the IMF until serious economic and democratic reform take place; not one dime until subsidies to Cuba are stopped; and not one dime until Baltic independence is met with talks, not tanks." And the United States linked any chance of future membership in the IMF to serious reform in the Soviet Union.[31]

Finally, relating to both requirements, in 1995 Assistant Secretary John Shattuck testified to the U.S. House that the State Department "oppose[s] loans by international financial institutions to countries that have a pattern of serious human rights abuses, excepting loans for basic human needs." He pointed out that the United States has opposed loans to Equatorial Guinea, Mauritania, and Sudan for these reasons.[32]

We have established that there are good reasons to believe that U.S. decision makers are willing to influence decisions on IMF conditional loans on human rights criteria and that they have the opportunity to do so. Indeed, if we are to believe decision makers' rhetoric, such decisions have been manipulated by U.S. foreign policymakers on the basis of human rights concerns, at least in some cases. Convinced of the relevance of IMF loans to our purposes, we will soon set out to evaluate the impact of these loans on repression. There is, however, some relevant empirical literature on IMF programs that should be addressed briefly before we continue.

Previous Research on IMF Stabilization Programs

Most of the research-related conditional loans have focused on the question of whether the conditions imposed in these programs achieve their goal of economic stabilization.[33] Only a very few studies have dealt with questions that bear directly on the present inquiry, which link these programs to political variables such as repression of human rights and the closely related issue of political instability.

Bienen and Gersovitz point out that the idea that "the International Monetary Fund's conditions for its loans create problems of political stability for developing countries" is widely held by both academic scholars and policymakers. They suggest that the Fund's conditions are perceived "as 'bitter medicine,' that will lead to economic austerity, which in turn will provoke instability."[34] The Senate Foreign Relations Committee also seems to accept this relationship in its 1977 report, which, in noting the correlation between economic hardship and political repression, suggests that "the Carter Administration may . . . have to choose between pressing its international human rights effort, and supporting creditor demands for drastic austerity programs that can only be achieved at the expense of civil liberties."[35] The literature cites an abundance of examples of political instability — most of which appear to be protests (in the form of demonstrations, strikes, and riots) against IMF and the implementation of IMF-mandated austerity measures.[36]

Only a few research efforts have attempted to systematically analyze the relationship between the IMF agreements and these outbreaks of political instability. And only Walton and Ragin and Sidell have engaged in any sophisticated statistical analysis. Both of these studies suggest that the presence of an IMF agreement does not significantly increase the probability of political instability. However, each of these studies has sufficient limitations as to suggest that these results are far from conclusive.[37]

To our knowledge only one published study has evaluated, systematically, the question of whether IMF's loan agreements are related to increased political repression.[38] David Pion-Berlin's research evaluates the impact of IMF policies on repression in Argentina between the years 1958 and 1980.[39] Analysis is limited to acts of repression against organized labor groups, because these groups represent the strongest Argentine opposition to the IMF policies. Pion-Berlin reports that the impact of stabilization programs on acts of repression is statistically significant, even while controlling for the effects of military rule and other international assistance. Though such findings indicate that IMF policies led to repression against labor groups in Argentina, the question of a more general relationship, existing in other countries and with regard to repression affecting other kinds of groups, is not addressed by this study. Therefore, another look at the issue, with a more general scope, is called for. Next, we will embark on an empirical investigation of this issue, first discussing our measures of the independent variable, IMF stabilization programs, and of the dependent variable, abuses of personal integrity rights.

Measuring the Independent Variable of Interest: IMF Stabilization Programs

For this analysis two dichotomous variables will be constructed to measure the presence or absence of an IMF stabilization program during each year between 1980 and 1987. These variables will identify countries that were participants in either of three major IMF programs, available during all or some portion of this time period: standby arrangements, extended fund facilities EFF, and structural adjustment facilitiesSAF.[40] IMF's annual reports were used to obtain information concerning the dates and types of IMF programs that had been initiated in each country.

Two dichotomous (0,1) variables were constructed. The first identifies with a "1" all cases, or country-years, in which an IMF loan program was initiated, with all other cases coded AO." The second variable is coded as "1" for every country-year in which a nation-state participated in an IMF stabilization program excluding the initiation year and "0" for all other cases.[41] We constructed a separate variable for the initiation year, because we believed that the effects of conditional aid programs on human rights, as captured in the published reports we will use to tap that concept (discussed below), might not be evident in the year of the loan. This, it seems, would be particularly probable in cases when such loans were given very late in the year. Another reason for a separate measure for the first year of a loan is that, consistent with the idea that regimes play two-level games, it may be that in some cases regimes do take seriously the U.S. stance against giving such loans to human rights abusers, and thus "clean up their acts" prior to the IMF decision.[42] Constructing a separate variable for the initiation year may allow us to capture this effect, if it exists. It will also serve to prevent this effect from muddying the findings with regard to the impact after the agreements go into effect.

Measuring the Human Rights to Personal Integrity

Even though consensus on the definition and measurement of human rights remains elusive, some agreement has developed concerning the particular subset of human rights we examine as the dependent phenomenon in this study. Personal integrity rights have generally been defined as a category of coercive activities on the part of the government designed to induce compliance in others. Abuses of such rights would include such activities as murder, torture, forced disappearance, and imprisonment of persons arbitrarily, or for their political views.[43] To measure levels of personal integrity rights abuses, we employ a standards-based measure to rate each country on a five-point ordinal human rights scale (1 to 5, with the worst abusers rated 5), based mainly on coders' reading of Country Reports in the Amnesty International Reports. This measure has been referred to as the political terror scale by Stohl, Gibney, and their co-researchers.[44] The categories are as follows:

1. "Countries . . . under a secure rule of law, people are not imprisoned for their views, and torture is rare or exceptional . . . political murders are extremely rare."

2. "There is a limited amount of imprisonment for nonviolent political activity. However, few persons are affected, torture and beating are exceptional . . . political murder is rare."

3. "There is extensive political imprisonment, or a recent history of such imprisonment. Execution or other political murders and brutality may be common. Unlimited detention, with or without trial, for political views is accepted. . . ."

4. "The practices of [Level 3] are expanded to larger numbers. Murders,

disappearances are a common part of life. . . . In spite of its generality, on this level terror affects primarily those who interest themselves in politics or ideas."

5. "The terrors of [Level 4] have been expanded to the whole population. . . . The leaders of these societies place no limits on the means or thoroughness with which they pursue personal or ideological goals."[45]

Most of the data were those that were shared generously by Gibney and Stohl, but they were augmented by the authors of this chapter and their co-researchers to make the sample more global in its coverage.[46] The content of the Country Reports issued by the U.S. State Department and of the Amnesty International Reports was analyzed and scores given to countries for which sufficient information was available.

For the purposes of this paper we choose to present mainly the result of analyses conducted on the data gathered from the reports issued by Amnesty International. We give the Amnesty variable the nod for our current purposes, because those who believe that the State Department Reports are biased would find analyses of an Amnesty International index more persuasive. However, in the cases in which Amnesty did not report on a particular case, we substitute the coding we gained from the State Department Reports because of the serious problems with selection bias that would be raised if those cases were left out.[47] We don't believe that the use of the U.S. State Department Reports in these cases will be a major problem, because critics who have argued the reports are biased have frequently concluded that the biases typically affect a relatively small number of cases, involving leftist countries or strong U.S. allies.[48] Again, these data cover the 1980–87 period.

Are Human Rights a Consideration
in Determining Who Receives IMF Support?

We will now briefly digress from our main purpose of examining the impact of IMF programs on human rights to briefly address a related and important question. The two variables already described give us the opportunity to conduct a simple test of the assertion made by U.S. legislation, Shattuck, and others that the United States works through IMF to deny loans to repressive countries. Testing such statements is also a policy-relevant endeavor from the perspective of our hypothetical decision maker who wanted to know about how things work "in the real world" and is also highly relevant from

Table 12.1. Does the IMF Give Conditional Loans to Human Rights Abusers?

| | Initiation of IMF Loan Time$_t$? | | | |
| | No | | Yes | |
Personal integrity abuse level time$_{(t-1)}$	Count	%	Count	%
1 Rule of law, no prisoners	233	91.4	22	8.6
2 Limited imprisonment	262	84.5	48	15.5
3 Extensive imprisonment	266	77.1	79	22.9
4 Extensive imprisonment, killing, torture	85	77.3	25	22.7
5 Worst abuses, killing affects whole population	46	90.2	5	9.8

Note: Human rights data are from 1980–86. IMF data are from 1981–87.

the perspective of citizens who deserve to know if their governments' rhetoric and policy statements are reflected in their real-world behavior.

In table 12.1 we see a simple cross-tabulation of countries' ratings on the personal integrity abuse scale and a variable indicating whether or not they received any of the three kinds of conditional IMF loans in an immediately subsequent year. We find that countries with recent histories of extensive human rights abuse are *not* excluded from those agreements. Indeed, countries with extensive political imprisonment were actually more apt to receive loans than countries with better human rights practices, as they received loans 22.9 percent of the time in the early and mid-eighties. Countries where killings, disappearances, and torture were a common part of life (Level 4) were also more apt to receive loans (22.7 percent of the time) than countries in categories 1 and 2. Only in the final category, where such abuses characterize conditions for individuals regardless of whether they are interested or involved in politics, there was a decrease in the percentage of countries receiving loans to 9.8 percent.

Admittedly, this is a very simple, initial test of an hypothesis that deserves further examination. Because we fail to control for other potentially important variables, it could be that loans are an important determinant of human rights abuse, but that the relationship is hidden. Our intuition is that countries with lower levels of abuses tend not to receive IMF loans, because, generally, they are less needy. Countries with greater levels of human rights abuses may receive IMF assistance, because they, on average, are more needy. Thus the apparent relationship between human rights and IMF loans may be spurious, arising due to the linkage of economic development (which has been found to be associated with human rights abuse by Poe and Tate and others) and participation in IMF programs.[49] A more in-depth examination of the impact of human rights on IMF decisions would consider the countries' level of economic development and other potential confounding factors in the context of a multivariate model.

It is also possible that the conditions imposed on countries with serious human rights problems include provisions that actually encourage or require regimes to improve their human rights practices. And it could be that, consistent with Shattuck's claim, loans to abusing countries are directed toward improving basic human needs.

We have some anecdotal information that indicates that countries have been excluded from these programs due to human rights concerns. Nevertheless, this simple bivariate analysis leads to the conclusion that abusing regimes are not systematically excluded from IMF conditional loan programs. The percentages suggest that only the most serious abusers (Level 5) tend to be excluded, and even then some countries make the grade.

Building a Multivariate Model to Test the Impact of IMF Loans: Control Variables

We will now return to our primary purpose, which is to find the consequences of IMF loans for recipient countries' human rights conditions. On this question we will go beyond simple bivariate tests to construct a multivariate model of human rights abuse. The advantage of a multivariate model is that it "controls for" other factors that are important determinants of personal integrity abuse. Thus, a relationship that is hidden in bivariate tests may be isolated, or a relationship that might appear in simple bivariate tests can be shown to be spurious, if other explanatory variables, tapping other factors that have been shown to lead to repression, are also considered.

As controls we will consider six factors found to have had statistically significant and substantively important impacts on levels of repression in one of the co-authors' previous studies. These factors, the expected direction of their impacts on levels of human rights abuse, and our operationalizations are summarized in table 12.2. Because our main purpose here is to isolate the impact of the IMF program variables on levels of repression, we do not provide a complete discussion of the theoretical justification of each of these variables. Those desiring a more in-depth discussion of these theories should

Table 12.2. Control Variables Used to Explain Personal Integrity Abuse

Variable and expected effect	Expected effect	Operationalization
Lagged dependent variable	Positive	Five-point ordinal scale gathered from either State Department or Amnesty International reports, depending upon model
Democracy	Negative	Freedom House's seven-point political rights index, inverted (1 = no democracy, 7 = maximum democracy)
Population size	Positive	Logged population
Economic standing	Negative	Per-capita gross national product
International war	Positive	Adapted Small and Singer's definition (1982): total of 1,000 deaths. Participant countries had 1,000 personnel involved, or suffered 100 fatalities.
Civil war	Positive	Adapted Small and Singer's definition (1982): government involved as a combatant and an effective resistant must be present, in the form of a group organized for violent conflict, or able to inflict 5% of the fatalities it receives.

see the earlier study by Poe and Tate.[50] Thus the multivariate model we shall test, with OLS regression, is as follows:

Personal Integrity Abuse$_{tj}$ = a + b$_1$Personal Integrity Abuse$_{(t-1)j}$ + b$_2$Democracy$_{tj}$ + b$_3$Population Size$_{tj}$ + b$_4$Economic Standing$_{tj}$ + b$_5$International War$_{tj}$ + _b$_6$Civil War$_{tj}$ + _b$_7$Initiation of IMF Stabilization Program$_{tj}$ + b$_8$Ongoing IMF Stabilization Program$_{tj}$ + e$_{tj}$

The model will be tested with a cross-national data set, covering 153 countries for each of the years in the 1980–87 period. Thus the unit of analysis will be the country-year. The lagged dependent variable — personal integrity abuse during the previous year (t−1) — is included in the model in part to deal with the statistical problem of autocorrelation. Its inclusion led us to otherwise exclude the first year of the data set, 1980, from the analysis. For reasons discussed in an earlier study, White's Panel Robust Standard errors were employed to control the effects of heteroskedasticity.[51] Heteroskedas-

Table 12.3. A Test of IMF Stabilization Programs' Impact on the Abuse of Personal Integrity Rights

Independent variables	Coefficients	std. error	T-ratio	Level of significance
Constant	-.01	.12	-.11	.4547
Personal integrity abuse(t-1)	.74	.08	9.30	.0001
Democracy	-.05	.02	-3.17	.0008
Population size	.05	.02	3.11	.0009
Economic standing	-.01	.01	-1.35	.0877
International war	.19	.07	2.63	.0043
Civil war	.33	.11	2.86	.0020
Initiation of IMF program	-.02	.06	-.28	.3906
Participation in IMF program	.10	.06	1.71	.0437
R-squared	.77			
N	1071			
Average contemporaneous correlation of errors	.42			

Note: Main entries are unstandardized OLS coefficients, generated using RATS386 version 4.02.

ticity potentially biases the standard errors, which leads to incorrect t-scores and probability estimates unless White's Robust errors or other appropriate techniques are employed.

Statistical Results of the Multivariate Model

Table 12.3 reports the results from the analysis using the political repression scale based on Amnesty International Reports. As expected, findings obtained with six control variables are almost identical to those that arose in the previous study, which suggested them as controls.[52] The results for these variables suggest that a country that had a recent history of repressive behavior, was engaged in civil or international war, or had a large population size is, ceteris paribus, more apt to abuse personal integrity rights than would a country that did not have such a history, was not engaged in civil or international war, or had a small population size. A higher level of political democracy continues to greatly decrease the likelihood of political repression. These results again suggest that economic standing has an impact on repres-

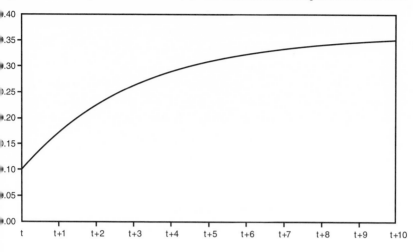

Figure 12.1. The Impact of the Initiation of an IMF Loan on Human Rights Abuse over Time

sion. A coefficient identical to that found in the Poe and Tate study is produced, but it is statistically insignificant at only the .10 level (one-tail test).

The variable identifying years in which IMF loans were initiated has a coefficient that is negative, a finding that would be consistent with the argument that regimes may act to improve their human rights conditions when being considered for IMF loans. However, the weak coefficient ($-$.02) and the fact that the relationship is far from reaching conventional levels of statistical significance (p < .39, one-tail test), lead us to reject this hypothesis. In contrast, the participation period variable produces a coefficient of .10, which achieves a .04 level of significance. This result suggests that even while controlling for other conditions, such as democracy, economic standing, and wars, the addition of an IMF agreement would independently produce an impact of .10 on the human rights scale. This impact, admittedly, is rather small; to estimate the importance of this variable, though, we, should also consider its lagged impact over time, through the lagged dependent variable. In Figure 1 we assume a country in which an existing IMF agreement lasts for ten years, and we find that its impact would be .36 at the end of that period.[53] When this impact is compared to an impact of civil war continuing over ten years (almost 1.2) or the impact of a country slipping from the highest point of democracy index to the lowest point on the index over the same time period (almost one point), the impact of an IMF conditional agreement seems somewhat insubstantial. However, of all the independent variables that are shown to affect political repression, this variable certainly appears to be the condition that would be most easily manipulable — especially compared to conditions such as economic development, the level of political democracy, or war.

Initially, the addition of the IMF variables does not appear to improve the overall performance of the original Poe and Tate model. The R^2, which is a measure of the percentage of the variance explained by the model, or its explanatory strength, is an identical .77 after rounding. The fact that the addition of these variables does not substantially increase the R^2 led us to wonder whether the impact of IMF programs added anything to our explanation, or whether it was just accounting for variance that had already been explained by other variables.[54] To test the possibility that the addition of the IMF variable does not add to the explanatory strength of the model, a joint-F test was used. The inclusion of the IMF variable was found to be statistically significant at the .04 level. This result allows us to conclude that this variable did add significantly (statistically speaking) to the explanation of the abuse of personal integrity rights. Substantively, the significance of its impact appears, at best, to be only weak or very moderate when compared to the effects of other factors stemming from "root causes," which are generally not as easily controlled by U.S. foreign policymakers.[55]

The results of previous empirical research have indicated that abuses to the rights of personal integrity will tend to decrease as a state of economic development and democratic governance is reached. They also suggest that these abuses could sometimes be avoided by settling international and domestic conflicts short of war. Unfortunately, though these findings are interesting and arguably are relevant from both the theoretical and practical political standpoints, they are not factors that U.S. foreign policy decision makers can typically manipulate. Thus, practitioners interested in improving respect for human rights around the world might argue that the results mentioned above are of questionable utility in their efforts. In this chapter we investigated the impact of a variable that is manipulable by the United States, by virtue of its voting strength in the International Monetary Fund: the provision of IMF conditional loan programs. We made a theoretical argument that could reasonably lead us to expect that we might find a linkage between these programs and the abuse of human rights to personal integrity. We also rehearsed anecdotes indicating that the provision of these loans has in some cases been followed by increased repression.

How important are IMF conditional loan programs in determining levels of abuse of personal integrity rights, and whether increases in the abuse of those rights will occur? Our empirical analysis indicates that there is a slight tendency toward short-term increases in repression associated with the initiation of these programs once other factors are controlled. The results emerging from our multivariate regression analysis suggest that an ongoing IMF program had a contemporaneous impact of .10 in a 5 point abuse scale, which would increase as that program continued throughout time, up to .36 if that program carried on for a full decade. In comparison to the impact of the "root cause" explanations, such as democratic institutions and civil and international wars, the impact of IMF stabilization programs is relatively small.

When interpreting these findings it is important to keep in mind this study's limitations. We improved over previous studies that have examined the linkage between IMF programs and human rights by focusing on a global sample of countries for the 1981–87 period. Though consideration of a longer time span gave us some advantages over previous work, the seven year period is insufficient for us to estimate the impact of such programs in the long term. If such programs do have the desired effect of improving the economic situation in the recipient country, our results with regard to the effect of economic development suggest that this would serve to decrease levels of repression. Empirical studies investigating the economic impacts of IMF programs have yielded only very mixed results.[56] Still, we cannot in good faith argue that these programs should be discontinued. To make such a recommendation we would first have to assess empirically the degree to which economic development has been advanced by these programs and then proceed to weigh these possible improvements (and any resulting decreases in human rights abuse) against the short-term tendency of IMF programs to lead to a somewhat greater probability that personal integrity rights will be abused.[57] At the very least, though, policymakers should attempt to find ways to temper the tendency of these programs to encourage more personal integrity abuse, especially in cases in which opposition groups are considered by the regime to constitute a serious threat to the existing order.

We chose to focus on IMF stabilization programs because we thought they were apt to be somewhat important in an explanation of human rights abuse and because they are manipulable by U.S. policymakers. Thus we believed an investigation of their effects would be policy relevant. We conclude that, unfortunately, the variables that account for the vast majority of the variation in levels of human rights abuse tend to be those which are much less amenable to change. Clearly, future research needs to focus on the complex inter-relationships between our "root cause" explanations of human rights abuse: governmental institutional arrangements, international and domestic violence, and levels of economic development.

Though we have attempted to be practical in this chapter, we cannot pretend to have addressed all or even most of the issues policymakers, real or fictitious, would raise with the body of quantitative research on the determinants of human rights abuse. If our fictional policymaker were to read this study we suspect she might observe that, though we have shown her the factors that have a tendency to lead to more human rights abuse, we have not specifically addressed what she should do in particular cases, such as her example of Jordan. She might argue that because of this our study is of questionable utility to her practical pursuits. To this assertion we would simply reply that we have said something that should be of interest to policymakers dealing with Jordan and every other country in the world where human rights conditions are a concern. It is true that wars do not in every case lead to greater repression. It is also the case that some nondemocratic governments and the governments of many poor countries have not abused personal integrity rights. Certainly, there are many cases in which IMF conditional loans have not led to an increase in repression. But we would remind our policymaker that the statistical connection between smoking and lung cancer does not manifest itself in every individual case either, as the father of one of the co-authors, a healthy and athletic seventy-year-old smoker, attests. Does this mean the conclusion that there is a linkage between smoking and lung cancer, established by many unbiased scientific studies, is irrelevant to individuals interested in healthy living? Evidently not, if the collective advice of a generation of medical doctors is any indication.

The policymaker might also be quite exasperated with our use of statistical terminology (for example, heteroskedasticity, autocorrelation) in some sections of this paper. Foreseeing this criticism, we tried to be as clear as possible in presenting our results, while saying enough to satisfy those informed and interested in statistical issues. But if we had written this paper in the hope of having it published in the American Political Science Review, or if we did not happen to have a previous publication to which we could refer readers in order to answer their statistical questions, the policymaker would find it to be a much tougher read.

We are afraid there is no easy approach toward making the primary literature of quantitative political science accessible to policymakers who lack statistical expertise. And perhaps this is as it should be. The focus on methodology and design in much quantitative research and the associated terminology does serve as a barrier that effectively keeps many practitioners out of this realm. But at the same time this terminology, when properly used, is a shorthand that allows specialists interested in creating a body of empirically falsifiable theory to communicate efficiently with one another. Two close siblings of foreign policy studies, the public administration and public policy subfields, deal with this problem by having journals in which social scientists can publish empirical research that is aimed toward policymakers. Unfortunately, in contrast, the journals that are commonly held to be read by foreign policy practitioners, *Foreign Affairs* and *Foreign Policy*, continually shun quantitative social scientific research. Quantitative researchers wishing to do practical research concerning foreign policy are left without a publication outlet that is apt to be read by the audience they wish to reach. Perhaps this is part of the reason why, as Raymond has noted, scientific policy evaluation is a "neglected task" in the field of foreign policy research.[58] It may be that a necessary step to learn, in order to publish policy-relevant empirical studies on foreign policy, is for the research community to first develop a publication outlet in which it could do just that.

Notes

1. See James M. McCormick and Neil Mitchell, "Is U.S. Aid Really Linked to Human Rights in Latin America?" *American Journal of Political Science* 32 (1988): 231–239; Neil J. Mitchell and James M. McCormick, "Economic and Political Explanations of Human Rights Violations," *World Politics* 40 (1988): 476–498; Conway W. Henderson, "Conditions Affecting the Use of Political Repression," *Journal of Conflict Resolution* 35 (1991): 120–142; Conway W. Henderson, "Human Rights and Regimes: A Bibliographical Essay," *Human Rights Quarterly* 10 (1993): 525–543; Steven C. Poe and C. Neal Tate, "Repression of Human Rights to Personal Integrity in the 1980s: A Global Analysis," *American Political Science Review* 88 (1994): 853–872. In this paper, for the sake of ease of expression, we sometimes refer to the abuse of these rights as "repression," even though we realize repression may involve the suppression of other classes of rights. We also, at times, refer to personal integrity rights as human rights, even though we realize that term, too, has a much broader meaning.

2. The first published work out of this project was Poe and Tate, "Repression." In that piece we tested a multivariate model of human rights abuse on a global, cross-national data set covering the 1980–87 period. We found that democratic political institutions, civil and international wars, population size, and economic development

were statistically significant and at least somewhat important determinants of repression. In a follow-up piece we tested the model on regional subsystems and found some important variations by region. See Steven C. Poe, C. Neal Tate, Linda Camp Keith, and Drew Lanier, "Domestic Threat and the Abuse of the Human Right to Personal Integrity," paper presented at the Annual Meeting of the Midwest Political Science Association (April 18–21, 1996). In another more recent piece, we built a more sophisticated causal model, testing it with path analysis and found that other factors, such as population growth, affect levels of repression indirectly, through their effects on democracy, which is an intervening variable. See C. Neal Tate and Steven C. Poe, "Democracy and the Human Right to Personal Integrity: A Causal Model" (1996), unpublished manuscript. In a piece focusing on domestic threats we conducted analyses that illustrate that a whole range of internal threats increases the probability of increases in repression during subsequent time periods and that such increases tend to endure several periods after the threats took place. See Steven C. Poe, C. Neal Tate, Linda Camp Keith, and Drew Lanier, "Domestic Threat and the Abuse of the Human Right to Personal Integrity," paper presented at the Annual Meeting of the Midwest Political Science Association (April 18–21, 1996). Finally, we explored the impact of international agreements on human rights practices around the world, finding that the act of signing such agreements had little impact on countries' human rights practices. See Linda Camp Keith, "The United Nations International Covenant on Civil and Political Rights: Does It Make a Difference in Human Rights Behavior?" (1996), unpublished manuscript. Our research draws substantial insights from the research of Mitchell and McCormick, *U.S. Aid*; Henderson, "Human Rights and Regimes"; and Davenport, among others. See Christian Davenport, "Multi-Dimensional Threat Perception and State Repression: An Inquiry into Why States Apply Negative Sanctions," *American Journal of Political Science* 39 (1995): 683–713.

3. We do not mean to suggest that researchers should give up efforts to understand the causal nexus between human rights abuse, democracy, and international and domestic violence. Nor do we mean to suggest that U.S. foreign policymakers are always unable to manipulate such factors, even though the empirical research conducted thus far seems to indicate that U.S. foreign policy has not been particularly successful in promoting either democracy or human rights. On the impact of U.S. aid on human rights see Patrick M. Regan, "U.S. Economic Aid and Political Repression: An Empirical Evaluation of U.S. Foreign Policy." *Political Research Quarterly* 48 (1995): 613–628. For an empirical study concluding that U.S. foreign assistance has failed to promote, and in some cases actually has undermined, democracy see Stephen A. Lohse, "U.S. Foreign Assistance and Democracy in Central America: Quantitative Evaluation of U.S. Policy, 1946–1994," unpublished masters thesis, University of North Texas, (1996).

4. Research on public policy indicates that there are numerous other factors that

determine whether a study is apt to be used by policymakers. See, for example, the discussion of Martin Bulmer, *The Uses of Social Research: Social Investigation in Public Policy-Making* (London: George Allen and Unwyn, 1982), 111–127. Though this study relates to the consumption of social science literature in the British case, some of his conclusions would seem to apply equally well to the American case.

5. A considerable literature has been devoted to the question of the motivations behind U.S. foreign policy and whether human rights are an important consideration. Much of this literature has focused on the empirical question of whether human rights influence the allocation of foreign aid. The bulk of the findings on this issue seems to show that human rights are considered in the allocation process but that their impact is at best moderate, and they are overridden if more vital U.S. interests are at stake. For example, David L. Cingranelli and Thomas E. Pasquerello, "Human Rights Practices and Distribution of U.S. Foreign Aid to Latin American Countries," *American Political Science Review* 29 (1985): 539–563; Steven C. Poe and Rangsima Sirirangsi, "Human Rights and U.S. Economic Aid to Africa," *International Interactions* 18 (1993): 309–322; Steven C. Poe and Rangsima Sirirangsi, "Human Rights and U.S. Economic Aid During the Reagan Years," *Social Science Quarterly* 75 (1994): 494–509; Steven C. Poe, Suzanne Pilatovsky, Brian Miller, and Ayo Ogundele, "Human Rights and U.S. Foreign Aid Revisited: The Latin American Region," *Human Rights Quarterly* 16 (1994): 539–558; Shannon Blanton, "Impact of Human Rights on U.S. Foreign Assistance to Latin America," *International Interactions* 19 (1994): 339–358. However, see Michael Stohl and David Carleton, "The Foreign Policy of Human Rights: Rhetoric and Reality from Jimmy Carter to Ronald Reagan," *Human Rights Quarterly* 7 (1985): 205–229; McCormick and Mitchell, *U.S. Aid*; and Daniel J. B. Hofrenning, "Human Rights and Foreign Aid: A Comparison of the Reagan and Carter Administrations," *American Politics Quarterly* (October 1990): 514–526, for dissenting views.

6. 22 U.S.C. §2151n (1982).

7. 22 U.S.C. §2304 (1982).

8. 22 U.S.C. §262d (1982).

9. Patrick M. Regan, "U.S. Economic Aid and Political Repression: An Empirical Evaluation of U.S. Foreign Policy," *Political Research Quarterly* 48 (September 1995): 613–628.

10. Margaret Garritsen De Vries, *The IMF in a Changing World: 1945–85* (Washington DC: International Monetary Fund, 1986).

11. John Williamson, "Reforming the IMF: Different or Better," in *The Political Morality of the International Monetary Fund: Ethics and Foreign Policy*, ed. Robert J. Meyers (New Brunswick: Transaction Books, 1987), 2.

12. Irving S. Friedman, *Toward World Prosperity: Reshaping the Global Money System* (Lexington MA: Lexington Books, 1987), 299; Andrew Crockett, *International Money: Issues and Analysis* (New York: Academic Press, 1977), 38.

13. Henry S. Bienen and Mark Gersovitz, "Economic Stabilization, Conditionality, and Political Stability," *International Organization* 39 (1985): 736.

14. Richard N. Cooper, *Economic Stabilization and Debt in Developing Countries* (Cambridge MA: MIT Press, 1992); Friedman, *Prosperity*; Williamson, "Reforming the IMF"; and John Williamson, *IMF Conditionality* (Washington DC: Institute for International Economics, 1983).

15. John Williamson, "On Judging the Success of IMF Policy Advice," in Williamson, *IMF Conditionality*, 665.

16. *Europa Yearbook* (London: Europa Publications, 1986), 3188.

17. *Europa Yearbook* (1984), 139.

18. *Europa Yearbook* (1984), 515.

19. The theoretical base from which we draw these expectations is spelled out in some detail in Poe et al., "Domestic Threat."

20. David Pion-Berlin, "The Political Economy of State Repression in Argentina," in *The State as Terrorist*, ed. Michael Stohl and George Lopez (Westport CT: Greenwood, 1984), 105.

21. For example, Mitchell and McCormick, "Explanation," and Poe and Tate, "Repression."

22. Benjamin J. Cohen, "International Debt and Linkage Strategies: Some Foreign-Policy Implications for the United States," *International Organization* 39 (1985): 707.

23. George Shultz, "Restoring Prosperity to the World Economy," *Current Policy*, no. 451 (Washington DC: U.S. Department of State, Bureau of Public Affairs, 1983).

24. See Tyrone Ferguson, *The Third World and Decision Making in the International Monetary Fund: the Quest for Full and Effective Participation* (London: Pinter Publishers, 1988), 62; and Peter Körner, Gero Maass, Thomas Siebold, and Rainer Tetzlaff, *The IMF and the Debt Crisis: A Guide to the Third World's Dilemma* (Atlantic Highlands NJ: Zed Books Ltd., 1986), 43.

25. Ferguson, *Quest*, 62.

26. Ferguson, *Quest*, n.24; Körner et al., *The IMF and the Debt Crisis*, n.24.

27. Körner et al., *The IMF and the Debt Crisis*; Walter S. Mossberg and Marcus W. Brauchli, "U.S. Plan for Third World Debt May Set Stage for Greater Japanese Role at IMF," *Wall Street Journal* (March 20, 1989), no page citation available.

28. Cohen, "International Debt," 507.

29. David P. Forsythe, "Congress and Human Rights in U.S. Foreign Policy: The Fate of General Legislation," *Human Rights Quarterly* 9 (1987): 391.

30. Susuma Awanohara, "U.S., Japan Block IMF Effort to Support Vietnam," *Far Eastern Economic Review* (September 28, 1989): 27–28; Susuma Awanohara, "U.S. Hurdle to Vietnam's IMF/World Bank Ties," *Far Eastern Economic Review* (October 17, 1991): 13–14; Jonathan Friedland, "U.S. Out on Limb in Blocking Vietnam's IMF Borrowings," *Far Eastern Economic Review* (October 31, 1991): 74.

31. Alan Murray, "Politics and Policy: Group of 7 Didn't End, Only Postponed, Debate over Financial Aid for U.S.S.R," *Wall Street Journal* (July 25, 1991), A10.

32. John Shattuck, Testimony on Human Rights and Democracy in Africa before the Subcommittee on Africa Committee on International Relations, February 22, 1995.

33. For example, see Malcolm Crawford, "High Conditionality Lending: The United Kingdom," in *IMF Conditionality*; Adolfo Diz, "Economic Performance Under Three Stand-by Agreements," in *IMF Conditionality*; Reginald Herbold Green, "Political Economic Adjustment and IMF Conditionality: Tanzania, 1974–81," in *IMF Conditionality*; Stephan Haggard, "The Politics of Adjustment: Lessons from the IMF's Extended Fund Facility," *International Organization* 39 (1985): 505–534; Tony Killiick, "Kenya, the IMF and the Unsuccessful Quest for Stabilization," in *IMF Conditionality*; Jorge Marhsall, Jose Luis Mardones, and Isabel Marshall, "IMF Conditionality: The Experiences of Argentina, Brazil, and Chile"; Joan M. Nelson, "Poverty, Equality, and the Politics of Adjustment," in *The Politics of Economic Adjustment*, ed. Stephan Haggard and Robert R. Kaufman (Princeton: Princeton University Press, 1983); Manuel Pastor Jr., "The Effects of IMF Programs in the Third World: Debate and Evidence from Latin America," *World Development* 15 (1987): 249–262; Karen Remmer, "The Politics of Economic Stabilization: IMF Standby Programs in Latin America, 1954–1984," *Comparative Politics* 19 (1986): 1–24.

34. Bienen and Gersovitz, "Economic Stabilization," 709.

35. U.S. Senate, Committee on Foreign Relations, International Debt, the Banks, and U.S. Foreign Policy, Staff Report (Washington DC, 1977), 7.

36. Haggard, "Adjustment"; Bienen and Gersovitz, "Stabilization"; John Walton and Charles Ragin, "Global and National Sources of Political Protest: Third World Responses to the Debt Crises" (1990); Chris Carvounis, *The Foreign Debt/National Development Conflict* (New York: Quorum Books, 1986); Joan M. Nelson, "Poverty, Equality."

37. See Walton and Ragin, "Political Protest." See Scott R. Sidell, *The IMF & Third-World Instability: Is There a Connection?* (New York: St. Martin's, 1988).

38. See Haggard, "Adjustment," 512. See Michael Stohl, David Carleton, George Lopez, and Stephen Samuels, "State Violations of Human Rights: Issues and Problems of Measurement," *Human Rights Quarterly* 8 (1986): 597. See Charles Taylor and David A. Jodice, *World Handbook of Political and Social Indicators*, 3rd. ed. (New Haven: Yale University Press, 1983), 62. See James Franklin, "*Protest, Political Repression and the International Monetary Fund.*" Paper presented at the Annual Meeting of the Southwestern Political Science Association, March 22–25, 1995, 10.

39. Pion-Berlin, "State Repression in Argentina," 99–122.

40. Initially, dichotomous variables were constructed to test the impact of each type of arrangement both separately and combined. The variable that measured the

presence of any of the three types of IMF program performed better than the individual variables; therefore, the combined variable was chosen for the final model.

41. Participation for any portion of the year was included unless the participation was less than one-half of a month. A third dichotomous variable was constructed that identified the presence of an IMF stabilization program in each year, regardless of whether it was a year in which the program was initiated or one in which the program continued. As we expected, stronger results were achieved when the variable was analyzed with the initiation period separated out. In addition, if a country canceled its IMF arrangement, its participation in the arrangement was considered to end at the time of cancellation.

42. On two-level games see Robert D. Putnam, "Diplomacy and Domestic Politics: The Logic of Two-Level Games," *International Organization* 42 (1988): 427–460.

43. See note 1 above for citations of studies focusing on personal integrity rights.

44. For just a few of the many studies using these data, see Stohl and Carleton, "Rhetoric and Reality"; Mark Gibney and Michael Stohl, "Human Rights and U.S. Refugee Policy," in *Open Border? Closed Societies? The Ethical and Political Issues*, ed. Mark Gibney (Westport CT: Greenwood, 1988); Mark Gibney and Matthew Dalton, "The Political Terror Scale," in *Human Rights and Developing Countries*, ed. David L. Cingranelli, forthcoming; and Henderson, "Human Rights and Regimes."

45. Raymond D. Gastil, *Freedom in the World: Political Rights and Civil Liberties* (New Brunswick NJ: Transaction Books, 1980), as quoted in Stohl and Carleton, "Rhetoric and Reality," n.5.

46. For the fullest presentation of the data gathered by Gibney and Stohl, see Gibney and Dalton, "The Political Terror Scale," n.44. See Poe and Sirirangsi, "Aid to Africa," for a discussion of our augmentation of the data set provided by those researchers.

47. See Poe and Tate, "Repression," 869 n.8.

48. See, e.g., Judith Eleanor Innes, "Human Rights Reporting as a Policy Tool: An Examination of the State Department Country Reports," in *Human Rights and Statistics: Getting the Record Straight*, ed. Thomas B. Jabine and Richard P. Claude (Philadelphia: University of Pennsylvania Press, 1992).

49. Poe and Tate, "Repression."

50. Poe and Tate, "Repression."

51. See Poe and Tate, "Repression," 859–860; and Nathaniel Beck, Jonathan Katz, R. Michael Alvarez, Geoffrey Garrett, and Peter Lange, "Government Partisanship, Labor Organization, and Macroeconomic Performance: A Corrigendum," *American Political Science Review* 87 (1993): 945–948; and the sources cited therein.

52. A few of the variables achieve a higher level of statistical significance in this study, which is probably due to the removal of the variables that had been shown to be statistically insignificant in the earlier Poe and Tate study.

53. This impact is calculated by multiplying the effect of the agreement at time$_t$ by

the coefficient of the lagged dependent variable and then adding the direct effect of an IMF agreement at time$_{t+1}$. This process is repeated for each successive lag.

54. The model tested here does have in its favor the fact that it had fewer variables. Adding more variables tends to increase R-squares somewhat, even if the impact of those variables is insubstantial, by decreasing the degrees of freedom.

55. Some may argue that we should focus our analyses on only lesser developed countries, which tend to be candidates for IMF stabilization programs, and that including developed countries in our work biases the study toward positive findings. We still prefer the more general approach that focuses on a global sample, because we are seeking to build a highly generalizable model that would allow us to determine the conditions under which repression is most likely to occur.

56. See Pastor, "Effects of IMF Programs," and sources cited therein, and Remmer, "The Politics of Economic Stabilization."

57. We would certainly prefer to have gained enough knowledge about the possible positive impacts of IMF loans on economic development to make such a recommendation, but that task was simply too large to undertake here. By isolating the relatively small impact of IMF stabilization programs on human rights, we have suggested a variable that should be considered by policymakers in their deliberations and future quantitative researchers who would wish to take on the task of conducting such a cost-benefit analysis.

58. Gregory A. Raymond, "Evaluation: A Neglected Task for the Comparative Study of Foreign Policy," in *New Directions in the Study of Foreign Policy*, ed. Charles F. Hermann, Charles W. Kegley Jr., and James N. Rosenau (Boston: Unwin Hyman, 1987), 96.

13

The United States, Development, and Indigenous Peoples

•

ROBERT K. HITCHCOCK

No assistance may be provided under this part to the government of any country which engages in a consistent pattern of gross violations of internationally recognized human rights, including torture or cruel, inhuman, or degrading treatment or punishment, prolonged detention without charges, causing the disappearance of persons by the abduction and clandestine detention of those persons, or other flagrant denial of the right to life, liberty, and the security of person, unless such assistance will directly benefit the needy people in such country. — U.S. Foreign Assistance Act of 1961, Section 116

In the 1970s and 1980s the United States was the largest provider of foreign economic assistance to developing countries. Some of the funding and technical assistance (or "foreign aid") was given to countries with questionable human rights records. This was done to meet U.S. foreign policy objectives or, in some cases, to provide assistance to "the needy people" of specific countries. A target population for a portion of U.S. development aid has been those people who are characterized by themselves and others as indigenous.

Indigenous populations include those groups that are known as native peoples, aboriginals, tribal peoples, Fourth World peoples, or "first nations." Thus South American Indians are considered indigenous peoples, as are the Aborigines of Australia, the Adivasis ("Scheduled Tribes") of India, the Penan of Malaysia, and the San (Bushmen) of the Kalahari Desert region of southern Africa. Recent estimates indicate that there are over 350,000,000 indigenous people residing in some seventy-five of the world's countries, comprising roughly about 5 percent of the world's population. These peoples tend to have some of the lowest living standards, highest rates of mortality and illness, and poorest records of treatment of the various segments of the world's population.[1]

The United States prides itself on its human rights record as it relates to indigenous peoples. The U.S. government has taken strong rhetorical stances on behalf of the rights of indigenous peoples in Latin America, Africa, Asia, and the Pacific.[2] In practice, however, the United States has sometimes engaged in actions deleterious to the well-being of indigenous peoples in countries ranging from Vietnam and Thailand to El Salvador and Guatemala. U.S. agencies have also implemented development programs and policies that have had negative economic, social, and environmental impacts on indigenous peoples.

The United States has chosen not to be a signatory to international human rights conventions on indigenous rights, because doing so would, according to U.S. foreign policy experts, violate state sovereignty.[3] The United States has yet to ratify the International Covenant on Economic, Social, and Cultural Rights, an international instrument that is considered crucial by indigenous groups because of its emphasis on socioeconomic rights. An underlying reason for U.S. failure to support these conventions is that they would require the United States to treat its own indigenous people in accordance with international human rights standards, something that in many ways it has been reluctant to do.

The U.S. has a mixed record when it comes to dealing with indigenous peoples in foreign countries. It has provided sizeable amounts of economic and humanitarian assistance to help alleviate stressful situations affecting indigenous groups and others in places ranging from Ethiopia during the 1984–85 drought to Bangladesh during the floods of the early 1990s. U.S. financial assistance in the form of loan guarantees through the Export-Import Bank to Indonesia was withdrawn in 1996, in part because of issues raised by indigenous and environmental groups who argued that the Indonesian government was engaging in human rights violations against tribal peoples in Irian Jaya (West Papua).[4] On the other hand, U.S. development assistance has been provided to projects that have had indigenous peoples as their direct beneficiaries.[5]

Development and Indigenous Peoples

Development can be defined as the strategy whereby the social and material well-being of people is raised. It should be stressed, however, that there are different perspectives on how to define the concept development. On the one hand, development is seen as being synonymous with economic growth and modernization as measured by increases in gross national product (GNP) or gross domestic product (GDP). On the other, it is viewed as a holistic process in which not only are incomes and access to social services enhanced, but so, too, are literacy rates, health conditions, employment opportunities, and social equity.[6]

Indigenous groups, similar to others, especially in the Third World, see development as a fundamental right of all people. The United States, for its part, has been reluctant to accept the principle that socioeconomic rights are equally as important as civil and political rights, at least insofar as indigenous peoples are concerned.[7] The U.S. government, for example, has not imposed sanctions on countries that refused to provide fair and just compensation to indigenous peoples for the loss of assets as a result of development projects.

U.S. government policy toward its own indigenous peoples differs somewhat from its policy toward indigenous peoples in other countries. The U.S. government espouses the idea that federally recognized American Indian tribes are "sovereign nations," ones that theoretically have the right to self-determination. In practice, however, the federal government treats Indian tribes as "dependent nations," reserving for itself the right to exercise veto power over tribal council decisions with which it disagrees. The U.S. Congress has plenary power, which means that at any time it can abrogate unilaterally any agreements with Indian tribes. The U.S. federal government can declare eminent domain and take land from Indian tribes for purposes of undertaking public projects such as roads, dams, and reservoirs. The U.S. government has the fiduciary responsibility to manage Indian resources (for example, land, the trust funds, mineral resources, water, timber). Thus Indian tribes in the United States are sometimes described as "dependent nations," because they receive funds from the federal government and must contend with external jurisdiction issues, as is the case with hunting, fishing, and water rights, and the extension of civil and criminal jurisdiction over nontribal members. Every agency of the U.S. government has a trust responsibility to American Indians (for example, Housing and Urban Development, Health and Human Services, and Education). The relationship between the U.S. government and Indian tribes has been characterized in various ways, including measured separatism, semi-autonomy, and domestic dependency.

It should be noted that the term autonomy lacks international legal recognition. It means the right to be different, to be left alone, and to be able to

preserve, protect, and promote values that are different from the rest of society. It may also imply protection from discrimination and preservation of
cultural, linguistic, or other values from majority assault. American Indians
would argue that they have not had true autonomy nor have they had true
sovereignty, the right of a group to make its own decisions independently of
other groups, states, or nations.[8]

Whereas the United States opposes true self-determination for Ameri-
can Indians, it has supported efforts to seek autonomy and gain the right to
self-determination on the part of such indigenous groups as the Miskitos of
Nicaragua, the Tigreans and Eritreans in the Horn of Africa, and the Kurds
of northern Iraq. Such support, however, is highly political. The United
States assisted the Miskitos, for example, because of their opposition to the
Sandanista government in Nicaragua in the 1980s. U.S. support of the Iraqi
Kurds since the end of the Gulf War in 1991 was a function of their opposition (at least until recently) to the government of Saddam Hussein.[9] On
the other hand, the United States gave economic and military support to
countries such as Brazil, Guatemala, Indonesia, the Philippines, Somalia,
and Turkey with the full knowledge that their governments were engaged
in actions that violated the basic human rights of indigenous peoples and
others.[10]

The American government institution that deals most directly with indigenous peoples outside the United States is the U.S. Agency for International
Development (USAID) in the Department of State. USAID is a *bilateral* (country to country) aid agency. Established in 1961, USAID has as some of its objectives the promotion of economic and social development in Third World
countries, the reduction of poverty, illness, and hunger, the protection of
the environment, and the enhancement of participatory democratic governance. The U.S. law that covers aid provided through USAID is the Foreign
Assistance Act (FAA) of 1961, an act that is amended relatively regularly, de-
pending on political, economic, and other conditions. The budget for USAID
is controlled by Congress, which has budget hearings every year that determine the finance to be provided to the agency.

The U.S. Agency for International Development was envisioned originally
as a nonpolitical institution that would provide aid to developing countries on the basis of need. In the 1960s, however, pressures were exerted on
the agency to engage in actions that served U.S. interests in the Cold War
struggles with the Soviet bloc. This can perhaps best be seen in the case of

USAID's role in Southeast Asia during the Vietnam War. USAID officials were directly engaged in recruiting the Montagnards of Vietnam to take part in counterinsurgency operations during the 1960s.[11] USAID's activities in Thailand in the 1960s ranged from training and supplying units of the Thai police to carrying out community development and constructing physical infrastructure (roads, air bases) in rural areas.[12]

Paramilitary units were established at the village level in both Vietnam and Thailand. Local peasants were conscripted to take part in antiguerilla patrols, the costs of which had to be borne by the people themselves. Participation in these units was risky; not only were people engaged in activities that could result in serious bodily harm or death, but they were also put in precarious social situations with other members of their communities, some of whom supported the opposition. Failure to take part in the antiguerilla patrols sometimes led to retribution by government forces and U.S. Special Forces personnel, including imprisonment, torture, and extrajudicial killing.[13] Similar situations were faced by members of indigenous communities in Central America in the 1980s and 1990s, especially in Guatemala where USAID had a large office and where substantial amounts of covert military and intelligence assistance were invested in counterinsurgency efforts.[14]

In the late 1960s Congress revised the Foreign Assistance Act to disallow the use of American economic and humanitarian assistance for military purposes. Funds were not supposed to be spent for the purchase of weapons or for training and support of foreign armies, police, or paramilitary units. In spite of these restrictions, there were numerous instances in which U.S. economic assistance was used to support dictatorships that were involved in oppressing their citizens or that were misusing or appropriating U.S. funds for private purposes. This was the case, for example, in Haiti, the Philippines, Somalia, and Zaire. In Somalia in the 1980s the United States was well aware of the sale of food given to refugees under Title I of the Food for Peace Act (Public Law 480). The funds that were generated from the sale of the food were used to purchase weapons for Somali paramilitary units that were supposed to assist in the overthrow of the Mengistu regime in Ethiopia. Instead, these groups turned their guns on the U.S.-supported government of Siad Barre, toppling it in 1991 and contributing to the famine of the early 1990s in the Bay region that led to the deaths of over half a million people, many of them women and children.[15]

The United States generally has tended to follow a model of development that favors economic growth over socioeconomic equity. What this has meant for indigenous peoples in those countries that receive U.S. funds and technical assistance is that few benefits of U.S. development aid have actually reached them. One reason for this situation has to do with the structure and organization of indigenous institutions. According to U.S. law, before an organization can receive U.S. funds, it has to go through an audit and it must meet fiscal management standards set by the General Accounting Office. Many indigenous communities lack the financial and management structures required by U.S. law and thus are unable to gain access to U.S. funds. Another problem is that USAID requires that organizations receiving U.S. assistance have to be registered officially with their governments. Many governments are reluctant to give official recognition to indigenous organizations, because they are wary of their desire for greater autonomy in decision making or in some cases are vying with them for access to land and resources.

Capitalist, "free-market" development strategies have been pursued aggressively by the United States in its bilateral aid programs and by such multilateral donors as the World Bank (the International Bank for Reconstruction and Development, IBRD), the International Development Association (IDA), and the International Monetary Fund (IMF). Structural adjustment programs (SAPS) and economic policy reforms may have helped stabilize or enhance some developing countries' national economies, but they have also had the effect of seriously exacerbating problems of poverty, inequality, and environmental degradation. In many cases, it is the people at the bottom of the socioeconomic system, some of whom are indigenous, who are hurt the most by structural adjustment and free market strategies.[16]

Indigenous peoples generally have not been comfortable with the type of development that places major emphasis on capital-intensive strategies and free market economics. Indigenous leaders have argued repeatedly (for example, in meetings of the Working Group of Indigenous Populations [WGIP] in the United Nations) that economic development has not, in fact, resulted in their being made better off; rather, in many ways it has resulted in them becoming much worse off. An examination of indigenous peoples' socioeconomic statuses reveals that there are substantial numbers of people who are living at or below the Poverty Datum Line (PDL), or "the minimum income needed for a basic standard of living." There are rising inequalities between the poor and the wealthy in many indigenous communities; this situation has served to contribute to rising social tensions, inter- and intra-

community conflict, and grassroots movements aimed at bringing about
better living situations for local people, some of which, such as those in Mexico, are having significant political and economic effects.

Bilateral and multilateral development projects have sometimes had extremely negative impacts on indigenous peoples. Perhaps the best known of
these projects are large dams, some of which have displaced tens of thousands, and in a few cases, hundreds of thousands of people, most of whom
were made worse off.[17] In India, 40 percent of all those people displaced by
the Narmada Dams are *adivasis*, tribal people. Indigenous groups in Brazil,
China, Vietnam, the Philippines, and Laos all face displacement because of
large dams, and some of them have already suffered significant losses of income, land, and resources to advanced infrastructure projects related to dam
construction.[18] There are a number of cases in which opponents to dam construction were beaten, jailed, and sometimes killed for their opposition to
the dam building.

In the 1960s, USAID had some involvement in dam projects, but it with-
drew from these kinds of projects over time, in part because of the criticism
of nongovernment organizations at hearings in Congress and because of
local resistance. Many of the world's dams today are built with funds from
consortia of private banks and other financial institutions. The World Bank,
which has been criticized heavily for its involvement in large dam projects,
has instituted guidelines for handing involuntary resettlement.[19]

Although USAID lacks guidelines on resettlement, it has a whole series of
stipulations about how to go about handling project identification, design,
implementation, monitoring, and evaluation. Some of these stipulations
have included doing detailed surveys and assessments prior to the initiation
of projects. These strategies, however, have not always ensured that the projects were positive. A number of bilateral and multilateral development projects have had negative effects on indigenous peoples (see table 13.1). These
projects range from large-scale resettlement efforts in Indonesia to agricultural substitution projects aimed at getting farmers to stop growing coca in
Bolivia.[20] In some cases, human rights violations occurred directly as a result
of project implementation; this was the case with the Manantali Dam on the
Bafing River Mali, for example, where conflicts occurred over land access
and local people were killed.

Some USAID projects have also contributed to the impoverishment of local people and the degradation of the habitats in which they were located.

Table 13.1. Bilateral and Multilateral Development Projects That Have Had Negative Impacts on the Human Rights of Indigenous Peoples

Project	Country	Impacts
Chapare Valley Regional Development Project	Bolivia	Efforts to reduce production of coca included development of agricultural substitutes and lumbering, combined with raids by Bolivian and U.S. troops, led to outmigration and impoverishment of local people.
Grande Carajas Project and Tucuri Dam	Brazil	Dispossession, loss of natural resources, expansion of land conflict and competition, local people impoverished
Bastar Technical Assistance Project	India	A forestry project aimed at creating employment that led to deforestation, increased foraging effort, poor worker-management relations, and local-level resistance
Transmigration Program	Indonesia	Environmental damage, local populations forcibly dispossessed, conflict expansion
Manantali Dam	Mali	Forcible resettlement of 10,000 people and increase in conflicts over land and resources
Kor Jor Gor (Land allocation project for the poor in degraded forest reserve areas)	Thailand	Dispossession of farmers, no compensation paid, no social infrastructure replacement, excessive cutting down of trees by military-owned businesses, oppression of local populace
Rwenzoris National Park	Uganda	Bakonjo and Batoro communities excluded from the park, women arrested for local resource exploitation
Zimbabwe Natural Resources Project	Zimbabwe	Local residents were displaced by a district wildlife area, and a dam refurbishing led to the expansion of livestock numbers and overgrazing, resulting in hardship for local people

Hearings before Congress in the 1980s and suggestions for reform from both inside and outside the agency led to changes in the ways in which USAID approaches its projects. One outgrowth of these reforms is the expansion in the emphasis on local people's participation in the project identification, formulation, and implementation process. USAID now has guidelines that ensure that projects take into consideration the attitudes, ideas, and recommendations of people to be affected by development projects.[21]

International Trade, Development, and Indigenous Peoples

Over the past decade a dramatic upsurge has taken place in efforts to promote international trade of agricultural products, pharmaceuticals, timber, nontimber resources such as plant-based dyes and indigenous craft items made from wild natural resources, and, in some cases, human genetic materials. The passage of the General Agreement on Tariffs and Trade (GATT) (now the World Trade Organization, WTO) and the expansion of commercial exploitation of resources have begun to have significant effects on biodiversity and both indigenous and nonindigenous societies. U.S. foreign policy has attempted to promote international trade and free market economics.[22]

As resources have declined in more populated parts of the world, the frontier regions that support indigenous populations have become increasingly attractive to companies and international development agencies hoping to profit from exploitation of plant, mineral, and other valuable resources. North American, European, and Asian drug companies have begun to tap the knowledge of indigenous healers (shamans, traditional doctors) in their efforts to find new species with medicinal value. Some of these species, such as the rosy periwinkle in Madagascar and the grapple plant (devil's claw) in the southern Kalahari region of Namibia and Botswana, have proved to be highly profitable to nonlocal companies who generally have provided little in the way of returns to the local people who occupied the lands where they were found and who, in many cases, actually did the work to obtain them.

The expansion of tourism in indigenous regions and the sales of crafts to visitors and marketing organizations have had a profound effect on the livelihoods of local people. The rising popularity of baskets made from the vegetable ivory palm (*Hyphaene ventricosa*) has led to a decline in the distribution and numbers of palm plants and a threat to its survival in such places as the Okavango Delta of Botswana and the Caprivi region of Namibia.[23] The overexploitation of valuable wild plants by people on the payrolls of handicraft marketing agencies, some of them funded with grants from USAID and other bilateral and multilateral development agencies, has resulted in a loss of important fall-back income. This is particularly the case for indigenous households headed by women. The commercialization of craft production has also contributed to increased work effort of indigenous women, cutting into the time that they can spend in other pursuits such as agriculture, household maintenance, and child care.

One of the major difficulties that indigenous groups as primary producers must contend with is that frequently they are excluded from taking part in the marketing of high-value goods (for example, crafts, export crops). To make matters even more complicated, members of indigenous communities generally do not benefit directly from the value that is added to their goods as they move through the system. To overcome marketing and other constraints, indigenous people in Africa, Latin America, Asia, and the Pacific have organized themselves into cooperatives, self-help groups, and marketing associations. These organizations have helped to provide credit to their members and have assisted them in gaining access to development assistance and training.[24] The problem, however, is that all too often highly capitalized transnational corporations outcompete small-scale local producer associations.

Agency-supported agricultural development projects aimed at producing large amounts of cash crops for the world market have led to a reduction in subsistence crop production in many parts of the world. Indigenous agriculturalists, a large proportion of whom are women, maintained agrodiversity through careful seed selection and planting of a number of different types and varieties of crops. As monocropping spread, however, rural people found themselves at greater risk because of the vulnerability of nonindigenous crops to drought, pests, disease, and the effects of pollutants. Another consequence of monoculture has been a reduction in diversity in the diet and vitamin deficiencies at the local level.[25]

One of the areas in which USAID received considerable criticism was in the implementation of water and livestock development projects. This was seen, for example, in the case of the Sahel region of Africa in the 1970s, where the drilling of boreholes and the initiation of animal health projects contributed to an increase in livestock numbers. The expansion of livestock, in turn, led to a worsening grazing situation. When the Sahel drought of 1973 struck, large numbers of livestock died, and the people dependent on them suffered greatly as well.[26]

USAID has undergone significant changes over time in the kinds of projects that it has supported and the ways in which it has pursued economic development. Some of these changes have come about because of the pressure of human rights and environmental organizations. They have also occurred because of questions raised by Congress. This was the case for live-stock projects in the 1970s, when, because of the criticisms of the role of USAID-supported projects in possibly contributing to the Sahel famine situation, the United States made a policy decision to no longer engage in livestock development projects. As noted previously, USAID also shifted its focus away from the construction of large-scale infrastructure projects such as dams. When USAID did take part in dam projects, as it did in the case of the Manantali Dam in Mali, it was generally to provide support for assessments of the social and environmental impacts of the projects and to programs aimed at providing assistance to those people who were resettled.

The U.S. Agency for International Development, the World Bank, and the European Union (EU) through the European Development Fund (EDF) provided low-interest loans to African, Caribbean, Latin American, and Pacific countries to undertake livestock development projects. One result of these projects has been a reduction in the numbers of breeds raised by local producers, a process, which, in turn, has affected genetic diversity adversely. The susceptibility of livestock to disease and other hazards such as drought increased concomitantly.

Another impact of livestock development projects is the loss of tropical forests. Forested areas, especially in South and Central America, have been turned into cattle ranches, a process that has resulted in the dispossession of indigenous peoples and reduction in the densities of wild resources crucial to the incomes and subsistence of local households.[27] Some of the peasants who lost their lands migrated further into the forest, establishing new agricultural plots and engaging in mining activities, some of which had devastating impact on indigenous groups such as the Yanomamo of Venezuela and Brazil.[28]

A third effect of livestock projects has been the reform of land tenure in an attempt to shift the basis of land-holding from communal to individual or private. This has sometimes resulted in losses of land access for poorer members of indigenous communities. One way of getting around this problem, it was hoped, was to expand the number of communally owned ranches. This strategy was pursued with some vigor, particularly in Africa (see table 13.2). The group ranches had some unforeseen impacts, including the exclusion of noncommunity members and the transfer of title over the land to commercial interests, thus reducing local people's access to land.

In some instances, the livestock projects exacerbated ethnic conflicts; this was the case, for example, with the Rwanda Mutura Agriculture and Live-

13.2. Allocation of Pastoral Land under International Development Aid Programs in Africa

try, region, period	Social organization unit to which land allocation was made	Area of land allocated to organization (km2)	No. households participating in organization	No. livestock units grazed on
wana 1970s–80s	Group ranch	49–64	10+	200–400+
'a				
do 1976–77	Group ranch	230 (40–690)	160 (30–420)	8,000 (550–89,000)
nda				
ra 1970s	Group ranch	4	15	NA
gal				
Senegal 1980s	Pastoral unit	264	c. 83	NA
alia				
no 1980s	Refugee association	17.64	186	930
alia				
ral Rangelands	Grazing associations	300	NA	NA
)s				
ania				
sailand 1960s–70s	Ranching association	1675 (500–2700)	484 (250–1000)	23,000 (19,000–30,000)

s: Livestock units (lu) are estimated on the basis 1 lu - 1 bovine or equine (of any age) = 5 sheep or goats / age = 0.77 camel (of any age). Some of the figures quoted here are the average of several figures given.

ces: Adapted, with additions, from Clare Oxby, Group Ranches in Africa (Rome: Food and Agriculture Organization, 1981); John Galaty, Dan Aronson, and P. C. Salzman, eds. The Future of Pastoral Peoples (Ottawa: international Development Research Center and McGill University, 1981); Stephen Sanford, Review of World Livestock Activities in Dry Tropical Africa (Washington DC: World Bank, 1981); Stephen Sanford, Management of Pastoral Development in the Third World (London: John Wiley and Sons and Overseas Development Institute, 1983, 115, Table 6.1); John W. Bennett, Steven W. Lawry, and James C. Riddell, Land Tenure and Livestock Development in Sub-Saharan Africa, AID Evaluation Special Study No. 39 (Washington DC: U.S. Agency for International Development, 1986).

stock Development Project, which was aimed at promoting land settlement and establishing cattle ranches for some 9,000 people. The project failed to take into consideration the prevailing social situation, and as a result, two groups, the Hima and Tutsi, ended up in a disadvantaged position relative to Hutu settlers. Efforts by an anthropologist to bring this situation to the attention of the World Bank and other agencies were ignored, a situation that was repeated in Somalia with the Central Rangelands Project and in other cases in Africa with similar adverse consequences.[29] One of the lessons that USAID learned in the process was the importance of doing social impact assessments (SIAS), something that is now a legal requirement in all USAID project preparation and design efforts.

Efforts to control the trade of wild products have sometimes resulted in difficulties for indigenous communities. The placing of elephants on Appendix 1 of the Convention on Trade in Endangered Species of Flora and Fauna (CITES), which was supported by the U.S. Fish and Wildlife Service, meant that the collection, processing, and sale of ivory became less viable as a source of income. While this action may have helped reduce pressure on elephants, it also caused frustration and a certain amount of economic hardship both at the national and local levels in eastern and southern African countries. Rising numbers of elephants in Kenya, Zimbabwe, and Botswana have also led to increased elephant-human conflicts, and people have been killed trying to protect their crops and homes.

To get around some of the problems of local people being affected adversely by the control of the sale of wild products and the imposition of hunting laws, efforts were made by various nongovernment organizations, often with support from USAID and other donor agencies, to establish community-based natural resource management projects (CBNRMPs), also known as integrated conservation and development projects (ICDPS). These kinds of projects have been implemented in many parts of the world with USAID and other donor funding.

The problem has been that conservation efforts have sometimes had negative effects on local people, including violations of basic human rights.[30] As a result, indigenous peoples and others have called for a new approach to wildlife preservation, management, and development, one that does not cause them harm but which instead leads to improvements in their standards of living.[31]

In the 1970s and 1980s, as the concern over the loss of elephants, rhinoceros, and other large mammal species increased, there were greater efforts by African governments to put pressure on people who they defined as poachers. Local people were arrested and jailed by police, wildlife department officials, and military personnel. In some cases, suspected poachers were badly mistreated during questioning or while they were in custody.[32] There were also cases in which local people were shot and killed as anti-poaching operations were conducted. Data obtained in the field suggest that at least some of those shot were simply gathering wild plants, obtaining water, or visiting friends.[33] Exact numbers of people killed by government officials in the pursuit of biodiversity preservation are difficult to come by. Some officials have suggested off the record that there may have been as many as ninety-six people shot and killed in a single year in one country in southern Africa. The hard-line shoot-to-kill policy has served to anger local people and has resulted, in some cases, in attacks on game scouts and tourists by local people. It has also led to what some feel are politically motivated spearings of rhinoceros and other large mammals, as occurred, for example, in the Ngorongoro Conservation Area in Tanzania and some of the Kenya national parks in the 1970s and 1980s.[34]

The antipoaching operations arguably have served to slow down the rate of destruction of such endangered or threatened species as rhinoceros and elephant. There is a major question, however, as to whether or not the mistreatment and killing of people is really the most effective way to promote conservation. Some local people in Africa have suggested that the actions of government and military agencies are genocidal in intent. Others have argued that preservationist actions have been undertaken to get them off the land so that it can be used for other purposes, including ranching and recreation. Still others have argued that the arrests and killings of local people have actually had the effect of exacerbating poaching problems.[35]

USAID is aware of many of the implications of the various consequences of wildlife preservation actions and has taken steps to ensure that USAID funds are not used to support anti-poaching efforts directly. It can do this by enforcing sections of the Foreign Assistance Act that stipulate that U.S. assistance is not to be used to purchase arms or to engage in paramilitary training activities. At the same time, by giving governments financial assistance to use for conservation purposes, it frees up other government funds to be used in anti-poaching efforts, so USAID still must bear responsibility for its actions.

The United States and Participatory Development

The nature of U.S. interaction with indigenous peoples outside the United States has varied and might be characterized best as being extremely fickle. At the same time, the U.S. has provided funds and technical assistance to programs in which indigenous peoples are the direct beneficiaries. This has been the case, for example, with the Regional Natural Resource Management Project (NRMP) (USAID Project No. 690-0251, SADCC Project No. 5.0.18) in southern Africa. For NRMP, funds have gone to support resource extraction and conservation activities in Zimbabwe, Botswana, Namibia, and Zambia. Financial and technical assistance has been provided to Ju/'hoansi San (Bushmen) and other indigenous community organizations, and efforts have been made to promote empowerment and expand local skills in governance and broad-based decision making. The United States has also taken stances on behalf of indigenous rights, as was the case in March 1996, when members of the Appropriations and Foreign Relations Committees of the U.S. Senate sent a letter to the government of Botswana urging it not to forcibly relocate the Basarwa and Bakgalagadi from the Central Kalahari Game Reserve.[36]

In spite of the greater attention to human rights and more participatory forms of development on the part of USAID, the status of indigenous people in some places where there are AID projects has declined so seriously as a result of competition that a number of them have organized their own self-help groups and have sought assistance from local development organizations, church groups, and human rights NGOs. Some of them are using the media to positive effect, as was the case in March 1996 when various indigenous groups spoke before the Human Rights Commission of the United Nations in Geneva.

The problems facing indigenous peoples today have brought about greater awareness of the urgent need to address issues relating to social, economic, and cultural rights and opportunities. Numerous indigenous communities and individuals have called for a different kind of approach to development — one that is not socially and environmentally destructive. They argue that they have a right to sustainable development, development that has been defined as that which, as the World Commission on Environment and Development puts it, " . . . meets the needs and aspirations of the present without compromising the ability of future generations to meet their own needs." This approach is seen by many indigenous individuals and groups as the only way to overcome the difficulties people are experiencing.[37]

A strategy for promoting sustainable rural development currently being debated is the use of local common property resource management (CPRM). Common property resource systems combine local control of resources with measures to promote sustainable use. More and more communities and nongovernment organizations are arguing in favor of community-based resource management as a sustainable development strategy. There are growing numbers of projects and community activities in various parts of the world that are engaged in implementing community-based resource management projects that are participatory in their orientations. Some of these projects have been relatively successful, and others have faced constraints ranging from lack of sufficient resources to the unwillingness of higher-level institutions to decentralize authority to grassroots-level organizations.[38]

There are relatively few examples of truly participatory development and community empowerment programs and projects in which local people have been fully involved in processes of change. One reason for this situation is that often development projects have short life spans, whereas institutional development and community empowerment requires long periods of time and a great deal of patience. Another reason is that often the development or conservation programs being advocated do not lay the groundwork necessary to ensure that the local people have a stake in the projects (they do not gain the support of the government so that legislation is changed to make possible local control over resources).

A third reason that participatory approaches to development are overlooked is that easily definable project outputs such as infrastructure construction or agricultural yield increases are given preference over less precisely quantifiable indicators such as institutional strength and resource management capacity. Often, greater emphasis, funding, and technical support are given to outside agencies (contracting groups, nongovernmental organizations) rather than to community-based organizations (CBOs). If local communities are to be empowered and participatory development actually carried out, then there will have to be a significant change in the ways that development agencies, donors, and voluntary organizations deal with local people and their concerns.

It has become a truism that the failure of many development projects is a result of lack of direct and indirect participation of local people who theoretically are supposed to be beneficiaries. In some cases, development agencies take a "top-down" approach in which local people are not consulted before, during, or after the implementation of the project. In other cases, people may be asked whether they agree with the project goals, but they do not have any say in the ways in which the project is implemented.

The most effective development projects are those that incorporate local people in decision making at every stage of the development process. Consultation alone, however, is insufficient. Local people must play a role in the identification of problems and constraints; they must assist in designing interventions to address those factors; and they must be part of the management of whatever programs or projects are established.

There are a number of examples of projects in which management authority is ceded over target areas by government agencies to NGOS. There are relatively few examples of situations in which governments have allowed local people or community-based organizations total control over resource management and development action. Local communities do sometimes get control over specific resources (for example, grazing in the case of pastoral associations in eastern or southern Africa, or water in the case of irrigation organizations in Morocco and Tunisia). Governments can assist local communities through passage of enabling legislation, as occurred in the case of Appropriate Authority status granted to District Councils in Zimbabwe under the Parks and Wildlife Act or the establishment of multiple-use areas in Niger and Uganda. USAID has played a positive role in a number of instances in promoting policies that ensure local control over resources. USAID country programs have also made efforts to see to it that local communities receive direct benefits in exchange for the costs that they bear.[39]

One area in which indigenous peoples would like to see the U.S. government take a stronger stance is in imposing sanctions on private companies that harm indigenous populations and the habitats in which they live. The United States has been notably reluctant to withdraw tax subsidies for oil companies engaged in activities that result in negative social and environmental impacts in places such as the Amazon Basin and Southeast Asia. The Clinton administration has been reluctant to penalize U.S.-based multinational corporations engaged in projects that lead to dispossession, loss of resources, and oppression of opponents. One of problems with the U.S. failure to take issue with these companies' actions is that it sends the message that it is acceptable for private companies to violate basic human rights and engage in environmentally destructive activities.[40]

The civil rights movement in the United States and the moves toward decolonization in the Third World in the 1960s helped fuel efforts to promote economic development and support indigenous peoples' rights. The "Development Decade" of the 1960s did not bring about many of the improvements in the lives of local people that were hoped for, especially the poor. Changes in the Foreign Assistance Act in the late 1960s and the early 1970s legislated that greater attention be paid to human rights issues. These changes were in part a product of events in Southeast Asia, where U.S. economic and humanitarian assistance programs were used to promote counterinsurgency actions and to support certain groups and individuals over others.

In the 1970s there was a certain amount of depoliticization of foreign aid, and a number of stipulations were written into foreign aid enabling legislation geared toward ensuring that the aid was used in more positive ways. Environmental and social impact assessments became part of the USAID approach to the development planning and implementation process. Greater emphasis was placed on meeting the needs of disadvantaged groups in Third World countries, some of whom were indigenous. USAID regulations required that greater efforts be made to improve the lives of women, and women in development (WID) officers were appointed at the country (mission) level in various parts of the world.

The 1980s saw a return to the political use of foreign aid and aid institutions, especially in Central America where tens of thousands of indigenous people died at the hands of U.S.-supported government forces and death squads.[41] Indigenous peoples spoke out against U.S. actions at international forums and at local level meetings. Some of the indigenous leaders argued that there had to be a more direct link made between human rights and development and a better balance between civil and political rights and social, economic, and cultural rights.[42]

Indigenous peoples have been more than willing to protest the mistreatment that they feel they have experienced at the hands of development agencies such as USAID and the World Bank. In the late 1980s and 1990s a number of representatives of indigenous groups have testified before Congress, and they have held their own press conferences to which they invited journalists and representatives of human rights groups. USAID, the World Bank, and other development institutions have had to deal more directly and more carefully with members of indigenous communities, some of whom have substantial support not only among members of the public but in Congress as well.[43]

In part because of the criticism it was receiving, combined with difficulties encountered in overcoming development constraints and the outright failures of some of its projects, USAID began to employ new strategies. USAID missions embarked on what some people termed a participatory extension approach to development. This kind of approach placed emphasis on community involvement in all aspects of policy formulation, project and program planning, and project implementation. This type of approach resulted in the formation or strengthening of local institutions such as indigenous farmers' associations or women's groups. It also provided opportunities for local people to share ideas and information and to formulate new strategies based on public consensus. In some ways, USAID's approach to development has been much more participatory than that of the World Bank. It is ironic that just as participation has become more than a simple catchphrase in USAID, the political and financial support for the agency has declined.

The U.S. government supported indigenous rights in theory, but in practice it has often worked to undercut them.[44] The United States has dragged its feet in discussions of indigenous peoples' rights at the Inter-American Commission on Human Rights and at the Human Rights Commission of the United Nations. In spite of U.S. attempts to weaken its provisions, the Inter-American Commission on Human Rights (IACHR) of the Organization of American States (OAS) passed a draft declaration of the rights of indigenous peoples at its 1278th session held on September 18, 1995. It is likely that the United States will continue its efforts to water down the provisions of the IACHR declaration as it moves through the consultation process prior to its being presented to the General Assembly of the OAS. The United States has also indicated its opposition to aspects of the Universal Declaration of Indigenous Peoples' Rights, which is making its way through the UN system after having been drafted by the Working Group on Indigenous Populations, especially those sections relating to land and resource rights and collective rights.[45]

The problem that USAID as an institution is having to deal with today is that it is once again facing the possibility of being politicized. If the agency is incorporated directly into the Department of State, as has been suggested by some members of Congress, then there is a chance that once again U.S. foreign assistance will be used for purposes other than for what it was intended. The concern of many indigenous peoples is that once again they will have to contend with an agency that places more emphasis on "winning their hearts and minds" and trying to counter their efforts to seek self-determination than on providing high quality social and economic development assistance. As one indigenous leader from Latin America put it, "We want USAID, the World Bank, and other development and finance institutions to help us, not violate our human rights." Without some effort to ensure that the primary goal of U.S. economic assistance is development, it is likely that sizable numbers of indigenous peoples could find themselves living in even greater social, economic, and political insecurity than they are at present.

Notes

Support of the research upon which this paper is based was provided by the U.S. National Science Foundation (grants SOC75-02253 and BNS76-20373), the Norwegian Agency for International Development (NORAD), the United States Agency for International Development (USAID), the Ford Foundation and the Research Council of the University of Nebraska–Lincoln. I would like to thank Dave Forsythe, Anne Pitsch, Alan Osborn, Beth Ritter, Ralph Hartley, Suzy Prenger, Bob Epp, Karen Griffin, Patrick Morris, Victor Montejo, Ted Scudder, Sandy Davis, Barbara Belding, Michael Painter, Sonia Arellano-Lopez, and the members of the Committee for Human Rights (CfHR) of the American Anthropological Association for their insights, information, and assistance. It would not have been possible to discuss many of the issues in this paper without the assistance of numerous indigenous people and organizations, and I wish to acknowledge my deep appreciation for their contributions.

1. For overviews of the socioeconomic statuses of indigenous peoples, see Alan B. Durning, *Guardians of the Land: Indigenous Peoples and the Health of the Earth* (Washington DC: Worldwatch Institute, 1992); Marc S. Miller, ed., *State of the Peoples: A Global Human Rights Report on Societies in Danger* (Boston: Beacon, 1993); and David Maybury-Lewis, *Indigenous Peoples, Ethnic Groups, and the State* (Boston: Allyn and Bacon, 1997).

2. The United States has argued for indigenous rights in forums ranging from the Human Rights Commission of the United Nations and the Inter-American Commission on Human Rights of the Organization of American States (OAS) to hearings in Congress.

3. This was the case, for example, with Convention 169 of the International Labor Organization, The Indigenous and Tribal Peoples Convention, which was brought into force on September 5, 1991, without U.S. ratification.

4. The situation in Irian Jaya (West Papua) is complicated. There were protests about local people having been beaten and killed by Indonesian government forces, including members of the Amungme tribe. Tribal groups protested these actions. Criticism was also leveled at a U.S.-based mining company, Freeport MacMoRan Copper and Gold, Inc., which was extracting resources in Irian Jaya. It was argued that the company colluded in the human rights violations that occurred and that there had been large-scale environmental destruction as a result of the mining operations. Background information on this situation can be found in David Hyndman, *Ancestral Rain Forests and the Mountain of Gold: Indigenous Peoples and Mining in Indonesia* (Boulder CO: Westview, 1994).

5. Examples of such projects include those supported under the Regional Natural Resources Management Project (USAID Project 690-0251) in southern Africa and a number of integrated conservation and development projects (ICDPs) in the developing world. See International Institute for Environment and Development, *Whose*

Eden? An Overview of Community Approaches to Wildlife Management (London: International Institute for Environment and Development and Overseas Development Administration, 1994). For a critical view of these projects, see Clark C. Gibson, and Stuart A. Marks, "Transforming Rural Hunters into Conservationists: An Assessment of Community-Based Wildlife Management Programs in Africa" *World Development* 23 (1995): 941–957.

6. Discussions of development can be found in Robert Chambers, *Rural Development: Putting the Last First* (London: Longman, 1983); Michael P. Todaro, *Economic Development*, 5th ed. (New York: Longman, 1994). A useful discussion of development assistance can be found in Sarah J. Tisch and Michael B. Wallace, *Dilemmas of Development Assistance: The What, Why, and Who of Foreign Aid* (Boulder CO: Westview, 1994).

7. For a discussion of socioeconomic rights and civil and political rights, see Russel Lawrence Barsh, "The Right to Development as a Human Right," *Human Rights Watch* 13 (1991): 322–338; David P. Forsythe, ed., *Human Rights and Development: International Views* (London: Macmillan, 1989).

8. For discussions of the issues of American Indian sovereignty, self-determination, and autonomy, see John R. Wunder, *"Retained by the People": A History of American Indians and the Bill of Rights* (New York: Oxford University Press, 1994); and David E. Wilkins, *American Indian Sovereignty and the U.S. Supreme Court: The Masking of Justice* (Austin: University of Texas Press, 1996).

9. See Organization of American States, *Report of the Situation of Human Rights of a Segment of the Nicaraguan Population of Miskito Origin* (Washington DC: OAS, 1984). Some Miskitos believed that they had been manipulated by the United States, the Sandanistas, and the Contras, the coalition of groups funded in part by the Central Intelligence Agency that was attempting to force the Sandanistas from power in the 1980s. Information on the Kurds and their struggles can be found in Mehrdad Izady, *The Kurds: A Concise Handbook* (Bristol PA: Crane Russak, 1992).

10. Discussions of the support for countries violating the rights of indigenous peoples and others can be found in the annual reports of Amnesty International, Survival International, the Minority Rights Group, and the International Work Group for Indigenous Affairs, and summaries of the human rights situations in various states are contained in the *Country Reports on Human Rights Practices* done on an annual basis since the 1970s by the Department of State and presented to Congress.

11. For a discussion of the situations faced by the Montagnards and other Hill Peoples of Vietnam, see Gerald Cannon Hickey, *Shattered World: Adaptation and Survival among Vietnam's Highland Peoples during the Vietnam War* (Philadelphia: University of Pennsylvania Press, 1993).

12. See Eric Wakin, *Anthropology Goes to War: Professional Ethics and Counterinsurgency in Thailand* (Madison: University of Wisconsin Center for Southeast Asian Studies, 1992).

13. Information on these actions is contained in Hickey, *Shattered World*, 1993; and Wakin, *Anthropology*, 1992. Data were also obtained on the village patrols and the functions of "strategic hamlets" in Vietnam in the form of personal communications from Vu Niem (a pseudonym) in Lincoln in 1993 and 1994.

14. For discussions of the impacts of development and counterinsurgency operations in Central America, see Robert M. Carmack, ed., *Harvest of Violence: Guatemala's Indians in the Counterinsurgency War* (Norman: University of Oklahoma Press, 1988); and David Stoll, *Between Two Armies in the Ixil Towns of Guatemala* (New York: Columbia University Press, 1993).

15. Data on Somalia were obtained from fieldwork in 1983–84 and from USAID/Somalia and nongovernment organization files, as well as from interviews with Somali clan members, USAID/Somalia Director Louis Cohen, and U.S. Ambassador to Somalia Robert Oakley.

16. For discussions of the impacts of international finance institutions' policies, see Susan George and Fabrizio Sabelli, *Faith and Credit: The World Bank's Secular Empire* (Boulder CO: Westview, 1994); and David P. Forsythe, "The United Nations, Human Rights, and Development," *Human Rights Quarterly* 19 (1997): 334–349.

17. There is a huge literature on the impacts of dams; see, for example, E. Goldsmith and N. Hildyard, *Social and Environmental Effects of Large Dams*, 2 vols. (Camelford, Cornwall: Wadebridge Ecological Center, 1984); Patrick McCully, *Silenced Rivers: The Ecology and Politics of Large Dams* (London: Zed Books, 1996); and the newsletters and reports of the International Rivers Network.

18. See, for example, McCully, *Silenced Rivers*, 70–72; and Patrick E. Tyler, "Cracks Show Early in China's Big Dam Project," *New York Times*, July 15, 1996, pp. A1, A5.

19. The World Bank policy on resettlement is contained in "Operational Directive 4.30: Involuntary Resettlement," in *The World Bank Operational Manual* (Washington DC: The World Bank, 1990). An example of World Bank experience with resettlement can be found in World Bank, *Early Experience with Involuntary Resettlement: Impact Evaluation on Thailand Khao Laem Hydroelectric (Loan 1770-TH)* (Washington DC: Operations Evaluation Department, World Bank, 1993). For examples of criticism of the World Bank's resettlement and development policies, see Alex Wilks and Nicholas Hildyard, "Evicted! The World Bank and Forced Resettlement," *The Ecologist* 24 (1994): 225–229; Catherine Caufield, *Masters of Illusion: The World Bank and the Poverty of Nations* (New York: Henry Holt and Company, 1996).

20. The data on development project impacts were obtained from a large number of sources, including the *Urgent Action Bulletins* of Survival International, the bulletins and annual reports of the International Work Group for Indigenous Affairs, *Cultural Survival Quarterly*, reports of the Minority Rights Group, Human Rights Watch, Amnesty International, and the Institute for Development Anthropology, along with reports of international finance institutions such as the World Bank, and documents of bilateral aid agencies such as USAID.

21. These guidelines are presented in the *AID Handbook* (Washington DC: U.S. Agency for International Development, Department of State, 1982 and subsequent updates).

22. International trade issues have been addressed in a number of contexts, including the debate over the North American Free Trade Agreement (NAFTA); see, for example, M. Delai Baer and Sidney Weintraub, eds., *The NAFTA Debate: Grappling with Unconventional Trade Issues* (Boulder CO: Lynne Rienner, 1994).

23. For a discussion of these issues, see Ministry of Wildlife, Conservation and Tourism, *Namibia's Green Plan (Environment and Development)* (Windhoek, Namibia: Ministry of Wildlife, Conservation, and Tourism, 1992).

24. See, for example, Alan B. Durning, *Action At the Grassroots: Fighting Poverty and Environmental Decline* (Washington DC: Worldwatch Institute, 1989); and Robert K. Hitchcock, "Africa and Discovery: Human Rights, Environment, and Development," *American Indian Culture and Research Journal* 17(1): 129–152.

25. Discussions of the Green Revolution have emphasized many of the negative social, environmental, and economic effects of monocropping; see, for example, Susan George, *How the Other Half Dies: The Real Reasons for World Hunger* (Montclair NJ: Allanheld, Osmun and Co., 1977).

26. For a discussion of the role of development aid in contributing to the environmental degradation and famine situations in the Sahel, see Claude Meillassoux, "Development or Exploitation?: Is the Sahel Famine Good Business? *Review of African Political Economy* 1 (1974): 27–33.

27. See Stephen G. Bunker, *Underdeveloping the Amazon: Extraction, Unequal Exchange, and the Failure of the Modern State* (Chicago: University of Chicago Press, 1985); and Michael Painter and William H. Durham, eds., *The Social Consequences of Environmental Destruction in Latin America* (Ann Arbor: University of Michigan Press, 1995).

28. The Yanomamo have been affected adversely by encroaching groups, especially miners, over the past decade; see, for example, Bruce Albert, "Gold Miners and Yanomami Indians in the Brazilian Amazon: The Hashimu Massacre," in *Who Pays the Price? The Sociocultural Context of Environmental Crisis*, ed. Barbara Rose Johnston (Covelo CA: Island Press, 1994).

29. Information on the Central Rangelands Project was obtained from Somali residents of the region where the project was based and from members of the team that implemented the project. Other projects in Africa for which data were obtained are listed in table 2.

30. Human rights violations in the context of conservation programs have been dealt with in the following: Nancy L. Peluso, "Coercing Conservation? The Politics of State Resource Control," in *The State and Social Power in Global Environmental Politics*, ed. Ronnie D. Lipschutz and Ken Conca (New York: Columbia University Press, 1993), 46–70; and Robert K. Hitchcock, African Wildlife: Conservation and

Conflict," in *Life and Death Matters: Human Rights and the Environment at the End of the Millennium*, ed. Barbara R. Johnston (Thousand Oaks CA: AltaMira Press, 1997), 81–95.

31. See, for example, Hanne Veber, Jens Dahl, Fiona Wilson, and Espen Waehle, eds., "... *Never Drink from the Same Cup.*" Proceedings of the Conference on Indigenous Peoples in Africa. Tune, Denmark, 1993. (Copenhagen: IWGIA and Center for Development Research, 1993).

32. See, for example, Alice Mogwe, *Who Was (T)here First? An Assessment of the Human Rights Situation of Basarwa in Selected Communities in the Gantsi District.* Occasional Paper No. 10. (Gaborone, Botswana: Botswana Christian Council, 1992).

33. See Douglas B. Lee, "Okavango Delta: Africa's Last Refuge," *National Geographic* 178 (December 1990): 38–69. Data on the human rights impacts of anti-poaching operations were drawn from interviews done in 1988, 1989, 1990, 1991, and 1995 in Botswana. See Robert K. Hitchcock and Stuart A. Marks, *Traditional and Modern Systems of Land Use and Management and User Rights to Natural Resources in Rural Botswana. Part I: Field Data and Analysis.* (Gaborone, Botswana: Natural Resource Management Project, 1991); data on western Zimbabwe was obtained in 1989 and 1992; see Robert K. Hitchcock and Fanuel M. Nangati, *Zimbabwe Natural Resources Management Project Community-Based Resource Utilization Component: Interim Assessment.* (Harare, Zimbabwe: U.S. Agency for International Development and Department of National Parks and Wildlife Management, 1992).

34. Henry Fosbrooke, Daniel Stiles, personal communications. See also P. Arcese, J. Hando, and K. Campbell, "Historical and Present-Day Anti-Poaching Efforts in Serengeti," in *Serengeti II: Research, Conservation, and Management of an Ecosystem*, ed. A. R. E. Sinclair and P. Arcese (Chicago: University of Chicago Press, 1995), 506–533. Although the Ngorongoro environment has been protected, the status of the Maasai in the area has declined; see J. Terrence McCabe, Scott Perkin, and Claire Schofield, "Can Conservation and Development Be Coupled among Pastoral People? An Examination of the Maasai of the Ngorongoro Conservation Area." *Human Organization* 51 (1992): 353–366.

35. Statements along these lines have been made at a number of international conferences on indigenous peoples such as one held in Gaborone, Botswana ("The Second Regional Conference on Development Programs for Africa's San Populations," October 11–13, 1993; they were also raised at the Human Rights Commission meeting in Geneva in March 1996.

36. For a discussion of the effects of a community-based natural resource management project on indigenous people in southern Africa, see Barbara Wyckoff-Baird, "Democracy: Indicators from Ju/'hoan Bushmen in Namibia," *Cultural Survival Quarterly* 20 (1996): 18–21; see also cases in Barbara Wyckoff-Baird, ed., *Devolution of Authority, Responsibility, and Funding Capability: Links to Biodiversity Conservation* (Washington DC: Biodiversity Support Program, 1999).

37. World Commission on Environment and Development (the Brundtland Commission), *Our Common Future* (Oxford: Oxford University Press, 1987). For other discussions on sustainable development, see the special section on sustainability issues in the *Annual Review of Ecology and Systematics*, vol. 26, 1996.

38. For a discussion of common property resource management and the kinds of projects that are being done in various parts of the world, see David Western and R. Michael Wright, eds., *Natural Connections: Perspectives in Community-based Conservation* (Covelo CA: Island Press, 1994); and Richard Margoluis and Nick Solafsky, *Measures of Success: Designing, Managing and Monitoring Conservation and Development Projects* (Covelo CA: Island Press, 1998).

39. See Associates in Rural Development, *Decentralization and Local Autonomy: Conditions for Achieving Sustainable Resource Management* (Burlington VT: Associates in Rural Development; and, Washington DC: USAID, 1992).

40. For discussions of the issue of the negative effects of multinational corporations on indigenous peoples and their habitats, see Al Gedicks, *The New Resource Wars: Native and Environmental Struggles Against Multinational Corporations* (Boston: South End, 1993). An overview of the environmentally harmful effects of governments and private companies can be found in Aaron Sachs, *Eco-justice: Linking Human Rights and the Environment* (Washington DC: Worldwatch Institute, 1995).

41. For an excellent, if disconcerting, discussion of the situation facing the Quiche Maya and other indigenous peoples in Guatemala, see Ricardo Falla, *Massacres in the Jungle: Ixcan, Guatemala, 1975–1982* (Boulder CO: Westview, 1994).

42. See Leo van der Vlist, ed., *Voices of the Earth: Indigenous Peoples, New Partners, and the Right to Self-Determination in Practice* (Amsterdam: The Netherlands Center for Indigenous Peoples, 1994).

43. Public and Congressional support of indigenous rights is apparent in the support for investigations into the deaths of indigenous and other people in such countries as Guatemala, Iraq, and Rwanda; see, for example, H. Jack Geiger and Robert M. Cook-Deegan, "The Role of Physicians in Conflicts and Humanitarian Crises: Case Studies from the Field Missions of Physicians for Human Rights, 1988 to 1993," *Journal of the American Medical Association* 270 (1993): 616–620. An example of pressure brought to bear on multinational corporations can be seen in the case of Unocal, which constructed a pipeline in Mayanmar (Burma) that allegedly was being done with slave labor; see Karl Schoenberger, "The Human Rights Pipeline," *Los Angeles Times*, April 11, 1994, p. D1.

44. It has done this in a number of ways, arguing on behalf of indigenous peoples' land rights in Brazil, for example, and then turning around and giving advice to the Brazilian judicial system about how to get around provisions of its own constitution as it relates to indigenous rights (Terry Turner, Linda Rabben, personal communications).

45. This declaration has been produced as appendix 2 of van der Vlist, *Voices of the Earth*, 305–316. A discussion of individual rights, group rights, and collective rights can be found in Douglas Sanders, "Collective Rights," *Human Rights Quarterly* 13 (1991): 368–386. The issue of participation in development has been addressed in Michael M. Cernea, ed., *Putting People First* (Washington DC: World Bank, 1991).

14

U.S. Targeting of International Humanitarian Assistance

•

GEORGE KENT

Many people around the world suffer as a result of armed conflict, genocide, exploitation, and disasters of different kinds. In some cases the international community provides humanitarian assistance in the form of food, health care, and shelter to alleviate their suffering. The system under which international humanitarian assistance (IHA) is provided has become increasingly effective, significantly reducing the misery. However, there is room for improvement. My purpose here is to examine prospects for improvement in one important aspect of IHA policymaking, the targeting of humanitarian assistance. In a world full of people with many different kinds of needs, where should the resources that are available for humanitarian assistance be used? Who should be helped? The question is viewed here from the perspective of one major donor country, the United States.

This study is not about the radical social change that may be needed to prevent suffering in the world, but rather it is about the need to relieve suffering immediately. The analysis is on symptomatic relief; it ignores the roots of the problems. The premise here is that while we work to forecast and prevent future crises, we should not neglect the many severe crises that are currently ongoing.

The United States plays a strong role in IHA, not only through its direct bilateral assistance but also through its participation in the global IHA system. At the global level the lead agency for IHA is the UN Department of Humanitarian Affairs. Other global organizations such as the UN High Commissioner for Refugees, the UN Children's Fund, the World Food Program, and the Food and Agriculture Organization of the United Nations play major roles. The International Committee for the Red Cross plays a major role in armed conflict situations. The United States has substantial influence in many of these organizations.

This chapter examines the way in which the United States government decides which problematic situations in the world are to receive assistance. I then suggest that a rights-oriented system for targeting assistance might help to make global IHA more effective and efficient, and also more just.

Types of Assistance

There are many different kinds of assistance. This study focuses specifically on *humanitarian* assistance, defined here as *assistance whose primary motivation is to provide relief for people in situations of extreme need*. It can take many different forms including, say, rescuing a child who has fallen down a well, offering a coin to a beggar, providing certain kinds of foreign aid, or undertaking military intervention to release hostages. It can be provided by individuals, local and national governments, and international governmental and nongovernmental organizations. International humanitarian assistance may be private or public; that is, it may be supplied either by private agencies (nongovernmental agencies [NGOs], or private voluntary organizations [PVOs]), or by governmental (public) agencies.[1] Governmental agencies often work with and through nongovernmental agencies, sometimes on a contract basis.

Frequently, the humanitarian motivation is mixed with other motivations. IHA may be used to strengthen political alliances or to increase sales of domestic products. Governments may provide international food aid not only to help others but also to provide an outlet for the nation's agricultural surpluses and thus provide assistance to their agricultural sectors. In some cases, humanitarian motivations may be claimed to justify actions wholly motivated in other ways. Nevertheless, no matter how difficult it may be to discern in concrete situations, humanitarian assistance is understood here as action driven primarily by compassion, by concern for the well-being of others who are in extreme need.

Foreign assistance agencies and analysts often count humanitarian assistance as a subcategory of development assistance, but it is useful to distinguish the two. Humanitarian assistance is mainly about directly meeting extreme human needs, especially (though not exclusively) in the short term. In contrast, development assistance is mainly about economic benefits, usually in the long term. Humanitarian assistance is often based on delivering immediate benefits in the form of food, medicine, or shelter.

Some analysts suggest that development assistance is humanitarian, because "economic growth is bound to trickle down to the poor and the disadvantaged."[2] However, in many development assistance efforts economic growth is the primary motivation, and the "trickle down" — if there is any — is incidental. Development assistance projects are assessed primarily in economic terms.

Military units may be involved in international humanitarian assistance in several different ways. They may be used as combat forces in humanitarian *interventions*, which means humanitarian assistance without the consent of the government of the receiving nation. Military units also may be used to help provide food, medicine, or shelter in noncombat situations. For the purposes of this study, that part of the effort used for the direct provision of such services may be counted as humanitarian assistance. Combat operations themselves are not counted as humanitarian assistance, regardless of their objectives. Thus where there is humanitarian intervention of the sort undertaken in Iraq, Somalia, and Bosnia, the overall combat operation is not regarded here as humanitarian assistance. Only that portion involving the direct provision of food, medicine, shelter, and the like would be counted as humanitarian assistance. Combat operations devoted specifically and exclusively to securing the delivery of humanitarian assistance might be counted as part of the humanitarian effort, provided it was wholly impartial with regard to the parties in conflict.[3]

U.S. International Humanitarian Assistance Programs

Private agencies within the United States have always provided food relief and assistance of other forms to people overseas, but through much of the nation's history there was a general belief that the Constitution did not give Congress the power to use public funds for that purpose. Active government involvement did not begin until after World War I, and especially after World War II. In 1954 a provision of the Mutual Security Act allowed funds to be used to respond to foreign disasters. In that same year Public Law 480, the Food for Peace program, allowed the government to sell or donate surplus agricultural commodities to needy people throughout the world.

U.S. foreign assistance overall is driven primarily by its political, strategic, and economic motives. During the Cold War, it was largely driven by the anticommunist impulse. Humanitarian assistance accounts for only a small share of the total foreign assistance budget. Nevertheless, it is still a substantial amount, especially when compared with the amounts offered for international humanitarian assistance by other countries. Moreover, U.S. hu-

Figure 14.1. U.S. Government Humanitarian Assistance Agencies

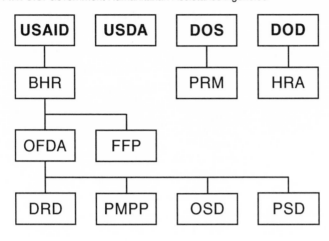

manitarian assistance has been managed with a high level of skill and sophistication by very dedicated professionals.

The current institutional structure of U.S. assistance programs is set out in the Foreign Assistance Act of 1961 and its subsequent amendments (22 U.S.C. Section 2151b, 1990). On November 3, 1961, President Kennedy created the U.S. Agency for International Development (USAID) as the lead agency for administering U.S. foreign assistance programs. Under a National Security Council Directive of September 15, 1993, the USAID administrator serves as the President's Special Coordinator for International Disaster Assistance and thus serves the major interagency coordinating function for the U.S. government.[4]

The major agencies of the U.S. government involved in international humanitarian assistance are described in the following paragraphs.[5]

Within USAID, the Bureau for Humanitarian Response (BHR), and under it, the Office of Foreign Disaster Assistance (OFDA) has the leading role in managing U.S. humanitarian assistance. OFDA, in turn, is organized into four divisions. These are the Disaster Response Division (DRD) and the Prevention, Mitigation, Preparedness and Planning Division (PMPP), both of which work with the Operations Support Division (OSD) and the Program Support Division (PSD). DRD manages most of OFDA's assistance programs. PMPP oversees projects designed to prevent or reduce the impact of disasters. PMPP helps countries develop their own disaster management systems.

Humanitarian assistance from the United States is generally launched with the declaration of a disaster by the U.S. ambassador. OFDA then works with the local USAID office. When the situation is warranted, OFDA sends a Disaster Assistance Response Team (DART) to the country to manage the IHA operations. Stockpiles of emergency relief commodities are maintained in Maryland, Panama, Italy, Guam, and Thailand.

The Office of Food for Peace (FFP), also located under BHR, is responsible for managing the U.S. government's foreign food aid programs under Public Law 480, Titles II and III. Title II emergency food aid programs are targeted to vulnerable populations suffering from food insecurity as a result of natural disasters, civil conflict, or other crises. Title III food aid programs are intended to promote long-term food security in selected countries.[6]

The U.S. Department of Agriculture (USDA) works closely with BHR/FFP in allocating surplus food commodities to developing countries. These commodities are often used for emergency feeding programs.

The Department of State (DOS) provides humanitarian assistance through its Bureau for Population, Refugees, and Migration (PRM). PRM was formerly known as the Bureau for Refugee Programs.

The Department of Defense (DOD) provides humanitarian assistance through its Office of Humanitarian and Refugee Affairs (HRA). DOD has been involved in hundreds of humanitarian assistance missions since the close of World War II, but it did not have a formal IHA policy. HRA was established in 1985 to coordinate DOD efforts with other agencies, especially BHR/OFDA.[7] With HRA coordination, the DOD undertakes humanitarian and disaster relief (HDR) missions. These are not combat missions and should not be confused with humanitarian interventions, which are combat missions.

DOD's IHA activities are divided into four categories: foreign disaster assistance, distribution of DOD excess property, humanitarian assistance for nation building, and space-available transportation of nongovernment supplies. Each is separately authorized by law.[8]

DOD's regional commanders in chief (CINCS) have authority to immediately use local military resources to save lives, even without waiting for a disaster declaration. The CINC's response is usually short-term, designed to respond to the immediate effects of a disaster until the OFDA-coordinated response is under way. Subsequent support from DOD may be provided as part of the OFDA assistance plan. DOD assistance prior to the declaration of a disaster may or may not be reimbursed by OFDA. Assistance provided by DOD following the disaster declaration is normally reimbursed by OFDA.[9]

Apart from DOD's direct foreign disaster assistance efforts, there are three other DOD programs contributing toward IHA. Excess property such as tents, blankets, medicines, and meals-ready-to-eat may be donated for IHA purposes. In FY91 and FY92 DOD donated excess property worth over $150 million. Under the heading of nation building, DOD is authorized to conduct humanitarian and civic assistance activities in conjunction with its overseas training exercises and deployments. In FY93, $25 million was allocated to the program. DOD is also authorized to transport IHA supplies on a space-available basis.[10]

IHA Operations and Fundings

Worldwide, donor governments provide humanitarian assistance directly (bilaterally) or through UN and other international agencies (multilaterally). In 1993 donor nations that contributed to humanitarian assistance in three or more receiving countries were Australia, Austria, Belgium, Canada, China, Denmark, the European Union, France, Germany, Indonesia, Iran, Italy, Japan, Netherlands, Norway, Pakistan, Russia, Saudi Arabia, Spain, Sweden, Thailand, Turkey, United Kingdom, United States, and the Vatican.[11] Direct aid totaled more than $3 billion in 1992 and 1993. The largest direct donors were the United States, the European Union, Germany, Italy, and the United Kingdom.[12] Some countries spread their resources around, while others concentrate on particular receiving countries. Saudi Arabia, for example, has contributed more than $200 million to Afghan refugees since 1980.

The major contributors of IHA are members of the Development Assistance Committee (DAC) of the Organization for Economic Co-operation and Development (OECD). For the DAC group, in 1994:

> Bilateral expenditure on *emergency and disaster relief* (excluding food) rose to an all-time high of $3.5 billion. If DAC Members' emergency food aid and their contributions to multilateral institutions for emergency purposes are included, the total would be about $6 billion, or roughly ten percent of their total ODA [Official Development Assistance] expenditures.
>
> Within this total, DAC Members' expenditure on developing country *refugees* rose to $2.5 billion in 1994.[13]

For DAC members, in 1993 emergency aid (other than food aid) was about 6.1 percent of their total Official Development Assistance. Food aid accounted for another 2.8 percent.[14]

In FY1994 (October 1, 1993, to September 30, 1994), U.S. bilateral assistance given in response to disasters and crises overseas amounted to over $1.3 billion. The magnitude and distribution of U.S. efforts through BHR/OFDA are shown in table 14.1. There were sixty-nine relief operations, with sixty-five new declared disasters in forty-nine countries. There were eighteen different disaster types. Studying the table, in column V we see that there were a large number of small operations, and fourteen operations costing more than a million dollars each. Five operations — in Angola, Burundi, Rwanda, Somalia, and Sudan — cost more than 10 million dollars each. Column VIII shows the proportion of BHR/OFDA operations in the total U.S. assistance.[15] This can be taken as a rough indicator of the extent to which the assistance was humanitarian.

For many of the small operations the expenditure amounted to $25,000. This is due to the fact that when a U.S. ambassador or the Department of State declares a disaster, BHR/OFDA can immediately provide up to $25,000 to the embassy or USAID mission to purchase relief supplies or to contribute to a local relief organization. Larger amounts require more paperwork and more approvals from other parts of the government.

IHA Targeting Maps

Resources are limited, so choices must be made among different situations in which assistance might be offered. Where should U.S. or other IHA resources be used? The concern here is with situations in which IHA might be provided if the government of the target country welcomed it. It is not about the targeting of combat-oriented interventions, whether humanitarian or otherwise.[16]

Targeting means systematically identifying options and then choosing among them in a reasoned way. A targeting map for the global IHA system is suggested in table 14.2. Each row identifies a broad type of IHA situation, and each column identifies particular providers of IHA. With a finer-grained matrix the rows could be broken out to identify concrete situations at a particular time. In a first cut, the targeting map could be filled in with x's to show which providers were operating in which situations. With more detailed information, the map could show how much was being spent by each agency in each situation. With still more information, it might be possible to show how many lives were saved in each situation, and at what cost.

To establish the coordinates of the map, clear categories of IHA situations

14.1 BHR/OFDA Response Obligations in FY 94

	II Disaster type	III No. dead	IV No. affected	V BHR/OFDA obligation ($)	VI Other USG assistance ($)	VII Total USG assistance ($)	VIII BHR/OFDA as % of Total
gional	—	—	—	610,934			
	Earthquake	114	10,000	25,000			
	Civil strife	100,000	3,600,000	19,367,530	70,483,778	89,851,308	21.6
	Food/fuel shortage	—	—	25,000			
	Emergency	—	3,500,00	25,000			
an	Displaced persons	—	50,000	25,000			
& Serbia	Civil strife	—	3,340,000	30,620,914	357,248,688	387,869,602	7.89
	Civil strife	50,000	1,600,000	7,081,586	54,707,800	61,789,386	11.5
	Drought	—	300,000	25,000	3,274,900	3,299,900	0.8
	Floods	1,400	73,000,000	25,000			
a	Earthquake/landslide	271	5,000	26,544	700,000	762,844	3.5
	Civil strife	1,000	250,000	39,000			
ica	Floods	5	35,000	1,371			
	Civil strife	—	690,000	0			
	Food shortage/DPs	—	2,030,000	2,775,745	30,919,100	33,694,845	8.2
	Food shortage	—	6,700,000	886,917	43,340,800	44,227,717	2.0
	Civil strife	—	200,000	331,421	5,613,00	5,944,421	5.6
	Civil strife	—	150,000	0			
	Cholera	311	24,000	25,000			
Bissau	Cyclone	—	1,722	10,000			
	Emergency	—	2,000,000	5,253,129	66,734,546	71,987,675	7.3
as	Floods	150	15,150	25,064			
	Earthquake	10,000	150,000	747,492	992,508	1,740,000	43.0
ia	Earthquake	207	40,000	23,899			
	Civil strife	—	250,000	2,482,818			
	Drought	—	1,200,000	1,189,532	27,108,600	28,298,132	4.2
	Epidemic	1,000	6,500,000	25,000			
tan	Landslide	111	45,000	25,000			
	Civil strife	—	1,000,000	9,914,794	66,449,373	76,364,167	13.0
nia	Food shortage	—	25,000	25,000			
scar	Cyclone	231	500,000	295,000			
	Drought	—	3,000,000	25,000	8,775,000	8,800,000	0.3
a	Floods	47	25,000	33,513			
pique	Displaced persons	—	3,500,000	381,812	431,131,200	43,513,012	0.9
pique	Cyclone	2	1,500,000	579,272			

Table 14.1 *continued*

I Country	II Disaster type	III No. dead	IV No. affected	V BHR/OFDA obligation ($)	VI Other USG assistance ($)	VII Total USG assistance ($)
Nicaragua	Floods	31	61,190	2,900		
Niger	Floods	60	62,052	25,000		
Nigeria	Floods	30	400,000	25,000		
Northern Iraq	Displaced persons	—	750,000	212,254		
Papua New Guinea	Earthquake	41	9,600	25,000	607,599	826,023
Papua New Guinea	Volcano	4	100,000	25,000		
Peru	Flood	52	89,000	25,000		
Philippines	Lahars*/floods	333	2,936,009	25,000		
Philippines	Typhoons	514	2,967,550	25,000		
Philippines	Lahars	50	757,000	543,960		
Rwanda	Refugees	—	350,000	25,000		
Rwanda	Civil strife/DPs	500,000	4,500,000	39,963,789	236,157,158	276,120,947
St. Lucia	Tropical storm	4	600	25,000		
Sierra Leone	Civil strife/DPs	—	1,437,000	3,003,805	8,243,800	11,247,605
Somalia	Displaced persons	—	1,000,000	12,195,044	26,849,619	39,044,663
Sudan	Civil strife	—	4,280,000	28,475,137	66,330,400	94,805,537
Swaziland	Drought	—	150,000	0		
Tajikistan	Floods	—	8,200	34,445		
Tajikistan	Floods	—	5,000	50,000		
Uganda	Earthquake	7	50,000	25,000		
Ukraine	—	—	400,000	25,000		
Ukraine	Floods	6	100,000	25,000		
Ukraine	Epidemic	71	1,333	0		
Venezuela	Mudslides	—	400,000	20,000		
Vietnam	Typhoons	120	6,000	36,072		
Yemen	Civil strife	—	375,000	51,000		
Zaire	Displaced persons	—	3,000,000	11,137,660		
Zaire (N. Kivu)	Refugees	48,000	1,000,000	25,000		
Zaire (S. Kivu)	Refugees	—	312,000	25,000		
Total		714,410	141,681,406	179,029,353		

Source: U.S. Agency for International Development, BHR/OFDA Annual Report FY 1994 (Washington DC: U
1995).

*Lahars are volcanic mud flows.

Table 14.2. Mapping International Humanitarian Assistance

	IHA providers																	
	IGOs							Bilaterals								INGOs		
IHA situations	ICRC	UNDHA	WFP	UNHCR	UNICE	WHO	etc	USAID	OFDA	USDOD	JAICA	NORAD	SIDA	ARC	etc	MSF	CARE	etc
Earthquakes																		
Civil strife																		
Food shortages																		
Fuel shortages																		
Displaced persons																		
Epidemics																		
Cyclones																		
Typhoons																		
Floods																		
Droughts																		
Landslides																		
Volcano eruptions																		

must be established. The row labels tentatively suggested in table 2 are adapted from those used in table 1 by bhr/ofda. Other agencies suggest ways of using broad categories and then finer subcategories. For example, some studies distinguish between manmade and natural disasters, and some further divide natural disasters into those that are geophysical (earthquakes, volcano eruptions), and those that are meteorological (cyclones, floods, droughts).[17]

It should be possible to locate the work of every iha provider on a comprehensive map such as suggested in table 2. However, if we survey, say, the annual reports of the major national and international agencies involved in iha, we find that they don't mesh together. Each of them has a different way of categorizing iha situations. Even within the United States itself, different agencies use different languages to talk about work they commonly label as humanitarian. There is nothing wrong with agencies having particular approaches and areas of specialization, but currently this partitioning is not the result of an orderly division of labor. The turf battles — whether to gain or to avoid specific areas of responsibility — have not been completed. If there is to be orderly targeting of iha resources, potential iha situations need to be identified in terms of well-defined, consistent, widely accepted, mutually exclusive, and collectively exhaustive categories. This is not simply an issue of linguistic orderliness; it is an important basis for effective policymaking.

It is not difficult to construct an orderly list of labels for IHA situations. However, if it is actually to be adopted, the system should be devised by the agencies themselves. The formulation of such a system would help to achieve a more coherent division of labor among the providers of IHA.

Some IHA agencies focus on "complex humanitarian emergencies," defined as internal conflicts with large-scale displacements of people, mass famine, and fragile or failing economic, political and social institutions."[18] These are important situations and get special attention largely because these pockets of instability can lead to serious regional security concerns. There is a problem, however, if it is suggested that complex humanitarian emergencies are the entire domain of IHA. This sort of misunderstanding can lead to the neglect of other important kinds of situations, especially the pockets of quiet suffering that continue on a chronic basis in several parts of the world. In the Indian state of Orissa hunger and poverty are so intense that families sell their children for small sums of money.[19] In places such as Malawi, Niger, and Togo the disasters seem to have no beginning and no end.

Some agencies speak as if they were covering all of IHA when in fact they are selective, operating only in one specific area of the map of possibilities. There is a tendency to equate international humanitarian assistance with action taken under international humanitarian law (IHL), or action taken by the international Red Cross system, especially the International Committee for the Red Cross (ICRC). Similarly, some observers seem to assume that international humanitarian assistance takes place only in situations of armed conflict. This sort of shrinking of the domain of IHA can result not only in confusion of terminology but also in real neglect of some types of situations in which humanitarian assistance is needed.

The possibilities of gains through reallocation of resources are suggested by the grand totals. According to the International Federation of the Red Cross, "worldwide disasters, excluding war, kill over 150,000 people a year."[20] More than $3.5 billion a year is spent currently on IHA. At the same time we know that around 12 million children die each year before their fifth birthdays, most from a combination of malnutrition and disease. Yet the budget of the United Nation's Children's Fund (UNICEF) runs at only about $1 billion a year. Is the chronic pattern of massive child mortality not a disaster?[21]

In FY94 BHR/OFDA obligations in Iraq amounted to $212,254.[22] This was 0.55 percent of the total U.S. government assistance to Iraq in FY94, $38,212,254. The vast amounts expended on military interventions in difficult situations such as Iraq could save many more lives if they were spent in other, quieter situations for humanitarian purposes.

Targeting Guidelines

What are the bases for targeting international humanitarian assistance from the United States, or indeed, from any IHA agency? There is little explicit guidance. Assistance is now provided in some situations and not in other seemingly comparable situations. There have been many disasters of the types enumerated in table 1 for which the United States has not provided assistance. Why? There is also the question of why the United States should attend to the types of disasters enumerated in table 1 and not to other types. Is there some common feature that distinguishes these from disasters such as, say, failed economies or genocidal massacres or situations of chronic malnutrition? Where other types of disasters are identified, is the U.S. government responding to them through agencies other than BHR/OFDA, or are they simply excluded from U.S. coverage? Is the exclusion deliberate, or is it a matter of neglect?

In examining targeting policy it is important to know not only where the IHA system has responded but also where there have been comparable situations in which no assistance has been provided. Maps of options should be produced, not simply with generic categories of IHA situations but with lists of specific, current, potential IHA situations. Some surveillance studies have been made to identify areas of potential need, but most have been issued only sporadically.[23] All such studies have been selective, highlighting the interests of particular IHA providers.

There has not been any systematic assessment of IHA operations and, as the International Federation of the Red Cross observes, the objectives of humanitarian assistance "have become more complex, opaque and confused since the end of the Cold War era."[24] What are potential IHA situations, and how can the effectiveness of IHA operations be assessed?

U.S. policy on foreign disasters is to respond quickly to help alleviate human suffering. The response generally begins with a determination by the U.S. ambassador that "a great number of lives are at risk, and . . . an appropriate response is beyond the capacity of the affected country."[25] The International Federation for the Red Cross says "relief work is about the 'bottom line' of ensuring basic minimal necessities to keep people alive."[26] It might be useful for IHA agencies in the United States and globally to formally adopt the view that *the primary purpose of international humanitarian assistance is saving lives.* If that is accepted we would see that IHA *is potentially needed in any situation in which mortality risks are, or are likely to become, extraordinarily high.* In this approach, disasters would be defined as life-threatening situations.[27] The U.S. government has found that "Premature mortality is an appropriate health status indicator for allocating federal funding for the core public health functions administered by the states."[28] Much the same reasoning could be used to guide the global allocation of assistance by the international community.

With this explicit focus, the effectiveness of any IHA operation would be estimated in terms of the number of lives saved. Where IHA is provided, the actual mortality rate would be compared with an estimate of the mortality rate that would have been likely in the absence of the IHA operation. The cost-effectiveness of such operations could be estimated in terms of the cost per life saved. With experience it should be possible to make reasonable estimates. Techniques of estimation could be borrowed from specialists who assess the effectiveness of public health interventions.[29]

One could ask whether different allocations of funds across life-threatening situations might have resulted in more lives saved and whether allocations for other than direct humanitarian purposes might have yielded greater social benefit if devoted to lifesaving.

Most of the guidelines available with regard to IHA now focus on the management of ongoing IHA situations. They say little about the selection of situations. Taking the core purpose of IHA to be saving lives would help in formulating targeting guidelines. Those who call in IHA would have to present the case that lives were at risk and that assistance could substantially reduce that risk. With experience, guidelines could be formulated to help providers of IHA to more systematically assess and decide which situations to select.

Rights to Assistance

Every organization has internal policy guidelines, whether formal or informal, to help direct its work. There is always some shared understanding within the organization regarding the organization's goals and the means for achieving them. However, in addition to internal guidelines, organizations also need systematic pressure from the outside, some form of accountability. Without accountability, organizations tend to lose their sense of mission and go off track. Institutional arrangements to assure accountability can be provided through the creation of auditors, inspectors general, and the like. Under the Reinventing Government campaign and the National Performance Review (based on the Government Performance and Results Act of 1993) in the United States, government agencies are being pressed to clarify their objectives, and increasingly they are being held accountable for their performance in pursuing those objectives. IHA agencies, in the United States and elsewhere, should be examined in much the same way.

One good mechanism of accountability is to give the customers, the purported beneficiaries of the agency's service, a clear say. Agencies should make explicit commitments of service to their customers, and when there is a failure to deliver, the customers should have available a mechanism for lodging complaints and obtaining redress. People should have a *right* to particular services. If, for example, your mail carrier decides not to deliver your mail for a week, there should be a systematic way in which you can complain and have that situation corrected. You are not supposed to get mail only when the carrier feels like it. You are *entitled* to a specific level of service.

Under some conditions people should have a right to assistance. If I have a fire at my home, I want to know that I have a right to expect firefighters to come. The firefighters should have a counterpart obligation to come. These rights and obligations should be clearly specified in the law. There should be some rights to assistance in relation to IHA as well. Some analysts believe that such a right already exists in armed conflict situations, under international humanitarian law, but in my view the law is now so vague that it cannot be regarded as a real right.[30] Where there are clear rights to assistance there should be specifications regarding who has what obligations to provide assistance.

With an entitlement the needy can know what sorts of assistance they are supposed to receive under particular circumstances. They should have some means of legal recourse, some means for lodging effective complaints, if they do not receive what is due them. Many public assistance (welfare) programs within nations are based on the principle that the needy have specific rights to assistance; they have an *entitlement*. Without such rules, public assistance is likely to be arbitrary and used as a political tool by those in power.

Providers' Motivation

Many government agencies have to deal with systems of accountability imposed on them from above. In the global IHA system, however, there will be no systematic accountability unless the providers of assistance themselves agree to it. Why should they agree? Accepting that the needy have specific rights, and thus the providers have specific obligations, would reduce the providers' freedom of action. Why should IHA providers agree to a rights-based system? How can the granting of entitlements to the needy be viewed as advantageous to the providers of assistance?

The question of why donors would want to recognize that the needy have a right to assistance in some circumstances may be viewed as a special case of the broader question of why anyone, or any government, would want to recognize that others have human rights. The answer is based not on conceptions of narrow self-interest but on some form of enlightened self-interest. We all benefit from social order rather than anarchy. We recognize that in some circumstances we get better results when we limit our freedom. Anyone who joins an organization or signs a contract gives up some freedom in exchange for other kinds of benefits. The argument here is that an entitlements-based IHA system can achieve effectiveness, efficiency, and justice beyond what can be obtained with guidelines that do not include entitlements.

However, for a single donor nation such as the United States, there would be no reason to agree that the needy in other countries have authoritative claims on its resources. The prospect has been considered and rejected by USAID:

> Some favor an entitlement approach premised on a fundamental U.S. obligation to provide basic human needs to the vulnerable peoples of the world. Universal rights to health and education have become a byword in these circles, the implication being that the U.S., as the world's wealthiest nation, should be the provider of last resort. . . . Americans like to see progress around the world, but our commitment to doing anything about it falls far short of any consensus on global entitlements to automatic U.S. aid.[31]

But consider this argument with the term "international community" substituted for "U.S." Though it might not make sense for the United States alone to shoulder the burden, a system of entitlements would make sense for the global IHA system taken as a whole, at least for some kinds of extreme circumstances.

The international community should accept some level of obligation to assure the well-being of all people, at least up to some minimal level. The world should look after its most vulnerable just as national governments are expected to look after the most vulnerable within their particular jurisdictions. If we see looking after the weakest among us as a common, shared global responsibility, and not just a U.S. responsibility, the proposal of entitlements becomes much more palatable.

The IHA donor countries as a group should adopt a collective, self-imposed obligation to provide assistance to the most needy under specific extreme conditions. They should commit themselves to creating a global "rescue squad," which would operate under specific obligations. The reasoning is similar to that behind the creation of a village fire brigade. There was a time when villages had no systematic fire protection. If someone's house started to burn, he would run out and yell for help. The help might come or it might not. During and after the fire people would help out, sometimes providing emergency shelter, and possibly offering funds to rebuild.

Each incident was treated as if it were an entirely unpredictable surprise. However, after each incident, procedures for managing fires would be discussed and reconsidered. After a while it was recognized that such incidents occurred often, and institutional arrangements — fire equipment and fire brigades — were set in place, on standby, in anticipation of future fires. Community members willingly contributed to the effort. These contributions were motivated in part by the recognition that each individual would benefit from this protection. They would benefit directly or indirectly. Even though the need for protection may have been uneven (some had solid brick houses while others had flimsy wood houses), all recognized that having institutionalized fire protection made the village as a whole a better place to live.

An important element of this story is that the fire brigade was required to respond to all fire alarms. It was not free to choose, responding only to fires in brick houses or only to owners of particular ethnic or political affiliations. The brigade's responsibility was to the community as a whole, not to any selected segment of it. To assure that there would be no such discrimination, it was established in the rules that any villager was *entitled* to have the services of the brigade if needed. Anyone not served properly could bring a complaint to the village council. On finding that a complaint was warranted, the complainant might be awarded damages, and the rules regulating the fire brigade's operations might be tightened up. Thus there was a system of accountability to assure that the fire brigade performed its mission.

The global system of international humanitarian assistance is beginning to be institutionalized. However, there is still a need to negotiate procedures and policies anew with almost every incident. Rather than stationing substantial standby resources "at the ready" throughout the world, new resources must be solicited with each incident. The rules of engagement are being standardized, but slowly. The global IHA system does not yet have arrangements comparable to the United States' pre-deployed stockpiles of relief commodities or its DART teams.

The global IHA system is evolving slowly, because some national participants want to maintain their own control and do not want to be subjected to a centralized authoritative command structure. This difficult political problem might be resolved partly by working out a clear division of areas of responsibility and authority for different aspects of IHA. There already exists some informal partitioning of responsibility, with some providers concentrating on disasters in certain geographic areas or in countries with particular cultural affinities.

There is a need for clarity regarding the IHA obligations not only of individual nations but also of the global community taken as a whole. On the basis of the fire brigade analogy, the providers of global IHA should collectively agree that there are some kinds of situations to which they *must* respond collectively, through joint action. They can do this by creating a standing institutional arrangement to provide rapid and effective responses, a global rescue squad. If it is to maintain its effectiveness, that institutional arrangement should be held accountable, based on the idea that people in certain kinds of disaster situations are entitled to specific services. If the required service is not provided, there should be some forum in which the disaster victims or their representatives could voice their complaints.

Structurally, the fire brigade analogy here is a variation of Garrett Hardin's "tragedy of the commons." [32] It is based on his insight that in some situations we benefit from arrangements of mutual coercion, mutually agreed on. That is the best institutional mechanism we have for balancing the fundamental political tension between the desire for freedom and the desire for order.

The international community should systematically recognize global obligations to protect the most vulnerable. The UN Department of Humanitarian Affairs, the International Committee for the Red Cross, the World Food Program, the United Nations' Children's Fund, the World Health Organization, and many other international governmental and nongovernmental organizations have begun to establish an effective global IHA system. That system could be strengthened by systematically recognizing that the international community, as a whole, has specific obligations to provide IHA.

Implementation

It has been argued here that, as a matter of principle, some people under some conditions ought to have a recognized legal right to assistance. Such rights should be recognized both within nations and internationally. Although specific designs cannot be elaborated on here, it may be useful to suggest some ways in which such rights could be implemented.

One approach would be to focus on children's mortality. Under current policy: "The UNICEF programme budget in each country is allocated according to three criteria: under-five mortality rate (the annual number of deaths of children under five per 1,000 births); income level (GNP per capita); and the size of the child population."[33]

Although UNICEF allocates its resources on the basis of these clear guidelines and publishes the amounts allocated to each country, the receiving countries cannot claim they are entitled to these sums. They have no legal recourse if they should receive less than they feel is due to them, and the amounts vary from year to year because the contributions made by national governments are voluntary. The system could be strengthened by establishing that the countries with the worst child mortality rates have a right to at least a minimal level of assistance. The donor countries could meet in a kind of anticipatory pledging conference. At this conference they could commit to providing at least a specified level of support every year for, say, the twenty countries with the worst child mortality rates in the world. The obligation on the part of the donors could be firmed up by having them agree to contribute in accordance with an agreed formula based on factors such as gross national product and population size.

Serious malnutrition can result in significant increases in mortality rates. Work is under way in many quarters on the clarification and implementation of rights to adequate nutrition. Most of that work focuses on the challenge of implementation within nations, but there are efforts to press for clearer commitments by the international community to support nutrition rights.[34]

Another much-neglected issue that deserves clear advance commitments to action is genocide and related crimes. The mass killings in Rwanda in the 1990s have been only a portion of a long history of genocidal activity in that region and throughout the world. There is an effort under way to establish a permanent International Criminal Court to punish perpetrators of genocide, war crimes, and crimes against humanity such as rape, torture, and murder. There is also a need to regularize the international community's relief response to such incidents with serious advance planning and explicit commitments to action.

Policies with regard to IHA are most fully developed in relation to armed conflict situations. International humanitarian law provides the framework, and the ICRC serves as the recognized lead agency for humanitarian assistance in such situations. The ICRC should continue to press for fuller articulation of victims' rights to assistance and the international community's obligations to provide assistance in armed conflict situations.

One area in which the international community's obligations are distinctive is in relation to refugees, because refugees, by definition, are no longer under the care of their home states. Work is under way to articulate the rights of refugees. In this context, it would be useful to consider ways in which refugees might have effectively implemented nutrition rights.

U.S. Policy

To retain its freedom of action, the United States has invested most of its IHA resources into its bilateral operations. It should give more attention to strengthening the global IHA system as a whole. With a better-managed global system, other nations will be more willing to take their share of the burden.

In combat operations under the auspices of NATO or the UN Security Council, the United States is not willing to place its forces under any but U.S. command. With regard to IHA resources, however, the U.S. should recognize that it would be best for all concerned if it were willing to relax its control and permit those resources to be used under other authorities. The United States should play a full role in working out appropriate rules of engagement, at the policymaking stage, but it should be willing to delegate operational activities to a central global rescue squad. For the United States to insist on retaining control would be akin to having a village council that wanted to direct every fire engine or ambulance that went out. U.S. and other nations' participation in an international arrangement of this sort should be viewed not as a sacrifice of sovereignty but as a well-calculated act of sovereignty.

The global IHA system should be designed as a central agency managing a global rescue squad. The donors would sit on its board of directors, participating in the shaping of policy. The rules under which IHA operations would be undertaken would, in effect, articulate the rights of needy people to receive assistance under particular circumstances. To keep the agency on track, there should be some mechanism through which the needy or their representatives could complain and call for corrective action. The creation of such a global rescue squad, operating under explicit, agreed on rules of engagement, would mark an important step forward in the governance of the global order.

Notes

1. Private foreign assistance has a long history. See Landrum R. Bolling and Craig Smith, *Private Foreign Aid: U.S. Philanthropy for Relief and Development* (Boulder CO: Westview, 1982); and Brian H. Smith, *More Than Altruism: The Politics of Private Foreign Aid* (Princeton NJ: Princeton University Press, 1990).

2. The Human Rights Council of Australia, Inc., *The Rights Way to Development: A Human Rights Approach to Development Assistance* (Marricksville NSW, Australia: HRCA, 1995), 7. The Council points out that this belief makes it easy to claim that programs in education and health are humanitarian when in fact they are trade promotions for Australian industry.

3. An attempt was made to use combat forces for purely humanitarian purposes in Somalia in 1992, but its mission was soon expanded to include more political goals. On the difficulties in maintaining neutrality, see Denise Plattner, "ICRC Neutrality and Neutrality in Humanitarian Assistance," *International Review of the Red Cross*, no. 311 (March–April 1996), 161–179.

4. Assistance from the federal government for disasters within the United States is very different in that the Federal Emergency Management Agency's (FEMA) public assistance is geared mainly to funding the repair of eligible public and private nonprofit facilities (such as roads, government buildings, utilities, and hospitals) that are damaged in natural disasters. FEMA spends around a billion dollars a year for such services.

5. Much of the following information is drawn from U.S. Agency for International Development, BHR OFDA *Annual Report FY 1994* (Washington DC: USAID, 1995). Also see Development Assistance Committee, Organization for Economic Co-operation and Development, *Development Co-operation Review Series: United States* (Paris: OECD, 1995).

6. Concerns related to USAID's management of these programs are examined in U.S. General Accounting Office (GAO), *Food Aid: Management Improvements Are Needed to Achieve Program Objectives* (Washington DC: GAO NSIAD-93-168, 1993).

Also see U.S. General Accounting Office, *Foreign Assistance:* AID *Strategic Direction and Continued Management Improvements Needed* (Washington DC: GAO NSIAD-93-106, 1993).

7. Congressional Research Service, *Providing Humanitarian Assistance: Using the U.S. Military Overseas* (Washington DC: Government Printing Office, 1992).

8. Frank J. Cook III, Jeffrey A. McChesney, Gary R. Stephens, Gregory G. Wilmoth, and William M. Wilson, *The Defense Department's Role in Humanitarian and Disaster Relief* (Cambridge MA: National Security Program Policy Analysis Paper 93-02, 1993).

9. Congressional Research Service, *Providing Humanitarian Assistance*, 4.

10. Cook et al., *The Defense Department's Role*.

11. Directorate of Intelligence, *Worldwide Humanitarian Aid: An Overview of the Relief System* (Washington DC: Central Intelligence Agency, Intelligence Research Paper RTT 94-10009, February 1994), 15–16.

12. Directorate of Intelligence, *Worldwide Humanitarian Aid*, 4.

13. James H. Michel, *Development Co-operation* (Paris: Organization for Economic Co-operation and Development, 1996), 95.

14. Michel, *Development Co-operation*, A46.

15. Columns 1 through 5 of table 1 are from the summary table on pp. 56–69 of USAID's BHR/OFDA *Annual Report* FY *1994*. Columns 6 and 7, on other U.S. government assistance, are from the brief narratives on these disasters provided on pp. 19–54.

16. On the targeting of combat-oriented interventions, see Richard Haass, *Intervention: The Use of American Military Force in the Post-Cold War World* (New York: Carnegie Endowment, 1994).

17. U.S. Mission to the United Nations, *Global Humanitarian Emergencies* (New York: U.S. Mission to the United Nations, 1996); International Federation of Red Cross and Red Crescent Societies, *World Disasters Report 1996* (New York: Oxford University Press, 1996), 126–127.

18. U.S. Mission to the United Nations, *Global Humanitarian Emergencies, 1995* (New York: U.S. Mission to the United Nations, 1995), 1.

19. Ruben Banerjee, "Children on Sale for Rs 20," *India Today* (February 15, 1993): 80–81.

20. International Federation of Red Cross and Red Crescent Societies, *World Disasters Report 1996*, 124.

21. I discuss these issues in *The Politics of Children's Survival* (New York: Praeger, 1991) and *Children in the International Political Economy* (London and New York: Macmillan and St. Martin's, 1995).

22. USAID, BHR/OFDA *Annual Report* FY *1994*, 48.

23. See, for example, U.S. Mission to the United Nations, *Global Humanitarian Emergencies*, 1996.

24. International Federation of Red Cross and Red Crescent Societies, *World Disasters Report 1996*, 63.

25. Congressional Research Service, *Providing Humanitarian Assistance*, 3.

26. International Federation of Red Cross and Red Crescent Societies, *World Disasters Report 1996*, 47.

27. The Red Cross's *World Disasters Report 1996* distinguishes between natural and man-made disasters (120–121) but does not define disasters as such.

28. U.S. General Accounting Office, *Public Health: A Health Status Indicator for Targeting Federal Aid to States* (Washington DC: U.S.GAO, GAO/HEHS-97-13, November 1996), 4–5.

29. Rather than evaluating humanitarian assistance in terms of lives saved, it might be more appropriate to count the number of life-years saved. A more sophisticated approach would be to estimate the Disability-Adjusted Life Years (DALYs) saved. The relative cost-effectiveness of public health interventions is sometimes assessed on the basis of estimated DALYs saved. See World Bank, *World Development Report 1993: Investing in Health* (New York: Oxford University Press, 1993), especially 25–29; and Christopher J. L. Murray and Alan D. Lopez, "Global Mortality, Disability, and the Contribution of Risk Factors: Global Burden of Disease Study," *Lancet* 349 (May 17, 1997): 1436–1442.

30. Yves Sandoz, "'Droit' or 'Devoir d'Ingerence' and the Right to Assistance: The Issues Involved," *International Review of the Red Cross*, no. 288 (May–June 1992): 215–227; Olivier Corten and Pierre Klein, *Droit d'ingérence ou obligation de réaction? Les Possibilités d'action visant à assurer le respect des droits de la personne face au principe de non-intervention* (Brussels: Emile Bruylant, 1992); "Guiding Principles on the Right to Humanitarian Assistance," *International Review of the Red Cross*, no. 297 (November–December 1993), 519–525; Yves Beigbeder, *The Role and Status of International Humanitarian Volunteers and Organizations: The Right and Duty to Humanitarian Assistance* (Dordrecht, Holland: Martinus Nijhoff, 1991); Peter Macalister-Smith, *International Humanitarian Assistance: Disaster Relief Actions in International Law and Organization* (Dordrecht, Netherlands: Martinus Nijhoff, 1985). Also see my unpublished manuscript, *Rights Regarding Humanitarian Assistance*, Honolulu, August 1996.

31. USAID, *Development and the National Interest: U.S. Economic Assistance into the 21st Century* (Washington DC: USAID, 1989), 16–17.

32. Garrett Hardin, "The Tragedy of the Commons," *Science* 162 (no. 3859): 1243–1248. This paper has been republished in many anthologies on the environment and related issues.

33. UN Children's Fund, *UNICEF Annual Report 1996* (New York: UNICEF, 1996), 81.

34. The March 1996 *Food Policy* is a special issue devoted to Nutrition and Human Rights. I edited a Special Issue on Food and Nutrition Rights of the *International Journal of Children's Rights* 5, no. 4 (1997).

15

Human Rights, UN Institutions, and the United States

•

PATRICK FLOOD

Over the past half century the United States has joined with other member states of the United Nations to establish a variety of structures to carry out the Charter mandate to promote practical respect for human rights. This chapter examines the development of these mechanisms, focusing particularly on the creation of the Human Rights Commission's Working Group on Disappearances and the office of high commissioner for human rights, and on the U.S. role in this process. It also seeks to draw broad conclusions about the value of UN human rights institutions for the pursuit of U.S. human rights policy objectives.

First, I discuss the historical background and the authority for creation of UN human rights institutions and briefly compare the advantages and disadvantages of treaty-based and Charter-based UN mechanisms, concluding that the latter are more effective because of their direct link to political bodies. Generally, a state wants to be thought well of by other states — its peers — and by influential publics in key countries; most want to be seen as civilized and humane polities and as cooperative and responsible members of the community of states. While some revolutionary regimes reject these values during their early years, most return to them because complete disregard for the good opinion of other states usually leads to political isolation. As members of a community, states pursue goals whose achievement depends significantly on avoiding such isolation. This need has been a necessary (though not sufficient) condition for human rights activist states, including the United States, gradually to develop UN mechanisms that can bring steady, year-round pressure on a state to reduce abuses. As enduring parts of the external political environment within which states make choices, these mechanisms have influenced some state choices in ways that benefit human rights.

This chapter then looks at the case of the creation and operation of the Working Group on Disappearances. I contrast the policies of the Carter and (first) Reagan administration and how these fit into U.S. policy toward the Argentine military regime. I address such issues as the willingness to use multilateral human rights forums to advance U.S. geopolitical goals and the salience of human rights as a U.S. foreign policy value vis-à-vis other values that influence policy-making.

I then turn to the creation of the post of UN high commissioner for human rights, the U.S. role therein, and the potential significance of this office for the pursuit of U.S. human rights policy goals.

Historical Background

In the second half of the twentieth century many people have come to think of human dignity as something that can be better understood, and therefore more effectively safeguarded, when considered under the aspect of human rights. This happened mainly because totalitarian states, having decided to exclude rights absolutely from official recognition and protection, made human dignity seem almost to disappear in the lands they ruled. The concentration camps and gulags demonstrated the ultimate consequence of abandoning human rights as a normative value.

During and after World War II, U.S. and other political leaders and thinkers focused increasingly on human rights. The first step was identifying and affirming allegiance to them as a "common standard of achievement" in the Universal Declaration of Human Rights (1948), a project that enjoyed strong support from the United States. U.S. support included outstanding leadership by Eleanor Roosevelt, the U.S. Representative, who served as chair of the commission and, with Rene Cassin, as cochairperson of the drafting committee that produced the declaration. Since the mid-1970s, emphasis has shifted to the question, "How can a state be influenced to observe human rights in practice?" The United States has included UN institutions among the channels through which we pursue this goal.

After the Second World War, many states recognized the need for some kind of global institutional framework and procedures to respond on behalf of the international community to massive violations of human rights. Wartime atrocities against civilians and other noncombatants (such as prisoners of war) during wartime were to be addressed through the new Geneva Conventions, under which the International Committee of the Red Cross played the central implementing role. But what about during times of international peace? Although the powerful example of the Nuremberg Trials, with their forthright insistence on individual accountability for acts performed under color of state authority, could have served as a precedent deterrent to later crimes against humanity, states did not invoke the trials' principles in subsequent cases until mass savagery in the former Yugoslavia and in Rwanda seared the conscience of mankind.[1]

The community of states began the task of institution building by creating the UN Commission on Human Rights, of which governments, rather than individual experts, are members. As noted earlier, the United States played an important role in the commission's early work. In 1966 the commission and the General Assembly, again with strong U.S. support, completed preparation of the Covenants on Civil and Political Rights and on Economic, Social and Cultural Rights; both entered into force in 1976. In subsequent years the commission drafted other legal instruments with implementation mechanisms, and in December 1993, after a long struggle in which U.S. involvement was crucial at key stages, the General Assembly created the office of high commissioner for human rights.[2]

I will use the term international community to mean the community of states, including the governments that represent them. However, I fully recognize that nongovernmental organizations and the media participate in the ongoing dialogue on human rights issues and that they contribute importantly to the momentum to create international human rights institutions and to the shape of these new institutions. But I do not include them here in the term "international community," because in the literal sense they are not rule-making, rule-implementing actors.[3]

Authority

The authority for UN efforts to implement human rights standards is found either in the Charter or in subsequent international agreements. Though these subsequent treaties apply only to states that have acceded to them, legal obligations based directly on the Charter apply to all member states of the organization, which are accountable to one another as members of this community.

Article 55 of the Charter states clearly that "the United Nations [that is, the Organization] shall promote . . . universal respect for, and observance of, human rights and fundamental freedoms for all without distinction as to race, sex, language or religion." And Article 56 reads: "All Members [that is, States] pledge themselves to take joint and separate action in cooperation with the

Organization for the achievement of [these] purposes" (emphasis added). Later articles specify that these functions are to be carried out by the General Assembly and the Economic and Social Council, which in practice usually means by the Council's Human Rights Commission.

Over a dozen treaty-based implementation mechanisms have been established under the two Covenants, the Convention on Torture, the Convention on the Rights of the Child, and similar instruments.[4] For instance, the Covenant on Civil and Political Rights provides for an eighteen-member Human Rights Committee comprised of independent experts elected by the states parties, but its powers are not terribly impressive.[5] Committee sessions are little noticed by the press, and, once the hearing is over, nothing much happens. The required public reports attract little attention. Even the "general comments" of the committee have been fairly safe, politically speaking (see the chapters by Schabas in this book). The treaty-based committees have no authority to initiate investigation of reported violations; they cannot act in urgent situations, even when emergencies occur while the committee is in session. They cannot perform a "good offices" role, nor are they authorized to conduct onsite visits. Their agenda and their reports are linked to the states' own reports. A state need do nothing, really, until the next report is due, usually in two or three years. The knowledge that there will be a next report, and a next hearing, probably has a slight moderating effect on some aspects of state conduct, but the nature of this forum and its very limited powers suggest that such influence is indeed slight. The basic problem is that the experts have no organizational power behind them — not of the United Nations' political bodies and not of the secretary general; they speak only in their own name.

The Civil and Political Rights Covenant also contains a provision allowing one state party to bring a complaint against another state party for failure to observe the Covenant and for resolution of the complaint by the committee either directly or through an ad hoc Conciliation Commission.[6] That no state has invoked the provision is probably due to the fact that states already have ample opportunity in other UN forums to complain about each other's shortcomings.

Also, the machinery of treaty-based institutions applies only to states parties. For nonparties, it may as well not exist. The United States took an active part in drafting the two Covenants, and President Carter signed them in 1977 and sent them to the Senate. It was not until 1992, however, that the Senate gave advice and consent to ratification of the Civil and Political Covenant (with some major reservations and understandings), and the Economic, Social and Cultural Covenant still languishes unratified. We might recall that it took forty years for the Senate to approve the Genocide Convention; even moderate or liberal chairs of the Foreign Relations Committee have seldom exercised leadership in the effort to ratify human rights treaties. They have other priorities.

The Human Rights Commission's work has traditionally been divided about equally among four categories: (1) political warfare — bilateral conflicts replayed in a multilateral setting; (2) standard-setting, that is, formulating new international declarations and conventions; (3) efforts to improve and strengthen implementation procedures and institutions; and (4) efforts to act on specific human rights problems and cases.

In the first category, representatives of sovereign states, including the United States, see it as their first duty to protect their own government from censure by fellow sovereigns.[7] Most of these sessions are public. There is also about a week of confidential sessions, which only member states of the commission may attend.[8] Here also, governments are "charged" with various offenses against human rights and given an opportunity to defend themselves; in this case the charges reach the commission through a careful screening process by a subcommission of independent human rights experts. The proceedings are highly adversarial, and governments behave essentially as they do in public, although the tone is more businesslike. For those in the dock, the aim is to have one's country's case dropped or at worst merely "kept under review," and not made the subject of an in-depth investigation.

In the second area, standard-setting, the commission has managed to produce an impressive number of international human rights instruments. Since 1980, these include, for example, the Declaration on the Elimination of Religious Discrimination, the Convention against Torture, and the Convention on the Rights of the Child, in all of which the United States played an active and supportive role at the drafting stages. The United States played an opposing (and usually isolated) role in connection with the Declaration on the Right to Development, which was adopted overwhelmingly in 1986; among the developing-country majority, U.S. negativism on this issue eroded receptiveness to our own multilateral initiatives. It continues to impede our efforts to build trust and support among developing country delegations, who find it extremely difficult to understand why we cannot accept a declaration on a matter of such fundamental importance to them.

In the third area of the commission's work, the search for better tools and methods of implementation, and the fourth, the attempt to come to grips with actual violations, the commission has in the last decade or so ventured into new institutional experiments. These differ in fundamental respects from treaty-based expert committees. The earliest such efforts concerned the "pariah states" of South Africa, Israel, and Pinochet's Chile. Because the goal of the sponsors of these country-specific resolutions was to discredit the governments concerned, it was almost inevitable that subsequent efforts to create such institutions would be viewed as attempts to dump additional states into the pariah category. This led to the idea of creating thematic mechanisms that are to oversee impartially, on behalf of the whole community, the observance by all states of a single right. It is more difficult for a state to argue that a proposed thematic mechanism is actually directed at it.

The United States has usually supported proposals to create thematic mechanisms but, for geopolitical reasons, has picked and chosen among country-specific proposals. As we shall see in looking at the Working Group on Disappearances, U.S. policy under the first Reagan administration regarding even thematic mechanisms was strongly affected by geopolitics.

Disappearances, Argentina, the United States and the United Nations: Phase One

How did the United States seek to deal with the issue of disappearances in Argentina through the UN Human Rights Commission in the late 1970s and early 1980s? How did the other member states respond? How did the United Nations then proceed?

In the 1970s there was growing awareness among Western governments, parliaments, press, nongovernmental organizations and the general public of enforced disappearance, which is in fact a multiple human rights violation: abduction and clandestine detention by official forces means not only arbitrary deprivation of liberty but also denial of judicial due process and of access to family and counsel. In Argentina, Chile, and some other countries, it usually also meant torture and arbitrary and summary execution.

Daniel Livermore and B. G. (Bertram) Ramcharan pointed out that the Argentine junta in the mid-1970s expanded and systematized the practice of enforced disappearance, which had been employed by the Pinochet regime in Chile a few years earlier.[9] Pinochet's excesses, which included about six hundred well-documented cases of enforced disappearance during the period 1973–78, brought condemnation by the General Assembly in 1974 and the subsequent establishment by the Human Rights Commission of a country-specific working group to investigate this and other abuses.[10]

In an earlier contribution to the literature on human rights, I assessed the effectiveness of the U.S. government response to the issue of disappearances and other grievous abuses in Argentina. In that essay I argued that a combined bilateral-multilateral effort made more sense from many standpoints, and in the end was more effective, than bilateral efforts alone. I will return to this point, which I continue to believe is valid.[11]

The Argentine military regime committed about 9,000 confirmed disappearances between 1976 and 1980.[12] Thanks to work by Argentine human rights activists — especially the Permanent Assembly for Human Rights and the Mothers of the Plaza de Mayo — by Amnesty International, and other international nongovernmental organizations, and by some governments — notably the United Kingdom, Canada, the United States, and France — the story reached the UN General Assembly in 1978.[13] By this time there were also credible reports of disappearances in countries other than Argentina and Chile.

By adopting Resolution 33/173 (1978) formally identifying the practice of enforced disappearance as a major human rights violation and calling for states and intergovernmental organizations to take measures to halt the practice, the General Assembly set the stage for the implementation machinery established in 1980 that has functioned ever since.[14] But the 1978 resolution itself set up no machinery, and this omission led to a protracted battle by the Argentine government to fend off any meaningful UN intercession.[15]

Historian Joseph Tulchin writes of the junta that seized power in Argentina in 1976 that, "Like so many of its predecessors, civilian and military, [it] was obsessed with international prestige."[16] The new military government also pursued economic policies designed to build up hard-currency reserves and reinsert the economy into the international market. At the same time, it was dedicated to a doctrine of the national security state that led it to wage a campaign of "total extirpation of subversive elements from the body politic by whatever means necessary."[17]

Tulchin is probably right that a desire for international acceptance and respect underlay many Argentine foreign policy attitudes and actions during the period of military rule from 1976–82. This desire also helps to explain Argentina's sustained efforts to escape UN scrutiny for its human rights abuses.

Between autumn 1978 and February 1980 the Argentine government fought to ensure that any UN activity concerning disappearances would take place under the confidential "1503" procedure, after the number of the Economic and Social Council (ECOSOC) resolution that established it with U.S. support in 1970.[18] The resolution provided for the first time a UN procedure to deal with reports of "consistent patterns of reliably attested gross violations of human rights." Though the 1503 procedure at least provides a forum in which states can be held to a limited sort of accountability by and to their peers, this calling to account, and indeed all the steps that lead to this stage, have to take place under conditions of strict confidentiality. States members of the commission learn of complaints against themselves and have a chance to respond, but the complainants — usually the victims of alleged abuse, or nongovernmental human rights organizations — never see the government response, nor do they know the ultimate disposition of the complaint. Only the other member states of the commission learn of a complaint and then only if the subcommission decides to forward it to the commission.[19]

Few complaints have much chance of being considered by the full membership of the commission. And even if they reach this stage, nothing happens beyond a decision to conduct a "thorough study" or "investigation" of the situation, or merely to keep the matter "under review," that is, on the agenda for discussion next year — again, with no public knowledge of what is going on or of the results of a "thorough study." The original idea for confidentiality was that governments could be expected to cooperate with the commission only if their dignity as sovereign states were never in the slightest questioned in public.

Extensive documentation on disappearances in Argentina was submitted to the subcommission under the 1503 rules, and in 1979 that body forwarded this material to the commission for consideration at its 1980 session. The Argentine military regime had submitted confidential replies to the accusations against it, in an effort to ensure that its case would remain under the cloak of confidentiality. Argentine representatives argued that a case could be considered by UN institutions under only one procedure and that Argentina's cooperation under the 1503 system exempted it from being considered in any other UN forum.[20] Chile had earlier attempted to "forum-shop" on human rights issues by claiming that its submission of a report to the expert-level Human Rights Committee of the Covenant on Civil and Political Rights exempted it from having to answer to any other UN body.[21] Chile's claim was rejected by the commission; so, eventually, was Argentina's.

As I have noted, the Argentine government was deeply concerned about its international image. The junta said it had undertaken its war against subversion to save Western civilization from the international communist conspiracy. It did not want to be seen as undermining such important foundations of Western civilization as justice and respect for human dignity or to be thought of as a gang of inhumane barbarians. A panel of senior navy officers emphasized precisely that sentiment to me during my official visit to Buenos Aires in April 1979.

Joseph Tulchin says that "By 1979 the refutation and rejection of the international 'campaign' against Argentina had become an obsessive issue in foreign policy and had spilled over into areas of economic and political policy. The issue of human rights had assumed significant proportions by 1978. The accusation touched the very heart of the military's sense of its mission and threatened its long-term objectives" (emphasis added).[22] Tulchin outlines the junta's public relations efforts to protect its image. In 1978 the government-controlled press ran a postcard campaign in an Argentine magazine designed to influence U.S., UN, and Amnesty International officials, and the following year the junta hired a U.S. public relations firm, launched a monthly bulletin from their embassy, and established strong ties to certain influential conservatives in Washington. The next year they hired a private publishing firm to distribute printed materials and to conduct American-Argentine seminars on public policy.[23]

According to Jacob Timerman, the junta believed that "Argentina [was] alone and misunderstood by those who ought to be her natural allies, the Western democracies. Hence [inferred the regime] the unleashing of the anti-Argentine campaign" by certain democracies and the Vatican.[24] Timerman was, of course, a prominent victim of the junta's antisubversion campaign, but I do not think his analysis here is distorted by his personal experiences; it conforms with the public record and with my own observations during the time I shared responsibility for U.S. human rights policy toward South America.

Once the junta had decided it was at war, but a war without the usual features of uniformed combatants and defined battlefields, it decided that the agreed ethical rules governing armed conflict — the Geneva Conventions — did not apply. The cleansing of society and the security of the state were the only goals, and the methods could therefore be as ruthless as those used by the terrorists. Indeed, they had to be, in the junta's view; because otherwise the war could not be won. As Tulchin, Alison Brysk, and others point out, the regime found it hard to understand why Western countries did not appreciate this line of thought.[25]

Disappearances, Argentina, the United States, and the United Nations: Phase Two

By 1979 the phenomenon of enforced disappearances had become so widely known that a strong feeling began to develop within the U.S. government and among member states of the Human Rights Commission that the junta must no longer be allowed to hide behind confidential procedures. Moreover, the remoteness of Argentina from the U.S.-Soviet front line created favorable conditions for the United States and other activist pro-human rights states on the commission to break new ground in shaping human rights machinery. Although it proved impossible to establish a mechanism on disappearances at the 1979 session, later that year the Economic and Social Council and the General Assembly urged the commission to take definitive action at its meeting in February–March 1980.

Argentina was at the time a member of the commission. The United States decided that our first priority for action that year was to establish a mechanism that could help end disappearances in Argentina and elsewhere and provide a neutral means for governments to transmit information to families about the fate of their missing relatives. A multilateral thematic approach made sense for three reasons: (1) governments would presumably prefer to cooperate with a multilateral organization (the United Nations) of which they were members rather than appear to be submitting to bilateral pressures; (2) the problem had reached multiregional dimensions; and (3) it was risky to expect that succeeding U.S. administrations would be prepared to invest the same amount of political capital on this problem.

To achieve consensus adoption of a resolution at the 1980 session, the group of human rights activist states first introduced a separate resolution specifically on disappearances in Argentina and Chile, mentioning both countries by name. By no means was Argentina willing to be lumped together with Chile. The two countries had nearly gone to war over the Beagle Channel a little over a year earlier. Chile had long since acquired pariah status at the United Nations and could not have resisted the new draft resolution. Argentina, on the other hand, although actually a worse human rights offender, had thus far escaped any special public attention from UN human rights organs. This was due in part to the greater skill of its diplomats (Pinochet had heavily militarized Chile's diplomatic service), and because the Soviet Union and its allies had not targeted Argentina as they had Chile.[26] (The Soviet angle is discussed below.)

The United States and several other countries indicated informally that we would support the country-specific resolution, even though we preferred a universal, thematic approach. At the time I was in temporary charge of commission matters in the Department of State's Bureau of Human Rights and Humanitarian Affairs and led a successful fight within the department rapidly to clear an instruction to support the draft resolution, to arm our Geneva delegation with a valuable negotiating tool. When it became clear that such a resolution would pass if put to a vote, Argentina agreed to consensus adoption of a universal mechanism — the Working Group on Enforced Disappearances — in return for withdrawal of the other proposal.[27]

The following year, Argentina thought it might be able to reverse the decision to set up the new Working Group because of the change in U.S. presidents. Ronald Reagan had criticized Jimmy Carter's human rights policies during the campaign, and one of his first acts was to appoint Jeane Kirkpatrick as ambassador to the United Nations. Ambassador Kirkpatrick had made no secret of her belief that the Carter administration had been too hard on Argentina, Chile, and other authoritarian states.[28]

At the 1981 session of the Human Rights Commission, Argentine Ambassador Gabriel Martinez took the floor for an hour and a half in an attempt to deny that his government practiced enforced disappearance. Instead, he asserted, many reported disappearances were actually cases of death in armed combat with security forces, execution by fellow terrorists, desertion, travel abroad, or simply a "descent into clandestinity." While he, nevertheless, acknowledged during his remarks that some disappearances were caused by "official excesses," he emphasized repeatedly that Argentina would provide individual case information to the commission only under the 1503 rules concerning admissibility and confidentiality.[29] Lord Colville (United Kingdom), the Working Group chairman, told the Western delegation caucus that acceptance of the Argentine demand would completely change the character of the Working Group and its operations.[30] In the end the commission upheld the integrity of the group's procedures and rejected the renewed Argentine bid to hide its activities under the 1503 rules.

The fact that Argentina had supplied information to the commission under the confidential procedures does not mean that it actually accounted in this manner for disappeared persons. As noted earlier, Resolution 1503 was designed to provide a way for the commission to evaluate situations amounting to "consistent patterns of gross violations," and not as a way to resolve individual cases of abuse. A state responding to complaints under the 1503 procedure customarily focuses its reply on this situational aspect, citing laws and procedures that protect rights, in an attempt to weaken the credibility of the charges made against it and to avoid becoming the target of continuing attention by the commission. Often, a state that makes a show of cooperating under the confidential procedures finds that it can thereby escape being singled out for treatment in public proceedings — that is, the commission will be unlikely to appoint a public country-specific rapporteur, Working Group, or similar mechanism. And it did not do so in the Argentine case, despite the fact that the commission rejected Argentina's formal request to limit scrutiny to the confidential forum.

At the 1981 commission session, the new pro-authoritarian U.S. policy made us an ally of the Argentine junta's efforts to weaken the Working Group. As Argentina was still a member of the commission, consensus renewal of the Working Group's mandate would require Argentine acquiescence. The U.S. delegation, led by Reagan administration appointees, sent many signals of support to the Argentines, thereby causing strains within the Western caucus. The delegation reported to the State Department at the close of the annual session that:

> Our position favoring a consensus decision [on renewing the mandate] . . . was obviously a factor in the willingness of France and Lord Colville to go almost the last mile to achieve consensus. The issue at stake was the extent to which the Working Group would be obligated to keep its proceedings confidential. The compromise language is subject to varying interpretations. . . . The shift in the U.S. position on this issue [from that of the Carter administration] caused strain with our Western allies, who favored the original French proposal and opposed the effort to impose rules which could provide a basis for claiming confidentiality.[31]

But the group itself subsequently chose to interpret the resolution as not imposing confidentiality and indeed as not changing its mandate in any respect. And the United States decided not to further irritate our Western allies by challenging the Working Group's interpretation; instead, we let the matter drop. I should add that from the outset the Working Group took to heart the need to balance carefully the value of public disclosure with the value of discretion in the decisions it took regarding both its meetings and the content of its public reports.[32]

The Role of the Soviet Union

Even during the Carter administration the hope of inducing Argentina to participate in the grain embargo against the USSR following the Soviet invasion of Afghanistan created new pressures to relax our human rights policy. The Soviets were trying to capitalize on Argentina's estrangement from the United States by supporting Argentine positions in the United Nations and by other means. This alarmed the White House, which sent two high-level missions to Argentina in the spring of 1980 to see what could be done to rebuild the bilateral relationship. On the first mission, although Gen. Andrew Goodpaster raised human rights concerns strongly, he mixed up some key details about what we were seeking at the commission, whose session was about to open. Although we were able to sort that out in Geneva, the failure of the head of the second special mission, Ambassador Gerard Smith, to do more than barely mention the topic of human rights left the Argentine leaders with the impression that human rights had lost their high priority on our policy agenda. The Argentines now felt that they could use the Afghanistan crisis to keep us off balance on human rights issues. Still, a presidential policy review in spring 1980 reaffirmed and in some ways strengthened our human rights policy toward Argentina, and we were able to maintain a consistent and firm stance until the change of administrations.

In December 1981, nearly a year into the first Reagan administration, the U.S. mission in Geneva was able to report that:

> "The WG has continued to operate effectively and discreetly during 1981. Lord Colville . . . has told us that Argentina — which formerly declined to cooperate with the WG — has begun to change its attitude and is unlikely to oppose extension of the mandate. However, he expects the Soviets to make trouble, as they did last year. . . ."[33]

Lord Colville's reference to the Soviet Union requires a brief explanation. The anti-Communist Argentine junta did not single out the Moscow-backed Argentine Communist Party as a particular target in its war against domestic opposition groups. The Soviet Union obtained a measure of protection for its client party in Argentina by refusing to join in international condemnation of the junta's practices and by giving the junta quiet support at UN Human Rights Commission sessions. This is not to say that no Argentine Communist Party members were victims of disappearance. But more often they were left alone, and they were not very active in the opposition to the junta. After the Soviet invasion of Afghanistan in December 1979, the USSR relied on Argentina for grain imports far more than it had previously. The junta did not join the U.S.-led grain embargo imposed against the USSR, and Argentina made a great deal of money from sales to the Soviet Union during this period.[34]

How Well External Pressure Worked in the Argentine Case

In any external effort to influence a government to change its human rights policies, bilateral and multilateral approaches are mutually reinforcing. And just as bilateral pressure is heightened if exerted by several countries, so multilateral activity is more effective when carried out through more than one channel. Moreover, these approaches should be maintained over an extended period — often several years — to demonstrate seriousness of purpose and the priority external actors attach to the human rights issue. In the case of Argentina, I believe that the eventual halt in disappearances was due largely to this combination of sustained external pressures. Internal factors seemed to have less impact because of the relatively low profile taken by the churches, unions, political parties, and press. Thus most of the usual institutions through which popular resistance can be channeled either could not or would not take initiatives. Only the human rights organizations themselves took the risk. And, as the experience of the Mothers of the Plaza de Mayo illustrates, they began to have impact only when their story reached an international audience, through which their activity added to the external pressures on the military government.[35]

I believe that the combination of pressures from the United States and other Western governments, the United Nations, OAS, Amnesty International and other nongovernmental organizations, and the Vatican eventually made the regime understand that human rights was a serious priority of the international community and that until abuses halted, they would affect Argentina's external relationships. Maintaining a policy of disappearance was not to be a cost-free exercise in terms of Argentina's ties with the world. The immediate cost was primarily in terms of a badly degraded image of the nation, an image that would take some time to repair; the immediate material costs were largely limited to the U.S. restrictions on military sales and assistance and economic assistance.[36] Still, the latter were not trivial, and the Argentine junta was aware that they could be followed by similar actions by other Western states, some of which had already begun to follow the U.S. lead in refusing to support Argentine loan applications in the multilateral development banks. The regime thus had to consider the possibility that material costs could rise significantly. This helps explain why they fought so hard against being the target of any public human rights procedure in the United Nations.

In the State Department we believed that prompt intercession in disappearance cases worked fairly often in new cases, because the central government — the entity with which we dealt, after all — had some interest in preventing a worsening of our already bad bilateral relations and of its own deteriorating international image. The regime had gone from attempting to explain disappearances as an effect of the war against terrorism ("There are always some missing in action after a battle," Argentine Army General [and later President] Bignone told me in April 1979) to stating that it would take measures to halt disappearances. By the time of my conversation with General Bignone, in fact, Argentine officials were making both statements simultaneously, thereby creating a bizarre situation in which they half-denied and half-accepted responsibility for the practice. It seemed that international pressure was beginning to have some effect.

Also, Argentina's hemispheric peers in the Organization of American States were growing more critical, and the publication of the report of the 1979 visit by the Inter-American Commission on Human Rights further raised public consciousness in Latin America, where it received considerable press attention. In April 1980 the military government felt constrained to publish a rebuttal of the report.[37]

Iain Guest cites an unnamed Argentine Foreign Ministry official's comment in October 1980 on the effectiveness of international human rights institutions: "We can predict adverse consequences from the machinery now in place in the international organizations. To counter this, we will need decisive support from the other countries." Guest adds that this comment "showed again that the very qualities that rendered the UN an object of contempt in the West — the delay in acting, the ponderous bureaucracy — made it an object of acute concern in Argentina."[38]

The Vatican lent early support to the cause of human rights through quiet diplomacy, and in early 1979 the Pope started to make public statements focusing on the disappearance issue in Argentina and Chile. The Vatican statements encouraged the Argentine hierarchy to take a more forthright public posture, which it did, albeit gradually. Catholic bishops and priests and Jewish rabbis were among the most active members of the Permanent Assembly for Human Rights; a Catholic bishop served as vice president of the assembly.

Effectiveness of the Working Group

Livermore and Ramcharan point out that during the first eight years of operation of the Working Group, "the total number of cases resolved or clarified [is] some 7 or 8 percent of all cases processed, some 25 percent of urgent cases. . . ." They acknowledge that, although this "remains small relative to the total caseload of the Working Group, the success rate is higher than that of any other body within the UN system, many of which have few procedures for dealing with individual cases in effective ways." [39]

In January 1981 the U.S. mission in Geneva reported to the Department of State that "As the number of new disappearances declined significantly after the establishment of the Working Group, many Western observers believe the very fact of the Group's existence has helped to curb the practice." [40] While this statement accurately reflected the situation as the mission understood it, we also hoped that it would help educate the incoming Reagan administration as to the real value of the Working Group. We wanted to get the facts in the hands of the transition team and of incoming officials so that actual policy decisions would not be made hastily or in ignorance.

The news continued to be positive. In June 1981 Thomas McCarthy (U.S.), the UN official in charge of the staff supporting the Working Group, told me that "there have been recent cases where the Working Group's rapid intercession seems to have been effective." [41] In other words, it had saved lives. A year and a half later, in December 1982, the mission reported to the department that "The Working Group Chairman, Lord Colville (UK), recently told us that the number of new disappearances seems to be decreasing and that nearly all governments are cooperating with the Working Group." [42]

Iain Guest has written that the publication in early 1981 of the Working Group's first report ended an era: "The group had intervened to save lives. It had named governments, bypassed confidentiality, and taken information from people because they had suffered and not because they had been given 'consultative status' [by ECOSOC]. . . . By taking up a theme as opposed to a country, it had also broken the mold of discriminatory, single country probes on Israel, South Africa, and Chile and made the UN less 'selective.'"[43]

The group is authorized to "seek and receive" information from all sources that the group considers credible, including nongovernmental organizations, governments, intergovernmental organizations, and individuals. In a key phrase that authorizes the group to act rapidly on its own initiative, it is to "bear in mind the need to be able to respond effectively to information that comes before it." It is to make a public report to the commission, "together with its conclusions and recommendations," but it is given flexibility to determine how much should be in the report and how much should remain in the file cabinet.[44]

It is the word "seek" in the phrase "seek and receive" that is crucial; this word gives the group authority to demand information from governments about the location and status of a person believed to have been abducted by official forces. This, taken together with affirmation of the need for urgent action ("be able to respond effectively"), encouraged the group to adopt the practice of sending telegrams or telexes immediately on receipt of a disappearance report from a relative, a generally reliable nongovernmental organization, a responsible press source, and so forth. In the beginning, dispatch of such a telegram involved obtaining concurrence from all five members, but as there was consensus on every such telegram the members decided to streamline the procedure by letting the chair act in this matter on their behalf without prior consultation. The group thus adopted a technique already employed with good effect by Amnesty International, which had instituted an "urgent action procedure" a few years earlier to respond to reports of torture.

The Working Group discovered that governments often responded promptly to their urgent-action cables. They did not, however, respond quickly, or sometimes at all, to the Group's inquiries about people who had been missing for some months. The U.S. government had a similar experience. Whenever the Department of State instructed one of our embassies officially to request a government to provide information about the whereabouts and situation of a missing person believed to have been taken into official custody, we received a prompt and positive response usually only in "current" cases — that is, of people who had been taken in the past few days or weeks. The more recent the event, the more likely we would receive a positive response, for example, a report that the individual was in fact in custody at a specific location and was going to be charged or released. From that moment, of course, the individual was protected from further danger of summary killing. He or she could be found and communicated with by family and attorneys and friends and supporters. The individual was no longer "disappeared" and thus was no longer in a situation of absolute vulnerability to state power.

By 1979 many in the State Department had come to believe that most of the longer-missing people had probably been killed. The Argentine, Chilean, and other governments that we approached for information concerning specific long-disappeared individuals told us, typically, that the office responsible for handling such inquiries had checked with all police and military authorities and that no information was available on the person concerned or, sometimes, that the government understood that the individual had "gone abroad." (The latter assertion was rarely true, although in fact a tiny number of the disappeared did surface in foreign countries.)

In a dozen or so cases in early 1979, prompt intercession by the American Embassy in Buenos Aires on behalf of someone just abducted led to pressure by the central military authorities on regional and local military and police commanders to acknowledge the detention. They did so, thereby halting in these cases the usual sequence of torture followed by killing. This enabled the Argentine junta to demonstrate its intention to seek a more cooperative bilateral relationship with the United States. At the same time, the rate of disappearances declined sharply from the 1978 rate of about fifty a month. Other concerned Western and Latin American governments also made representations on behalf of individuals. When the UN Working Group began to function in early 1980, the United States and other Western countries made it clear to the Argentine military that prompt and positive responses to Working Group inquiries were just as important to us as positive resolution of cases in which we had interceded on a bilateral basis.

One could say, of course, that the Working Group is a failure, because it is unable to resolve 75 percent of the cases it undertakes under its most productive form of operation (its urgent-action procedure). But as there was, until establishment of the high commissioner's office, no other agency within the UN system with the authority or ability to undertake this task, the real alternative was probably close to 100 percent failure. The Working Group continues to carry out its responsibilities on the basis of the commission mandate, in coordination with the high commissioner. The existence of a UN entity charged with this politically sensitive responsibility has been, for states, a valuable way to pursue an essentially humanitarian task that otherwise would not be performed by an agency responsible to the international community as a whole.

By responding in a cooperative spirit, a government may at least control the damage to its reputation that often is already beginning to appear by the time the Working Group becomes involved. It is safer for a government to provide information to an international agency responsible only to the intergovernmental entity that appointed it, and of which the state is a member, than to provide that information to the press, to a nongovernmental organization, or to another government, all of which might sensationalize their treatment of it or use it to attack the government concerned. It is also easier to use such an agency as an intermediary to pass information to relatives. I share the conclusion of Livermore and Ramcharan that: "the Working Group has . . . helped to mobilize international public opinion . . . to exercise diplomatic influence in some countries, and to save lives in some circumstances. . . . [It] has broken new ground with its fact-finding procedures. . . . [This] is tangible proof that perseverance can result in effective international cooperation."[45]

Creating the Office of UN High Commissioner for Human Rights

After the collapse of the Argentine junta, the Reagan administration supported continuation of the Working Group without making further trouble for our Western Group and Latin American partners at the commission. By the time of the second Reagan administration, this policy had become routine, and it has continued unchanged throughout the Bush and Clinton administrations.

This was not the case, however, with other efforts to strengthen the capacity of the United Nations to deal effectively with human rights abuses. Notably, the Reagan administration was at best lukewarm about the proposal to establish an office of high commissioner for human rights — which had enjoyed enthusiastic U.S. support since at least the mid-1960s. At the outset of the Carter administration in 1977, the United States joined with Costa Rica and Sweden in relaunching the initiative at the UN General Assembly, very nearly succeeding in winning approval. But by 1977 the majority of UN members were recently independent ex-colonies. The Soviets were able to play effectively on these countries' sensitivities concerning their colonial past to portray the high commissioner proposal as a neocolonialist Trojan Horse. They found willing allies among the leaders of the Non-Aligned Movement: India, Algeria, Yugoslavia, and Cuba. These factors, plus a poorly organized lobbying effort by pro–high commissioner forces, led sponsors to withdraw the resolution to prevent its being laden with hostile amendments that would have made it unacceptable to the original sponsors.[46]

Italy joined Costa Rica, Senegal, and others to try again in the early 1980s. At that time I became involved in this effort in the course of my service at the U.S. Mission to the United Nations in Geneva, where I became convinced that establishment of the post was essential to give the United Nations the capacity to act swiftly and effectively. Debating human rights abuses six months or a year after they had occurred was simply an inadequate response by the international community.

While the Department of State officially supported the concept of a high commissioner, and the U.S. delegation voted for every resolution that actually came to a vote, there were times between 1981 and 1984 when I had to work hard to keep the department, and especially the Reagan administration's political leadership of the U.S. delegation, even minimally committed to the project. While this made my job more difficult in advocating the measure with other delegations, I went forward as vigorously as circumstances allowed, believing that in the long run something like this was crucial to enable the UN human rights effort to reach its potential.[47]

In June 1993 the Clinton administration decided to give the project high priority at the World Conference on Human Rights in Vienna. An intensive U.S.-led lobbying effort finally succeeded in gaining a consensus for establishing the post, and that momentum carried forward to the General Assembly, which in December adopted a consensus resolution actually creating the post.[48] Success came in 1993 and not in 1983 or 1984 because of a number of factors:

The end of the Cold War removed the obstacle of Soviet intransigence; while this obstacle could have been overcome earlier by majority vote, its removal now made it thinkable to try to achieve consensus.

The passage of an additional decade allowed the colonial era to fade further into the past, and the prospect of new human rights machinery began to appear less threatening to ex-colonial states.

The high commissioner's terms of reference include an explicit mandate to promote a people's right to development in addition to traditional individual rights.

And, energetic support by the U.S. lifted this topic from "one among many" to the number one priority issue at the World Conference and a few months later at the General Assembly. Official U.S. support, under the leadership of Secretary of State Warren Christopher and Assistant Secretary for Human Rights John Shattuck, was enhanced by the personal intercession of former President Jimmy Carter.

The effectiveness of Charter-based human rights procedures depends on the notion that states are members of an international community to which they are accountable, to some degree, for their conduct toward their own citizens. They are designed to enhance a climate in which this sense of accountability is acceptable to states. The aim is to bring to bear a structured international diplomatic presence and influence on a government to cease violations and to restore respect for human rights. Military force and economic sanctions are not the normal instruments of choice of the community of states for protecting and promoting human rights; rather, persuasion, in its many public and private forms, is the United Nations' principal method. The approach includes ethical and legal elements as well as appeals to the target states to act in a way that makes it easier for other states to conduct normal international dealings with them — and thus to avoid actions that could lead to or prolong their political isolation.

An individual government can appeal to its fellow sovereign on the basis of interest: "If you want to do business as usual with my government, you will need to forswear this abuse," or on the basis of traditional friendship and cultural links. A state seeking to persuade another state through bilateral channels to halt human rights abuses can combine ethical appeals with elements of material interest (trade, aid, credit, arms sales, military training, alliances, and the like). But it is very difficult to frame a bilateral appeal on ethical grounds without appearing to be engaging in a form of cultural imperialism. The appeal is seen as more legitimate if it is initiated by an agent that has a specific international mandate to apply international standards; it is almost always more efficacious to be able to say that one is supporting a community initiative rather than one's own.

An appeal by an international agent, such as the high commissioner or a Special Rapporteur, has no direct relationship with positive or negative material incentives, but it has sufficient moral authority that a government may weigh whether refusal to cooperate with the agent might lead indirectly to material repercussions in the policies of states of importance to it. A target state is aware that the agent will report at intervals to the body of states, that his or her reports will provide material for criticism or praise by that body, and that such praise or criticism can have further impact on national attitudes and policies of important states.

The high commissioner has the authority to employ all the techniques and methods of fact finding, good offices, negotiation, advisory services, conciliation, and public pressure available to the various thematic and country-specific mechanisms developed earlier. In addition, the high commissioner has direct authority over the resources of the un Human Rights Center (in 1996, some seventy professional and thirty-five supporting staff plus short-term experts, and a budget of $23 million, in addition to a voluntary fund amounting to $16 million). Finally, the commissioner is given specific authority to coordinate human rights protection, promotion, education, and information activities throughout the un system and to "adapt [and] strengthen" un human rights machinery "with a view to improving its efficiency and effectiveness."[49]

The concentration of diplomatic, operational, budgetary, personnel, program, and system-wide coordinating authority in a single high-ranking international official symbolizes a commitment by member states to strengthen the practice of state accountability to the international community in the human rights field. As the resolution makes clear, the General Assembly intended that the commissioner stand at the apex of the United Nations' human rights system, under the authority only of the secretary general and of the assembly itself.

Unfortunately, the world has not yet developed a way to provide positive material incentives to states to improve human rights practices beyond a limited advisory services/technical assistance program, which consists mainly of projects for training judges, prosecutors, and prison officials, providing law libraries, helping to write constitutions, and so forth. Still, these small programs — involving in the aggregate about $16 million dollars a year in 1995 — are becoming increasingly well integrated with other un human rights mechanisms, thereby reinforcing the impact of diplomatic efforts.[50]

Negative economic incentives, in the form of denial of loans by multilateral banks, and trade and financial restrictions, have not yet been fully utilized by the United Nations for human rights purposes except in the cases of

South Africa, Rhodesia, and most recently (1994–95) Haiti. The same is true of arms embargoes.

Recent Developments at the Commission

At the 1994 and 1995 sessions of the Human Rights Commission, the United States tried unsuccessfully to get the Commission to condemn human rights violations in China, despite a major lobbying effort.[51] In both years the United States found itself the target of successful Cuban resolutions criticizing the U.S. embargo on Cuba; these were adopted by 23-18-12 (1994) and 24-17-12 (1995). On the brighter side, as a result of the U.S.-brokered Palestinian-Israeli agreements of 1993 we were able to vote for some of the resolutions concerning the Middle East, loosening the traditional pattern of negative, and usually isolated, votes on resolutions criticizing Israeli human rights practices. We still found ourselves opposing some resolutions on this subject, however, including texts supported by our allies and friends in the European Union. And the United States continued to oppose resolutions concerning the right to development, following the policy of the Reagan and Bush administrations and earning us nothing but suspicion and ill will among the developing-country majority. We were successful in including anti-Semitism in the portfolio of the new special rapporteur on racism. This rapporteur also made an official visit to the United States in late 1994, which may have been the first time that a UN thematic mechanism reported to the commission on human rights practices in the United States.[52]

The record of these two recent sessions of the commission shows that the United States and other countries continue to look on the annual session as a way to advance national political objectives. Or try to advance them. Meanwhile, the impartial implementation machinery already established is working to achieve its purposes outside the framework of the annual sessions, in the form of the two dozen thematic mechanisms and country-specific rapporteurs. Most important, the new office of the high commissioner has begun to fill the huge gap in the UN human rights program that long weakened its effectiveness and credibility. It still matters what goes on at the annual sessions in Geneva, but the main action has shifted from the meeting room of the commission. Resources are still far short of needs, but they are growing — and the United States has been there to support funding for the special field missions in Rwanda, the former Yugoslavia, and Burundi and for the new international criminal tribunals for the first two of these.[53]

The high commissioner has established field missions of investigators and advisors in such places as Rwanda, Burundi, the former Yugoslavia, Zaire, Georgia/Abkhazia, and Colombia.[54]
The commission has undertaken some procedural innovations. With strong U.S. support, it has convened emergency special sessions to deal with the situations in the former Yugoslavia and in Rwanda. At the 1995 regular session the high commissioner supplemented his formal report with a question-and-answer meeting with delegates. He has also started to hold regular meetings with all the thematic and country-specific agents.[55] The high commissioner issues a bimonthly newsletter, and he has begun to publish material on the Internet. He has made numerous onsite visits himself and has sent representatives to many other countries. The high commissioner and his staff are becoming a tangible presence in a great many parts of the globe, shattering the previous image of the United Nations' human rights action as too often confined to the comfortable quarters of Geneva.

As an integral part of the constellation of international institutions in the political universe within which states function and interact, UN human rights mechanisms constitute an increasingly significant structural deterrent to abuse by states. The very presence on the world scene of these mechanisms, and their activities, has become a factor in the decision-making process of most governments. The methods of persuasion have not helped all victims, but in combination with other pressures they have become important factors influencing state conduct. Although UN human rights institutions cannot force a change in conduct by a state, they can potentially affect interests of that state. States deal with each other in a multiplicity of bilateral and multilateral activities and structured relationships. If a government becomes a pariah because of human rights abuses, it is likely to find its foul reputation becoming entwined with other aspects of its bilateral and multilateral relationships. This raises the level of discomfort of the state concerned and increases the psychological and political price it must pay if it chooses to continue its conduct.

Beginning in the late 1970s, with strong U.S. support the Human Rights Commission greatly strengthened its implementation activities. The high commissioner for Human Rights is building on the experience of earlier mechanisms to further improve the United Nations' ability to carry out the Charter mandate to promote respect and observance of human rights and fundamental freedoms for all. The UN human rights system continues to provide the United States an effective, relatively inexpensive means to promote human rights policy objectives within a framework in which we share the political and economic burden of this fundamental responsibility with other members of the international community.

Notes

1. The International Tribunal for the Prosecution of Persons Responsible for Serious Violations of International Humanitarian Law Committed in the Territory of the Former Yugoslavia was established by the Security Council in Resolution 827, acting under chapter 7 of the Charter. The Tribunal met for the first time in November 1993 to elect its officers and to begin work on its rules of procedure and evidence. A chief prosecutor was named in July 1994. The first indictments were returned later that year.

2. In addition, two of the Specialized Agencies — the International Labor Organization (ILO) and the UN Educational, Scientific, and Cultural Organization (UNESCO) — have also evolved human rights procedures. On the regional level, the postwar period saw the establishment of an Inter-American Commission on Human Rights under the auspices of the Organization of American States (OAS) and comprised of individual experts serving in their personal capacity, and a similarly constituted European Commission set up within the framework of the Council of Europe. Each is now linked with a regional Human Rights Court, for which there is no counterpart in the United Nations. In the 1980s an African Commission on Human and People's Rights was formed, and somewhat less systematized arrangements have come into existence under the auspices of the Arab League and among some Asian countries. The Office of Democratic Institutions and Human Rights and a high commissioner for Minorities function within the framework of the Organization on Security and Cooperation in Europe.

3. In saying this, I do not mean to imply that individuals or groups have no standing in international law; to the contrary, I hold that individual human beings have rights under international law, that these are guaranteed by the international community, and that the latter has undertaken an obligation to promote and protect them.

4. As of September 1995 the Covenant on Civil and Political Rights had 131 parties, and the Covenant on Economic, Social and Cultural Rights had 122. The Optional Protocol to the Civil and Political Covenant had 85. The United Nations had over 180 member states.

5. Covenant on Civil and Political Rights, Articles 28, 31, and 40.

6. Articles 41 and 42 in the Covenant, *Covenant on Civil and Political Rights*.

7. This includes observer states, which have the right to speak and to co-sponsor

resolutions (provided at least one member state is a sponsor). Nongovernmental organizations in consultative status with ECOSOC are entitled to attend all public meetings and to speak, but not to cosponsor resolutions.

8. These are the "1503 Procedures," so named, because they are spelled out in ECOSOC Resolution 1503 (of 1970), which set up a four-tier system to screen and evaluate the thousands of human rights complaints submitted to the United Nations annually. The resolution directs the commission and its expert-level subcommission to focus on abuses that constitute "a consistent pattern of gross violations of internationally-recognized human rights."

9. J. Daniel Livermore and Bertram G. Ramcharan, "'Enforced or Involuntary Disappearances': An Evaluation of a Decade of United Nations Action," in *Canadian Human Rights Yearbook 1989–90* (Ottawa: University of Ottawa Press, 1990), 217–230.

10. The figure of six hundred is based on information from the UN Working Group on Chile, the *Vicaria de la Solidaridad* (Vicariate of Solidarity) of the Archdiocese of Santiago, and the International Committee of the Red Cross. See UN document E/CN.4/1363, February 2, 1980, esp. paras. 87–89.

11. Patrick J. Flood, "U.S. Human Rights Initiatives Concerning Argentina," in *The Diplomacy of Human Rights*, ed. David Newsom (Lanham MD: Institute for the Study of Diplomacy/University Press of America, 1986), 129–139.

12. In April 1979, F. Allen Harris, human rights officer at the American Embassy in Buenos Aires, showed me about 8,500 case files on which the Embassy had acquired detailed information, much of it provided by family members. At that time, estimates of the number of disappeared persons by nongovernmental organizations ranged from 5,000 to 30,000. The Embassy files eventually reached about 9,000 cases, a figure that later proved to be accurate as a result of investigations conducted by the InterAmerican Commission on Human Rights of the Organization of American States (1979) and, after the restoration of democratic governance in Argentina, by the official Argentine National Commission on Disappeared Persons. The UN Working Group on Disappearances used the same figure. However, other sources insist that the number is probably higher — perhaps much higher. See, for instance, Alison Brysk, *The Politics of Human Rights in Argentina* (Stanford: Stanford University Press, 1994), 37–40, 70–72, 216 n.8.

13. By 1979 at least eight Argentine organizations were dealing with the problem of enforced disappearance, not counting exile groups. In addition to the Mothers and the Permanent Assembly, they included Christian Service for Peace and Justice (of Nobel Laureate Adolfo Perez Esquivel) and the Grandmothers of the Plaza de Mayo. For a thoroughly researched, well-documented sympathetic account of the Argentine human rights movement, see Brysk, *The Politics of Human Rights in Argentina*. For an extensive if highly enthusiastic appreciation of the Mothers of the Plaza de Mayo, see Marguerite Guzman Bouvard, *Revolutionizing Motherhood: The Mothers*

of the Plaza de Mayo (Wilmington: SR Books, 1994). Guzman Bouvard lists the eight organizations on p. 94.

14. General Assembly Resolution 33/173, adopted by consensus on December 20, 1978. Although the Geneva Conventions of 1949 prohibit clandestine detention, mistreatment, and killing during wartime, they do not cover such abuses during peacetime, nor do they address violations of human rights by a state against its own citizens and residents.

15. In 1976 the military government tried to choke off preliminary action by the expert-level UN Human Rights Subcommission on Discrimination and Minorities. Antonio Cassese, then a member of the UN subcommission, recounts blatant attempts of intimidation by the Argentine ambassador in Geneva. Antonio Cassese, *Human Rights in a Changing World* (Philadelphia: Temple University Press, 1990), 128–129.

16. Joseph S. Tulchin, *Argentina and the United States: A Conflicted Relationship* (Boston: Twayne, 1990), xv–xvi, 143.

17. Tulchin, *Argentina and the United States*, 141–142.

18. Livermore and Ramcharan, "Enforced or Involuntary Disappearances," 220. See also David Forsythe, *The Internationalization of Human Rights* (Lexington MA: Lexington Books, 1991), 65–69.

19. There is a minor exception to this statement: Member states of the commission also had access to a periodic summary list of complaints received by the secretariat. These, too, were UN-confidential.

20. Iain Guest, *Behind the Disappearances: Argentina's Dirty War against Human Rights and the United Nations* (Philadelphia: University of Pennsylvania Press, 1990), 232.

21. Report of the Special Rapporteur on Human Rights in Chile, UN Doc. A/34/583, November 21, 1979, paras. 1–13.

22. Tulchin, *Argentina and the United States*, 146–147.

23. Tulchin, *Argentina and the United States*, 148–149.

24. Jacobo Timerman, *Prisoner Without a Name, Cell Without a Number* (New York: Alfred A. Knopf, 1981), 101–102. See also Juan Carlos Torre and Liliana de Riz, "Argentina Since 1946," in *Argentina Since Independence*, ed. Leslie Bethell (London: Cambridge University Press, 1993), 324–327; David Rock, *Argentina 1516–1982: From Spanish Colonization to the Falklands War* (Berkeley: University of California Press, 1985), 352–366; and Tulchin, *Argentina and the United States*, 134–139. But Brysk, *Politics of Human Rights in Argentina*, 32, asserts that the Montonero and ERP guerrillas "never posed a serious threat to the territorial or institutional integrity of the state," and that whatever threat did exist "had substantially diminished before the 1976 coup."

25. Tulchin, *Argentina and the United States*, 155. Also see Brysk, *Politics of Human Rights in Argentina*, 33.

26. Guest, *Behind the Disappearances*, contains a comprehensive account of the operations of Argentine diplomats at the United Nations in New York and Geneva during this period, in chs. 14–18.

27. Human Rights Commission Resolution 20(36), February 29, 1980.

28. Ambassador Kirkpatrick is best known for her 1979 *Commentary* article, "Dictatorships and Double Standards," which Candidate Reagan said had a formative effect on his view of an appropriate U.S. human rights policy. Also see Forsythe, *The Internationalization of Human Rights*, 126–129.

29. U.S. Mission Geneva telegram 1645, February 18, 1981.

30. U.S. Mission Geneva telegram 1542, February 16, 1981.

31. Geneva telegram 2796, March 17, 1981.

32. For instance, U.S. Mission Geneva telegram 11211 of August 19, 1980, to the Department of State: "UN Human Rights Division Director told Mission . . . Working Group prefers private session this time because of sensitive and controversial nature of material to be considered. WG plans to invite NGO's and other interested parties to appear. . . . WG would probably hold a third session later. . . . WG would decide whether this session would be public or private. . . . He expects the WG's report to the UNHRC to be public."

33. Geneva telegram 12616, December 24, 1981.

34. Tulchin, *Argentina and the United States*, 150; also see Gaddis Smith, *Morality, Reason and Power: American Diplomacy in the Carter Years* (New York: Hill and Wang, 1988), 128–129.

35. Guzman Bouvard, *Revolutionizing Motherhood*, 82, 86–87.

36. Smith, *Morality, Reason and Power*, 128–129.

37. Government of Argentina, *Observaciones y Comentarios Criticos del Gobierno Argentino al Informe de la CIDH sobre la Situacion de los Derochos Humanos en Argentina* (Buenos Aires: Circulo Militar, 1980).

38. Guest, *Behind the Disappearances*, 238.

39. Livermore and Ramcharan, "Enforced and Involuntary Disappearances," 226–227.

40. U.S. Mission Geneva telegram 108, January 6, 1981.

41. Memorandum from the writer to Warren Hewitt, director of the Office of Human Rights, Bureau of International Organizations, Department of State, June 30, 1981.

42. U.S. Mission Geneva telegram 12546, December 29, 1982.

43. Guest, *Behind the Disappearances*, 234.

44. Human Rights Commission Resolution 20(36), February 29, 1980.

45. Livermore and Ramcharan, "Enforced and Involuntary Disappearances," 230.

46. This account comes from a conversation in 1981 in Geneva with B. G. Ramcharan, then special assistant to the director of the Division (later Center) of Human Rights, who was present at the 1977 General Assembly debate.

47. After the 1982 subcommission session, for example, I reported to the Department of State (U.S. Mission Geneva telegram 9832, September 30) that "If the project is approved by the Commission, ECOSOC and the GA, it will significantly improve the way the UN does business on human rights issues by adding a capacity for prompt action in urgent situations, particularly through vigorous quiet diplomacy. . . . We urge the Department to give it high priority in our pre-Commission consultations with Western and selected Third World colleagues." For the record, I can state that high priority was not forthcoming. I was left largely to my own devices in the lobbying effort.

48. General Assembly Resolution 48/141, Annex H.

49. General Assembly Resolution 48/141, Annex H.

50. For many years, some states and nongovernmental organizations have urged, vainly so far, that all UN economic institutions be brought into the United Nations' human rights work, and vice versa. See particularly, the *Vienna Declaration and Programme of Action* (A/CONF.157/23).

51. Barbara Crossette, "China Outflanks U.S. to Avoid Scrutiny of Rights Record," *New York Times*, April 24, 1996.

52. John R. Crook, "The 50th Session of the UN Commission on Human Rights," *American Journal of International Law* (October 1994): 806–821; Crook, "The 51st Session of the UN Commission on Human Rights," *American Journal of International Law* (January 1996): 126–138.

53. *New York Times*, April 2, 1996; U.S. Department of State *Dispatch*, November 21, 1994, June 2, 1995.

54. For instance, A/50/566 of October 26, 1995; GA/SHC/3328 of November 21, 1995; E/CN.4/1996/103 of March 18, 1996; E/CN.4/1996/111 of April 2, 1996; and s/1996/644 of August 9, 1996.

55. E/CN.4/1996/50/Add.1, October 24, 1995.

Postscript
U.S. and Asian Views on Human Rights

•

Prospects for Convergence

•

AMBASSADOR MARK HONG

As one solitary Asian, I cannot presume to speak on behalf of Asia, a huge, diverse, and populous continent. I seek to explore the areas of convergence in human rights between the West and Asia and merely note areas where deeply held beliefs do not permit much movement. I would like to move the debate forward, rather than get mired in sterile debate over different approaches to the issue of human rights. No one, no country has a monopoly on wisdom. My approach is that, where we disagree, we should have the courtesy and graciousness to acknowledge that there might be some truth or merit in the opposing view.

A False Debate

A study for the Centre for Strategic and International Studies by David Hitchcock shows that there is a perceptible difference in preferences and perceptions between Asians and Americans interviewed on the importance of various societal values. I believe that there is in fact more convergence than divergence on these issues. In my view, there are three main key points in the trans-Pacific debate on human rights:

(1) Asians value democracy and human rights as much as the West. They have, however, a different approach to such issues, for example, stressing more the economic human rights (jobs) or civil rights (personal security) and basic needs (rights to clean water and air). Although the United States and Asia may have different views and approaches to various aspects of democracy and human rights, nevertheless we should work together to evolve a balanced and common approach to the Rights of Society and the responsibility of the individual.

(2) Rights need to be balanced by responsibility if a society is to develop and maintain communal and individual cohesion. This applies to both Asian and Western societies. Too much stress on the individual leads to anarchy and anomie. Too much stress on the role and importance of the community and society leads to conformity, sterility, and passivity. The trick is in finding and maintaining the right balance. I believe that the individual in every society should behave more responsibly in areas such as the protection of the environment, in conservation of resources, in social behavior, in helping to maintain law and order, and civic virtues.

(3) Although many of the so-called "Asian values" are also to be found in other societies, it is the emphasis and role accorded to such values by Asian countries that make them Asian and particular. Secondly, such values can be considered as Asian values, because in many Western countries they have disappeared or gone out of fashion, although there are some attempts to re-discover and re-establish the old Western values. Third, while such values as filial love are universal, the way Asians fulfill them makes them different. This stems from the role and importance accorded to the individual. In the West, the individual is accorded primary importance. In Asia, the individual is also regarded as important but within the context of family and community. This difference of perspective fundamentally affects family, communal, and societal relationships. It should be stressed that these values will be affected by the modernization of Asia, but equally important, Asian countries are trying to preserve this value system and make it compatible with modernization.

The debate about Asian values is important as it involves basic issues such as the organization of society. It has also internal and external implications as it involves power relationships within and between states. In philosophical terms, the debate has focused on the correct balance between the respective rights of the community and the individual. Also, how countries view human rights is conditioned by national culture and conditions. In my view, human rights will continue to evolve and adapt to new needs. For instance, a new human right was established at Habitat II (Istanbul, June 96), namely the right to adequate housing. Although in theory all people should enjoy human rights, the reality is very different in developing and poor countries. Finally, in my view, the West may have overprivileged the individual to the point where the rights of society are undermined, for instance, a criminal has become a "victim of society" rather than a transgressor of laws.

Human Rights and Foreign Policy

Democracy and human rights are deeply linked and are highly sensitive and politicized issues, because they involve national sovereignty and independence, how societies are governed, and relationships between individuals, communities, and governments. This politicization is enhanced when the West places its tremendous political influence and economic weight behind such concepts. There are also legal and moral dimensions of human rights that complicate the implementation of human rights issues in foreign policy. Briefly stated, all member states of the United Nations are legally bound to abide by the UN Charter, which includes human rights that have been elaborated in such documents as the Universal Declaration of Human Rights and the Vienna Declaration of Human rights. A wise government respects and fulfills its international human rights obligations, consistent with its national sovereignty, independence, and specific national circumstances. In the moral context, the issue of promoting human rights internationally is essentially the question of morality in foreign policy. Does morality play a role in foreign policy? Each country answers this question differently. Some argue that foreign policy is amoral, and is driven solely by national interests and power relationships. Others, including George Kennan, argue that evil needs to be contained and opposed actively.

Extra Territoriality

A solely human rights–based foreign policy is extremely problematic. (One good example is the problem faced by Germany in July 1996 when it faced protests and pressures from China, which objected when Germany raised the issue of Tibetan human rights). It raises difficult dilemmas of extra-territoriality, respect for other countries' sovereignty and independence, the questions of mandates and double standards, and conflicts of interest between one's economic/trade interests and human rights/political interests.

Responsibility for Consequences

The issue of responsibility for the consequences of an external intervention because of human rights violations needs to be highlighted. When a powerful country intervenes in another country, there are two possible outcomes.

The first is positive, such as in the case of Haiti, where UN intervention improved the human rights situation. The consequences for this should be that the United Nations needs to continue for some years to help nurse Haiti back to socioeconomic and political health. After saving a person from death, the Good Samaritan should remain engaged. The second consequence is negative, as in the case of Somalia where humanitarian intervention while alleviating famine, has been unable to resolve a complex, factionalized political problem. Other examples are Rwanda, Burundi, Bosnia, and complex situations elsewhere where human rights intervention may exacerbate ethnic tensions, divide a country, or slow down socioeconomic development.

Can the intervening country be morally absolved of the disastrous consequences if intervention results in negative consequences? This is a complex, moral problem: it should not be misconstrued to imply that gross violations of human rights should be tolerated by the international community. What is being stressed is the need to be aware of the possible consequences of human rights interventions and to ask whether the intervening state is prepared to carry the enormous burdens and responsibilities that follow the initial actions, and remain engaged for years. Secondly, it is also important to note that there are ambiguous situations: the twilight zone of human rights wherein several communities claim competing rights. In such morally ambiguous situations, there is legitimate debate, and ultimately each country will have to decide on its own policy.

Economic Pressures

When overpopulation makes huge and increasing demands on shrinking resources, as in East Asia and elsewhere at present and in the world in a few decades, the role of the individual and the role of the team or community comes under scrutiny. In certain areas such as entrepreneurship and leadership, the individual still plays a key role. In other areas such as protection of and access to the environment and to scarce resources (food, water, energy), the group or community should take precedence in access, sharing, and conserving. Japan is a good example of how mankind evolves strategies and behavior for the individual and the community to cope and balance between overcrowding and an inadequate resource base. Individually, the average Japanese is as good as any other worker in other countries, but it is Japanese teamwork that makes the difference with superior results. Contrast this to the primacy and importance accorded to the individual in the West. Yet the world of the future will look more like overcrowded Japan than the generous space and resources of the West.

Singapore and the United States

When we compare the United States and Singapore, the dissimilarities could not be more striking in terms of size, population, and resource endowment. Furthermore, the two countries operate on different philosophical systems: one stresses individualism, the other communitarian and family values. Yet both are consistently rated the two most competitive economies by international companies such as the World Economic Forum. Does this mean that value systems play no role in economic productivity and efficiency? In the case of Singapore, due to its small size and lack of resources, it has no choice but to stress responsibility, discipline, and unity. If Singapore can manage to become the second most competitive economy after the United States, despite all its handicaps, this may indicate that its system has certain strengths and advantages. In the case of the United States, with its space, rich resources, and origins in religious dissent, it could afford to stress individualism. Yet as the United States becomes more populated, and as the family and its values come under attack, more Americans understand the need for greater individual responsibility and discipline. They have understood that responsibility and discipline are paradoxically also human rights! Human rights are essentially expressions of values, and responsibility and discipline are as much values as freedom.

It may be difficult to convince an American audience that there are possibilities of convergence, but there are some encouraging signs and trends. Admittedly, there are major differences of views on key issues such as the place of the individual. There are some signs of convergence nevertheless between the views of Singapore and the West in various areas. Take, for example, the stress on the family. In Singapore, much stress and importance is placed on the family as a transmitter and nurturer of values, as a social and economic support system, as a basic unit of society and the nation. Singapore has identified as family values the following: love, care and concern, mutual respect, filial responsibility, commitment, and communication.

Family Values

In the United States, President Clinton has likewise lent his support to the institution of the family. In June 1996 he and his wife, Hillary, presided over the fifth-annual family reunion in Nashville. Second, according to the *Los Angeles Times* (June 6, 1996), 92 percent of Americans would like the government to help strengthen families and family values. However, Americans are still divided and uncertain about how much of a role the government should play in promoting values. Third, *Newsweek* (June 3, 1996) reported that a national radio talk-show hostess carried on more than three hundred North American radio stations, Dr. Laura Schlessinger, is getting more popular because she emphasizes "character, courage and conscience." She emphasizes responsibility as "an antidote to a pop-psyche movement that many people feel is short on ethics and long on excuses." Victimology and mollycoddling are out, and values and responsibility are in. Fourth, in the United States, organizations such as Character Education Partnership in Washington and the Character Counts Coalition in California have widespread support, including President Clinton, in teaching values such as honesty, responsibility, self-discipline, respect, and caring in public schools.

Welfare State Reforms

Another example is the attitude to the welfare state. Singapore practices the minimal welfare state, with subsidies only in education, healthcare, and public housing. In Singapore we try to strike a good balance between individual responsibility and community support, for instance in healthcare. In Europe both Germany and France have begun to realize that the overgenerous welfare state is no longer affordable and is an economic burden to productivity and competitiveness. This new attitude was shown in the first anniversary speech by President Chirac. He declared that "France must move from a culture of assistance to a culture of responsibility. In a country where recourse to the state is second nature, we must have a revolution in thinking." In the United States (August 1, 1996) President Clinton has signed a welfare bill ending federal aid to poor Americans, limiting benefits to five years, and forcing recipients to work. Thus, there are many areas where Singapore and the West can cooperate to produce a Pacific Way that fits the needs of the new century, a new convergence in human rights to restore the balance toward the responsibility of the individual. Indeed when Singapore advocates Asian values, it is trying to counter the overemphasis on the individual's rights and to re-emphasize the point about responsibilities of the individual to family and society. Speaking up about Asian values is not about condoning oppression in East Asia or providing philosophic cover or support for oppressive regimes. Essentially, Asian values is about responsibility and accountability to the community and society.

Different Priorities

How do changing ideas on the family and welfare affect our differences of views on human rights? My answer: such trends help to narrow the gap. In Asia modernization and socioeconomic development will give the individual a greater social space and role to play. In the West the ongoing restructuring of the welfare state will give the family and community a greater role in taking back some of the functions handled previously by the state, for example, healthcare. Asians are as concerned about human rights as the West, but the emphases and the approaches are different. In Singapore, as in many other developing countries, we place as much emphasis on economic human rights as on political and civil rights. Asian countries are at different levels of development, and each level has its own priorities: nation building, modernization, and socioeconomic development. In Asia the rights of man include the right to a home, to a job, and to personal security in a community. Many in the West who suffer from high unemployment and crime may agree with this approach.

New Pacific Harmony

Singapore is pointing in the direction toward a new Pacific combination of individualism and communitarianism: wherein approximately equal importance is given to both the individual and the community; wherein equal stress is given to responsibilities and to rights; wherein economic human rights are accorded as much weight as political human rights; and wherein democracy is balanced with discipline. This harmonious balance may be the appropriate combination for the future world, overpopulated and under siege.

My objective is not to convince the readers of the rightness of one particular view but merely to show that there are alternative approaches that may be

equally valid. Only history will show which system of organizing society —
the individual or communitarian — will be successful. Perhaps it might even
be a false debate, and both approaches could be combined in a happy synthesis. Thus I seek to move the human rights debate forward, to be future
oriented rather than to get mired in sterile and endless debates on current
human rights questions. Lastly, being different does not mean being wrong.
I realize that the gap is wide between those who emphasize the primacy of the
individual and those who stress the importance of family and community.
But I believe that such views are not incompatible or irreconcilable.

NOTE: This paper reflects my personal views and does not represent the views of the
Singapore government.

Contributors

Ambassador Harry G. Barnes Jr. is director of the Human Rights and Conflict Resolution Programs at the Carter Presidential Center of Emory University in Atlanta, Georgia. Mr. Barnes received his B.A. from the College of Amherst and an M.A. from Columbia University. He entered the U.S. Foreign Service in 1951, becoming ambassador in Romania, India, and Chile. In the latter post, especially, he was prominently active on a variety of human rights issues. He also served as the director general of the U.S. Foreign Service and director of personnel.

Christina Cerna is senior human rights specialist at the Inter-American Commission on Human Rights of the Organization of American States (OAS). She has been with the OAS since January 1979 and is the author of over forty articles on human rights, in general, and the inter-American system, in particular, which have been published in the *British Year Book of International Law*, the *Annuaire Francais de Droit International*, the *N.Y.U. Journal of International Law and Politics*, and other journals. She was seconded to the UN Centre for Human Rights (1992–94) to collaborate in the preparation of the UN World Conference on Human Rights held in Vienna. She has a law degree from American University and an LLM from Columbia University.

Audrey Chapman is the director of the Science and Human Rights Program of the American Association for the Advancement of Science (AAAS). She is the author or editor of ten books, including *Health Care Reform: A Human Rights Approach* (Georgetown University Press) and the forthcoming *Health Care and Information Ethics: Protecting Fundamental Human Rights* (Sheed and Ward). Her articles on human rights have appeared in the *Human Rights Quarterly*, the *ICJ Review*, the *American University Law Review*, and other journals. One of the projects that she is currently directing involves the development of methodologies and resources for monitoring economic, social, and cultural rights.

Jack Donnelly is currently Mellon professor at the Graduate School of International Studies at the University of Denver. He received an M.A. from Georgetown University and his Ph.D. from the University of California–Berkeley. His most recent books are *International Human Rights*, *Universal Human Rights in Theory and Practice*, and the *International Handbook of Hu-*

man Rights. He has published articles in such journals as the *American Political Science Review, International Organization,* and *Ethics and International Affairs.*

Ellen Dorsey is the national field director for Amnesty International — USA. She is also an adjunct assistant professor at the School of International Service at American University. She holds her advanced degrees from the University of Pittsburgh. She has contributed to the *Politics of Global Governance* and also to the *Human Rights Education Handbook.*

Patrick Flood began his academic career after serving as a U.S. Foreign Service officer with the Department of State, receiving a doctorate in political science from the University of Massachusetts–Amherst in 1995. While in the Foreign Service, Professor Flood worked extensively on human rights and international organizations issues in Washington and abroad, wrote several articles on these subjects, and contributed to the *Diplomacy of Human Rights* (Georgetown University, Institute for the Study of Diplomacy). He has recently taught international relations and foreign policy at the University of Massachusetts and the Budapest Economic University and is currently senior lecturer in international relations at Western New England College.

David P. Forsythe is Charles J. Mach Distinguished Professor of political science at the University of Nebraska–Lincoln. He holds a B.A. from Wake Forest University and a Ph.D. from Princeton University. Among his recent books are *Human Rights and Peace* and *Human Rights in the New Europe.* His recent articles have appeared in journals such as *Human Rights Quarterly* and *Ethics and International Relations.* His forthcoming book is *Human Rights in International Relations.* He recently served as a vice president of the International Studies Association and is directing a research project for the United Nations University on human rights and foreign policy.

Mark Gibney is the Belk Professor of political science at the University of North Carolina–Ashville. He is the author of *Strangers or Friends: Principles for a New Alien Admission Policy* and the editor of *Open Borders? Closed Societies?: The Ethical and Political Issues.* Professor Gibney has published articles on immigration and refugee issues in such journals as *Human Rights Quarterly, Georgetown Immigration Law Journal, International Migration Review,* and *Journal of Refugee Studies.*

Robert Hitchcock is chair and associate professor of anthropology and coordinator of African studies at the University of Nebraska–Lincoln. He is the author of a number of books on indigenous peoples' rights, including the forthcoming volume *Organizing to Survive: The Politics of Indigenous Peoples' Human Rights Struggles* and *Kalahari Communities: Bushmen and the Politics of the Environment in Southern Africa*. He has had other papers on human rights and indigenous peoples published recently in *Human Ecology*, *Colorado Journal of International Environmental Law and Policy*, and *Development and Change*. Professor Hitchcock is a founding member of the Committee for Human Rights of the American Anthropological Association.

Ole Holsti received his Ph.D. from Stanford University in 1962. He has taught at Stanford, at the University of British Columbia, and, since 1974, at Duke University, where he is George V. Allen Professor of International Affairs and director of undergraduate studies in the Department of Political Science. He served as president of the International Society of Political Psychology. His most recent books are *Public Opinion and American Foreign Policy* (1996) and *Encyclopedia of U.S. Foreign Relations*.

Ambassador Mark Hong is currently Singapore's ambassador to the Russian Federation. He was educated at Cambridge and Georgetown Universities, being a president (the leading award for Singapore's best students) and Fulbright scholar. He has served in Singapore's embassies in Cambodia, Hong Kong, Paris, and New York and in the Ministry of Foreign Affairs of Singapore in various capacities. He has presented numerous papers at over forty international conferences and seminars and has contributed individual chapters to five books. Ambassador Hong has had articles printed in the UN *Journal of Disarmament* and the *East Asia Institute of Columbia University*. He is on the advisory board of a Canadian journal on peacekeeping.

Christopher Joyner is professor of government at Georgetown University. He holds a B.A. and two M.A. degrees from Florida State University and a Ph.D. from the University of Virginia. He is coeditor of the two-volume study, *United Nations Legal Order*. He is the author of other books, including the forthcoming *Managing the Arctic Commons*. His articles have appeared in such journals as the *Duke Journal of Comparative and International Law*, *Vanderbilt Journal of Transnational Law*, *Michigan Journal of International Law*, and *Israel Yearbook on Human Rights*. Professor Joyner is a member of the Executive Committee of the American Society of International Law.

Linda Camp Keith is a graduate student in political science at the University of North Texas. Her research interests include international human rights and the U.S. court system. She was winner of Pi Sigma Alpha's national award for best graduate student research paper in 1995. Her dissertation research focuses on the impact of constitutional law and the judiciary on human rights behavior.

George Kent's professional work addresses finding remedies for social problems, especially looking for ways to strengthen the weak in the face of the strong. He works on international relations, peace, development, and environmental issues, with a special focus on issues relating to nutrition and to children. He has written several books, including *The Political Economy of Hunger: The Silent Holocaust*; *Fish, Food, and Hunger: The Potential of Fisheries for Alleviating Malnutrition*; *The Politics of Children's Survival*; and *Children in the International Political Economy*. He is co-convener of the Commission on International Human Rights of the International Peace Research Association and coordinator of the Global Task Force on Children's Nutrition Rights. He has worked as a consultant with the Food and Agriculture Organization of the United Nations, the United Nations Children's Fund, and several nongovernmental organizations.

Kelly-Kate Pease is an assistant professor of history, politics, and law at Webster University, St. Louis. She holds a Ph.D. from the University of Nebraska–Lincoln. Professor Pease has coauthored articles in *Human Rights Quarterly* and the *Austrian Journal of International Law*. Her research and teaching interests are in the fields of human rights, international organizations, and international political economy.

Steven C. Poe is an associate professor of political science at the University of North Texas, where he has won several departmental and university teaching honors. His research on human rights has appeared in the *American Political Science Review*, *American Journal of Political Science*, *Social Science Quarterly*, *International Interactions*, *Journal of Peace Research*, and *Human Rights Quarterly*. He is now working on a book with C. Neal Tate on why governments violate human rights.

William Schabas is a professor in the Law Department at the University of Quebec in Montreal. He is the author of *The Abolition of the Death Penalty in International Law*, *The Death Penalty as Cruel Treatment and Torture*, and *International Human Rights Law and the Canadian Charter*. His recent articles have appeared in *Human Rights Quarterly*, the *Human Rights Law Journal*, and the *Revue universelle des droits de l'homme*. He has taken part in several human rights monitoring missions, notably in Africa.

Barbara Stark is a professor of law at the University of Tennessee–Knoxville. She is the author of the forthcoming *Critical Theory and Economic Rights in the United States: The Other Half of the International Bill of Rights* and has contributed chapters to *International Women's Human Rights: A Reference Guide* and *Feminist Approaches to Social Movements, Community, and Power*. Her articles on economic rights have recently appeared in *Harvard Women's Law Journal*, *Hastings Law Journal*, and the *Michigan, Vanderbilt, and Virginia Journals of International Law*.

Stephen Zunes is an assistant professor of politics at the University of San Francisco. He is an author of several articles addressing U.S. Middle East policy, which have appeared in *International Journal of Middle East Policy*, *Arab Studies Quarterly*, *New Political Science*, and other publications. He is editor of *Peace Review* and is the author of a forthcoming book on conflict in the Western Sahara.

Index

regarding humanitarian assistance, 344–345

U.S. human rights policy: bilateral relations and, 182–185; death penalty issue and, 98, 101–102, 108 n.34; during Cold War, 76–77; Economic Covenants ratification and, 79–84; gap between American exceptionalism and, 153; history of international treaty ratification and, 110–111; inconsistency of, 38; international opinion/domestic constituencies and, 82–83; on joining unions, 44–45, 46; multilateralism of, 185–187; nature of alien claims and, 54–55; nonrefoulement principle and, 54; political/civil vs. economic/social, 34–39; post–Cold War marginalization of, 78–79; UN High Commissioner for Human Rights and, 370–372. *See also* American Convention on Human Rights; human rights

U.S. international humanitarian assistance programs, 328–331

U.S. refugee policy: creation of new, 67–69; distinctions among alien groups and, 53; end of the Cold War and, 67; human rights and, 56; human rights and post–Cold War, 59–66; possible scenarios of, 66–67; refugee admissions/asylum adjudications (1980s) and, 56–59; U.S. immigration history and, 52–53

U.S.S. St. Louis incident (1938), 56

values: comparing Singapore and U.S., 381; human rights and changing, 383; human rights debate and Asian, 377–378; U.S. promotion of family, 382

Van Dyke, Vernon, xix

the Vatican, 362–363

Vienna Convention on the Law of Treaties, 115–120, 121–122, 179

Vienna Declaration and Plan of Action (1993), 82, 111, 379

Vienna World Conference on Human Rights, 367

Vietnam War syndrome, 131, 187

Vogelgesang, Sandy, xx

Voting Rights Act, 37

wages: minimum, xv–xvi, 42–43, 44; trade-off between unemployment and, 43

Walton, 281

War Crimes Tribunals (former Yugoslavia/Rwanda), 185–186, 372 n.1

Welfare Reform Act, 80

welfare state: entitlement rules in, 339; human rights in liberal democratic, 206–209; justification for, 220; market democracy and, 223–224; markets civilized under, 221; neoclassical economic theory on, 39; reforms in model of, 382–383; rise of European, 37–38; scaling back of U.S., 40–41; U.S. debate over, 79–80; U.S. as liberal democratic, 223

Wenders, Wim, 84

White's Panel Robust Standard errors, 287, 288

Wilson, Woodrow, xx, 132

Wings of Desire (film), 84–85

Wofford, Harris, 13

women: human rights and rights of, 192; improving lives of indigenous, 317

women in development (WID) officers, 317

Women's Affairs Technical Committee, 259

Women's Convention (CEDAW), x, 75, 110

women's organizations (Arab world), 258–259

women's rights movement, 192

Women's Union of Jordan, 258

Working Group on Enforced Disappearances, 358, 359–360, 363–366

Working Group on Indigenous Populations, 318

World Bank: compromise of imbedded liberalism and, 33; developing state' complaints against, 42; development strategies used by, 305; low-interest development loans by, 310; questionable human rights record of, xxiii; resettlement policy of, 321 n.19

World Commission on Environment and Development, 314

World Conference on Human Rights (Vienna), 367

World Economic Forum, 381

In the *Human Rights in International Perspective* series